CHRISTIAN ART

IN THE PLACE AND IN THE FORM

OF

LUTHERAN WORSHIP.

By

Paul E. Kretzmann, Ph. D., B. D.

ST. LOUIS, MO.
CONCORDIA PUBLISHING HOUSE.
1921.

PREFACE.

The double volume which is herewith offered to the Lutheran liturgiologists and liturgists of America makes no claim of being an exhaustive presentation. It is merely, as the subtitle states, a hand-book for the student, for the busy pastor, and for all those interested in Christian art from the Lutheran standpoint and in the liturgical heritage of the Reformation. The references and foot-notes, however, may prove of value to such as wish to make a more detailed study of any section.

The author wishes to make grateful acknowledgment for suggestions and help received in preparing this study to Professor L. Fuerbringer, of St. Louis, Mo., to Dr. J. F. Ohl, of Philadelphia, Penn., to Dr. E. F. Krauss, of Maywood, Ill., to Dr. C. Abbetmeyer, of St. Paul, Minn., and to such others as have given encouragement and advice in any form.

THE AUTHOR.

TABLE OF CONTENTS.

Part II.
Hymnology.

Part III.
Heortology.

Part IV.
The Liturgical Content of the Lutheran Services.

BOOK I.

———

A HANDBOOK

OF

CHURCH ARCHITECTURE AND ECCLESIASTICAL ART

ESPECIALLY FROM THE STANDPOINT

OF THE

AMERICAN LUTHERAN CHURCH.

INTRODUCTION.

The number of books, tracts, and articles that have appeared in the last fifty years, and notably in the last two decades, on some phase of the subject "Christian Art," are evidence of the revival of a healthy interest in the proprieties of public worship, especially so far as the place of worship and its appointments are concerned. The Anglican Church has been especially active in this respect. Many a vestry has been ransacked, many a church account has been thumbed over, many a faded book has been cleaned of the dust of centuries, in order that the people might once more get an understanding of the expression of the ritual in the form of church art.

This movement has not been confined to the Anglican Church or to the Protestant Episcopal Church of our country. In the Reformed churches of various types, the bareness and barrenness of former times is, in many cases, being agreeably relieved by decorations and hangings which show the increasing interest and understanding of our times for a proper and significant ornamentation of the house of worship.

The fact that this tendency is also becoming more obvious within the Lutheran Church of America does not argue that innovations are being proposed or foisted upon a suspicious majority by a few well-meaning but formalistic reformers with high-church or even Romanizing tendencies. On the contrary, the Lutheran Church of America, having emerged from the years of poverty and privations which very naturally attended its establishment in a new country, is now in a position to gather up the treasures of the ages and to display them in such a way as to confound the scoffer and to convince the serious-minded. For the Lutheran Church was never an enemy of the arts, neither of the fine nor of the industrial arts. Luther, with fine tact and wise discrimination, insisted upon only one thing, namely, that every suspicion of idolatry in the houses of worship be removed and that the preaching of the Gospel be made paramount. To these principles the Lutheran Church assented.[1] So far as our day and age are concerned, the question of art for churches in its various forms could hardly be discussed in a more convincing manner than in the

---

1) Apologia Confessionis, Art. XXIV, De Missa, 41—50. Mueller, 258. 259.

words of the well-known liturgiologist, Dr. C. Abbetmeyer: "The
Lutheran Church, in the matter of seasons, decorations, and ritual,
with true conservatism and in the exercise of Christian liberty, has
avoided the idolatrous and heretical mummeries of Rome as well as
the extreme and unbecoming bareness of many Reformed churches
and, in order to bring the knowledge of God's grace to men's hearts,
has preserved those usages of the past relating to the seasons of the
church-year, the appointments of the church-buildings and the liturgical church-service, which, being 'good' and serviceable, suit the true
Church of God in all ages. To confess its faith it did not hesitate to
enlist the aid of pure and beautiful art forms, not only in the har-
monies of poetry and music, but also in architecture, sculpture, painting, bronze work, wood-carving, and embroidery, so long as these
aided its purpose of instruction and edification. In this it followed
the lead of Luther, who said with reference to the iconoclasts, to
counteract whom he left the safe precincts of the Wartburg: 'I do
not-believe that art is to be overthrown by the Gospel, as some hyper-
spiritual people maintain; but I should like to see all the arts placed
in the service of Him who made them." [2]

It is of architecture that we shall mainly treat in these pages,
though painting, sculpture, and the minor arts will receive the consideration which they deserve as the handmaidens of architecture.
And this in itself is a subject which may well engage the interest of
all that love the beautiful. For all art is creative and readaptative.
It is intelligent and serves a purpose. It is the beautiful expression
of intelligent truth. If this is true of every art, how much more appealing must it be in the case of architecture, in which we find the
principles of every art: theme, paragraphs, coherence, completeness,
plan, and unity, expressed in a most convincing and edifying manner.
"When a building entirely fulfils the purpose for which is it intended
and bears the impress of a genuine style, it takes rank as a work of
architecture." [3] "We may define architecture as the art which seeks
to harmonize in a building the requirements of utility and beauty . . .
Only when the idea of beauty is added to that of use does a structure
take its place among works of architecture." [4] In a similar way,
Smith,[5] Price,[6] and others have defined architecture. A building,
then, to be a work of art, to rank with the products of architecture,
must be appropriate to its use, strongly built, and pleasing to
look upon.

---

2) *Lutheran Witness*, XXXVI (1917), No. 13.
3) Mrs. A. Bell, *Architecture*, v.
4) Hamlin, A. D. F., *History of Architecture*, xxiii.
5) *Architecture, Classic and Early Christian*, i.
6) *The Practical Book of Architecture*, 20—24.

But there is another factor that should be emphasized. Mr. R. A. Cram, in his recent book "Church Building," says: "Art is the measure of civilization. If we have not an art that is distinctive, the natural expression of a healthy people, then we protest in vain. We do not possess a genuine, vital civilization. For art is a result, not a product." If this be true of art and architecture in general, it will be especially true of Christian, and specifically of Lutheran architecture. The charge which is so often made against the Lutherans in America, that their church edifices are merely utilitarian and that in many of them every law of beauty and expression, not to speak of doctrinal and liturgical significance, is violated, is one which is often only too well founded. The peculiar utilitarian ideas which appear in the church buildings of some of the ultra-modern anti-Christian congregations (Mormon, Christian Science, Institutional, and others) and characterize the church bodies to whom they profess allegiance, are only too often copied, at least in part, by the members of a well-meaning Lutheran building committee and carried out by an avaricious or, at least, unintelligent architect. It seems that in a good many so-called edifices of public worship the kitchen, the pantry, the dining-room, and, perhaps, the ball-room are of more importance than the church auditorium proper, which should receive first consideration. Such buildings are travesties, and their erection, in many cases, is little short of sacrilege. It is decidedly not without reason that we find a writer complaining: "One finds in so many, also in the newer churches, the disgrace that they often are more like a warehouse, a concert-hall, or a barn than a house of God. Some churches have no head, others are all vestibule. In a few the tower and main portal are behind the altar, at the head, instead of at the feet. . . In short, many churches are *disjecta membra,* a confused mass of pieces of a dismembered corpse, but no well-ordered organism full of spirit, reason, and life." [7] Of such a building, another writer says: "The designer seems purposely to have avoided an ecclesiastical expression, and to have undertaken to typify, in brick and stone, the wild, free theology of the West. He has so far succeeded that nobody could possibly take the results of his labors for a church in the usual acceptation of the term, but this negative attainment does not yet constitute a positive architectural success. It may be that western ideas in theology are thus far somewhat too sketchy to form a basis for the establishment of an architectural type, since mere negation is insusceptible of architectural expression." [8]

That conditions occasion such severe censure, also in Lutheran

---

7) Muehe, *Die pastorale Wuerde im Kirchendienste,* 8.
8) Schuyler, Montgomery, *American Architecture,* 178. 179.

circles,9) is a sad reflection upon the state of enlightenment in our midst. If a Church which has always encouraged and nurtured all the arts becomes guilty of such flagrant offenses, it shows that there is a lack of understanding as to the patrimony of the ages and the heritage of the Reformation. For it cannot be a question merely of money and willingness. Our people, for the most part, are now so situated that they are no longer obliged to be hewers of wood and drawers of water. Moreover, they are eager to learn all they can of

EL DEIR, TEMPLE AT PETRA.

the glorious riches of Christian church art and will respond nobly to every effort made in their behalf. If pastors, deacons, and trustees, teachers and boards, men's clubs and ladies' societies, young people's guilds and schools take up the questions involved, each in his own sphere and in relation to the part he is most interested in, the result ought to be a splendid revival of interest in the liturgical and artistic heritage of the Reformation.

9) *Lutheran Witness*, XXXVI (1917), No. 15; XXXIV (1915), No. 22. No. 25.

It is with this object in view that these pages are written. Not only shall the historical side of Christian art receive its proper emphasis, with all the subsidiary arts; not only shall the liturgical and doctrinal significance of the various parts in their relation to one another and to the entire church-building be shown; but the practical side also will receive due attention.

With this fact in mind, we shall therefore omit all discussion of the pre-Christian era, with the exception of the Jewish tabernacle and temples. The grandeur of the Egyptian temples, of Thebes, of Karnak, of Edfu and Philae, the majesty of those royal tombs, the pyramids of Ghizeh, the overwhelming silence of the Sphinx, had little or no influence on Christian architecture. The Assyrian palaces of Babylon, Khorsabad, and Persepolis left no impress on the art after Christ. The impressive beauty of the Greek temples with their fluted columns in the three orders has aroused only temporary interest in the Neo-Classic period. The Etruscan and Roman addition of somberness and dignity did nothing to make the temples more attractive to the Christians, associated, as these edifices were, with idolatrous practices. Some of them were, indeed, converted into Christian churches, but the history of their past still clings to them.

It is similar with sculpture, painting, and the minor arts. Phidias, Praxiteles, and Skopas, Polygnotos, Timanthes, and Apelles had indeed gone before, and that there was some influence of the antique, of the classic, in the development of Christian art cannot be questioned; but essentially it followed its own ideas, since it believed in and fostered other ideals. Even the Renaissance, in spite of its giant upheaval, did not influence church art in quite the same manner or to the same degree as it revolutionized secular art.

Our purpose will be, simply to follow the history of Christian architecture and art from the beginning, and to make the application of the historical, liturgical, doctrinal, and practical considerations to our own day and age. And since sculpture and painting, for the purpose of this book, are on a level with the minor arts, as being ancillary for the adornment of the places of worship, they will be considered in this respect only, in order that the exposition may stay well within the compass of a handbook.

PART I.
History of Church Architecture and Ecclesiastical Art.

CHAPTER 1.
The Tabernacle and the Three Temples of the Jews.

There are several reasons why the tabernacle and the three temples of the Jews are of particular interest to the believers of the New Testament. It is not merely that we feel the appeal of the past and that the fascinating study of archeology beckons us on. This factor can, of course, not be neglected in a study of this kind. It is undoubtedly the motive which prompted the investigations of De Vogue, De Saulcy, Perrot, Chipiez, Friedrich, Ewald, and others. But the interest of these men would probably have been just as great in the instance of a Hittite or Sassanian or Assyrian temple. The study of the past, the unveiling of mysteries which are shrouded in the veil of uncertain traditions engages their attention and challenges their ingenuity. We have reasons to be grateful to such students of antiquity. Their zeal in more than one instance has unearthed treasures which have often, in a most remarkable way, substantiated the evidence of Scripture. A mere archeological interest may, therefore, serve to stimulate investigations which will open up to us the testimony of the stones.

It is also not merely the fact of Jehovah's having planned the first edifice of His cultus on earth which especially engages our attention, though this fact is also interesting enough, in itself. It may be true, of course, that all attempts to fix the symbolism of the tabernacle, its furniture, and its appointments, outside of that revealed in Scriptures, are arbitrary. Certain it is, at any rate, that the explanations of Josephus, Philo, Maimonides, and the early Christian teachers have been challenged by recent scholars. That the general plan of the first sanctuary is to serve as a model for the houses of worship of all times, was stated by a writer not long ago.[10] According to this exposition, the tabernacle is a type of the human organism, which was designated by Jesus as His temple. The division into vestibule, sanctuary, and holy of holies is said to correspond to the limbs, trunk, and head of man. From this the writer argues that the Jewish houses of worship were types of the woman, the *alter Eva*, Mary, the

---

10) Muehe, *Die pastorale Wuerde im Kirchendienste,* 5. 6.

mother of Christ, and, therefore, in the last analysis, of the New Testament Church. Whether the author's reference to Ezek. 44, 1—3, to Daechsel's explanation, and to the significance of the "Golden Portal" be more than mere conjectures, can hardly be determined. It is safe to assert, however, that such arbitrary attempts can never evoke more than passing interest.

There are other reasons which compel our interest and make us eager for every possible source of authentic information regarding these Old Testament structures. The first is the reason of religious sentiment. For none of the structures of the Jews reached or even approached the magnificence of some heathen temples, in spite of the fact that the actual amount of gold used by Solomon exceeded the wildest dreams of the heathen. "The temple of Jerusalem, when isolated from its accessories, is a mediocre and small edifice, which can bear no comparison with the corresponding structures at Karnak, Luxor, the storied towers of Chaldea, the temples of Greece and Rome, or Gothic and Renaissance churches." [11]) It is rather that the temple, though "twice rebuilt and destroyed, aided, no doubt, by the sublime poetry of Holy Writ, — has taken such hold on the imagination of peoples reared on the teachings of the Bible, as to distance every other and assume colossal proportions. . . . It is a monument unique in the world in that, having left no traces on the site it once occupied, yet it has lived and lives in the memory of almost all classes of men." [12])

The other reason, however, is the most compelling for engaging and holding our attention, namely, because the tabernacle, and especially some of the places and vessels belonging to it, have become typical of Christ and of His sacrifice in the new dispensation, as the Epistle to the Hebrews and other passages of the New Testament show. If there were no other reason why we should feel the appeal of the tabernacle and the temples of the time under the Law, this one would be more than sufficient for every one interested in the great High Priest and Sacrifice of the Christian Church.

The *tabernacle* of the Jews actually possessed the distinguishing characteristic which so many heathen temples claimed for themselves, both the pattern for the sanctuary and of all the appointments thereof having been furnished by the Lord, Ex. 25, 8. 9. This sanctuary was designated by various names, which gave a clear indication of its character and of its purpose. It was called "house," or "tent," or "dwelling," because it was the place where the Lord dwelt in the midst of His people. In this capacity it served as a type for heaven, Heb.

---

11) Perrot-Chipiez, *History of Art in Sardinia, Judea, etc.*, 112. See also Baehr, *Symbolik des mosaischen Kultus*, I, 257—261.
12) Perrot-Chipiez, 113.

9, 2. 11. 24. It is also called the "tent of coming together," the "tent of witness," the "tent of testimony," Num. 17, 6—9. In this sanctuary, the Lord appeared in His glory before the people, who were gathered there for His service. Here He spoke to them by the mouth of the priests and gave evidence of His divine power and majesty. The place of God's dwelling among His chosen people is finally called "sanctuary" and "tabernacle," because it was a holy, a sanctified place, separated from common or secular use, dedicated entirely to Him whose presence in this sanctuary was promised.[13])

The tabernacle formed a rectangular parallelepiped, being thirty cubits long, ten cubits wide, and ten cubits high, inside measurement. Of this room, one-third was partitioned off as the "holy of holies." The framework consisted of forty-eight heavy planks or pillars, twenty of these being used for the north and south wall, respectively, and eight for the west wall. Each pillar was ten cubits long and one and

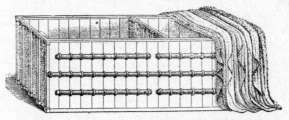

THE FRAME-WORK OF THE TABERNACLE.

one-half cubits wide, being furnished with two tenons at the lower extremity, which fitted into forty sockets of silver placed on the ground. These pillars were coupled or fastened together beneath and also above the head with bars of the same acacia wood of which they were made. The middle bar above reached from end to end, thus supplying the ridge-pole of the tent. All the boards were overlaid with gold, as well as the bars holding them together, and their rings were also of gold, Ex. 26, 15—30.[14]) The pitched roof of the tabernacle, as well as the walls, was formed of several layers of curtains. The inside curtain was of fine twined linen (byssos), "and blue, and purple, and scarlet, with cherubim of cunning work," Ex. 26, 1, and consisted of ten strips, each four by twenty-eight cubits in size, held together by loops or couplings. The middle of this large curtain was just over the partition of the tabernacle, thus permitting the "holy place" to be covered as far as the front opening, while the "holy of holies" was covered both on ceiling and sides. This curtain was covered by

---

13) Cp. Baehr, *Symbolik des mosaischen Kultus*, I, 75—91.
14) Cp. Rupprecht, *Bible History References*, 79—81; Josephus, *Antiquities of the Jews*, Book III, Chapter VI; Baehr, I, 55—57.

another of goat's hair, consisting of eleven strips, four by thirty cubits in size. The outside shelter of the tabernacle was provided by rams' and badgers' skins.

The partition between the two rooms of the tabernacle was formed by a richly-wrought curtain, hanging between the walls and reaching from the top to the bottom. This "veil," Ex. 36, 35; Lev. 16, 2, 2 Chron. 3, 14; Matt. 27, 51, or "second veil," Heb. 9, 3, was "very ornamental, and embroidered with all sorts of flowers which the earth produces, and there were interwoven into it all sorts of variety that might be an ornament, excepting the forms of animals." [15]

The tabernacle was surrounded by a court, one hundred cubits long by fifty cubits wide, whose enclosure was a screen, five cubits high, of fine twined linen. The curtains of the enclosure were sus-

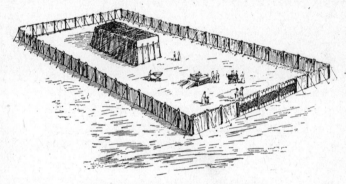

THE TABERNACLE AND ITS COURT.

pended from ropes drawn between pillars of brass, whose capitals were overlaid with silver, and which stood on bases of bronze. The fifty-six pillars were held in place by cords fastened to tent-pins of bronze. The entrance to the court was on the east side.

The position or orientation of the tabernacle with its court was included in the directions given by God. The locality and the condition of the ground were no determining factors, but the cardinal points of the compass. The front of the tabernacle was to face toward the east, and its length toward the north and south, respectively, Num. 3, 38; Ex. 26, 18; 20, 22; 36, 23—27. Around the tabernacle with its court, during the wilderness journey, were grouped the twelve tribes of Israel, Num. 3, 22. 29. 35. 38; 2, 2—25.

The sanctuary stood in the western half of the court, being divided, as stated above, into two parts, the "holy place" and the "holy of holies." The place of greatest honor and sanctity in the inner

15) Josephus, *Loc. cit.*, § 4.

sanctuary was occupied by the "ark of the covenant," Ex. 25, 10—16. It was made of acacia wood and measured two and one-half cubits in length by one and one-half cubits for the width and height. It was overlaid with pure gold and had a special decoration, a crown or girdle of gold at the upper rim, which served as a lip for holding the cover or mercy-seat, Ex. 25, 17—22; Rom. 3, 25; Heb. 9, 5. This cover was made of pure gold and was decorated with two cherubim of beaten gold in its two ends. The cherubim had their wings extended and faced each other over the center of the kapporeth. Above the mercy-seat, between the wings of the cherubim, the Lord communed with Moses, Ex. 25, 22. The ark at first contained only the tables of the testimony which the Lord gave to Moses, the ten commandments written in stone by the finger of God. Later there was deposited here a copy of the book of the Law, Deut. 31, 25. 26, a golden pot, in which three quarts of manna were preserved, Ex. 16, 33, and the rod of Aaron, which had miraculously budded and blossomed and borne fruit, Num. 17, 8. 10.

The sanctuary or holy place also had its sacred furniture, Ex. 25, 23—40; 37, 10—28; 31, 8; 35, 13; 40, 4. 22. In the northern corner, near the curtain separating the outer and inner sanctuary, was the golden table of show-bread, or the prothesis table, two cubits long by one cubit wide and one and one-half cubits high. It was made of acacia wood, like the ark of the covenant, and was overlaid with gold in the same manner. It was also carried in the same way, by means of staves that were passed through golden rings fastened on the four corners. The golden crown of which the text speaks was probably a decorated molding which served to hold objects on the plate of the table. This table served as a stand for the show-bread or the dozen bread-cakes, after the number of tribes in Israel, which were renewed every Sabbath. Across the room, on the side opposite the table of show-bread, was the golden seven-armed candlestick. Its size is not given in Scriptures, but according to Jewish tradition it was about three cubits high and two cubits wide. It was made of pure gold, but hollow inside, giving it a total weight of eighty-six pounds. Its richest decoration is described in the text as having consisted of knops or pomegranates and flowers, shaped like almond-blossoms, which served as sockets for the candles. Near the inner veil, in the middle, stood the altar of incense, Ex. 30, 1—10; 37, 25—28. It was made of acacia wood and measured two cubits in height, its plate being a square of the dimension of one cubit. It had a projecting rim to prevent the falling-off of coals or sacrifice, and its four corners were decorated with ornaments in the shape of horns. The entire altar, with its ornaments, was overlaid with gold and was furnished with golden rings to facilitate carrying. It was called the altar of incense, because the priests were required to burn incense on it at both the morning and the evening sacrifice. The fire needed for this sacrifice had to be taken from the altar of burnt offering in a golden fire-pan.

Out in the open court the altar of burnt offering was located, Ex. 27, 1—8. This brazen altar, as it is often designated, had a frame of acacia wood, which was overlaid, together with the horns, with brass. It was three cubits high, with a plate five cubits square. A peculiarity of this altar was a sort of walk suspended on three sides, which enabled the officiating priests to tend to the sacrifice. It is also very likely that there was a slanting approach to the altar from the south, Ex. 20, 26. Between this altar and the tent was the brazen laver, Ex. 30, 18; 38, 8. Its body as well as the stand were made of brass, to which were attached the mirrors which the women had given as a part of their contribution.[16]) The law required that the priests wash their hands and feet before offering sacrifice, on pain of death. All the small vessels used in the court, such as ash-pans, fire-pans, shovels, basins, flesh-hooks, etc., were made of brass, while those of the tabernacle proper, the dishes, bowls, spoons, covers, etc., were made of gold.

But even as the architecture of the tabernacle was prescribed by the Lord and all its vessels made according to the patterns which He showed to Moses on the mountain, thus also the garments of the priests were made according to the command and plan of God, even as to material and colors, Ex. 28. The garments of the high priest were especially costly and beautiful, consisting of "a breast-plate, and an ephod, and a robe, and a broidered coat, a mitre, and a girdle," v. 4. The colors were gold, blue, purple, scarlet, and the white of fine linen, v. 5. The dress of the priests was less elaborate, consisting principally of "a white linen tunic, reaching from the neck to the ankles, with tight sleeves, and held together around the waist with a linen girdle. On the head the priest wore a kind of tiara, of a round, turban-like shape."

The entire plan of God in regard to the place and manner of His worship had been committed to Moses during his stay on Mount Sinai. After his return to camp, he lost no time in executing the command of the Lord. Under the leadership of Bezaleel and Aholiab, wise-hearted men came together and fashioned the frame-work, the curtains, and all the paraphernalia of the tabernacle. It was a time of joyful sacrifice and of happy work. And when, finally, the sanctuary had been reared and dedicated, it became, as the Lord had intended, the center of the religious life during the long, trying march through

---

16) Baehr, *Symbolik des mosaischen Kultus*, I, 479—486.

the wilderness to the Land of Promise. When the Schechinnah, the cloud of God's glory, arose from the tabernacle, the people continued their journey. From it the Lord spoke, judged, and punished. The ark of the covenant belonging to the equipment of the tabernacle was the first to cross the river Jordan, and the tabernacle was established as the national center of worship at Shiloh, as soon as the conquest of Canaan was completed, Josh. 18, 1.

For more than four hundred years things remained practically unchanged, so far as the government of the people by direct or indirect theocracy was concerned. And during these centuries, the tabernacle remained the national house of worship. During that whole time, the Lord lived in the midst of His people in a tent, at first in Shiloh, Judg. 20, 18. 23. 27; 1 Sam. 1, 3; 3, 3; 4, 3; Ps. 78. 60; Jer. 7, 12. 14; 2 Sam. 7, 6. 7; 1 Chron. 17, 5, then at Gibeon or Gibeah, 1 Chron. 16, 39; 22, 29; 2 Chron. 1, 3, for a while even at Nob. Mark 2, 26; 1 Sam. 21, 6. It may be, however, that these latter names refer to the same locality on a hill (Gibea) situated between the four towns Gibeon, Gibeah, Kireath Jearim, and Nobe. King David had the ark removed to Jerusalem, 2 Sam. 6, 2—19, making there a provisional tabernacle of curtains until he might be able to build a temple. But the permission to carry out this plan was withheld by God, and so the first temple of the Jews was not built until the reign of Solomon, 1 Kings 5, 6—8, 11; 2 Chron. 2, 1—5, 14.

The resources of Solomon must have been remarkably large, according to the account of the Bible and that of Josephus, especially if one considers the relatively small size of the kingdom over which he ruled. Moreover, he enjoyed the friendship and secured the assistance of Hiram, the king of Tyre, with whom David had made a treaty. These facts enabled Solomon to expend vast sums of money and to employ a great army of men, which numbered, all told, 183,000 Jews and strangers, 1 Kings 5, 13—18.

The temple was built on the ancient Mount Moriah, one of the hills which forms the range of Mount Zion, the peak of this name being in the southwestern part of the city. The temple mount rises steeply from the Tyropoeon, on the south, and from the valley of the Kidron, also known as the Valley of Jehoshaphat, on the east. In order to obtain a horizontal space for the building, the top of the hill had to be leveled and filled up, finally serving as an enormous plinth. The area of the entire sanctuary was in the shape of a rough square or trapezium, averaging from 500 to 470 yards from east to west, and from 325 to 300 yards from north to south.[17] The wall of enclosure was laid on bed-rock and consisted in part of huge blocks of white

17) Perrot-Chipiez, *History of Art in Sardinia, Judea, etc.*

lime-stone, some of which measured more than twenty feet in length and weighed over one hundred tons. The blocks on the southeast angle are still in a good state of preservation. This angle is known as the place of wailing.

The architecture of the temple was borrowed from the art of the peoples with whom the Israelites had relations or with whom they came in contact. Egyptian conceptions are found in the successive courts and in the lofty entrance pylons, Phenician and Assyrian detail and workmanship is seen in the cedar wood-work, over-laid with metal work, and in the platform of stupendous masonry.[18]

The dimensions of Solomon's temple were just double those of the former sanctuary. The "holy of holies" was twenty cubits each

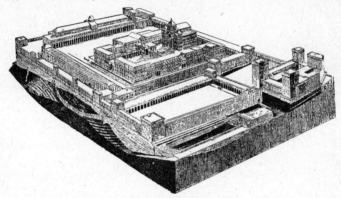

THE TEMPLE OF SOLOMON.

way, the "holy place" had the same height and width, but double the length, the porch and chambers were eighty by forty cubits, and thirty cubits high, and the court measured two hundred by one hundred cubits. The north, west, and south walls of the sanctuary proper were concealed by a three-storied structure of chambers or small cells, 1 Kings 6, 5. 6.

The material of which the temple was erected was stone, which had been so carefully prepared as to fit in place exactly, without the use of iron instruments. This stone wall received a veneering of cedar-wood, both inside and outside. The roof, ceiling, and floor were made of the same material. The floor and the ceiling were given a veneering of fir, 1 Kings 6, 15; 2 Chron. 3, 5. The entire sanctuary, on the inside at least, was overlaid with gold, whose weight amounted to six hundred talents. The windows were probably near the ceiling. They were windows of narrow lights, broad within and narrow without.

---

18) Hamlin, *History of Architecture*, Chapter V.

All the brass and metal work of the temple was made under the direction of Hiram of Tyre. The most conspicuous piece of work fashioned by this artisan were the ornaments of the temple's facade, two brazen pillars, called Jachin and Boaz, 1 Kings 7, 15; 2 Chron. 3, 15—17. These pillars were, at least at first, eighteen cubits high, twelve in circumference, and four fingers thick. According to the later account, they may afterwards have been lengthened to a height of thirty-five cubits. These pillars received ornamentation in the shape of chains and pomegranates. Their capitals were lily-shaped and five cubits in height. These famous pillars have been the cause of some very lively discussions among scholars who were anxious to discover some special purpose for them. The most ingenious explanation is that of Fergusson, who writes: "What Solomon erected was a screen (chapiter) consisting of two parts, one four cubits, the other five cubits in height, and supported by two pillars of metal, certainly not more than one cubit in diameter, and standing twelve cubits apart." [19]) But there is nothing in the text to support this conjecture. A far more plausible explanation is that given in Schaff-Herzog: "The purpose here may have been purely architectural, but the pillars are probably to be related to the obelisks and pillars that were characteristic of Phenician and Canaanitic temples."

The furniture which Solomon provided for the temple was of a design and workmanship harmonizing with the grandeur of the entire place of worship. The veil separating the "holy place" from the "holy of holies" was made of blue, and purple, and crimson, and fine linen, and was decorated with cherubim. There was also a door to the inner sanctuary, made of olive-wood, whose lintel above formed with the door-posts a pentagon. The double entrance doors to the "holy place" were of cedar and cypress and, according to the account of Josephus, were also supplemented by splendid curtains. The ark of the covenent or ark of the testimony was again assigned its place in the "holy of holies." But Solomon also placed into the inner sanctuary or *naos* two cherubim, made of olive-wood and overlaid with gold. They were ten cubits high, and their wings measured ten cubits from tip to tip. They stood facing the east, with their outstretched wings meeting over the mercy-seat and touching the walls on either side. All of the wood paneling and wainscoating was carved with figures of cherubim, and palm-trees, and open flowers.

The "holy place" again received the altar of incense and the table of show-bread. Instead of the single candlestick, however, Solomon had Hiram make ten, of pure gold, five on the right side and five on the left, before the oracle. The inner court, just before the sanctuary,

---

19) *A History of Architecture*, 223.

was the principal place of sacrifice. There stood the great altar of brass, whose height was ten cubits and whose top was twenty cubits square. Its elevation enabled great multitudes in the outer court to witness the sacrifices. The approach to this altar was probably by means of a long incline, and a platform surrounded the altar at the proper height for the officiating priests. Near the altar stood the brazen sea, a circular basin, ten cubits in diameter, five in height, and a handbreadth in thickness; its brim was slightly curved or flared outward. It rested upon twelve brazen oxen, which were arranged in groups of three, facing the cardinal points. In addition to this great basin for ceremonial washing, there were ten large lavers or kettles, which were set on ten bases of brass, four cubits square and three cubits high, placed on wheels for moving the instruments readily. The frame of these bases was decorated with figures of lions, oxen, and cherubim. The purpose of these lavers was to serve for the washing of sacrificial animals, 1 Kings 7, 27—39. Since so much water was used in the temple, it was necessary to have a full supply. This was provided by means of aqueducts leading from springs and built inside the rock. In a similar manner, the polluted water was carried off through underground sewers.[20] All the smaller vessels for use in the temple, the pots, the shovels, the flesh-hooks, the fire-pans, etc., were made of brass, and the corresponding vessels for the sanctuary, including also the tongs, the snuffers, the bowls, the spoons, and the censers, were of pure gold.

When this temple was finished, about 1005 B. C., it was dedicated with appropriate ceremonies, 1 Kings 8; 2 Chron. 5—7. For four centuries it served as the central sanctuary of the Jews, with varying vicissitudes, depending upon the character of the ruler. King Ahaz, for instance, made use of the oxen under the brazen sea to pay tribute to the king of Assyria, 2 Kings 16, 17. 18, besides performing other deeds of desecration, 2 Chron. 28, 24. 25. With Zedekiah came the end. Nebuchadnezzar, king of Babylon, destroyed the city of Jerusalem, took all the vessels of the house of God, both great and small, and burned the house of God, 2 Chron. 36, 17—19. This was about 586 B. C.

When the Jews, under the reign of Cyrus, and later under that of Darius, were permitted to return to their devastated country, they set about rebuilding the city of Jerusalem and also the temple, though it required some urging for the latter task, Hag. 1, 4. Under the leadership of the priest Zerubbabel the building was begun about the middle of the year 520 B. C. The altar was first erected, Ezra 3, 1—3.

---

20) Perrot-Chipiez, *History of Art in Sardinia, Judea, etc.*, Chapter II.

When the foundations of the temple had been laid, there was a great celebration, attended by shouts of joy from the younger generation, but by the weeping of those that had seen the first temple. In spite of the opposition of the Samaritans, who even managed to hinder the building operations for some time, the new temple was finished and dedicated with great joy about 516 B. C.

The accounts in regard to the second temple are so meager that any attempt to give a full description must be futile, resting, as it does to a great extent, upon conjecture. Fergusson, indeed, thinks that it was built after the description of Ezekiel, but that its materials and ornamentation were inferior to those of Solomon's temple.[21] But the prophecy of Ezekiel is undoubtedly a Messianic one and cannot be applied to the temple built by Zerubbabel. By comparing the Bible account with that of Josephus,[22] the following description may be given. Josephus quotes Hecataeus of Abdera, who wrote concerning the second temple: "There is, about the middle of the city, a wall of stone, whose length is five hundred feet, and the breadth a hundred cubits, with double cloisters, wherein there is a square altar, not made of hewn stone, but composed of white stones gathered together, having each side twenty cubits long, and its altitude ten cubits. Hard by it is a large edifice, wherein there is an altar and a candlestick, both of gold, and in weight two talents: upon these there is a light that is never extinguished neither by night nor by day." That the altar was of unhewn stone, is also related 1 Macc. 4, 44—47. The same account also speaks of the restoring of the cells of the priests, together with the sanctuary, of the making of the golden candlestick, the table of prothesis, and the altar of incense. "The ark having disappeared, its place in the 'holy of holies' was taken by a flat stone called the *shetiya,* upon which the high priest, on the day of atonement, placed the censer" (Schaff-Herzog).

The later history of the second temple has many dark pages. The sanctuary was desecrated under the reign of Antiochus the Noble, 1 Macc. 1, and restored by Judas Maccabeus after the defeat of Lysias, chapter 4. It is from this restoration that the Feast of Dedication dates. In the course of the years, the temple was fortified so strongly that Pompey was obliged to lay formal siege to it. After he had stormed it, he penetrated into the sanctuary, but did not touch any of the treasures belonging to the temple.[23] Later, Herod the Great took the city and the temple, and had much difficulty in restraining the soldiers from violating the sanctuary.[24]

---

21) *History of Architecture,* Book II.
22) *Antiquities of the Jews,* Book XI, I—IV; *Against Apion,* Book I, 22.
23) Josephus, *Antiquities of the Jews,* Book XIV, IV; *Wars of the Jews,* Book I, VII.
24) Josephus, *Antiquities of the Jews,* Book XIV, XVI.

When Herod had finally succeeded in establishing himself as king of Judea, under the sovereignty of the Romans, he conceived the plan of replacing the temple of Zerubbabel by a new and magnificent structure, rivaling in beauty the glorious temples of Greece. Accordingly, he began about 20—19 B. C. to carry out his design.[25] He first of all assured the Jews that he would not wreck any part of their temple till all the material for rebuilding the entire sanctuary had been assembled. It is probable that the sanctuary proper or *naos* was erected first, in order not to interfere with the religious cult of the people. Some of the priests became carpenters and stone-cutters, so that no profane hands need touch the sacred shrine. The old temple was taken down and the new one erected in the space of eighteen months. But much remained to be done, and the work dragged along until after Herod's death.[26] The entire temple was in process of

THE TEMPLE OF HEROD.

construction for forty-six years at the time of Jesus, John 2, 20, and the last details were not put into place until the year 64 A. D., only six years before its final destruction.

Herod practically doubled the area of the Solomonic temple by enlarging the hill and erecting foundation-walls of enormous blocks, some of them measuring twenty-five cubits long, twelve cubits wide, and eight cubits high. The various courts and approaches were laid out on successive terraces or elevations, thus affording a gradual ascent to the sanctuary. The entire temple area was enclosed by beautiful cloisters, with hundreds of slender Corinthian columns, for the architecture of the edifice followed classical lines. On the south was the Royal Court or Porch, and on the east that known as Solomon's Porch. The southern half of the temple area was known as the "Court of the Gentiles." A short flight of steps led to a second enclosure of stones. Bronze tablets bore inscriptions forbidding any

25) Josephus, *Antiquities of the Jews*, Book XV, XI.
26) Barton, *Archeology and the Bible*, 208.

persons but Jews to enter, on pain of death. This court, which was on the level just beneath that of the sanctuary, was divided into three parts, in terraces: the Court of Women, the Court of Israel, and the Court of Priests, the last surrounding the temple proper or the *naos*. In addition, there were galleries, in which the women could worship, since they were not permitted in the space before the great altar; a hall where the Sanhedrim met; chambers for treasures and offerings; and many architectural embellishments.

The vestibule of the sanctuary was one hundred cubits high and just as wide, though only twenty cubits deep. The measurements of the sanctuary were the same as in the temple of Solomon. There was a heavy double curtain or veil, which separated the "holy place" from the "holy of holies," Matt. 27, 50; Mark 15, 38; Luke 23, 45. The altar of burnt offering, in the priests' court before the sanctuary, was thirty-two cubits square at the bottom and twenty-four at the top, thus representing the frustum of a pyramid. The blood of the sacrifices was drained away through subterranean ducts into the Kidron. The altar, as well as its approach, were made of unhewn stone. Behind it was a bronze laver for ceremonial washing, and on the north was the place for the preparation of the sacrifices. The altar of incense, the table of show-bread, and the golden candlestick were assigned to their old places, but the inner sanctuary seems to have been bare, with the exception of the stone-plate mentioned above.

The glory of the third temple was only of short duration. According to the prophecy of Jesus, Mark 13, 2, not one stone of the temple was left upon the other. When Jerusalem was destroyed, 70 A. D., by the Romans under the leadership of Titus, the entire complex of temple buildings was razed. The golden candlestick, the table of prothesis, and other articles were carried to Rome as trophies, and their sculptured figures adorn the arch of Titus. They now very probably rest in the quicksands of the Mediterranean Sea, near the coast of Africa.

CHAPTER 2.

The Places of Worship of the Early Christian Church.

So long as the Savior was on earth, bringing the message of salvation through grace to the people of Israel, there was no need for special houses of worship. He preached the Word at all times and in all places: in houses, in synagogs, in the fields, on the sea-shore, in the wilderness, on the mountains, in the temple. His disciples at that time were still members of the Jewish church, and, with Him, performed the outward works of the cultus. After the day of Pentecost, indeed, the organic connection of the disciples with the Jewish Church was loosened and, in many cases, even severed. They were considered and treated as heretics by the religious leaders of the Jews. So long as they could, they continued to have assemblies in one of the many halls of the temple, Luke 24, 53; Acts 2, 46; 3, 11—26; 5, 12. 42. But reasons of prudence soon caused a withdrawal from such public places. It became the custom to meet in the houses of members of the congregation. We find the upper room, the *hyperoon,* mentioned as a place of assembly and worship, Acts 1, 13; 20, 8. There was a service of prayer in the house of Mary, the mother of John Mark, Acts 12, 12. The Christians not only celebrated the Holy Communion in the houses of the members, but conducted regular preaching services there as well, Acts 2, 46; 5, 42 *(kat'oikon).* The apostle Paul, indeed, on his missionary trips, had the custom of conducting services in the synagogs of the Jews, Acts 13, 14; 17, 1. 2. 10; 19, 8. In the course of these journeys he preached also on the banks of the river that flowed through or near the city of Philippi, Acts 16, 13. Later, when all his efforts in behalf of the Jews met with a cold reception, he spoke daily in the school of one Tyrannus, in Ephesus, Acts 19, 19. But the usual meeting-places of the little bands of Christians seem to have been the houses of members of the congregation. We are told that Justus of Corinth opened his house to Paul, Acts 18, 7. Peter preached in the house of Cornelius, Acts 10, 27. That the holding of services in private houses was the custom in Apostolic days, we learn from Rom. 16, 23, where Gaius is called the host of the whole congregation; from 1 Cor. 16, 19, where we read of a church or congregation in the house of Aquila and Priscilla; and from Col. 4, 15, where we are told that there was a church or congregation in the house of Nymphas. This custom continued into the second century and beyond. Clemens Romanus relates of a rich man, Theophilus of Antioch, that he offered his house to be dedicated as a church.[27] And the same is related of a senator in Tours at the time of Constantine.[28] In the case of small congregations, the *atrium* may have been large enough for the regular meetings; in other cases, the *tablinum* and even the *peristylium* could easily have been added to accommodate the larger number.[29]

In the meantime, we find evidence that the Christians began to dedicate halls and public assembly places for purposes of worship. Not all emperors were filled with the bloodthirsty hatred of Nero and Diocletian toward the Christians. Alexander Severus, 222—235, and his mother, Julia Mammaea, were more than lenient toward them.

27) Domus suae ingentem basicilam ecclesiae nomine consecraret. In Alt, *Der kirchliche Gottesdienst,* 41, note 1.
28) Gradmann, *Geschichte der christlichen Kunst,* 27.
29) Cp. Lowrie, *Monuments of the Early Church,* 98. 99.

The domestic chapel of the emperor was filled with the images of those heroes who, by improving or reforming human life, had deserved the grateful reverence of posterity. Among these heroes he reckoned also Abraham and Jesus. "Under the reign of Severus, the fury of the populace was checked; the rigor of ancient laws was, for some time, suspended; and the provincial governors were satisfied with receiving an annual present from the churches within their jurisdiction, as the price or as the reward of their moderation." [30]) It is not surprising, therefore, that this emperor, in a controversy between a Christian congregation and some liquor dealers with regard to a certain piece of public property, decided in favor of the former.[31]) It is altogether probable that indulgent governors and magistrates, especially under Caracalla and other lenient emperors, often gave the Christians permission to use the public halls for their services, since the latter, for reasons of conscience, could not use the temples with their altars of idolatry. Any suggestion, indeed, as though the cultus of the Christians had anything in common with that of the pagan religions, either as to places of worship or images used for idolatrous purposes, is repudiated with the greatest emphasis by Origen, Minucius Felix, Lactantius, Arnobius, and others.[32]) The decided disavowal of Origen was directed against the pagan sacrificial altars and the *naos* or niche with the image of the heathen god. He does not, as some scholars have thought, deny the existence of Christian houses or places of worship.

In this connection, mention must also be made of the catacombs as assembly places of the early Christians, especially during the persecutions, when the confessors of the new religion were often hunted like wild beasts. The catacombs were subterranean cemeteries (coemeterium — koimeterion), the sleeping places of those who died in the faith. They are found not only in Rome, but also in Naples, Syracuse, and other cities, even in Syria. The most noted ones are those along the *via Appia,* especially those of Balbina and of Callistus, that of Domitilla on the *via Ardeatina,* and that of Lucina on the *via Ostiensis.* The catacombs are subterranean corridors, with horizontal excavations in the walls, which are often widened out into cells or small rooms. Here the dead were deposited, usually in sarcophagi. The larger chambers, including the tombs of martyrs, were called *cryptae,* ordinary chambers *cubicula,* and the horizontal tombs *sepulcra* or *loca.* Some of the crypts were designed expressly for Christian worship, as, for example, that of Miltiades in S. Callistus;

---

30) Gibbon, *Decline and Fall of the Roman Empire,* I, 646.
31) Melius esse, ut quomodocunque illic Deus colatur, quam popinariis dedatur. In Alt, *Der kirchliche Gottesdienst,* 41, note 2.
32) Alt, *Der kirchliche Gottesdienst,* 42.

A still larger chapel is a crypt in the Ostrian cemetery, which is divided into nave, presbytery, and apse. Another very interesting chapel is the *Capella graeca* in S. Priscilla, especially on account of its fine decoration. After the year 410, in which the invasion of Alaric took place, the catacombs were no longer used as burial places, and a few centuries later even the crypts of the martyrs were abandoned, their bones having meanwhile been removed to the altar-crypts of various churches which bore their names.[33])

That there were special places, rooms, or buildings used expressly and exclusively for church purposes and designated by the name church at least as early as the latter half of the second century, is evident from several passages in the early church fathers. Clemens Alexandrinus calls the place where the faithful come together, *ekklesia*. Tertullian, in a sharp criticism of those Christians that made heathen idols for a living, calls the *domus Dei* the *ecclesia*. Hippolytus in one instance refers to the *oikos theou,* in another to the *ekklesia*. The remark of Eusebius in regard to the houses of prayer and the churches, which he calls *ekklesiai,* is well known. Even Origen, in a homily, speaks of such as bring gifts *ad ornatum ecclesiae.* A little later, Cyprian uses the designation *kyriakon* for the house of worship, and we find the word *conventiculum.* Still later, at the beginning of the fourth century, Optatus of Mileve makes the statement that there were more than forty churches in Rome to house the large number of believers.[34]) It is absurd to conjecture that these assembly-places were mere *cellae cimiteriales.* On the contrary, this statement comes in the nature of a climax to show that the Christians of the first three centuries, even before the toleration edict of Constantine, had actual church buildings, of whose size and beauty they had no reason to be ashamed. In addition to the circular church at Antepellius in Asia Minor and one of the basilican type at Silchester in England enough ruins have been uncovered in the last decades to remove all doubts as to the truth of this statement.

This introduces the question of the manner in which the development of Christian architecture took place. Various scholars have answered the question by pointing to the forensic basilica, to the private basilica, to the Roman house, and to the *cella cimiterialis* as the type. Others claimed for the early church building an architectural creation. That the rectangular form of the early church building, the so-called basilica, was patterned after the large public buildings thus designated, is stated with or without restriction by Meurer,[35]) Ham-

---

33) Cp. Gradmann, *Geschichte der christlichen Kunst,* 9—14; Meurer, *Der Kirchenbau,* 22—26; Lowrie, *Monuments of the Early Church,* 23—47; Hauck, *sub* Koimeterien.

34) Hauck, *sub* Kirchenbau; Alt, *Der kirchliche Gottesdienst,* 43. 44.

35) *Der Kirchenbau,* 28.

lin,[36]) Fergusson,[37]) Smith,[38]) and others. The idea of an independent artistic creation is championed by Ziegeler.[39]) But the more plausible conjecture of a gradual development of the classical dwelling, with subsequent additions and modifications, is held by Schultze,[40]) Hauck,[41]) Gradmann,[42]) and has been defended in a very convincing manner especially by Lowrie. The latter writes: "Certainly the most attractive theory of the development of the basilica which could be advanced is that which refers its origin to the private house, and the Apostolic custom of gathering there for worship. . . . We have every reason to believe that the Lord's Supper was, during the Apostolic age, and indeed through the first quarter of the second century, celebrated invariably in a private house. This was altogether natural in the case of a sacrament which was in its institution — still more obviously in its prototype, the Passover — a household meal, and represented the church in terms of the family. That the dwelling-house was the regular place for the celebration of the Eucharist throughout the first stadium of the development of the Eucharistic cultus is especially important in this connection, because the practices and ritual which centered in the Eucharist have always been one of the chief factors regulative of church architecture, and nowhere more obviously than in the case of the basilica. . . We may suppose that the earliest churches were either actually dwelling-houses which had been adapted and perhaps enlarged for Christian worship, or new buildings which preserved both without and within substantially the appearance of the private house. . . If we must recognize that the scheme of the basilica was prescribed by the necessities of the Christian cultus, we must recognize that the cultus was in turn determined in part by the arrangement of the private house." [43]) He then proceeds to show how the peristyle or *atrium,* together with the *tablinum,* and, in Roman houses, the *alae,* was changed by a colonnade surrounding the *impluvium,* permitting also the introduction of clerestory windows, into an ideal hall for the Christian assembly. The *tablinum* became the apse, the *alae* the transepts. The fundamental scheme of the structure, up to the fourth century, also the light construction and other factors, made the Christian basilica a building different from the public basilica used for market and court purposes [44]) In a similar way, Hauck describes the development of the early Christian

---

36) *History of Architecture,* Chapter X.
37) *History of Architecture in All Countries,* Part I, Book IV; Part II, Book I.
38) *Architecture, Classic and Early Christian,* Chapter XI.
39) *Einfuehrung in die christliche Kirchenbaukunst.* 1.
40) *Das evangelische Kirchengebaeude.* 5.   41) *Sub* Kirchenbau.
42) *Geschichte der christlichen Kunst,* 27.
43) *Monuments of the Early Church,* 94—96.   44) *L. c.,* 97—102.

basilica. He distinguishes a first period, during which the *atrium* of Greek and Roman houses served for church purposes; a second period, when the nave became rectangular, with apse; and the final stage, when the size of the congregations made the basilica-form of church possible, with certain modifications, however, which distinguished it from the public or forensic basilica (*sub.* Kirchenbau).

We cannot ignore the fact, of course, that a great many of the early Christian buildings used for purposes of worship had the circular form (Zentralbau), or, more properly speaking, there was a polygonal or circular base, and the entire arrangement was made with reference to a central perpendicular axis. "This principle is exemplified as well in the round buildings which consisted of concentric colonnades, covered by a conical roof, as in those, whether polygonal or round, which were surmounted by a dome. The dome, however, is the typical example of this principle, and, wherever it is employed, it exercises a strong centralizing effect." [45]) In order to understand this type of architecture, it should be remembered that the basilica was the normal type of churches built to serve congregations assembled for worship. "But special ritual observances or the desire to display princely pomp brought about the use of the circular structure, which became the normal one for baptisteries and memorial churches." [46]) The best designation for this form of churches is *oratory.* "As a sanctuary the rotunda, especially in the natural combination with the cupola vaulting, has in itself a powerful significance. It is the most impressive place of prayer, for the cupola is the most evident type of heaven." [47]) In the few instances in which the central building was used for preaching services and for celebrating the Eucharist, the builders added a semicircular extension with a radius considerably smaller than that of the building itself. In this apse were located the seats of the clergy, on a raised platform. In at least one case, that of the Church of the Apostles in Constantinople, the altar had the position which this form of building requires, namely in the exact center. In some cases heathen temples in this style were remodeled and then dedicated for Christian worship. The most notable case is the Pantheon of Agrippa, built by Valerian under the Emperor Augustus, which Boniface IV accepted as a gift from the Emperor Phocas and dedicated to the Virgin and the Martyrs. It is now known as the Chiesa di Sta. Maria dei Martiri, called Chiesa della Rotonda for short.

In most cases, however, there was no attempt at making these structures into regular churches. Their most frequent use was for baptismal chapels. Some writers have even thought that they were

---

45) Lowrie, *Monuments of the Early Church,* 131. 132.
46) Schaff-Herzog, *sub* Architecture.   47) Gradmann, *Op. cit.,* 48.

developed from the circular baths or *piscinae* of the classical age.[48])
The baptisteries were so necessary in the early days of the Church,
since most of the candidates for baptism were adults, and since the
sacrament was commonly, though not by any means always, administered by immersion. In other instances, buildings of this type were

ENTRANCE TO THE CHURCH OF THE HOLY SEPULCHER.

used for mausoleums, not only on account of their shape, but because
of their monumental solidity.

The central type of church building, in the early stages of Christian architecture, was a round or polygonal structure, whose heavy
dome construction required a very solid supporting wall. This was
usually broken or relieved by a series of niches, partly for artistic
considerations, but also for economy in the use of building material.

48) Ziegeler, *Einfuehrung in die christliche Kirchenbaukunst*, 13.

The exterior, in most cases, presented little ornamentation, but the interior was often decorated profusely with colored plates and mosaics. The semicircular niches also afforded opportunity for arches resting upon engaged columns. In some cases, elaborate paneling was employed, especially in the dome.

A few of these ancient buildings have remained, exhibiting their original structure and ornamentation. The Church of St. George, at Thessalonica, S. Stefano Rotondo, in Rome, and the Church of the Ascension, at Jerusalem, were used for general church purposes. The Church of S. Giovanni in Fonte, at Ravenna, the Arian Baptistery, of the same city, and the Lateran Baptistery, in Rome, are examples of baptismal chapels. They are also the types from which the later splendid baptisteries of Pisa and Florence were developed. S. Petronilla, one of the round buildings formerly adjoining the first Church of St. Peter, in Rome, is an example of a mausoleum in this type. And another name, which is still better known, is that of the Chiesa Sta. Costanza, in the same city, erected over the catacombs of Sta. Agnes, and originally the mausoleum of Constantia, the sister or daughter of Constantine the Great. The further development of the central type of church building resulted in the Byzantine style, which will be discussed below.

For the entire West and wherever its influence was potent enough, the basilica in its Christian form became the model. It was an edifice eminently suited for the cultus of the Christian religion. The preaching service of the congregation was, in its essential parts, modeled after that of the synagog, and consisted of prayers, Scripture readings, and exposition. It demanded an elevated position for the elder, a reading desk for the lector, a place where the assembly could hear well. In addition to this, the Christian service demanded a table for the Eucharist. All this could be provided for by a division of the church building as had been suggested by St. John, who distinguishes between the *thysiasterion,* or altar, the *naos,* or temple nave, and the *aule he exothen,* the outside hall, Rev. 11, 1. 2.[49])

In agreement with these fundamental factors, the Christian basilica consisted of three main parts. In front of the entrance of the church was the *atrium* or fore-court. It was an open space surrounded by a covered arcade, portico, or cloister. In the center of this court was the *cantharus,* a fountain or basin of pure water. Here the ceremonial ablutions of hands, face, and feet took place. The practise is continued in the Catholic Church in the custom of making the sign of the cross with holy water before entering the church. The *cantharus* was usually surrounded by a balustrade of

---

49) Cp. Gradmann, *Geschichte der christlichen Kunst,* 28.

PLAN OF THE LATER BASILICA.

sculptured marble; it was very frequently surmounted by an ornamental roof supported on columns.[50]) The *atrium* was the place of the *poenitentes,* the *locus lugentium sive hiemantium,* for such as were being disciplined severely were not permitted to enter the church proper until their time of penance was over. Here also the instruction of the catechumens and the feeding of the poor took place.[51]) The arcade in front of the building formed a porch or vestibule, which was called *narthex.* Since the *atrium* was not indispensable, this vestibule fully compensated for its absence, especially in the Orient. It was often constructed in several stories, and then usually contained the stairway to the galleries of the church. In some cases, baptisteries or round towers were built adjoining the *atrium.*

The church proper was usually a rectangle, known as the body or nave. The very name indicates the symbolical conception. The church was conceived as a ship under full sail, riding forward to heaven and eternity. For that reason, the principle of length was always observed. And the length of the church building was commonly orientated, as we learn from the Apostolic Constitutions, except where local considerations, the position of a martyr's grave, the location of bodies of water, etc., made a deviation from the rule permissible. Since the Romans and Greeks had built their temples so that the morning sun shone through the opened doors, the Christians, avoiding even the appearance of evil, had the doors of their churches in the west and the altar in the east, signifying that the light of the Gospel came from the Orient. The width of the church hall was commonly broken by either three or five aisles, of which the central one was the widest, and was called the nave proper. Its roof was raised above the aisles, thus forming clerestory walls with windows. The width of the side aisles was usually about half that of the middle. The height of the nave was not great in proportion to its length; throughout the building there was a preponderance of horizontal lines.

Immediately inside the doors, in the rear of the nave, was the place for those who were not yet members of the congregation, the catechumens, the *poenitentes* of the lesser grade, and the Jews and Gentiles, all of whom were mere *audientes* (hearers). A little farther forward, and in the side aisles, the *consistentes,* who were refused the Sacrament for a time, as the mildest form of penance, and beyond them, the men and women members of the congregation had their place. Those who were held in high honor in the congregation, widows, virgins, deaconesses, and those whom their age and social position rendered worthy of peculiar regard, had their place in the forward end of the aisles or in the transepts. In the east end of the

---

50) Lowrie, *Op. cit.,* 179.   51) Gradmann, *Op. cit.,* 29.

nave was the choir, sometimes on a level with the nave, then again
even with the floor of the apse, and enclosed by a balustrade, which
was often designated as the chancel, just as the screen or railing of
the apse was later. There was an ambo or reading pulpit on either
side of the choir, the one on the south side being devoted to the reading of the Epistle, and the other for the reading of the Gospel. The
space inside the nave chancels or curtains was set aside for the choir
and the other inferior clergy, such as acolytes and subdeacons. Even
in the early days, but oftener after the coalition of the Gallican
Church with that of Rome, the transept was added in the eastern end
of the nave, giving to this part of the church the form of a capital T,
which was considered by many the shape of the cross of Christ. But
the transept was probably not added for symbolical reasons only, but
was rather suggested by, or developed from, the *alae* of the classical
dwelling.

The entire arrangement of the church building, especially the
observation of the principle of length and the orientation, drew attention to the altar space or chancel, as it is now called. This part
of the church building was a round or polygonal extension on the
eastern end. The large entrance arch leading from the nave to the
apse was called the triumphal arch. The chancel or apse was called
the *presbyterium,* since it contained the *sedilia* of the higher clergy;
apsis, exedra, or *concha,* on account of its form; *tribuna* or *tribunal,*
because the magistrates occupied a similar room in the civil basilica;
and *bema,* because its floor was raised several feet above that of the
nave. The bishop's chair or *cathedra* stood at the head of the apse,
elevated several feet, so that the bishop could easily be seen above the
altar, which stood at the entrance to the apse, below the triumphal
arch. On either side of the *cathedra* were the seats of the presbyters,
while the deacons stood near the altar.

The basilicas were usually constructed of brick or stone. The
pillars supporting the clerestory walls and separating the nave from
the aisles were often taken from classical buildings, although this
form of vandalism was not practised so much as has been alleged.
The roofs were made of wood, supported on trusses, the ceiling, as a
rule, being constructed of paneling. The small openings of the wood
or stone windows were fitted with colored lights. There were variations, of course, some churches being more pretentious, others less so
than the type described here. For such is the description which we
obtain from an oration by Eusebius,[52] from the regulations of the
Apostolic Constitutions,[53] and from the extant churches of the type,

---

52) *Church History,* X: 4.   53) Book II, Chapter 57.

since some of them have been preserved in essentially the same form as they were built.[54])

Of the many interesting basilicas of the early Church which have been preserved or restored, as nearly as possible, to their original form, the following may receive mention here. In the year 326 Constantine erected the Church of the Holy Sepulcher at Jerusalem. There was a great five-aisled basilica for the assembly of the worshipers. A very interesting structure was the old basilica of St. Peter's, in Rome, which preceded the present monumental edifice. Other basilicas of Rome were Sta. Maria Maggiore, Sta. Agnese, S. Lorenzo, S. Clemente, Sta. Sabina, and S. Paolo fuori le Mura, which was destroyed by fire in 1823, but immediately rebuilt. Noteworthy examples were also in Ravenna: S. Apollinare in Classe, Sta. Agata, and S. Spirito. Among the churches of the Orient which had this form were the basilicas in Kalb-Lused, Turmanin, and Ruweha, Syria, and those of Tyre, Nicomedia, and especially S. Demetrio, of Saloniki, which was recently destroyed in the great fire which swept the city. The Church of the Nativity at Bethlehem is hardly to be distinguished, in its strict adherence to type, from the western basilicas. Recent explorations and excavations in Africa have shown that basilicas were comparatively common in the early centuries of the Christian era.

CHAPTER 3.

The Byzantine Style.

It is a peculiar fact based upon the liturgical ideas of the Eastern Church that the ecclesiastical structures of the Orient followed an essentially different line of development than those of the West. And since architecture, in a measure even more than the other arts, is an expression and revelation of the cultus of the respective ecclesiastical organization, this development is particularly interesting. The Greek liturgy is a drama of great intensity and symbolical presentation,[55]) and the Byzantine churches bear a strong resemblance to theaters. The nave is reserved for the audience, the sanctuary or apse with its side chapels is the stage. There are also a number of doors and curtains, each of which has its symbolism. Even the *narthex* is employed for a portion of the dramatic representation. The cupola or dome is a picture of heaven, bathed in a flood of light to draw the attention

54) Gradmann, *Op. cit.*, 27—35; Ziegeler, 2—7; Schultze, 5—8; Meurer, 27—37; Alt, *Der kirchliche Gottesdienst*, 51—55; Lowrie, 101—131; Hamlin, Chapter X; Smith, Chapter XI; Collett-Sandars, Book II, A, Chapter I.
55) Alt, *Der kirchliche Gottesdienst*, 204.

upward. The heavy columns upon which the weight of the dome rests in such an obvious manner, are the priests that form the means of communication between earth and heaven.

These ideas found their best expression in the central type of building, although the basilican principle of length is sometimes introduced. The simple polygonal or circular church was not large enough to accommodate large assemblies. In order to gain more room without interfering with the fundamental idea of the building, the niches were often extended into small alcoves, as in the Church of S. George at Esra. In the church at Bosra the apse with the choir extends to the center of the edifice, and there are two small chapels, one on either side of the sanctuary. In some cases, the churches were built in the form of a Greek cross, with a polygonal or circular dome over the center. To this class belonged the Church of the Apostles at Constantinople, built by Constantine as a mausoleum for himself and his family. This church was the model for one built by St. Ambrose in Milan, in 382, as well as for some smaller ones. The cross-shaped church surrounding the well of Jacob in Samaria also belonged to this type.

For a few centuries after the Council of Nicea, the importance of the sermon was still recognized, and therefore some churches made allowances for this requirement. A notable instance is the Church of Sta. Irene at Constantinople, where some effort seems to have been made to indicate horizontal direction. But the result is altogether unsatisfactory, since neither the central disposition is maintained nor the requirement of length satisfied. The ceiling is a compromise, doing justice to neither idea. S. Vitale in Ravenna is another example. But here the massive supporting columns and piers interfered very decidedly with the idea of length. And whenever the concept of the central type was accentuated, as in the Church of S. Lorenzo in Milan, the addition of the apse and of chapels give the entire plan a disjointed appearance, entirely at variance with the principle of unity. Half domes, set over the arms of the church, rising gradually to the great central cupola, were a great aid to the external symmetry of the building, but proved of no help for the further improvement of the interior.

It was not until the oblong plan of church building was introduced that a satisfactory solution of the question of combining the Byzantine idea with the basilican principle was reached. At the same time, the application of the pendentive, the spherical triangle of masonry arising from the pier below and forming, with its mates, a solid circle, from which the dome could rise like a beautiful hemisphere, was most successful. This culmination of the first period of

Byzantine architecture had not only the characteristics of a vaulted or domed basilica and the use of the pendentive, but it also made use of buttresses and had the interiors richly decorated, with carved details.

The most perfect building embodying the ideas and characteristics of this style is the *Hagia Sofia,* at Constantinople. The first

HAGIA SOFIA, CONSTANTINOPLE.

Church of the Holy Wisdom (the divine Logos, Jesus Christ) was built by Constantine as his cathedral shortly after the first Council of Nicea. When this church was destroyed by fire during the Nika Rebellion, in the year 532, the emperor Justinian resolved to replace it with the most perfect as well as the most splendid church palace ever erected. Since he spent the greater part of his reign in building large and beautiful churches, each of which was considered a master-

Kretzmann, Christian Art. 3

piece by the historian Procopius, his enthusiastic ambition made use of all resources to realize his ideal. He employed Anthemios of Tralles as architect and builder. On the 26th of December, 537, this masterpiece of the art of architecture was dedicated. And so thoroughly had the ambition of Justinian been realized, so exactly had his ideas been executed that he had some cause for his proud exclamation, "O Solomon, I have surpassed thee!" But twenty-two years after its completion, a part of the dome was destroyed during an earthquake. Justinian immediately charged Isidorus of Milet with its reconstruction. The execution of this commission fully measured up to the standard of the first dome. On Christmas Eve of the year 563 the church was dedicated for the second time. This splendid building, used as a mosque by the Turks since the capture of Constantinople in 1453, will now probably be reconverted into a Christian church. In that case, the beautiful mosaics and inscriptions that have been covered by a coat of paint will again be restored, and the minarets and other exterior additions which have nearly transformed the appearance of the church will be removed.

The ground-plan of *Hagia Sofia* shows a three-aisled, oblong basilica. Its center is a circle inscribed in a square. On either side of this square is a half-circle of the same diameter as the center one. The half-circles, in turn, open out into three semicircular cells. One of these is the apse. Opposite this concha is the opening to the narthex and the atrium. There are nine doors to the narthex, five to the atrium, and there was probably a special vestibule with three great portals.

The dimensions of the church are in themselves almost enormous. The building proper has the shape of a rectangle, being approximately 250 feet long by 235 feet wide. The distance between the four pillars whose pendentives directly bear the weight of the dome, is 110 feet. The nave is just twice as long as it is broad, measuring 200 by 100 feet, and the ceiling of the dome rises 180 feet above the center of the floor. The area enclosed is approximately 70,000 square feet.

The illumination was unusually generous. "Windows are pierced freely, not only in the high side walls, but in the half-domes, in the apse, and in the niches, while the crown of windows which illuminates the whole circumference of the dome seems to isolate it, as though it were suspended in the air." [56] Enormous sums of money were expended for decoration, in order to make this church the finest the world had ever seen. The surface of the walls and the vaulting, as well as the floor, was constructed of elaborate work in mosaics, inlaid with gold. The ornamentation was gorgeous to an extreme degree,

56) Lowrie, *Monuments of the Early Church*, 158.

The bishop's chair was decorated with silver. There were pictures of angels, of apostles, of the Virgin. The altar was overlaid with gold and set with precious stones. Together with its ciborium it was

INTERIOR OF HAGIA SOFIA.

valued at 40,000 pounds of silver. One of the ambons is said to have been worth one year's income from Egypt. The illumination at night, according to Paulus Silentiarius, was made by means of three great circles of lights suspended from the dome, supplemented by

rows of lamps and candelabra along the walls. "Any one that ever
has seen a dome, for instance that of Venice or Padua, illuminated
by night, may have a faint conception of the vaultings of the *Hagia
Sofia* on the night of Easter, shining in the volume of light, apparently enlarged into infinitude, as the marble walls and gold backgrounds and precious vessels reflected the light, a wonderful picture,
in which all the glory of the ancient Oriental empire was exhibited
and consecrated through the mysteries of the church." [57])

Some writers on architecture seem almost unable to find the
proper expressions to describe their appreciation of this palace among
the ancient churches, and its effect upon the visitor. "Never has
stability and daring, the *éclat* of color and purity of lines, never has
the genius of Rome and that of the Orient, been associated in a more
astonishing and a more harmonious whole," says Choisy.[58]) Another
recent writer calls the *Hagia Sofia* "the most perfect and most beautiful church which has yet been erected by any Christian people.[59])
And a noted lecturer says of it: "There are few impressions more
powerful than that which one receives when the interior of this building bursts upon the astonished gaze. It is in some respects more
overpowering than that of Cologne Cathedral, or St. Peter's at Rome.
For there are here no such chapels or side-aisles as we find in most
cathedrals. Its immensity at once reveals itself. . . . When we examine the details of this historic shrine, we begin to realize the richness of its decoration. In one place are galleries resting on beautiful
shafts of jasper, porphyry, and alabaster, supporting in their turn
arches that must have once been resplendent in their continuous
coating of golden mosaics. These monolithic columns were part of
the spoils taken from pagan shrines in Greece, Asia Minor, and Syria,
all of which were plundered by the Christians that they might thereby
render this the richest sanctuary in the world. Its wealth was, therefore, almost fabulous. A thousand persons were employed in its
service. It boasted of golden cases to contain the Gospels, of chalice-
cloths embroidered with pearls, of altars encrusted with jewels, of
crucifixes of solid gold, and of doors of cedar, amber, and ivory. In
fact, it was called 'The terrestrial paradise,' 'The earthly throne of
the glory of God.' " [60]) Other writers, however, while fully appreci-
ating the unexampled splendor of this church palace, have maintained, and rightly so, that this structure can hardly be said to fulfill the requirements of a Christian church. With all its gorgeous-
ness, it has the fault which must be alleged against most churches

---

57) Gradmann, *Op. cit.*, 65.
58) *Histoire de l'Architecture*, II: 34; Lowrie, 158.
59) Fergusson, *A History of Architecture in All Countries*, I, 446.
60) Stoddard, *Lectures*, II, 54—56.

of the Byzantine style: they are not built for the preaching of the Gospel.

The Church of *Hagia Sofia* marked the climax of the first period of the Byzantine style. There are other examples of this golden age of church architecture, which at least deserve to be mentioned. The church in Thessalonica of the same name as that in the Oriental capital is evidently built in imitation of that great cathedral. There are some modifications, such as the continuation of the narthex along the sides of the building in the form of a cloister or ambulatory. Other churches that belong to this period are S. Nicolaus of Myra, in Asia Minor, and Hagios Johannes, of Ephesus. The ruins of the latter now cover a large area.

For several hundred years after this, there were no great works of art in the Byzantine style of architecture. Then, however, a rejuvenation took place. There was a second golden era of church building, chiefly in the Orient. The fundamental characteristics remained the same: massive piers and wide arches, and pendentives with a dome rising over them in the main space, and vaulted spaces in connection with it. Another characteristic is the including of all buttress work within the edifice by roofing such space over and making it an integral part of the building. Oriental ornamentation was adopted more and more in the course of time. The exterior was often built up in a striped effect by using various colors of brick, stone, or marble in successive layers. The interior walls and vaultings were smooth, affording excellent space for wall mosaics, marble decoration, or mural painting. The illumination was diminished in harmony with the mysticism of the Oriental cultus. There were the first indications of a tendency toward a conventionalism which finally resulted in a dead formalism.

The Theotokos-Church of Thessalonica embodies practically all the characteristics named above, but still exhibits the normal type. The Church of S. Elias has no aisles. There is a Theotokos-Church also in Constantinople. Many other examples are found on the islands of the Aegean Sea, on Mount Athos, in Athens, Mistra, and throughout Asia Minor before the Mohammedan conquest. But the most majestic church of the second period of the Byzantine style is the Church of St. Mark's, in Venice.

The history of *San Marco* is very closely connected with that of the halcyon days of Venice, in the era when this city was practically an Oriental metropolis. It was in the year 828 that the relics of St. Mark were brought from Alexandria to Venice. As a shrine for these precious relics the first Church of St. Mark, probably a basilica of the old style, was erected. It burned down in 976, whereupon a first restoration was undertaken. In the last half of the eleventh

century, however, a new church palace, probably entirely different in
conception and execution, was erected. It was dedicated in the year
1094, but changes were made in details and ornamentation for the
next three hundred years, thus adding to the building certain Romanesque and Gothic features.

The church is an imposing structure. It is built in the cruciform plan, the inside dimensions being 200 feet east and west by 164

ST. MARK'S, VENICE.

feet north and south. The central and western domes are 42 feet in
diameter, the other three only 33 feet. The cupolas, with the magnificent arches beneath them, create an imposing rhythm of space,
form, and illumination, giving a mystic impression of sanctity. The
splendor of the ornamentation, especially the mosaics inlaid with
gold, enhances the effect of magnificence.

Few churches have evoked such volumes of praise as St. Mark's.
It may be that the historic associations and the picturesque setting

contribute somewhat to the general effect. But this does not change the fact that the excellence of its proportions and the skillful disposition of its parts impress even the unsentimental art critic. It has been called an "unexcelled creation of art." Poets have sung of the

INTERIOR OF ST. MARK'S.

church that "the glory of the Orient" is embodied in it. Mrs. Bell writes of it: "St. Mark's of Venice rivals S. Sophia in exquisite beauty of interior and excels it in ornate richness of the exterior." [61] Stoddard says, in part: "What a façade is this! Here, massed in

61) *Architecture*, Chapter V.

serried ranks, are scores of variously colored marble columns, each
one a monolith, and all possessing an eventful history. Some are
from Ephesus, others from Smyrna, while others still are from Constantinople, and more than one even from Jerusalem. On one, the
hand of Cleopatra may have rested; another may have cast its shadow
on St. Paul; a third may have been looked upon by Jesus. St. Mark's
is the treasure-house of Venice, a place of pride as well as of
prayer. . . . It is an impressive moment when one passes beneath
these gilded steeds and enters the interior of the cathedral. A twilight gloom pervades it, well suited to its age and the mysterious
origin of all it contains. The walls and roof are so profusely covered
with mosaics and precious marbles that it is easy to understand why
St. Mark's has been called the 'Church of Gold,' and likened to a
cavern hung with stalactites of precious stones. Some of these ornaments are of pagan origin; others have come from Christian shrines.
All, however, have had to pay their contribution to St. Mark's." [62)]
But a veritable paean of praise is Ruskin's description: "Between
those pillars there opens a great light, and, in the midst of it, as we
advance slowly, the vast tower of St. Mark seems to lift itself visibly
forth from the level field of checkered stones. And, on each side, the
countless arches prolong themselves into ranged symmetry, as if the
rugged and irregular houses that pressed together above us in the
dark alley had been struck into sudden obedience and lovely order,
and all their rude casements and broken walls had been transformed
into arches charged with goodly sculpture, and fluted shafts of delicate stone. . . . And well may they fall back, for beyond those troops
of ordered arches there rises a vision out of the earth, and all the
great square seems to have opened from it in a kind of awe, that we
may see it far away; — a multitude of pillars and white domes, clus-
tered into a long, low pyramid of colored light; a treasure-heap it
seems, partly of gold, partly of opal and mother-of-pearl, hollowed
beneath into five great vaulted porches, ceiled with fair mosaic, and
beset with sculpture of alabaster, clear as amber and delicate as
ivory, — sculpture fantastic and involved, of palm-leaves and lilies,
and grapes and pomegranates, and birds clinging and fluttering among
the branches, all twined together into an endless network of buds and
plumes; and, in the midst of it, the solemn forms of angels, sceptred
and robed to the feet, and leaning to each other across the gates,
their figures indistinct among the gleaming of the golden ground
through the leaves beside them, interrupted and dim, like the morning light as it faded back among the branches of Eden, when first its
gates were angelguarded long ago. And around the walls of the

62) *Lectures*, I, 319. 322.

porches there are set pillars of variegated stones, jasper, and porphyry, and deep-green serpentine spotted with flakes of snow, and
marbles that half refuse and half yield to the sunshine, Cleopatra-
like, 'their bluest veins to kiss,' — the shadow, as it steals back from
them, revealing line after line of azure undulation, as a receding tide
leaves the waved sand; their capitals rich with interwoven tracery,
rooted knots of herbage, and drifting leaves of acanthus and vine
and mystical signs, all beginning and ending in the cross; and above
them, in the broad archivolts, a continuous change of language and
of life — angels and the signs of heaven and the labors of men, each
in its appointed season upon the earth; and above these, another
range of glittering pinnacles, mixed with white arches edged with
scarlet flowers, — a confusion of delight, amidst which the breasts of
the Greek horses are seen blazing in their breadth of golden strength,
and the St. Mark's lion, lifted on a blue field covered with stars, until
at last, as if in ecstasy, the crests of the arches break into a marble
foam and toss themselves far into the blue sky in flashes and wreaths
of sculptured spray, as if the breakers on the Lido shore had been
frost-bound before they fell, and the sea-nymphs had inlaid them
with coral and amethyst." [63]   In spite of this ecstatic utterance,
however, the glory of St. Mark's also is not that of an ideal Christian
church building.

There are other isolated instances of Byzantine influence in the
Occident. A notable example is the Cathedral of Pisa with its tower.
This church is not built strictly in one style. It has the basilican
principle of length and peristyle and the regular cruciform shape,
yet its principal and most conspicuous feature is the Byzantine dome.
It is thus a conglomeration of various styles and ideas. Ravenna is
another city which felt the Byzantine influence very strongly. In
Germany, the Minster of Aachen, built by Charlemagne as a mausoleum chapel for himself, is based entirely upon Oriental ideas, although he was otherwise an eclectic. Its center is an octagon with a
diameter of fifty feet and a total height of one hundred. This is
surrounded by a circular cloister, two stories high, and surmounted
by a splendid dome. The design of several small chapels in Germany
and Switzerland has also been traced back to Byzantine influence.
With the exception of these few instances, the Occident found nothing in the Oriental style which really expressed the symbolism and
the requirements of its cultus, a fact which the few sporadic cases
cited above tend to emphasize.

But in the Orient, the Byzantine style retained its influence,
although its vitality was soon sapped, leaving nothing but a con-

63) *The Stones of Venice*, I, 101—103.

gealed, dead formalism. It is this fact which stands out so prominently in the Neo-Byzantine churches of the Greek Catholic Church,
especially in Russia, although Armenia and the countries along the
Danube all show the same influence. The Cathedral of Wladimir is
a church combining Armenian and Romanesque features with the
Byzantine type. Other instances are the churches of Kiev, Now-
gorod, and Rostow. In the course of time, other influences made
themselves felt, especially from India, Persia, and Turkestan. This
combination of tendencies resulted in some rather peculiar constructions. One characteristic is the strange, collar-like constriction of
the dome below the lantern. Another feature is the introduction of
many strange arches, elliptical-pointed, horseshoe-shaped, inverted
double, and others. There is often a strong resemblance to the pa-
godas and mosques of India and China. The ornamentation shows
features of the baroque, and even of the bizarre. The domes are
painted in the most discordant hues or covered with gold and silver.
The towers for bells are usually not integral parts of the churches.
In the interior, the absence of proper illumination contrasts strangely
with the gaudy and flimsy ornamentation. The entire architecture
with all its subsidiary arts is a striking symbol of the decadent church
with its dead ritualism.

The most lurid example of florid excrescence in this style is
probably the Church of St. Basil, in Moscow, built by Iwan the Terrible in the middle of the sixteenth century. This structure is really
a conglomeration of eighteen chapels, agreeing with the number of
saints to which it is dedicated. The design is conspicuously irregular, even the domes being constructed in the most varying sizes and
shapes. There are various kinds of heterogeneous cells, sacristies,
and towers. Dormers, bays, arches, turrets, and spires are affixed in
the most unlooked-for places. Small wonder that is has been called
by Kugler "a miracle of tastelessness".[64]) Of course one may find,
even in such a structure, a certain sensuous, barbaric beauty, as Stoddard writes: "The architecture of this marvelous structure is inco-
herent and amazing, yet, in a certain sense, beautiful. One would,
however, never suspect St. Basil's to be a Christian church, if it were
not for the gilded crosses that adorn its towers. The especial glory
of the building is its coloring, the effect of which can hardly be exaggerated; for it is painted in all the colors of the rainbow. Red,
orange, yellow, green, blue, violet, gold, and silver are blended in one
amazing mass, like a fantastic castle made of prisms. From the roof
rise eleven towers, apparently bound together like an immense bouquet
of architectural flowers. Each cupola is different. One represents

---

64) Gradmann, *Op. cit.*, 144.

an artichoke, another a pineapple, a third a melon, while others suggest the turbans of Oriental giants." [65]

Fortunately, not all Russian churches show this extreme type.
The Cathedral of the Assumption, in Moscow, and the Church of the
Annunciation, of the same city, are far more unassuming, although
they also have the typical defects of the Russo-Byzantine architecture. The Church of the Savior, in Moscow, built in the first quarter of the last century, has the bulbous domes, but otherwise, it exhibits nothing of the extremely fanciful and grotesque found in so
many Russian churches. It is built in the form of a Greek cross, of
cream-colored stone. The interior is decorated with barbaric magnificence. Variegated marble, jasper, porphyry, malachite, and alabaster, all cut and polished, occur in a great variety of forms. Altogether,
this cathedral, together with the Renaissance structures of Petrograd,
must be considered one of the finest structures under the jurisdiction
of the Greek Church.

There are isolated cases of Byzantine churches in America, but
such churches are, in most instances, built by congregations of the
Greek Orthodox faith. Occasionally one sees a Roman Catholic
church with Byzantine features, but the exceptions are so rare as to
confirm the rule.

CHAPTER 4.
The Romanesque Style.

The names which the historian chooses to designate certain periods are not always so expressive as those which we meet with in the
history of architecture. The name Byzantine is eminently fitting,
since its birth-place was the old Oriental capital, Byzantium on the
Bosporus, and its most excellent memorial is situated there. And
the name Romanesque is narrow enough to include the Occidental
buildings of the ninth to the thirteenth centuries, and sufficiently
encompassing to embrace all structures whose basic principle was the
round arch and certain other fundamental characteristics. There is
the same relation between the architecture of these centuries and the
early Christian, including the Carolingian Renaissance, as between
the Romance languages and the Latin tongue. The name Romanesque, therefore, does not designate a new art, but it is a continuation, with creative additions, of the early Occidental Christian art of
building. And just as the Latin language was obliged to undergo
many variations and transformations in the various countries until
finally new typical languages were the result: the Italian, the Spanish,

---

65) *Lectures*, VI, 320. 321.

the French with its many dialects, so also the principle of the ancient
Christian basilica was used as a model by the Germanic peoples, especially in France and Germany, varied and transformed to suit the
symbolism of their cultus, and transmitted to other countries, wherever their influence reached. It is for this reason that many scholars
make subdivisions for the Romanesque or round-arched style. We
read of Lombard, Rhenish, Romance, Norman, Saxon, Tuscan, Sici-
lian Romanesque architecture. The Tuscan Romanesque style is
that found in Tuscany, the ancient Etruria, especially in the structures of Florence and Pisa. That the Byzantine influence was very
strong here, was stated in the preceding chapter. The decorative
element also prevailed, and the detached tower became the campanile,
so characteristic of this section of Italy. In the Lombard style,
Byzantine traditions are still more strongly marked. Venice and
Ravenna were centers of art, and their example proved an impelling
power. The entire valley of the Po and the Adige, as well as the
Venetian lowland show evidence of this influence. It may be due to
this fact that Moore makes the criticism: "An imperfect imitation
of a more logical system, the principles of which they did not understand." [66]) The Saxon or Anglo-Saxon style is found in ancient
churches in England, built in the tenth and the first half of the
eleventh century. Its chief characteristics, as given by Mrs. Bell,
are great height compared with length and breadth of the building,
massive square towers, unadorned angular or semicircular towers,
stunted columns with plain capitals, deeply recessed windows, massive walls without internal decoration, no aisles or transepts.[67]) The
Norman style, as the name implies, had its inception in northern
France. It employed massive piers, but little vaulting; the vaulted
side-aisles were low; the doorways were richly adorned with carved
moldings. This style was transplanted to England with William the
Conquerer and there absorbed some ideas of the Anglo-Saxon structures. The characteristics of the Anglo-Norman style are stated by
Mrs. Bell: cruciform plan, great length in comparison with breadth
of the nave, columns of greater girth and height, massive walls,
beautiful clerestories, finely decorated doorways, strong external buttresses, twin western towers.[68]) A strange excrescence of the Norman
style is that which was developed in Sicily and southern Italy during
Norman rule. It seems that the Normans intended to introduce
their art of building, but later yielded to local influences. The result
is a strange mixture of Byzantine, Arabian, and Norman-French
forms. Greek mosaics, Oriental cupolas, Italian roof-trusses with

---

66) *The Medieval Church Architecture of England*, Chapter I.
67) *Architecture*, Chapter VII.   68) *Architecture*, Chapter VII.

Arabian coloring and Moorish stalactite vaulting, — all these are found in the same church building.[69]) The German Romanesque style, of which the Lombard is really only a subdivision, is found especially in the region of the Rhine. It exhibits the basilica plan with vaulted construction, barrel vaulting being employed very generally; if there is a clerestory, flying buttresses are usually present; in later times, six-part ribbed vaulting is found. It is the Rhenish style which reached the full freedom of consistent, mature, and concluding development.[70]) Since all these types, which we have now briefly surveyed, are merely adaptations or excrescences of the fundamental style, we may include them all in the same chapter, especially in the present brief summary, and venture a more detailed discussion of their common fundamental principles and characteristics.

At the beginning of this period the usual form of the churches was that of the ancient rectangular basilica, with the added apse. In small churches, this form was usually retained without aisle division. In larger churches, there was, almost invariably, a division into a large central aisle, called the nave, and commonly two, sometimes four, side-aisles. Later, the cruciform plan was very generally adopted in place of the simple, hall-like structure. The reason for the introduction of the cross-nave or transept was partly an historical one, since it corresponded to the *alae* of the Roman house. Very likely, though, the symbolic significance had more influence than historical or artistic considerations. Other changes in the groundplan, which were found in larger churches, were the adding of apses, either on the east walls, or on the north and south walls of the transepts, thus forming chapels of these arms. A second transept, narrower and shorter than the first, symbolized the superscription on the cross. Extensions of the cross-nave formed an ambulatory around the sanctuary with the high-altar. In some instances, especially when a church had two patron saints, a second large apse was constructed at the west end of the church. The main entrances were then on the north and south, in the western part of the church.

In the earlier churches, the walls were very heavy, because they had to carry the weight of the flat roofs. The windows were small and usually widened obliquely toward the outside to catch as much light as possible. The heavy columns which marked the division of the aisles carried the galleries over the aisles and also aided in bearing the weight of the roof. The column of the Romanesque period was round, with circular extensions at the base, and rested upon a square plinth. The shaft of the column was generally smooth, though

---

69) Gradmann, *Geschichte der christlichen Kunst*, 229. 230.
70) Schultze, *Das evangelische Kirchengebaeude*, 9.

decorations in low relief are occasionally found. The capitals were either plain cubes or such with convex or concave edges. It was an easy matter to decorate these cubes with leaves or geometric figures. Much more common than the graceful column was the ponderous pillar, usually four-square and plain, though molding or beading appears on the edges in some cases. The columns or pillars carried the round arches which supported the clerestory walls and gave a ponderous effect to the whole interior. The great expanse of wall space between the small windows was commonly covered either with mosaic decorations, geometrical designs, or pictorial representations, or with mural paintings, some of which were artistic productions of great merit.

The arrangement of the interior was not made subject to many changes. The (high-) altar retained its position just inside the apse. The place of the chancel (cancelli) is taken by a stone structure which is used for the reading of the Gospel lesson. This lectorium (Lettner) was often so high that it obstructed the view of the altar. For that reason, a second altar was placed in the nave which was known as the lay altar. Where the number of chapels in the transepts and elsewhere was large, there were altars for each chapel. There were balconies over the aisles, sometimes also over the entrance (used as oratorium for nuns). The towers, like the baptisteries, were originally detached structures. But gradually the incongruity of this arrangement seems to have been felt. The final result was that the tower was made an organic, integral part of the church building. In most cases, at least two towers were constructed, flanking the vestibule or porch, and containing the stairways to the balconies. They were usually square below, with an octagonal spire. If there was a large central tower over the main entrance in the west, additional smaller towers were usually erected at the corners. In unpretentious churches, a large tower was erected over the crossing of the nave and transept. It was usually octagonal in form, with many windows to aid in illuminating the main auditorium. In a few instances, there were small towers even at the north and south end of the transepts, thus resulting in a total of seven for the whole church (Limburg). The division of stories was indicated on the towers by horizontal water tables or a similar device. The windows are grouped in twos or threes, surmounted by arches and flanked by columns. In this way, the bluntness of the earlier forms was agreeably enlivened.

The most important change from the old basilican church which distinguishes the Romanesque style is in the construction of the roof. There were so many objections to the flat roof, not only of a symbolical, but also of a practical nature, that a substitute was eagerly seized upon in the form of vaulting. This vaulting could be carried out entirely in stone or brick, thus reducing or eliminating the danger of fire, and it took away the depressing effect of a flat ceiling. The vaulting at first was the so-called barrel vaulting, with a semicircular or stilted arch effect. This served to enliven the building to a considerable extent. Since, however, the position of the columns or pillars in the church really divided the auditorium into quadratic spaces, it was soon found practicable to construct round arches diagonally over these spaces, thus producing intersecting or cross vaulting. This added much to the beauty of the ceiling, taking away the dead line of the square effect. But this vaulting of the ceiling, in turn, necessitated a different wall construction, since there had to be some limit to the thickness of the walls. The thrust of the cross-vaulting, also, was not distributed evenly along the walls. Therefore the more graceful column gradually was abandoned for the ponderous pillar, and since the pillar often obstructed the view and shut out the light, it was placed halfway into the wall and became a pilaster, sometimes with only one half-column, sometimes with three or more, capable of upholding a very great weight. In addition to this, since "an arch never sleeps," the thrust of the cross-vaulting was effectually held back by buttresses, set against the pilasters on the outside of the church.

Another advance was the beautifying of the exterior of the churches, which in early times had been almost severely plain. Successful efforts were made to break up and diversify the façades and side-wall surfaces with appropriate ornaments. The frieze along the gables and under the eaves was not only decorated with various forms of molding, but also broken up into small arches. The doorways, portals, and window openings were also beautified with sculpture work. A fine effect was gained by having columns bearing graceful arches gradually recede into the wall. A notable example is the so-called "Golden Portal" of Freiberg. In some cases, the windows were grouped in series of three, with the center one higher than the others, thus producing the effect of height. It also became the custom to place a large circular window over the main portal. This window was divided into leaves and received the appropriate designation "rose window."

A peculiar remnant of earlier days was the crypt below the sanctuary. This was really an underground chapel, with vaulting, columns and pillars, apse and altar. Originally, the relics of the saint after whom the church was named had been deposited here. The custom of building crypts was gradually discontinued, as the relics were deposited under the altar.

There are, fortunately, quite a number of churches of this style still standing in all the countries where this type of architecture flourished. A brief description of a number of these may serve to accentuate the specific Romanesque characteristics embodied in their construction. That part of France which is south of the Loire really had its own development of the vaulted basilican type, but there are instances throughout the country and in Belgium. St. Martin of Tours (997—1014) was the most pretentious church of its time on the western side of the Alps. Of this old abbey church, which was especially noteworthy on account of its beautiful choir, now only two towers remain. The Church of St. Remy, of Rheims, was modeled after this church. It had a five-aisled nave and a three-aisled transept, showing bold and majestic outlines. Other exceptional church edifices were those of Avignon, Notre Dame de Doms, St. Sernin of Toulouse, St. Benigne of Dijon, the church at Conques, and the Cathedral of Tournay. In spite of the opposition made by the order of Cluny, the development of the apse into elaborate proportions continued. It was at this time that the cloistered ambulatories with the wreath of chapels about the apse were introduced. This form persisted even through the Gothic period. In the course of time, the churches embodied and reflected all the artistic aspirations of their communities. The cathedrals of Angoulême, Angers, and Poitiers are masterpieces, the beauty of their façades being fully equaled by the disposition and ornamentation of the interior. In the case of the Cathedral of Puy, Byzantine influence is again apparent in the domed vaulting. It was built during the time of the crusades and, in all its parts, breathes the spirit of its time. A church which seems to have prepared the way for the transition was the Minster of Cluny (1088 —1131). Its size was that of the basilica of St. Peter in Rome. Its nave was five-aisled, and there was a double transept and an ambulatory. The nave had barrel vaulting, the transepts cross-vaulting. The pilasters and pillars were constructed with the greatest technical skill, to counteract the thrust of the arches.

The Romanesque churches of Normandy were constructed under the influence of Benedictine ideas from Dijon and Cluny. William of Ivrea, the builder of St. Benigne of Dijon, was called by the Duke of Normandy to take charge of the monasteries in that country. And therefore we find in all the larger churches the same design: cruciform plan with vestibule, towers in the west and over the cross-vaulting of the transept, threefold choir and secondary apses at the ends of the transepts. But the Normans impressed upon their churches their own individuality. Both the principles of ship-building and of fortress-building were adapted in their cathedrals. The nave is very long and narrow, and the polygonal apse almost completes the illusion of the bow of a ship. The towers are four-square and massive. The addition of buttresses enhances the effect of rugged strength. There are several rows of windows, since there is often a double gallery. An early example is Mont-Saint-Michel. Caen became a great center of church architecture at the end of the eleventh century. It was here that William the Conqueror, in 1066, began to build St. Stephen's, whose nave was originally covered with a square roof, but later received vaulting. St. Nicholas, of the same city, still retains the pyramidal covering of the apse. In St. Trinité a further development is anticipated, and St. Etienne was fitted with vaulting in the twelfth century, sexpartite vaulting being used in the nave and barrel vaulting over the aisles.

The Norman ideas were elaborated still further in England, in the so-called Anglo-Norman style, which was referred to above. An early example was Worth Church, in Sussex. It was here that the addition of the second transept became almost the normal form, after the beginning had once been made at Canterbury (1096). The transepts were broken up into chapels. Transepts and apses are square; vaulting is rare, except in crypts; the round arch is a dominating feature. The principle of height is sacrificed entirely for that of length. Finally, the long center aisle makes the impression of a cloister, especially since the heavy pillars obstruct the view into the side aisles. The illumination of the interior is poor. There were some changes from the Norman type, mainly in this that the western towers were omitted and only that over the transept retained. The façade was often built up in perpendicular niches which served to enliven the whole building to some extent. Most of the larger English churches have been reconstructed in the Gothic style. But the abbey churches of Tewkesbury and Waltham are monuments of this type, and especially the Cathedral of Durham. It is here that we find the flying buttress employed to rest against the wall of the clerestory and counteract the thrust of the main roof. Other examples are the transept of the Cathedral of Ely, as well as parts of the cathedrals of Peterborough, Chichester, and Rochester, and the ruins of Kelso, in Scotland.

So far as Sicily (and southern Italy) is concerned, the characteristics of the special Romanesque type found here have been referred to above. Its chief monuments are the palace chapel of Palermo, whose decoration especially reminds one of Bagdad, the Monreale Minster, which is just as extravagantly decorated with Saracenic ornamentation, and the cathedrals of Palermo and Cefalu. In the "other Sicily," the mainland of southern Italy, the churches of Salerno, Amalfi, and Ravello show the Norman characteristics, though the influence of other styles is also evident. On the Adriatic coast, this influence is hardly noticeable, except perhaps in the rose window. The domination of Thessalonica and Ravenna was too strong. But in northern Italy, the Romanesque style, influenced, in part, by German types and builders, is plainly marked. Among the churches which are worthy of study are S. Zeno, of Florence, S. Miniato, of Florence, S. Babila, in Milan, and the Church of Vercelli. Still more interesting, however, as an expression of the type, is S. Ambrogio, of Milan. Here we find cross-vaulting in all the parts, with pilasters and pillars fashioned accordingly. Instead of employing flying buttresses, the builders elevated the side aisles to the height of the nave, thus producing the hall church, after the model of the crypts. The thrust of the main vaulting is thus held by the aisle construction, and the thrust of the aisle vaulting is distributed to various strong buttresses. We have here the original of the German "Hallenkirche," which was followed in most of the Lombard churches. The fact that the clerestory windows were now eliminated interfered with the illumination of the interior, but this difficulty was later solved in the Church of St. Michael of Pavia.

The Romanesque churches of Germany show a regular, rhythmic, consistent development of the fundamental ideas of the style. Here the eleventh century was truly the heroic era, for its art was simple, strict, and majestic. The steady progress of architecture is especially noteworthy along the Rhine. The distinctive characteristic of the German Romanesque is the cube capital. It was first used in the basilica of St. Michael, at Hildesheim. The dome of Treves presents a strange anomaly: the continuation of the ancient Christian basilica, with the choir, as well as the main entrance, in the west. The capitol church of Cologne has vaulted aisles and ambulatories. The origin of its clover-leaf apse has not yet been explained. Hirsau, with its St. Aurelius Church modeled after the Cathedral of Cluny, exerted considerable influence, churches of Goslar, Hildesheim, Schaffhausen, and elsewhere receiving their design and practical detailed execution from this church of the Order of Cluny.

In the second half of the eleventh century further progress was made, with a partial disregard of the model of Cluny. The Cathedral of Speier was reconstructed twice, due to floods and faults in the vaulting. In its final form, it presented a three-aisled vaulted basilica with single transept and semicircular apse. The Cathedral of Mainz was modeled after that of Speier, with minor changes, such as the omission of the ornamental half-column in the case of pilasters that received no thrust. The third cathedral belonging to this group is that of Worms. The round towers of this church flanking both

CATHEDRAL OF WORMS.

the eastern and the western choir and the octagonal towers over the cross-vaulting of the transept and over the eastern apse are especially noteworthy. The main entrances were on the north and south sides. A new departure is evident in the abbey church of Maria Laach. The quadratic sections of the plan were here changed to rectangular, which, with the round arch, presented some difficulties, since the arch lacked the proper support. In all other respects, this church shows the same ponderous solidity which is characteristic of all Romanesque buildings. However, the grouping of the windows under trefoliated

MAGDEBURG CATHEDRAL.

arches in the main tower has a rather charming effect. This church has six towers, while that of Bamberg may boast of only four, that of Bonn exhibits five, and Limburg even seven.

The latter church, incidentally, is notable for another reason. At the beginning of the thirteenth century, an unrest, a peculiar dissatisfaction with the straight lines and the closed curves of the Romanesque, became apparent. A seeking after greater freedom of construction manifested itself. Certain elements were introduced which led away from the old style and gave promise of something better and more ideal than anything heretofore attempted. The Cathedral of Limburg is an example of this transition. We find in it the elements of the Romanesque style as well as those of a type which in its very lines symbolizes the breaking away from the fetters of an oppressing condition. In the Dome of Limburg, the round arches of the windows are very agreeably offset by the pointed arches on the inside wall and over the aisles. It is somewhat strange that the incongruity and lack of harmony and rhythm in the combination of two different arches did not suggest itself to the builders. However, the art which the church architects felt more than definite rules could fix, finally found its expression in a new style, which was fully introduced at the end of the thirteenth century.

CHAPTER 5.
The Gothic Style.

The thirteenth century was marked by the beginning of the great unrest, social, political, and religious, which culminated in the Renaissance and the Reformation. It was the century of the Magna Charta in England, it was a period presaging the humanistic revival, it was an era of growth for the guilds. The social consciousness was aroused and an increasing activity in every line of social endeavor was made possible by the growing wealth of the people, both in town and country. This activity was manifested especially in the realm of religion. Not even the costly and devastating wars of this and the following centuries could materially interfere with the aspirations nor dampen the ardor of the enthusiastic builders of churches and cathedrals. The craze for building (Bauwut) which had characterized the preceding period was rather intensified than abated. "It was a great era of strife and endeavor, when people, dissatisfied with past results, made use of the most varied forms, until they had found in the Gothic style that new principle which now was carried out in all its consequences to the final exhaustion." 71) "The struggle between the old and new methods of building very clearly reflected that of the people for greater freedom of thought and action in the countries in which it took place. The keynote of both was an aspiration after nobler things, and, in architecture, a yearning for religious expression, typified by the pointing upwards of the spires and pinnacles of churches and cathedrals, coincided with the craving of builders for increased lightness and grace of structure." 72)

It has been stated that the Gothic style is the result of the effort to find the best manner of cross-vaulting, to have the weight of the roof rest more vertically, thus eliminating the heavy walls and making

71) Meurer, *Der Kirchenbau*, 63. 65.
72) Mrs. Bell, *Architecture*, 60. 61.

them serve simply for the purpose of enclosing the space of the church building. Hamlin defines it as "that system of structural design and decoration which grew up out of the effort to combine, in one harmonious and organic conception, the basilican plan with a complete and systematic construction of groined vaulting." [73] It is thus in its fundamental principle a matter of structure, and not merely of ornamental detail. In accordance with this basic idea, the barrel vault and the round arch were replaced by the pointed arch. But the conscious or unconscious striving typified in the Gothic style meant more than a mere physical or material advantage. Even as the columns and pillars in the old forms of architecture were reproductions of the mature tree-trunk, thus the lines of force in the pointed arches were the reproduction of the living, growing plants in nature. Wherever there is life, growth, strength in nature, the lines of force are found. And thus the lines of force in the Gothic style represent life, growth, strength of the best type. "The Gothic," says Price, "is dually a structural and a decorative architecture. Its development was as natural and as consistent as the growth of a tree, rising up, putting forth branches, and these, in turn, putting forth leaves. . . . It is the sense of upward motion, reaching often to the height of the sublime, which has made Gothic architecture essentially the architecture of the Church, rendering, as it does, a remarkable expression of spiritual nobility in architectural terms." [74]

The Gothic style is a sequel and outgrowth of the Romanesque, but the pointed arch changed structure and symbolism entirely. It introduced the concentration of strains upon isolated points of support by groined instead of barrel vaults. It made the wall a mere enclosure of the church space. It transmitted thrusts by the flagrantly flaunted device of the flying buttress. It took up the matter of ribbed vaulting, carrying it to the very limit of graceful endeavor. It lifted up highly-pitched roofs and gables to heights never dreamed of in earlier times and crowned the entire edifice with slender spires and pinnacles, growing ever more decorative and ever pointing upward in joyful ecstasy, until the whole building seems more than a mere sermon, — rather a splendid symphony in stone. Small wonder that most students of architecture have become enraptured with this great achievement of the Middle Ages. "Gothic cathedrals," says Hamlin, "express perfectly the idea of vastness, mystery, and complexity." [75] The Gothic is the "expression of inward faith till it attains bold enthusiasm, ever pointing heavenward," is the statement of Rosengarten. "The Gothic church in its classical perfection is

---

73) *History of Architecture*, 196.
74) *The Practical Book of Architecture*, 47—49.
75) *History of Architecture*, Chapter XV.

the most ideal and finished creation of church architecture and, at
the same time, the most perfect expression of the medieval religious
feeling." 76) "The Gothic edifice, in spite of all its splendor, has the
character of the meek and humble in the Christian meaning of the
term." 77) "The Gothic style more correctly ought to be called the
Christian style, because it gives the most pregnant expression to the
fundamental ideas of Christianity. The Gothic style, through the
adoption of the pointed arch and the buttress, has easily solved all
the most difficult problems of architecture. In its interior as well as
in the exterior architecture the Gothic dome makes the impression of
the supernatural." 78) "The Gothic style is the most Christian and
the most beautiful of all," says Dr. G. Palm. "In the Gothic, the
highest and most adequate Christian form of church building has
been found," writes another prominent critic. "The essence of the
Gothic style and its imposing effect is to be found in the vertical
lines. The *sursum corda* is, as it were, embodied in this style. . . .
All narrow and depressing effects have been taken away. The high
pilasters and pointed arches bowing to one another attract the eye
upward and lead the gaze uninterruptedly to the highest part." 79)
A more detailed examination of the characteristics will show how
well these laudatory statements are founded and borne out by the
construction in the Gothic style.

So far as the groundplan is concerned, there was little difference
between the Romanesque and the Gothic churches. The shape of the
nave was rectangular, usually broken or divided into three aisles (in
some cases five). The transept, which gave the church its cruciform
shape, was not emphasized so strongly as in the Romanesque, being
sometimes merely indicated. In smaller churches, the transept was
often omitted entirely. Instead of that, the custom of continuing
the side-aisles around the apse in the form of an ambulatory, from
which small chapels radiated, became more general. Since the building of the crypt was now no longer practised, the elevation of the
choir was not so pronounced. A mere balustrade was, in many cases,
the only indication of the segregation of the lower clergy and the
people. On the other hand, the dividing wall of the lectorium grew
into a most elaborate form, symbolical of the great gulf between the
higher clergy and the laity. The apse no longer had a semicircular
form, but was commonly built on the octagonal or polygonal plan.
The vestibule was an integral part of the church building.

Vaulted construction was the rule in the Gothic style, the only
exceptions being the English parish churches, which were rarely

76) Schultze, *Op. cit.*, 17. 77) Schnaase, *in* Schultze, 18.
78) Gaulke, *Religion und Kunst*, 22. 79) *Der Kirchenbau*, 68, 71.

vaulted. The quadratic sections of the church were replaced by rect-
angles in the center aisles. The pointed arches of the vaulting showed
plainly the lines of force whose arc was considerably greater than the
radius of the circle of height. The cross-vaulting rested on pilasters,
which consisted of four, eight, or even twelve half-columns set in the
wall and braced on the outside by heavy buttresses. If the church
had three or five aisles, the inner pilasters, which rose higher for each
successive story, were supported from the outside walls below by
means of flying buttresses, which in themselves were graceful reali-
zations of lines of force. The side aisles were thus, in most instances, considerably lower than the center aisles, thus showing a gradual
ascent to the highest ridge in the center of the church. A peculiarity
found especially in German churches was the building of all aisles
in the same height, though the side-aisles were much narrower than
the center aisle. This form of hall church lacked the climactic factor,
although the interior presented wonderful vistas of height and extent.

The greatest advance in the Gothic style was in the vaulting.
At first the comparatively simple quadripartite or cross-vaulting was
common. Soon, however, the more difficult sexpartite vaulting became customary. And, the problems of construction having been
solved, architectural embellishment suggested fanciful and even fantastic forms. The continental builders were finally satisfied with web
and net vaulting, but the English architects went even farther, in-
venting the so-called fan vaulting.

Since the entire weight of the roof and the vaulting now rested
on the pilasters through the medium of the pointed-arch vaulting, it
was no longer necessary to make the walls so thick and heavy as in
the previous styles. They therefore became mere enclosing screens.
Instead of the small windows of former times, which had scarcely
been more than loop-holes, large expanses of window-surfaces could
now be inserted. These were constructed in the pointed-arch design,
broken by mullions and tracery which ranged from the simply beautiful to the fancifully extravagant. The windows were glazed with
stained glass in figures and geometrical designs. So distinctive did
this feature of the large and beautifully colored windows become that
one author has suggested the name "painted-glass style" as being
more appropriate than "pointed-arch style" or "Gothic style." [80]
The rose window of the western wall was also a feature of the Gothic
style, more so even than in the Romanesque, from which it differed
by the application of the lines of force. The grouping of three narrow, high windows in series of threes or more in a single opening
under one great arch proved to be a most effective device.

---

80) Fergusson, *A History of Architecture in All Countries*, Book III.

More than ever before, the decorating of the façade and side walls was emphasized. The immense portals with their gradual recessing, adorned with beautiful sculpture work, rising into graceful square pinnacles surmounted by pyramids; the wide expanse of the wall, enlivened with turrets and exquisite tracery, and set in its center with the gleaming rose window, all these combined in producing a feeling of awe and reverence in the beholder. The towers were detached in only a few isolated instances, forming usually integral parts of the churches. In Germany and northern France, the towers continued upward in the graceful beauty of the spires with their open tesselated structure. Some churches had but one gradated tower over the main entrance, but the larger ones on the continent had a tower on either side of the front portal. But there were deviations from this rule, single towers over the transept crossing being the rule in England. But we also find towers at either side near the east end of the church, or flanking either the eastern or the lateral apses, or a single one at either the northern or southern end of the transept.

The fine arts were made subsidiary and ancillary in the best sense of the terms, uniting with architecture in forming one beautiful harmonious whole. Not only were the windows in their harmony and color excellent works of art, but the floor and wall mosaics recall the beauty of the early Christian art, while the mural paintings, in the contrast of their color schemes were often of a very high order and served well as an introduction to the perfect productions of the next period. And not only did the portals and window openings receive the attention of the sculptors, but the tympanum, the spandrils, the ridges, the spires, the turrets, and pinnacles, — all were decorated with innumerable ornaments modeled after the leaves and flowers of the surrounding country. Each niche was provided with a statue, and the very waterspouts were rescued from the commonplace, being formed in figures of animals, gargoyles, demons, and all the fantastic creatures of the medieval mind.

Such, then, are some of the characteristics and features of the Gothic style. If we strip the discussion of all non-essentials and reduce it once more to its simplest terms, the one fact stands out that the essential purpose of the Gothic style was so to construct the pointed vaulting and so to support the superstructure by buttresses as to render the roof independent of the walls and also, by the use of cross-vaulting, of the quadrangular floor-space. In the Gothic style, the full development of height was reached.

One can hardly understand the full significance of the Gothic style, however, without tracing its history in a more careful outline, as to beginning and growth, full realization, and gradual decline.

The transition style, called by some writers the late Romanesque, by others the preparatory Gothic, has its most characteristic monuments in the first half of the thirteenth century, although some of its churches were built in the twelfth century. Not only does the Dome

CATHEDRAL AT FREIBURG.

of Limburg on the Lahn exhibit the peculiarities which presaged a new style, but also the Minster of St. Denis and the Cathedral of Laon, not to mention a great many smaller churches of northern France. But the full vitality, originality, and diversity of the new style did not appear until about the second quarter of the thirteenth century, the *Early Gothic* usually being placed between 1225 and 1300. The forms and outlines are still heavy, but well-proportioned. The horizontal lines are relatively more prominent than the vertical. Simple ribbed vaulting is customary; simplicity and vigor of design and detail is noticeable at every turn; the windows are narrow and gaining in height. It is in the *Middle Gothic,* from 1300—1375, that we find the Gothic principle consistently applied and vigorously carried out. The horizontal lines disappeared, graceful vertical lines are prominent; there is a free imitation of nature, a refreshing freedom, rhythm, and movement, as well as an evident unity. The hall-church is introduced more generally, and both its advantages and disadvantages are emphasized. The vaults are more perfect; greater slenderness and gracefulness appears; the decoration becomes much richer; the size of the windows is increasing. The transept in its full length is rare; the pinnacles are not applied so regularly. The capitals of

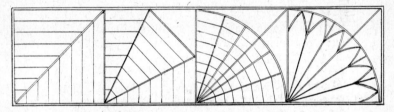

THE DEVELOPMENT OF FAN VAULTING.

the half-columns are omitted more and more, permitting the lines to run in an uninterrupted arch to the highest point of the ceiling. Lightness and fluidity appear, being exaggerated sometimes to an elegant mannerism. The perfection is often so obvious and consistent as to become monotonous. The combination of vigor and beauty of this period has seldom been equaled and never excelled. But after this culmination, a very gradual decline set in, which is represented in the monuments of the *Late Gothic,* from 1375—1525. The Decorated Style, as the Middle Gothic is often called, was followed by the Perpendicular Florid in England, and by the Flamboyant on the Continent, especially in northern France. The principles of vigorous construction upon which the Gothic style was built were relegated to the background, while the decoration became the center of interest. Star-, net-, and fan-vaulting was the order of the day; the double inverted arch appears more frequently. One cannot escape the impression that design and execution are, as a rule, entirely too ornamental, too decorative, too florid. The profuseness and minuteness of decorative detail is increased to mere ambitious arbitrariness on the part of the artists; flamboyant tracery arrests attention by its very pattern. The effort to hide the entire construction resulted in such abstract productions that some of them might be compared to magnificent bubbles suspended in mid-air, doomed to collapse at the first breath of air. In many cases, the ornamentation of the Baroque period can hardly be said to have been more absurd. A peculiar sequel of the Gothic style in England was the so-called Tudor style, whose characteristic is the bent or Tudor arch. This style was transitional between the last Gothic and the introduction of the Renaissance. It represents the breaking-down of pointed vaulting with its beautiful symbolism of life and growth, a process which had been inaugurated by the fan-vaulting. While a certain amount of beautiful dignity must be conceded to this style in church construction, it can never compare in challenging vitality with the most representative pointed-arch designs, especially on the Continent. And ostentation, such as marked by the Perpendicular and the Tudor styles, always marks a declining art.

It is a difficult undertaking to furnish an impartial estimate of the various monuments of the Gothic style, and yet even a summary can make no claim as to completeness without an enumeration of the most representative structures on the Continent and in England. The claim of France, or, more exactly, of the Isle de France, that it served as the cradle of the Gothic style, has rarely been disputed, although the ideas which were finally incorporated in its principles had found their expression long before and in various places. The classic building that marks the opening of this great epoch is Notre Dame de Paris, on the island of the Seine which was once the stronghold of the Parisii. It was built, with intermissions, from 1163—1235, and boasts of magnificent proportions. The western façade was the last to be built, the towers were carried up to their present height, but no spires added. Although the unity of the original five-aisled plan has suffered somewhat on account of restorations and changes, yet the simple beauty of the structure appeals to every visitor. "This old cathedral is a noble specimen of Gothic architecture. The long-drawn aisles, the fluted columns, the delicately pointed arches, the lofty intersections of the nave and transepts, the splendid windows of stained glass, through which the sunlight falls, apparently with the ruby and golden tints of autumnal leaves, — all these appeal to us with a mysterious charm that makes us speak in softer tones." [81] But while Notre Dame is still comparatively conservative, the buoyancy and effervescence of the French temperament was soon expressed

81) Stoddard, *Lectures*, V, 70.

NOTRE DAME, PARIS.

CATHEDRAL OF RHEIMS.

in increasing floridness of construction and overabundance of ornamentation. The Cathedral of Chartres (1195—1260) in its every line
expresses daring and pride, mixed with sternness. The apse received
an addition of three cells or niches, nave and transept were three-

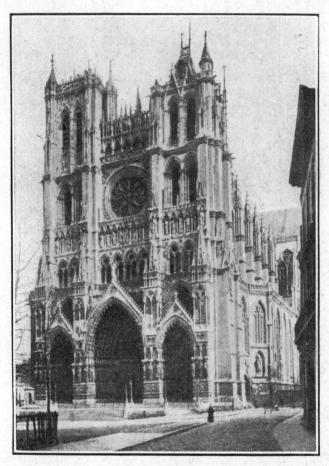

AMIENS CATHEDRAL.

aisled and of the same width. Altogether, it was an original and
epochal building. No less stately and beautiful was the Cathedral of
Rheims (1211—1295), whose interest was enhanced by its historical
associations, but which has now shared the misfortune of so many
works of art, having been made a victim of the great war. This
church belongs to the period of the best development in France.
Everything is designed to aid the idea of length and growth. The

INTERIOR OF AMIENS CATHEDRAL.

eye is lost in its vast depths, where the echoing chords of the mighty organ die away in mystery. The outstanding feature of the building was its elegance and symmetry, combined with vigor and loveliness. Behind the picturesque gables of the portals the sculptured beauty of the façade, surmounted by the glory of the spires, rose to heaven "like a fervent prayer." The Cathedral of Amiens (1220—1288), in spite of all the splendor of its parts, marks the turning-point of Gothic art in France. It is 521 feet long, and its vault rises in a tapering arch to a height of 140 feet. But the excellent proportions of its construction are made secondary to the elaborate decoration of the arches and tympanum, with scriptural reliefs, figures of saints, apostles, martyrs, and angels. One cannot get rid of the impression that deliberate ostentation has been practised throughout. Aside from this criticism, "the Gothic idea of an organic skeleton without walls, supporting stone vaulting, is embodied on a vast scale, in utmost perfection, both structural and artistic." [82]) Other churches of France that deserve mention in this connection are the Cathedral of Laon, for the early period, S. Etienne of Beauvais, and S. Denis, near Paris. In the Netherlands, the Cathedral of Tournay has parts built in the Gothic style, in Belgium S. Martin of Ypres and the Cathedral of Brussels. In general, the Romanesque features of width and massiveness are never entirely absent in these countries.

In England, national characteristics and racial development combined in impressing upon the Gothic style a peculiar dignified and challenging stateliness, without the softening features of freedom and grace. "In beauty of detail and elegance of proportion the English cathedrals generally surpass their Continental rivals." [83]) "The English were the first to grasp the decorative side of the Gothic style, which they also developed independently. But the early English structures also permit one to estimate, especially as to the erection of the walls, how much the early French Gothic was dependent upon Norman architecture." [84]) Among the early structures which exhibit the features of successive periods are the Cathedral of Canterbury, that of Lincoln, and that of Salisbury. Although Gothic features preponderate, yet the other characteristics are strong enough to stamp their peculiarity upon the buildings. Next in order we have the Minster of Beverley, the Cathedral of Wells, and parts of the cathedrals of Rochester, Lincoln, Peterborough, and Ely. In all these churches, the length of the choir becomes abnormally great, terminating invariably in a straight wall. In many cases the vestibule is built up so high as to hide the west wall of the church entirely. As

---

82) Moore, *The Medieval Church Architecture of England*, Chapter X.
83) Fergusson, *Op. cit.*, II, 335.   84) Gradmann, *Op. cit.*, 332.

the development of the Gothic style progressed, the towers often received the crowning beauty of spires, as in the cathedrals of Norwich, Chichester, and Salisbury. But the most magnificent examples of the Decorated style are found in the cathedrals of Exeter (1280—1370), Litchfield (1296—1420), York (1291—1338), Ely, and Wells. The Cathedral of Exeter presents a distant likeness to the Minster of Strassburg. The vertical lines are prominent, but fan-vaulting has already been adopted. The Cathedral of Litchfield is notable for its extreme length in proportion to its height. But the decoration of the

WESTMINSTER ABBEY.

interior still preserves the upward tendency. The Cathedral of York is considered by many the best exponent of the Gothic style in England. Magnificent stateliness is expressed in almost every line of the building. The high slender aisles and the consistent vertical structure strike the true Gothic note. The façade is the most beautiful in England, although the enormous windows seem out of proportion. Very few people visiting England neglect to see Westminster Abbey, a church which is fairly representative of Gothic architecture in England. Aside from its historical associations, this noble structure is worth a visit on account of its dignified beauty. "After the bareness of St. Paul's, it is with genuine delight that we walk through the pillared aisles of this old Gothic pile, whose pointed arches, fluted columns, and immense rose windows, which fill the temple with a softened light and bring a flush of color to the time-stained walls, are all in harmony with the inspiring thoughts suggested by the hallowed shrine." [85]) The most beautiful description of Westminster Abbey, from a layman's point of view, is that by Irving in his Sketch Book. Unfortunately, the Perpendicular style with its attempt at expressing the full idea of height was all too soon superseded by the decline with its adoption of the Tudor style, which is reminiscent of secular architecture. This feature is presaged in the great window of St. George's Chapel at Windsor, and was developed very strongly in many of the parish churches throughout England. With all their quaint and appropriate beauty, these churches never rise to the full expression of soaring freedom, which transcends all human misery and earthly sorrow and finds solace and power in direct communion with God. Altogether, the idea of height was never fully developed in England. Houses of prayer and houses of worship their stately churches may be, but they are not appropriate for preaching, nor can the worshiper feel, in the very surroundings of the vast piles of masonry, the sense of untrammeled freedom which rises above time and place to commune, in sacrificial worship, with the God of his salvation Himself. Another feature which almost all English churches exhibit, is the great similarity to castles. The lightness and daintiness of construction, in the general aspect, is absent, and the grim dignity of the great churches, with their parapets rather resembling battlements, does not elicit the loving confidence of the beholder. Nevertheless, much may be learned from the decorative details of the interiors, especially as to art windows, furniture, and vestments.

The case of Italy is most remarkable, so far as the influence of the Gothic style is concerned. This country never was good soil for the development of a style essentially northern, which combined strength with freedom and delicacy. The ultramontane spirit does not agree with the principles of the Gothic style. "The Italians have never grasped the fundamental trait of the architectural style, whose nickname 'Gothic' is derived from them. For them it was an affectation. As remarkable as their architectural achievements in the Gothic period are, they still move in the direction of the 'fine art of building,' the Renaissance, a movement which had its inception in the Romanesque period and is only for the time being deflected by the Gothic." [86]) "Gothic never took root in Italy." [87]) "The Italian Gothic weakens the vertical principle, turns back to the horizontal idea of the Romanesque structures, delights in wide spaces, in large wall-spaces filled with mural paintings, in splendid façades, in a

---

85) Stoddard, *Lectures*, IX, 321.   86) Gradmann, 348.
87) Mrs. Bell, *Architecture*, 83.

luxury of marble, a forest of statues, — in short, the construction
becomes secondary to the decoration. . . . With what right this [the
Gothic] style has been claimed as the specifically Roman Catholic
style, is hard to understand; with its ideal trait it is really opposed
to Roman Catholicism, and it is surely not a matter of chance that it
never really became 'at home' in Italy, that German builders were
prominently interested in most Gothic buildings of the southern
countries, and that the popes gave to the Gothic style, which was
indeed strongly declining, the death-blow when they erected St.

CATHEDRAL OF MILAN.

Peter's." [88] These statements are borne out by the fact that there
are really very few pure Gothic structures in Italy. Santa Croce in
Florence represents an early effort. Its lines and ornamentation are
extremely simple and yet very effective. The same may be said of
La Certosa, of Pavia. A much more pretentious structure is the
Cathedral of Siena, whose alternate layers of white and black marble
have done much to spread its fame. The Cathedral of Orvieto (1310
—1330) still shows Romanesque influence. A feature of this church
is its façade with sculpture work in high relief by Giovanni. "Four
broad piers separate the portals and are covered with a series of re-

88) Meurer, *Der Kirchenbau*, 78. 66.

liefs representing a vast Christian poem in four scenes: Genesis; the Tree of Jesse, with a choir of the Prophets of the Redemption; the Life of Christ; the Last Judgment. This epitome of the world from the Creation is given in a charming poetic and at times dramatic style. The scene of the Last Judgment is particularly grand, and the Creation scenes the most exquisitely beautiful. There is nothing like it even in France. It is the incarnation of a poet's dream." [89]) The Cathedral of Florence, in a way, serves as a foil for the wonderful dome, although its façade, finished only some thirty years ago, is very striking in its dignified beauty, as is also the Campanile. The best example of Gothic art in Italy is the Cathedral of Milan, which was begun in 1386. Although the full idea of height is not realized, the Gothic principle is otherwise splendidly maintained. And the ornamentation is such as to surpass anything of the same class. It has been called "a mountain of marble, with a forest of pinnacles, inhabited by an army of statues, splendid by day and fairy-like by moonlight."

Spain received its stimulus in Gothic art from France, but it has never reached the artistic heights which the French builders attained in their greatest monuments. The churches which are commonly mentioned are Santiago di Campostella, the Dome of Barcelona, and the cathedrals of Salamanca, Leon, and Toledo. But the Cathedral of Burgos, designed after that of Paris, is really notable, although the low pitch of the roof detracts somewhat from the impression of the *ensemble,* and the pilasters make the impression of extreme heaviness. "The great object of attraction in Burgos . . . is its cathedral of white marble — unquestionably one of the noblest specimens of Gothic architecture in the world. Its pointed towers rise like slender pyramids into the blue air to the height of three hundred feet, and are so exquisitely cut in perforated stone that by night the stars gleam through the chiseled tracery as through the trees. Its splendid central tower resembles a grand tiara, adorned with scores of pinnacles and statues and turrets of wonderful lightness. This elaborate carving and wealth of decoration reminded us of the Milan Cathedral, and we could hardly wonder at Philip II's declaration that parts of it seemed the work of angels rather than of men." [90]) The Cathedral of Sevilla (1403—1506) is considered the Spanish national type. It is an immense rectangular building, surrounded by chapels, surmounted by a cupola over the cross-vaulting of the transept.

The idea of the Gothic style took root in Germany almost as soon as in France. But its development was along much more conservative lines. Here the Gothic principle, the stately beauty and quiet

---

89) Ruoff, *Volume Library,* 435.   90) Stoddard, *Lectures,* V, 261.

grandeur, the lightness and yet the strength of construction, the idea of growth and height, was most thoroughly appreciated and most consistently and successfully carried out. Thus Germany became the second home of the Gothic style. It was here that its final development took place, after the French soil had been exhausted. A feature of the German plans is the comparatively simple construction of the choir, in which they differ materially from the French and especially from the English cathedrals. Another feature is this that even the larger churches of a diocese bear the stamp of the parish church. The sharp division between the laity and the clergy in the

CATHEDRAL OF SEVILLA.

church building disappears gradually. One of the early examples is the Liebfrauenkirche of Treves (1227—1243). The builder evidently received many of his ideas from Rheims. He also managed to give to the plan the characteristics of the central type of church. The Cathedral of Strassburg has Romanesque characteristics in the transept, while the other parts are markedly Gothic in design and execution. Notre Dame of Paris served as a model for the façade. Only the northern tower has been completed with its spire. The most conspicuous part of the Minster of Freiburg is the apse. The later parts of the building are constructed after the model of Strassburg. But of all the German churches, the Cathedral of Cologne represents the highest pinnacle reached by Gothic art in the North. It was begun in 1248, after the model of Amiens, and building operations were continued with intermissions till 1516. In the last century the

CATHEDRAL, STRASSBURG.

building was finally completed according to the original sketches. Unity and absolute mathematical precision is expressed in every line of the building. The main aisle is three times as high as it is wide, two and one-half times as high as the side-aisles. The very perfection of the parts has almost a monotonous effect. Fergusson writes that it is "certainly one of the noblest temples ever erected by man in honor of his Creator. . . Notwithstanding its defects, we see in the completed design a really beautiful and noble building." 91) One can very well understand the rapturous description which has been given: "At present it has a glory and a majesty that lift it heavenward above all other churches in the world and make of it a vast stone arch, bridging the stream of time, down which the intervening years have swept on to eternity. It is impossible to gaze on either the exterior or interior of the stupendous edifice without feeling wellnigh crushed by an overpowering realization of the sublime. The spires reach the almost unexampled height of five hundred and twelve feet, which is just equal to the entire length of the cathedral; and the height of the gable in the transept exactly corresponds to the cathedral's width. It is, therefore, the most regular and stupendous Gothic structure in existence, the consummation of grandeur and religion. When one stands at night beside its base, and lets his gaze climb slowly upward over its enormous buttresses and towers, the effect is mountainous, and its architecture appears Alpine in sublimity, the mighty shafts (which seem as solid as the eternal hills, yet are as graceful as the elm) rising until their summits vanish in the gloom, like a colossal stairway leading up to heaven." 92)

The Minster of Ulm represents a later development, both in design and execution. Some of its proportions are more colossal even than those of Cologne Cathedral, although the regularity of the latter structure is absent. One other church deserves particular mention, not only on account of its historical associations, but especially by reason of its artistic spire, namely St. Stephen's of Vienna. The western end of this church shows Romanesque features; the Gothic sections were built from 1276 to 1446. The entire building is covered by one immense roof. Of its most conspicuous feature, the beautiful spire, Stoddard says: "Its graceful spire, four hundred and fifty feet in height, is the dominating feature of the landscape at a considerable distance from the city; while, upon close approach, it still remains an object of great beauty — tapering gradually from base to summit, and covered all the way with artistic stone carving and Gothic ornamentation. So straight does it appear that I could

91) *History of Architecture*, 268. 273.
92) Stoddard, *Lectures*, VII, 107. 108.

scarcely believe the statement that its apex leans toward the north, with a deviation from the perpendicular of more than three feet." [93]) And what the same author says of this church may be applied with equal truth to other Gothic cathedrals. "St. Stephen's is, unquestionably, one of the grandest temples ever reared for Christian worship, and few cathedrals in the world have left upon my mind such ineffaceable impressions of sublimity. I love to stand by one of its huge pillars in the twilight and silently absorb its solemn grandeur. At such a time the distant roof is lost in darkness, and the majestic columns rise into the gloom, like stately palms or tropic plants whose leaves and flowers are the delicately chiseled canopies, pinnacles, and statues that cling to the colossal shafts with countless filaments of stone." [94])

CHAPTER 6.

The Influence of the Renaissance and the Neo-Classic Movement.

It seems impossible for the human mind to continue indefinitely on the heights; the fire of genius cannot be sustained beyond a golden age; a great and violent emotion which is able to produce unexcelled master-pieces is followed by a reaction with only mediocre attainments or adaptations. Thus it was in the period of the Renaissance following that of the Gothic. "No longer was the soaring Gothic style to voice in stone the aspirations of worshipers for closer intercourse with the divine." [94b]) For the Renaissance was not the result of new principles of construction, it was merely the expression of a peculiar taste which grew out of the humanistic movement and tried to apply to Christian church buildings what may be properly employed only in secular structures. The Renaissance in church architecture is not a more perfect development of art, but an anachronism, suitable, in the symbolism of its churches, only for ultramontanism or other religions in which the mediation of priests is an essential feature. It is the readaptation of something which was really much better before, without understanding the nature of the original or the principles upon which the ancient art was based.

This is not to be understood as though we did not recognize the value of the Renaissance movement, of the endeavor to return to the beauty of classical times and to re-create the art of antiquity with special reference to the modern needs. In every other form of building, this admiration is commendable, but to foist the lines of trabeated architecture upon a church building after the glory of the

---

93) *Lectures*, VI, 173.   94) P. 176. 177.
94b) Mrs. Bell, *Architecture*, 89.

pointed-arch vaulting had been demonstrated, — this is little short of sacrilege.

Fortunately, the development of this style cannot be charged to the Reformation. Luther and his coworkers were too busy with the elements of Christianity, with the restoration of the Church to its primitive purity, to take an active part in the fostering of the fine arts. But this does not mean that he was in any sense opposed to the arts or decried their influence. His classical saying as to placing all

PANTHEON, ROME.

arts in the service of Him who created them, and the fact that he advocated their adoption in the curriculum of schools, effectually disproves all such charges. We have only one direct statement by Luther in relation to the erection of churches. He is reported to have said in regard to large churches in general and the Cathedral of Cologne in particular: "They are unusual buildings and not arranged for the understanding of sermons. Medium-sized churches with low vaultings are the best for the preachers and the audience, because the purpose of churches is not the loud singing (Bruellen und Schreien) of the choir-members, but the Word of God and its preaching. St. Peter's of Rome, the churches of Cologne and Ulm, are very

CASTLE CHURCH AT WITTENBERG.

large and unsuitable." 95)   The prime desideratum as to a Christian church, as stated by Luther, was not essentially opposed to the Gothic style.   In fact, Luther himself must have preached in many of the beautiful Gothic parish churches of Germany, and he was far from advocating a general abandonment of these structures.   So far as the apostasy from the historical Christian styles of church architecture is concerned, the stimulus did not proceed from Wittenberg, but from Rome.   "In Italy, where the pagan sympathies, the antique traditions, had never wholly stopped, where the medieval viewpoints and also the medieval architecture had never found an intelligent appreciation and a delighted acceptance: there it was where people, in art in general, but especially in church architecture, reverted to antique principles and models with full consciousness." 96)   A short review of the development of the Renaissance style and its sequels will enable us to form a more perfect estimate as to the advantages and disadvantages of this style, and especially as to its unsuitableness for Christian church buildings.

As early as the fourteenth century there was evident a tendency in Italy to disregard the purely constructive side of church building and to emphasize the ornamental or aesthetic side.   At that time, it still made use of Gothic forms and is thus classed as the Italian Gothic.   With the throwing-off of Gothic forms and ornaments, however, this tendency resulted in the Early Renaissance or the Formative period, 1420—1490.   From the beginning, this style manifested an antipathy for the rectangular form of church with its idea of length, preferring instead, and employing, whenever possible, the central type of building.   The characteristic feature, therefore, is the cupola or dome, around which all the other parts of the church are grouped. There is a return to barrel-vaulting and even to the flat ceiling.   The latter is borne on classical pillars, usually by means of arcades.   The façade is gradually modeled after the antique temple.   In some cases, heavy pilasters or half-columns are surmounted by a triangular gable. All openings, doors and windows, are cast in antique forms, the heavy pediment increasing the idea of weight.   "Though quite a few churches of the Renaissance present themselves as beautiful structures in their circumstances and in individual parts, yet the whole movement, from the standpoint of church history, must be regarded as an aberration from church tradition, and condemned as a lapse into the profane and, in part, even into the pagan." 97)   This stage of the Renaissance was, fortunately, confined to Italy.   It produced the magnificently beautiful dome of the Cathedral of Florence, which

95) St. Louis, Ed., 22, 1698.   96) Meurer, *Op. cit.*, 87.
97) Gradmann, *Op. cit.*, 432.

so far overshadows the other parts of the building that the nave appears as a mere appendage to the dome.

During the second period of the Renaissance, the High Renais-

WITTENBERG AND THE CASTLE CHURCH.

sance or Formally Classic, 1490—1550, the movement reached its culmination. The secession from medieval ideals was now carried out absolutely. The Pantheon becomes the great model, and the chief ambition is to follow all the rules of Roman architecture with unabating strictness. The idealism which strove to represent even the

supernatural in art was discarded entirely. Without degenerating
into bland realism, the Renaissance of this period strove after full
expression of a lofty, classical dignity, which is unusually impressive.

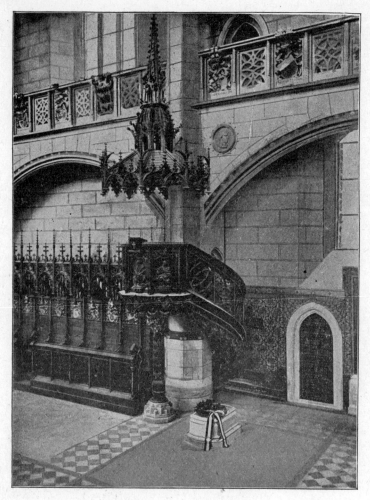

INTERIOR OF CASTLE CHURCH.

It was possible, in this style, to group great masses and attain to
colossal dimensions without interfering with the required proportion.
An artist that was able to combine beauty and harmony with the
former features had the opportunity to produce lasting works of art.
Since all the lines of a structure were simplified and arranged to have

the horizontal predominate, the niche became a very welcome aid for the enlivening of both the exterior and interior. In many cases, as in Or San Michele, of Florence, there was a great rivalry to place appropriate statuary into these niches. Some of the greatest artists

S. MARIA DEL POPOLO, ROME.

of the Renaissance, Brunelleschi, Bramante, Raffael, Michelangelo Buonarotti, and others, were actively engaged in building or decorating churches during the greater part of their careers. In spite of all the emphasis upon classical perfection in this period, there is still a marked difference between these structures and those of antiquity, since the builders could not altogether ignore the demands of the cultus.

In the Renaissance, as in the Gothic, the decline set in when ostentation became the prime object in building. This period is commonly called the Baroque, 1550—1625. Although critics have now become charitable enough to concede to this period a place in art development and find some admirable traits in certain works of art which have been preserved, it remains true, nevertheless, that arbitrariness and license characterize all its achievements. All the principles of construction are sacrificed for the sake of pictorial effect; columns and other architectural parts are not treated according to their structural purpose, but merely as decorative members, and all demands of proportion are coolly ignored. In many cases, the conglomeration of the most diverse members impresses one as the production of a horrible dream, and one may well understand the criticism of Burckhardt, who calls the architectural attainments of this period "fever phantasies of architecture." 98)

But the limit of arbitrariness had not yet been reached. Just how far builders would dare to go when they had once discarded the principles and ideals of true art was shown during the seventeenth and the first part of the eighteenth century, when the final decline set in with the period of the Rococo. It was in this period that all pretense even of definite architectural laws was given up. From pompous ornamentation the builders turned to light and liquid forms, which they combined in the most astounding patterns. Every form of curve and curvilinear decoration was introduced, everything was twisted and turned in the most senseless manner. The basic forms were so completely covered that only a disharmonious conglomeration of strange combinations is presented to view. There is ornamentation of the most arbitrary kind: foliage and shells, urns and snails, garlands and flowers and fruits, curves and geometrical figures, human and animal forms of all kinds alternate. All three kingdoms of nature are now represented and that mostly in stucco; for in place of the former sculpture work everything was now fashioned in stucco and then glued to the walls.99) A glance at the exterior and still more at the interior architecture of any building showing strong Rococo features is a surprising revelation, for in the niches, on the altars, on the pulpits countless saints, angels, and putti are standing, sitting, hanging, and balancing in strange and often impossible positions, solely for the purpose of decoration and architectural sport. Both the Baroque and the Rococo was much affected by the Jesuits in their churches, many of which, with their fantastic and luxurious adornments, present a veritable night-mare of form-combinations.

---

98) Meurer, *Der Kirchenbau*, 89.   99) Meurer, *Op. cit.*, 91.

The Jesuits also, in many cases, changed the orientation of their churches, preferring to place their altar at the western end.

If we should wish to summarize the characteristics of the Renaissance, the following features may be considered the most prominent. The plan was usually that of the central type, or as near an approach to this type as was possible. A rectangular basilica is often connected with the dome part of the structure. In addition to the Corinthian and Composite columns the Doric and Ionic again make their appearance. Horizontal lines: lintels and balustrades and entablatures according to classical models are adopted. The flat, paneled ceilings proved impracticable, and so the barrel-vaulting was gradually flattened down to the mirror-vaulting. Often a series of cupolas breaks up the ceiling. The decoration of the interior is richest in the frames of the panels, where arabesques and festoons are employed in the widest diversity. For the exterior decoration, pilasters and half-columns were used extensively. Round-arched and square windows and doors, with and without pediments, occur. Small round or oval windows are not uncommon, and twisted or broken curves are employed from the ground to the lantern. If one may venture a slight criticism, it is perfectly evident that, in the Baroque and Rococo at any rate, at least four of Ruskin's seven lamps of architecture are rudely shattered, and the others are pretty roughly handled.

There was a change for the better with the classic revival in the last century, which resulted in the Neo-Classic style. This movement differed from the Renaissance in this that it actually copied the ancient master-pieces, the arcades and porticos of Rome and the temples and colonnades of Greece. Depending upon the features which were emphasized, the style is often designated as the Greco-Roman or the Neo-Greek. All lines were forced to return to classical simplicity. The vulgar and lawless extravagances, the broken and contorted pediments, the huge scrolls, heavy moldings, ill-applied sculpture in exaggerated attitudes, all these evidences of the Jesuit style disappeared wherever the influence of the excavations in classical lands manifested itself. But the effect of such forms, when taken out of their historical and scenic setting, is strangely incongruent. There is a frosty aloofness about the classical buildings which rendered them unfit for Christian churches, as appropriate as we concede them to be for classical colleges, museums, and buildings of a similar nature. The attempt to fit the Christian cultus to the old pagan temples is bound to result badly for either the classical building or for the Christian service, probably for both, and seems a sacrilege from the standpoint of the latter.

In spite of the severe criticism which we are obliged to pass on the Renaissance and the Neo-Classic movements from the standpoint of the appropriateness of their monuments for Christian churches, we do not in any way wish to convey the impression as though none of them were worthy of being deemed works of art. Some of the church edifices of the High Renaissance and of the Classic Revival rank with the greatest master-pieces of all times, if dissociated from the use to which they have been put. The most costly Christian church in the world is St. Peter's of Rome. It represents the culmination of the High Renaissance in Italy. It was planned by Pope Nicolaus V in 1450, who chose for it the site of the old basilica of

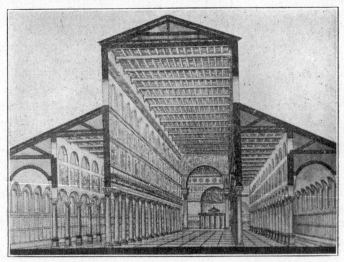

INTERIOR OF ST. PETER'S BASILICA, ROME.

St. Peter. But work had hardly been started when the pope died, and his successors were not interested in the project. But in 1506 Julius II commissioned Bramante to carry out the design. The first plan showed a Greek cross with apsidal arms. The large dome in the center was to be flanked by four smaller ones over the arms, while the corners were to receive slender towers. After the death of Bramante, Raffael, and later Sangallo, changed the plan to the rectangular form, but did not carry out the design. Michelangelo turned back to the plan of Bramante, with minor changes, such as the placing of the four small cupolas over the corners of the square. His dome was even larger and higher than the one originally designed. It was finished in 1604 under the direction of Fontana. Pope Paul V insisted upon having Maderna lengthen the nave, thus spoiling the idea of the central type. In 1626 Urban VIII could finally dedicate the great structure. The imposing approach with the double colonnades was added by Bernini, who finished them in 1637. The proportions of this great domed church are immense. The total length of the nave is 592 feet, with a span of vaulting 83 feet wide, the total width of this central aisle being 92 feet. The dome is 140 feet in inside diameter and has a total height of 405 feet. It is unfortunate that the imposing proportions of the great structure are marred by the lack of perspective. Only the dome presents the "most beautiful and exalted outline of any edifice in the world." In proud and haughty massiveness the Church of St. Peter to-day stands unsurpassed. It is a gigantic master-piece of architecture, whose *ensemble* cannot fail to impress every visitor, but which, viewed from the standpoint of its use as a Christian church, does not satisfy the heart. The hypnotism and witchery of its masses have caused it to become an example and a type leading to a false conception of a Christian church building.[100]) The following quotation is from the description of a layman, and therefore is doubly interesting. "It requires time to comprehend the immensity of St. Peter's, and it is usually only after several visits that one is able to appreciate its enormous size. It is so vast that we inevitably lose at first our sense of true proportion, and our bewildered minds must readapt themselves and grow to their new and strange environment. Thus, people in the distance, who appear to us like pygmies, are really men and women of the usual height. The bases of the columns, which seem low to us, we find to be on a level with our heads. The spaces in the huge pilasters look like slender flutings, but are in reality niches deep enough to hold colossal statues. Perhaps we think that the font of holy water in St. Peter's is no larger than those in ordinary churches; but when we examine it more closely, we discover that the marble cherubs supporting it, which at a distance look like children, are fully equal in dimensions to adults." [101]) Another Italian church of this period, which is worthy of mention, is Sta. Maria della Salute, of Venice. It is situated at the entrance of the great canal and is crowned with a cupola noted for its symmetry and elegance.

In England there is one great monument of the Classic Renaissance, or of the Anglo-Italian style, which stands out so completely from all the rest as to be considered in a class by itself. That is St. Paul's Cathedral, built by Sir Christopher Wren (1675—1710). It has the proportions of a Gothic cathedral, with rotunda and dome, the latter reaching the magnificent height of 360 feet. In area, it is the third largest church in the Christian world. A drawback of the dome, from the aesthetic viewpoint, is the fact that its inner drum

---

100) Meurer, *Op. cit.*, 87. 88.　　101) Stoddard, *Lectures*, VIII, 316.

gradually becomes narrower at the top, giving to the great supporting pillars an oblique position. The church is also conspicuously
bare of ornamentation. But in every other respect, the impression
of the cathedral is such that it "reflects, in its solemn and dignified
beauty, almost as clearly as did a medieval ecclesiastical Gothic edifice, the spirit of its age, during which the Puritan replaced the
Roman Catholic ideal, and a rigid Protestantism became the religion
of the people." [102])   The description which Stoddard offers is less en-

ST. PAUL'S, LONDON.

thusiastic, while giving full credit to the nobility and serenity of the
great English cathedral.[103])

In Germany no Renaissance church on such an enormous scale
was planned and executed. Nevertheless, there are many smaller
monuments which are worthy at least of passing notice. Among the
earlier examples are St. Michael's of Munich (1582), the Marienkirche at Wolfenbuettel, and the Marienkirche at Dresden. Of the
later churches, the Frauenkirche of Dresden (1721) is commonly considered a representative structure. It has the form of a square with
rounded corners. Its dome rests upon eight large pillars. The apse

102) Mrs. Bell, *Architecture*, 91.   103) *Lectures*, IX, 284—289.

is a semicircular extension behind the choir. But the entire arrangement is strongly reminiscent of a theatre. In Trinity and in St. Michael's, of Hamburg, the principles of the Renaissance style, with certain Baroque, and even Rococo, features, have been applied to the Protestant demands, especially as to cultus.

In France there is one example of the Renaissance which seems to point forward to the full classic revival. This is the Pantheon (1755). It is called by Hamlin "the greatest ecclesiastical monument of its time in France." [104] It shows, in almost every part, classical simplicity and directness, without the specifically extravagant features of the Baroque, which was then prevalent in France.

Even in far-away Russia we find monuments of the High Renaissance, which were carried out with all the magnificence and luxury of a splendor-loving people. Not only are the proportions of Our Lady of Kazan and of St. Isaac's vast and imposing, but the decorations and furnishings of the churches challenge the power of comprehension, assuming almost fabulous proportions. Of the latter church we read: "St. Isaac's Cathedral is an illustration of the fact that, when she makes the effort, Russia can surpass the world in the magnificence of her architecture; for the treasures of her quarries are exhaustless, and the skill of her lapidaries is unexcelled. It is, however, unfortunate, that there is no eminence in St. Petersburg [Petrograd] on which St. Isaac's could have been placed; since, at even a little distance, it is impossible to see to advantage the stairways leading to its various portals. Yet each of these steps is one gigantic block of rose granite, worthy of the Egyptian temple of Karnak; and every portico is supported by stupendous shafts of the same material, sixty feet in height and seven feet in diameter, and polished like the surface of a mirror. . . . But if this be the exterior, how shall I describe the interior of this temple of the North? Before its gilded altar-screen are ten columns of malachite, thirty feet high, and pillars of lapis-lazuli, each of which cost thirty thousand dollars. This exceeds every other display of these marvelous stones that the world knows. We are accustomed to regard a small fragment of either as a valuable ornament. Imagine, then, whole columns of them five times as high as ourselves! Yet this is only in keeping with the entire building; for in St. Isaac's we tread a pavement of variegated marble; we ascend steps of polished jasper; we clasp railings of pure alabaster; and are surrounded by walls inlaid with ver-dantique and porphyry, interspersed with vast mosaic portraits of the saints, and shrines of gold incrusted with jewels. One portrait

104) *History of Architecture*, Chapter XXIII.

of Christ is studded with diamonds, the largest of which is valued at thirty-five thousand dollars. The whole, in fact, is so magnificent as to appear incredible until actually seen." [105])

St. Paul's Cathedral, of London, and St. Genevieve, of Paris, later called the Pantheon, foreshadowed the Neo-Classic movement,

PEACE CHURCH AT POTSDAM.

which gained the ascendency, even for ecclesiastical architecture, at the end of the eighteenth century, at least in France and England. The most characteristic and representative monument is La Madeleine, in Paris. This church was built by Vignon as a classic temple, and surrounded with Corinthian columns. Viewed from the stand-

105) Stoddard, *Lectures*, VI, 237—242.

point of a lover of classical antiquity, the structure is a marvel of
symmetry and perfection. "It is a beautiful reminder of those classic lines which had the Acropolis for a pedestal, Pentelic marble for
material, and for a background the Athenian sky. Two thousand
years have rolled away since Grecian architects and sculptors placed

THE NEW DOME, BERLIN.

before the world those glorious models which have conquered time,
but we have not improved upon them. Wherever they are produced,
even with less attractive stone, less perfect statues, and less wonderful embellishment, they charm us still. . . . So much does it recall
the temples of antiquity that it at first seems incongruous that this
should be a Christian church." 106) The last statement is supported

106) Stoddard, *Lectures*, V, 14. 15.

very strongly by Hamlin, when he writes: "However suitable for a pantheon or mausoleum, it seems strangely inappropriate as a design for a Christian church." [107])

The last century has brought no new developments in church architecture. The parish churches of England are eminently suited to the demands of that country and its cultus. "Notwithstanding the infinite number and variety of our parish churches — size, design, construction, and plan — yet distinctly national types were evolved, characteristic of the English temperament and enshrining many of its best qualities, such as sturdiness, practical utility, and above all adaptability to circumstance." [108])   By adopting the fundamental principles of the Gothic style and adapting it, with certain modifications, to their own needs and wants, the English have thus evolved a style which is both characteristic and suitable. In France, exponents of the various styles endeavored to bring about a revival of interest. Even the basilica is again brought forward as a suitable form of Christian church building. In Germany, the case is much the same. The friends of the Gothic, both Catholics and Protestants, succeeded in bringing about a revival of pure Gothic. The Votive Church in Vienna is the result of such labors, as well as the completion of the Cathedral of Cologne and the Minster of Ulm. On the other hand, Protestants denounced the Gothic in its perfection as opposed to the Evangelical cultus. There was also some eclecticism and compromise. St. Luke's in Munich, St. Michael's in Bremen, and the Emperor William Memorial Church in Berlin are the result of the application of the Gothic principles to a rather liberal interpretation of the cultus. The resolution of the Dresden and Eisenach conference have served, in a way, to quiet the controversy and prepare for sound principles in church building. Much of the difficulty undoubtedly would be removed, if the various Protestant factions could come to a thorough agreement as to sound basis of doctrine and its expression in the cultus of the church.

CHAPTER 7.

Church Building in America.

It is only in late years that the history of American church architecture and the discussion of the principles of the various styles in this country have received closer attention. There are few cities, of course, that have no church buildings of some costliness and beauty, worthy of more than passing notice. But it was only through

---

107) *History of Architecture*, 371.
108) Cox, *The English Parish Church*, 15.

the work of Embury, Cram, and other friends of ecclesiastical architecture that attention was called to a feature of our country which is growing in importance every year, namely, the erecting of suitable parish churches throughout the length and breadth of our great land. In many cases, the interest may be more an historical than an artistic one, but a closer acquaintance with the places of worship of the various denominations is decidedly worth while.

The oldest Christian churches erected within the present boundaries of the United States are some Catholic chapels in and near Santa Fe, New Mexico. After Coronado and his famous band of explorers had opened up the territory in 1542, the priests followed. In the early years of the seventeenth century, they built quite a number of chapels in that section of the country. Most of these, if not all, were erected of adobe and may have been similar to that of Acoma, which is still standing, though sadly in need of repair. Rude as they were in construction, they served their purpose admirably and were also eminently suited to the climate and to the historical associations of their type.

The first Christian church in the East of which we have record is that which Captain John Smith described. "When we first went to Virginia, I well remember we did hang an awneing (which is an old saile) to three or four trees, to shadow us from the sunne; our walls were rales of wood; our seats unhewed trees till we cut plankes; our Pulpit a bar of wood nailed to two neighboring trees. In foule weather, we shifted into an old rotten tent, for we had few better, and this came by way of adventure for new. This was our church till we built a homely thing like a barne, set upon cratchets, covered with rafts, sedge, and earth; so was the walls." [109] How these men, who were almost without exception members of the Anglican Church, must have missed the cathedrals and even the parish churches of the old country! But the appearance of this rude log church would have seemed strangely familiar to some of the pioneer missionaries sixty or eighty years ago, and the chances are that the northernmost Lutheran church in Canada to-day is built in the same grand style, as a cathedral of faith and sacrifice.

When the Puritans landed at Plymouth a dozen years later, one of the first acts was the erection of a meeting-house, a large, square building with a flat roof, on which were mounted six cannon. As new settlements were made along the coast and in the interior, this square meeting-house became a characteristic feature of the village, especially since is was the original township hall and community center now so widely heralded as a twentieth century idea.

---

109) In Embury, *Early American Churches*, 7. 8.

When the Swedes landed on the Delaware less than a score of years later, they also made it a point to provide a place of worship at once as a forerunner of many which afterward dotted the landscape. It is probable that the rectangular form of church was immediately employed, since this is the plan in general use for the later churches in this region.

The meeting-house style, as it was subsequently called, with churches in the form of a square or a short rectangle with a low roof, became the governing style in New England, wherever the Puritan influence extended. But outside factors succeeded in introducing embellishing features which served, at least in a way, to enliven the exterior of the churches. The Ship Meeting House, of Hingham, Massachusetts, which dates from 1681, is square with a hipped roof and a small belfry. Copies or adaptations of this church may be found in many cities, towns, and hamlets along the North Atlantic coast.

In the early eighteenth century, this style, which was exceptionally bare and rude, was influenced to some extent by the last effort of the Renaissance period, thus resulting in the Colonial or American Georgian style. Old North Church of Boston (1723) is an early example of this style. It is a rectangle, with two tiers of circular-headed windows. The body makes a rather heavy impression, but the tower with its spire is slim, light, and elegant. Trinity Church, of Newport, and Old South Church also show these features, though the spire in the latter is not so graceful. King's Chapel, of Boston, has yielded more completely to Renaissance influence. It is their history rather than their art which makes these churches memorable, as also Christ Church, in Philadelphia. There are two other churches in the Middle Atlantic States which deserve mention, St. Paul's Chapel, of New York City, and the Lutheran Church of the Holy Trinity, Lancaster, Pennsylvania (1761—1766). Trinity, of Reading, and St. John's, of Philadelphia, also belong to this group.

The pure Colonial style, with the elimination of the essentially typical meeting-house features, had a better chance for development in the Middle and Southern States. St. Luke's, near Smithfield, Virginia (1632), indeed shows reminiscences of the Older Gothic. Its stepped gable has reappeared in some recent churches. The Gloria Dei Church, at Philadelphia (1697), the Old Swedes' Church, at Wilmington, Delaware (1698), St. Peter's, of New Kent County, Virginia (1700), and many Lutheran churches of Pennsylvania, Maryland, and Virginia are strongly Romanesque in appearance. But the so-called brick churches of Virginia and North Carolina, and the stone and stucco churches of South Carolina and Georgia

TRINITY CHURCH, NEW YORK CITY.

exhibit preponderating Colonial features. A typical example is
Bruton Parish Church, of Williamsburg, Virginia. It is, as Embury
says, a typical Virginia type, the brick being laid in Flemish bond,
and the cornice greatly reduced from the colonial pattern. The tower
is somewhat low and heavy. St. Michael's, of Charleston, though
purporting to be of a pronounced Renaissance stamp, is a trifle heavy,
especially in tower and spire. On the other hand, Christ Church, of
Alexandria, Virginia, and Pohick Church, historically interesting
because Washington was a regular worshiper there, are Colonial with

OLD ZION'S CHURCH, NEW YORK STATE.

a decided classical tendency, of which their Ionic and Tuscan columns bear witness.

In the meantime, the far Southwest was again becoming the
scene of Catholic missionary endeavors, with the attendant church
building. A Mallorca friar of the Franciscan order, Junipero Serra,
was sent to establish missions in Alta California, as distinguished
from Baja or Lower California. With only a little company he
marched overland, while supplies were sent by sea, until he reached
San Diego Bay, discovered by Cabrillo two hundred and twenty years
before. Here he founded the mission of San Diego de Alcala. It
was the first of a long row of stations which extended northward to
the Bay of San Francisco and eastward to the Colorado River. There
may have been some lines of the Romanesque style which served as

a model for the California mission churches, but, on the whole, they seem a spontaneous creation, simple, but most artistically effective, and fitting in thoroughly with the climate and the romance of the land. The mission chapel was usually one part of a group, which

OLD CHRIST'S CHURCH, ALEXANDRIA, VA.

included also living rooms and cloistered dormitories surrounding a patio. Not the least charm of the chapels lies in the manner in which the bells were suspended, in arched openings of the heavy walls. The beautiful quaintness and compelling interest of these churches is such as has impressed its stamp upon architecture, not only in California, but throughout the entire Southwest.

SAN GABRIEL MISSION, PASADENA.

The Classic Revival in the East, which extended from about 1810 to 1850, left its marks on a number of churches, some of them being built entirely in the Neo-Classic style. A fine example is the Monumental Church, of Richmond, Virginia, built in 1812. But this influence was by no means dominating, as the North Reformed Church, of Schaalenburg, New Jersey, which has a Gothic design, and others illustrate. There was even an Egyptian revival, leaving its mark on the First Presbyterian Church, of Sag Harbor, Long Island.

OLD CHURCH IN MACKINAC.

During the so-called War Period, which extended from 1850 to 1876, some more pretentious structures were attempted in various parts of the country. St. Patrick's, of New York City, is an example of Gothic design. It makes a somewhat cold and formal impression, lacking the vigor and spontaneity of the Gothic cathedrals. During this time, the churches of the Middle West were, for the most part, still of a more primitive kind. The days of the pioneer were not yet wholly left behind. But the last quarter of the last century marked a definite change. The age of the mere builders of churches drew to

a close, and we find more and more architects with a real understanding of the art of building. Trinity Church, of Boston, is generally
conceded to be a splendid example of the Romanesque revival, being
patterned after the Cathedral of Salamanca, in Spain. "The harmony
of both the exterior and interior proclaims this edifice one of the few
of first rank in America." [110])   The Cathedral of All Saints, at Al-

STANFORD MEMORIAL CHURCH, PALO ALTO, CAL.

bany, also deserves mention in this connection as a type of the metropolitan cathedrals in America whose number is increasing very
rapidly.

During the last two decades, the situation has improved in every
respect. In many sections of the country, indeed, a very arbitrary
eclecticism is still at work. Some architects or builders are persist-
ently seeking after the American Church style, a style which will, as

110) Ruoff, *Volume Library*, 428.

they confidently hope, express the great ideal which has been announced: One language, one God, one church! The results, up to the present time, have been little short of disastrous to the idea of true art which, though following fundamental rules, demands spontaneity of expression. At one time, the Mormon Tabernacle at Salt Lake City, which has been pronounced almost perfect, so far as acoustics are concerned, engaged the attention of building committees. Then again, the social features of a congregation's activities have been emphasized so strongly as to give the dominant note to the plan for a new church. In still other cases, the plan of a Greek theater has been adhered to with sufficient exactness to create a very definite illusion. In the Southwest, as mentioned above, the California Mission style is influencing a great many ecclesiastical structures.

On the whole, however, denominational characteristics seem to be governing the choice of style and the execution of the church buildings, both as to exterior and interior. The Reformed churches in general have retained the Meeting-house style, with modifications due to time and place. Their buildings in general, with square or low ceilings, make the impression of heaviness. The somber dignity and forbidding strictness of Puritan times is still evident, in a measure. The Unitarians, Universalists, and Christian Scientists are addicted to a plan which can best be described as a Renaissance temple. The Catholics are often governed by local considerations, but the pure high Renaissance, and the Romanesque and Middle Gothic are found oftenest in their larger churches, modified to suit their cultus. The Protestant Episcopal Church has practically adopted the Perpendicular Gothic and the Tudor Gothic for its own. Not only the larger cathedrals, but many of the smaller parish churches exhibit all the characteristics of these English styles, carried out with a marvelous fidelity of adherence to certain rules of their cultus. It is this church body which is doing more than any other in this country to enlighten the people as to artistic requirements in church design and ornamentation.

It is very difficult to make an appropriate selection of representative American churches. The following list, while by no means exhaustive, will still contain the names of some of the finest churches erected in recent years, or still in the course of construction. Of the Cathedral of St. John the Divine, of New York City, the chapels and the triumphal arch are now completed. The Roman Catholic Cathedral of Denver is a Gothic structure with a somewhat cold impression. The Cathedral of St. John, in the same city, is in the Perpendicular Gothic, carried out extremely well. The Cathedral of St. Paul, in St. Paul, is certainly one of the greatest monuments of the

High Renaissance in the Mississippi Valley. Built according to the central type, it occupies, with its great dome, a commanding position at the edge of the plateau overlooking the river valley. Other notable churches are St. Paul's Cathedral, of Detroit, the First Presbyterian Church, of Oakland, California, Calvary Church, of Pittsburg, the House of Hope Presbyterian Church, of St. Paul, the Chapel of the United States Military Academy, at West Point, St. Thomas's Church, of New York City, and the Cathedral of the Incarnation, of Baltimore.

CHAPTER 8.

History of Ecclesiastical Art: Sculpture, Painting, and Mosaics.

The insinuation which has often been made, especially by enemies of Christianity, and which often assumes the proportions of a direct charge, as though the spirit of Christianity is inimical to true art, is absolutely without foundation. "It was the natural result of the decay of Roman society, rather than enmity to sculpture, that eliminated it from the field of art at about the time when Christianity became the religion of the state under Constantine. . . . The decay was general throughout the Roman world, both East and West." [111] It is owing to this general decay of sculptural art that its Christian phase can hardly be said to have existed before the fourth century.

The earliest examples of the sculptor's art, which often indeed hardly deserve the designation, but are more like the imitations of artisans, have been placed by critics in the third century. Designs carved on the stone slabs of sarcophagi, known as *graffiti,* represent the earliest endeavors to portray Christian symbols or historical subjects. They show not only the conceptions of death and future life prevalent in the early Christian community, but also scenes from Bible and secular history. We find pictures of Ulysses and the Sirens, the Three Men in the Fiery Furnace, the Magi, Good Shepherd, Jonah, Noah in the Ark, Raising of Lazarus, Holy Trinity and Creation of Man, Logos between Adam and Eve, Daniel among the Lions, Denial of Peter, Moses with Tables of Law, Elijah's Ascent to Heaven, and many others. The design is often crude and the execution rude, the juxtaposition of unrelated scenes being the usual procedure. There is also an absence of true perspective. A feature of many sarcophagi is a central *orans,* or praying figure.

Beside this stone carving, some excellent work was produced in wood and ivory carving. Most of the monuments in wood have

---

111) Ruoff, *Op. cit.,* 433.

yielded to the ravages of time, but a few important examples have
been preserved. The finest work is that shown in the cypress-wood
doors of S. Sabina, in Rome. The artist employed great originality
in his designs, thus rendering the interpretation of many of the panels much more difficult than those exhibiting a more conventional
presentation, but it is evident that he wished to portray the principal
scenes in the cycle of redemption. The splendid cathedra of archbishop Maximianus of Ravenna, which dates from the middle of the
sixth century, is also a notable example of this work. The examples
of ivory carving are most interesting, because so many have been
preserved, of which a large number were later productions. The
diptych of Gregory, at Monza, shows beautiful detail work, but it can
hardly be said to surpass the diptych of Florence, or the ivory box at
Brescia. Ivory covers were also used extensively as coverings for
gospels, church books, and the like. In addition, there were marble
reliefs, pixes, patens, ampullas, vases of gold and silver, eucharistic
doves, altar fronts, and ciboria.

Of statuettes the most notable is that of the Good Shepherd,
probably of the third century, now in the Lateran Museum. It represents a young man bearing a sheep across both shoulders. The
statue of Hippolytus dates from the early years of the third century.
It is evidently a copy of a philosopher's statue of the classic age, and
was in the nature of a monument. The celebrated statue of St. Peter
with the Keys, now in the Vatican, gave rise to many interesting discussions. It was believed by some to have been a statue of Jupiter
Capitolinus, with the later addition of keys and nimbus. Since, however, the keys at least are an integral part of the statue, the theory
of Gradmann seems to be correct, that it was modeled after an ancient statue of a senator or philosopher. This first brief and uncertain expression of Christian art lasted only to the seventh century,
and included the Byzantine period, with Constantinople as the
art center.

Medieval sculpture is often reckoned as beginning in the eighth
century. But in reality, sculpture as an independent art remained in
eclipse for almost seven hundred years. From the fourth to the
eleventh century it hardly rose above the level of industrial carving.
During all this time, the church made use only of the cross and later
of the crucifix. The examples of evangelists and saints in high relief,
on portals, doors, altar frontals, etc., occasionally show glimpses of
genius, but usually they do not rise above the commonplace. Even
the dinanderie of the tenth and early eleventh century does not seem
to realize its possibilities.

But with the end of the eleventh century there is the first inti-
mation of the great revival of sculpture, which made "of the plastic

art an integral element, a logical coadjutor of architecture," as Ruoff
says.[112]) The first notable examples are the portals of St. Trophime
in Arles, those of Vezelay, and those of Autun, where not only the
arches are finely chiseled, but the tympanum, the columns, and the
façade on either side show beautiful work in high relief. But the
flood-wave of architectural sculpture came with the full introduction
of the Gothic style. Even in Notre Dame the tympanum of the main
portal, with its "Christ and the Last Judgment," was a wonderful
sermon in stone. And with each new cathedral, Le Mans, Chartres,
Amiens, Auxerre, Troyes, and others, the symphony of sculptural
embellishment rose to fuller orchestration, until it finally broke forth
in the fulness of loveliness and dignity in the Cathedral of Rheims.
Here we find not only each portal with its tympanum and columns
decorated with sculpture work, but also the buttresses, the galleries,
and the entire façade. There is a nobility, a vitality and freedom of
style, a picturesque and effective use of drapery, a multiplicity of
types which thoroughly flout the idea of a dead formalism. Single
statues have been chosen from the great mass as true works of genius.
"The 'Beautiful Christ' at Amiens, and the severer one at Chartres,
the dignified Virgin at Notre Dame, the smiling and coquettish Virgin at Amiens, and the rather self-conscious Grande Dame at Rheims
are all masterpieces." [113]) In Germany, the Rhenish school was especially active, producing such beautiful work as the sculpture of
Strassburg Cathedral, and also that of Cologne, Nuremberg, and Ulm.
The statue of "The Synagog," of Strassburg Cathedral, is famous
for the natural effect of its drapery, the gracefully bent head, and the
long curving lines, making it one of the most poetic figures of all
times. The Daniel and John the Baptist of the "Golden Portal" of
Freiburg, with their Byzantine costumes, are also often mentioned.
England is not so well represented at this time, the cathedrals of
Wells and Litchfield offering the best work in Gothic statuary.
Sculpture is here also an ancillary art, but there are no individual
specimens which stand out from the rest. On the whole, it may be
said of Gothic sculpture that the beauty of the individual statue was
sacrificed for the architectural effect as a whole.

    With the thirteenth century came the rise of Italian sculpture at
Pisa. The Pisani, Niccola (1205—1278), Giovanni, his son (1270—
1330), and Andrea, exerted a great influence with their revival of
the antique. This classicism is especially evident in the work of
Niccola, of which the pulpit of the baptistery at Pisa, with its scene
of the Nativity, and the pulpit of San Giovanni, at Pistoja, are particularly notable, while the work of Andrea shows a marked natural-

112) *L. c.*, 433.   113) Ruoff, 434.

istic tendency. A fine example of the work of the Pisani are the four piers of the Cathedral of Orvieto. Similar schools arose at Florence, Siena, and Naples. With the beginning of the fifteenth century, however, the work of the individual artists begins to stand out, although the schools do not lose much of their influence. At this time, sculptured altar-pieces, pulpits, choirs, galleries, fonts, ciboria, tabernacles, candlesticks, single statues of saints and angels, crucifixes, madonnas, large groups of statues, begin to appear in endless variety. It was at this time that Ghiberti won in a severe competition and cast the bronze door for the baptistery at Florence, with the scene of the Sacrifice of Isaac. He followed this up later with a second door of such beauty that Michelangelo pronounced it worthy of being a gate of paradise. Ghiberti's opponent in the first competition was Brunelleschi, the builder of the dome of Florence, also celebrated as sculptor. And not far behind them came Donatello, with his Pieta (in the sacristy of St. Peter's), S. Magdalene, S. George, and others. An artist noted primarily for his beautiful work in terra cotta (white, blue, gold) was Luca della Robbia. His Madonna and Child with Angels is a beautiful lunette, with a remarkably delicate tone. Other artists whose work is worthy of special mention are Jacopo della Quercia and Andrea del Verrochio.

With Michelangelo Buonarrotti, the Renaissance in sculpture reached its culmination. He was classicist, naturalist, idealist, all in one, the greatest artistic genius of his age. But with all his idealism he could not escape a brooding somberness. His Pieta at St. Peter's draws attention, not so much to the figure of the dead Christ, as to that of the mourning Mary. His Moses is one of the most impressive and overwhelming statues of all times, but it represents the law-giver only, not the prophet. His David has a vital appeal, but nothing about the head suggests the prophetic singer of the coming salvation. When Pope Leo sent the artist to Florence to execute the façade of San Lorenzo, he remained there for seventeen years. But in only one instance did he succeed in coming near to the ideal Christ. His statue of the Risen Christ shows the figure after the resurrection, nobly erect, clasping the cross with both arms.

After Michelangelo came the decadence; the humanistic revival having spent itself, the Catholic reaction resulted in the Baroque style, also in sculpture. Benvenuto Cellini was more of a goldsmith, an exceptional technician, than a sculptor. And the names of many other lesser sculptors might be added: Giovanni di Bologna, Bandinelli, Bernini, and others. With them, as Marquard says, "sculpture ran riot, exulting in its technical accomplishment and pushing plastic modes of representation to the furthest possible extreme." A similar criticism might be expressed with regard to the French and German monuments of the Renaissance sculpture, especially so far as the Church is concerned. Michel Colombe produced St. George and the Dragon, and Pierre Bontemps, Jean Goujon, Germain Pilon, François Girardon, and Antoine Coysevoux occasionally produced ecclesiastical sculpture. In Germany, Peter Vischer produced the beautiful shrine of St. Sebald in Nuremberg, and Michael Wohlgemuth, as engraver and sculptor, Veit Stoss, as wood carver, and Adam Kraft, as stone carver, deserve to be mentioned. In the seventeenth century, Andreas Schlueter carved the beautiful marble pulpit in the Marienkirche of Berlin. England has only Nicholas Stone, who executed some work for Westminster Abbey. Altogether, the art of this period was light and graceful, degenerating later into playfulness.

The Neo-Classic revival, with the prolific Canova as its apostle, gave a new impetus to sculpture. And while the art was now devoted mainly to secular purposes, for the private enjoyment of wealthy patrons, one man, at least, turned his attention to some extent to Biblical subjects. Berthel Thorwaldsen was the son of a carver of figure-heads in the royal dockyard of Copenhagen. His talent developed very early, and a prize won at the Academy of Arts enabled him to go to Italy, where he became a pupil of Canova. Here he came under the influence of the Hellenic. But his plaques and other relief work also show a quiet independence, with a romantic coloring giving these efforts a peculiar charm. His religious works, including a colossal group of Christ and the Apostles, St. John in the Wilderness, the Four Great Prophets, the Entry into Jerusalem, the Angel of Baptism, and others, have a powerful appeal which makes them interesting for all classes of Protestants. Many critics pronounce his The Blessing Christ the best work he has done. A spirit of divine dignity and loving tenderness seems to emanate from the face and the entire body, causing a feeling of the deepest devotion.

In England, Flaxman worked in much the same spirit of classicism. His Michael and Satan is vibrant with power and energy. The pose of the figures shows supreme triumph on the one side, abject defeat on the other. The presentation is thoroughly admirable. A German who deserves mention is Dannecker, whose statue of Christ the Mediator has a realistic touch, and may therefore be lacking somewhat in dignity. Rauch was the foremost sculptor of Germany since the Reformation. His historical monuments are splendid examples of the highest art. His one noted religious work is the group representing Moses with his hands supported by Aaron and Hur. His pupil Rietschel did not reach the level of the master, but his statue of Luther at Worms, of which there are several copies in America, has fairly made the great Reformer alive before our eyes.

Modern sculpture is almost wholly secular, as recent exhibits, especially at the San Francisco Exposition, have shown. Even Rodin's Gates of Hell and Brock's Eve are in conception and execution secular products. After the return of normal conditions, possibly the fact that large churches in the Gothic style are now being erected or planned in America, will cause a revival of interest in ecclesiastical sculpture.

*   *   *

It seems that from the very beginning pictorial representation in pigments (painting) and in colored stones (mosaics) was employed far more generally in the churches than sculpture. The frescoes or mural paintings of the catacombs are very decidedly under the influence of the classical, which was then in its decaying or degenerating stage. During the last decades, due principally to the work of Wilpert and other scholars, these paintings have been described and reproduced, so that both their execution and their symbolism is better understood than ever. The cemeteries of Priscilla on the Via Salaria, of Domitilla or SS. Nereus and Achilles on the Via Ardeatina, of Praetextatus on the Via Appia, and of S. Agnes on the Via Nomentana especially, have yielded works which have intrinsic as well as archeological value, although they do not rank with the world's great paintings. At first the purely decorative style of ornamentation, as it is known from the restored walls of Pompeii, prevailed. Its purpose was to give to the subterranean chambers the aspect of pleasant, home-like surroundings. Circles, arcs, and geometric figures of all kinds are combined in delightfully idyllic vignettes. In the middle of the second century, truly Christian art was developed, with a wide range of Biblical subjects. As this was the age of the persecutions, the subjects chosen still reflect chiefly thoughts of death and immortality. With the triumph of Constantine in the early fourth century, a new trend of thought was introduced into the art of the Church. A wider range of subjects is immediately noticeable, including not only a great variety of symbolical figures, but also a wide diversity of Bible scenes, supplemented largely by apocryphal material. Symbols of divine deliverance were Daniel in the Den of Lions, Three Children in the Fiery Furnace, Job in His Sufferings, Deliverance of Lot from Sodom, of David from the Hand of King Saul, Peter and Paul from Prison, and others. The name *orantes* in a general way applies to portraits of deceased and to representations of Biblical characters in the attitude of supplication. Of the Old Testament characters, Adam and Eve, Noah and the Ark, Moses, Daniel, Sacrifice of Isaac, Jonah, and Susanna were favorite subjects. Of the New Testament scenes, the miracles of Christ, especially the

Raising of Lazarus, the Woman with the Issue, the Feeding of the Five Thousand, the Samaritan Woman, are often found. The Good Shepherd was depicted with increasing frequency, as in sculpture, and both the Celestial Banquet and the Eucharistic Supper received their share of attention. Of the purely symbolical figures, the fish, the ring, the cross, and the monogram of Christ are found more than others. The Virgin is gradually given a more prominent place. At first she is represented merely as secondary figure in the Adoration of the Magi, but soon the Annunciation is treated, and the Madonna occurs with increasing frequency.[114])

The development of pictorial representation in mosaic work followed practically the same lines. Mosaic work was first used for floors or pavements. It consisted of figures constructed mainly of white and black cubes, though other colors are found. Geometrical designs were chiefly used, but representations of birds and beasts were also employed. Wall and ceiling mosaics were more rarely used in the early centuries. The lower walls were often embellished with incrustations of marble, cut and set in conventional designs. Toward the end of the third century glass mosaic came into use. It was an easy matter to cut glass paste of any color into cubes. An interesting form of this work was obtained by coating the cubes with gold leaf covered by a film of glass. It was not long till the purely decorative purpose of mosaic work became a secondary feature, while the object of edification, of instruction, of devotion came to the foreground. Some of the best examples of mosaic work during the ante-Nicean era and the period of the early Christian empire show Biblical subjects. In S. Pudentiana, on the Esquiline, there is a bearded Christ enthroned, with the right hand lifted in teaching and an open book on the left. In S. Sabina on the Aventine is a symbolical representation of the Church of the Jews and the Church of the Gentiles. In Santa Maria Maggiore there are figures of Adam and Eve, of Moses, and of Joshua. The Apocalypse is pictured in SS. Cosmas and Damian. The baptistery of San Giovanni in Fonte, at Ravenna, and San Apollinare Nuovo, of the same city, have fine examples of mosaic art. The mosaics of Hagia Sofia were of such remarkable excellence as to evoke poetical raptures, and those of S. George, at Saloniki, were also strikingly beautiful. With the passing of time, the mosaic decorations centered more and more in the apse. It was here that the glory of the Godhead, and especially of Christ, was depicted. Christ in the Glory of the New Jerusalem, Christ in His Majesty as Teacher, Christ on the Clouds of Heaven, Christ on the Globe of the World, are some of the subjects found.

---

114) Cp. Gradmann, *Op. cit.*, 14—24. 67—87; Lowrie, 187—247.

There can be no doubt that the outbreak of the iconoclastic discussions brought the early Christian period in art to a close. And when Leo III, the Isaurian, published his edict against image-worship (726), its influence was such as practically to paralyze Christian art in the East. There were still fantastic figures, sacred scenes and personages, there were even madonnas and saints and scenes from the Passion and from legends, but there was no spontaneity. Everything was steeped in the dead ritualism of the Mount Athos Handbook. In the West, conditions were not much better, although the so-called barbaric influence of Irish and Frankish elements gradually gained the ascendency. The age of Charlemagne brought a revival. There is a mosaic of Christ Enthroned at Aachen, there are mural paintings of considerable merit, there are many examples of the minor arts. But the flame which had given such promise soon died down and flickered out. Even the Romanesque movement failed to infuse new life, although a few specimens of painting and mosaics are notable as going beyond the designation of colored drawings. The great wall surfaces of the Romanesque churches afforded excellent spaces for mural paintings and frescoes. Such subjects as Christ the Teacher, the Evangelists, Ezekiel, the Crucifixion, the Seven Virtues, the Seven Vices, occur frequently. The ceiling of St. Mark's, at Hildesheim, has a representation of the Tree of Jesse, which became a very favorite subject in the Middle Ages. Wall mosaics are practically unknown in this period, especially in the North, but the pavement mosaics are found in many churches, both of Italy and the North. Some of the subjects used are David and Goliath, Joseph, Joshua, Samson. The mosaics of St. Mark's of Venice and of various churches in Sicily are particularly notable. S. Maria Novella, of Florence, has the Madonna Rucellai, painted by Cimabue. During the latter part of the Romanesque period, there is some evidence of breaking away from the stiff solemnity of the earlier times. Life, freedom, and joy are manifested in many of the monuments, relieving the dulness and unnatural coldness of the former age.

The full awakening came about the middle of the thirteenth century. The revival of mural painting in Germany, especially in the region along the Rhine, was followed by the rise of pictorial art in Italy. Giotto introduced the epic style. His Life of Christ still shows hard, impersonal faces, but the drawing is well executed, and the general effect is a most impressive one. His figures are strong, solid, quiet, and dignified. But his perspective is poor, as his Pieta shows. His influence was such as to render his rules of art a canon in Italy for more than a century. In Florence, Fra Giovanni da Fiesole succeeded in infusing a spirit of tender joyousness into his work, while the school of Cologne depicted piety, humility, loving-kindness, and enchanting idyls (Madonna with the Bean Blossom, Madonna in an Arbor of Roses).

The Renaissance had a wonderful effect upon pictorial art. After Masaccio and Masolino had broken away from most of the older rigidity and attempted a natural and almost realistic portrayal, and after Hubert van Eyck had demonstrated the rich effects of color and the results of excellent draftsmanship, the way was opened for the Renaissance proper. Brunelleschi, that versatile genius, had rediscovered the art of perspective painting, and this enabled the artists to combine conventionalism with realism. Fra Filippo Lippi was the first to use the faces of people about him as portraits. In his Coronation of Mary he even has his own portrait in the extreme foreground. His pupil Sandro Botticelli shows traits of originality and imagination which make his madonnas, especially that of the Magnificat, true impersonations of religious feeling. Ghirlandajo was a wonderful technician, but his work lacks the solidity and power of the perfect genius. Filippino Lippi had so much unbounded vitality that there is often an excess of movement in his pictures. Though he was also influenced by the dogmas of Savanarola, he lacks the mysticism and transcendentalism of Botticelli. The dominant note in the pictures of Perugino is peace and quiet. All his madonnas are humble maidens, with a complete realization of the glory of being the mother of the Christ. His compositions are graceful and his color rich. Padua also boasts a great artist in the person of Andrea Mantegua. He gave to the Biblical personages the dress of the Roman period in which they lived. Wherever he portrayed the nude, his figures show the full sinewy muscularity, with a sullen and silent expression, as in his Crucifixion of Christ. In Venice the Bellinis were prominent, Giovanni Bellini being the greatest in technical strength. The effect of his pictures is solemn, almost sad, but he paints feeling only, not action, as in his Pieta.

A new era in Italian art opens with Leonardo da Vinci. He was a man of many attainments, a mathematician and scientist as well as sculptor, architect, and painter. In all his pictures, his Baptism of Christ, his Resurrection of Christ, and others, he shows himself to be a master of light and shadow. He founded new laws of composition, and used also the hands as a psychological commentary. His fame rests principally upon his Last Supper, which is a psychological drama, "the grandest monument of religious art." Contemporaries of da Vinci were Fra Bartolomeo and Andrea del Sarto, the latter, as the best draughtsman of the Florentine school, being called "the faultless painter." Michelangelo, the great master of sculpture, was also a master of painting, which he imbues with all the massiveness

THE LAST SUPPER.
Leonardo da Vinci.

of the plastic art, as his Last Judgment and his series of Sibyls show.
His very opposite was Raphael Sanzio, a child of sunshine and joy,
"the harmonist of the Renaissance." His Burial of Christ is well-
known, but his fame rests principally upon the Sistine Madonna.

ECCE HOMO.
Guido Reni.

The beauty, dignity, and grandeur of the Virgin, and the appealing
charm of the two angel boys have never been surpassed. Of much
the same nature was Antonio Allegri, known as Corregio, whose appeal was almost entirely to the sensuous and artistic. His Holy Night.
is the very essence of the poetry of light and shadows.

The later Venetian school produced two great artists. The first was Tiziano Vecelli, known as Titian, whose madonnas are conventional in conception, but wonderful in execution. Perhaps his best-known picture is The Tribute Money, with its characteristic figures and psychological hands. Seldom has the irreconcilable contrast between Christ and the hypocritical Pharisee been brought out with greater force. Tintoretto's pictures show a solemn and majestic splendor, but the influence of the Baroque is also apparent, as in the Miracle of St. Mark. Other notable Venetians were Giorgione and Paolo Veronese, the latter a "brilliant colorist and a decorative painter of the highest order." After him the decay set in, and though there have been occasional flashes of genius, the glory and grandeur of the Italian golden age have never again been attained.

All the world learned from Italy, and therefore the results of art outside of Italy can be summarized. Spain has two great painters, whose work stands out from all the rest on account of its surpassing beauty and artistic perfection. Velasquez represents "icy pride and implacable ceremony." He was a realist, avoiding conspicuous color and brush-work, but none the less a master technician, as his Adoration of the Shepherds and Adoration of the Kings show. Later he turned almost entirely to portrait painting. Murillo was a master of purely artistic achievement, full of religious fervor and sentimentality. His Immaculate Conception is a charming picture of tender, caressing beauty.

The painting of the Netherlands is divided into the Flemish and the Dutch schools. In the former school Van der Weyden and Van der Goos are the first notable artists after the van Eycks. They were followed by Memling, a romanticist, whose Last Judgment is well known. A little later, Quentin Massys worked in the style of the Renaissance, after which the Italian influence gained ground. The greatest Flemish painter and one of the greatest of all times was Rubens. His was a truly sensual art, the apotheosis of the flesh. His Hellenic sensualism often becomes fiery sensuality. Even in his Adoration of the Kings, his Crucifixion of Christ, and his Last Judgment, this feature is prominent. But he was a master of technique, both in modeling and in drawing, with an artistic grasp of his personages. His pupil Van Dyck became prominent as a portrait painter. Elegiac sadness was expressed in most of his work. The later Flemish painters discarded religious subjects almost entirely and turned to portrait, genre, and landscape painting. Among the earlier Dutch painters Lucas van Leyden, a friend of Duerer, occupies a prominent place. After an interval during the sixteenth century, which produced mainly portraitists, a great painter arose in the person of Rembrandt. He was a master of his art, with exquisite taste and correct judgment, very skillful in the arrangement of light and shadow. His Holy Family and Presentation in the Temple are well-known religious works. After him, as in the Flemish school, came portraitists, genre and landscape painters.

England, due probably to Puritan influence, produced few religious paintings. In the eighteenth century, Thornhill painted eight scenes from the life of the apostle Paul for the dome of St. Paul's. Among the Pre-Raphaelites, Hunt is known for his religious pictures, which are carried out with careful attention to detail. In France the case was much the same. Nicolas Poussin, who was the founder of the classic and the academic in French art, painted scenes from both the Old and the New Testaments, with a careful realism. In the last century, Delacroix, in his Christ on Mount Olive, is romanticist, Ingres classicist, Delaroche, in his Mater dolorosa, realist, and Dore, with his Bible illustrations, shows the same tendency. Millet, in his Angelus, shows a pantheistic tendency.

In Germany, religious painting was carried on with varying success, influenced largely from Italy. Some of the earliest artists are not known by name, as the master of the Lyversburg Passion. But Stephen Lochner, and then Michel Wohlgemuth, were heads of schools with more than local fame. The latter was a great artist, though he approached nature rather rigidly and coldly, but his principal fame rests upon the fact that he was the teacher of Albrecht Duerer, one of the world's greatest artists, both in painting and engraving, besides being a philosopher and a poet of sorts. He is the father of post-Reformation art in Germany and has very properly been called the Leonardo da Vinci of Germany. He published many illustrated pamphlets, whose text agrees well with the realistic, rough figures adorning the pages. But his fame rests chiefly upon his truly Christian art, especially after he had come under the influence of the great Reformer. It has been asserted, in the last few years, that Duerer was the original cubist painter, and some of his sketches seem to confirm this impression at first glance. But a study of Duerer's letters and of his diary shows that these sketches are the result of his measurements of the anatomical proportions of the human body, and are not the miasmatic contortions of a diseased mind. The best-known series of Duerer's is that of the life of Mary, consisting of twenty separate sketches. Of this series, the Flight into Egypt and the Sojourn in Egypt are the ones most frequently offered in collections. Other pictures by the same prolific artist are The Prodigal Son, Adam and Eve, Adoration of the Three Kings, Christ on the Cross, and The Four Apostles. The last picture especially is characterized by a formal simplicity and a majestic, statuesque repose. The other artists of this age, Hans Suess of Kulmbach, Martin Schaffner, Matthias Grunewald, and Hans Baldung Grien, never reached the eminence of the great master. They were dominated by the Italian influence, instead of merely permitting this influence to direct their art. Albrecht Altdorfer was a romanticist of a peculiar type, who loved the portrayal of forest and nature, without, however, using them as models for his paintings. He was master of certain light effects. His The Birth of Christ, at Bremen, and The Holy Night, at Berlin, are pictures of peculiar interest, though they appeal more on account of their romantic touch than their psychological realism. The artist Lucas Cranach, the painter of Wittenberg, is very sympathetic to the Protestant mind, since he gave to the world the portraits of Luther and of other men interested in the Reformation. His style is dainty, sedate, naive.

The Swabian school was founded by Hans Burgkmaier, a contemporary of Holbein the Elder. Both of these men pale almost into insignificance beside Hans Holbein the Younger, who represents the culmination of the artistic ideals of his age and is considered by some critics the greatest painter that Germany ever produced, and one of the greatest of all times. He was not merely skillful in design, but also decidedly happy in color execution. Moreover, he had the faculty of choosing the psychological moment in a story and of portraying this with singular vividness. His most noted series is that of the 94 illustrations to the Old Testament. His realistic portrayal is tinged with an ideal, sometimes almost sentimental coloring, making his characters peculiarly sympathetic, especially his prophets. His illustrations of the New Testament are not so good, the seriousness and loftiness of conception being absent. During the seventeenth and eighteenth centuries Germany produced no painters of the first rank, though Elsheimer, Sandrart, and Mengs are often mentioned, the last being noted for his pastels.

With the "golden age" in German literature came also the revival in art, ushered in by Overbeck and Cornelius. An artist that followed in the footsteps of Cornelius and succeeded admirably in winning for himself a delighted audience throughout the Protestant world is Julius Schnorr von Carolsfeld. Although he painted other pictures, his Bilderbibel is still enjoying the most enviable popularity. Some of its pages show the very essence of true art. A woman artist of the first rank in this period was Angelica Kauffmann. Wilhelm Kaulbach combines refined beauty with dramatic effect. Pictures of his that are well known, also in America, are The Tower of Babylon, From God, and To God. Ludwig Richter produced the popular picture Christmas Night, Lessing Luther Burning the Papal Bull, and Rethel the series A Mighty Fortress is our God. Two men that are enjoying great popularity are the Protestant classicists Hofmann

CHRIST IN GETHSEMANE.
Hofmann.

and Plockhorst. Christ Taking Leave of His Mother and The Consoling Christ, of the latter, and The Adulteress, Christ in Gethsemane, and Christ and the Doctors of the former, are among the most common religious pictures in Protestant homes and churches. The last picture is considered "one of the most beautiful of all conceptions of

THE RISEN CHRIST AND MARY MAGDALENE.
Thoma.

the youthful Jesus," sharing with the Sistine Madonna the greatest
popularity of the Dresden Gallery. Hans Thoma has worked largely
in the style of these classicists. His Sinking Peter and The Risen
Christ and Mary Magdalene are known as favorably as any religious
paintings of the last century. Eduard von Gerhard was opposed not
only to the classicists, but also to the Oriental realism of Tissot and
others. In his pictures he has German scenes, German people. His
distinctive *forte* is the singling-out of a characteristic expression to
typify his conception of the psychological moment, as the joy of
Mary, in The Awakening of Lazarus, and Christ's greeting of the
bride and groom, in The Marriage Feast of Cana. Even radical
realism has its able exponents, among whom Fritz von Uhde, with
his popular pictures Come, Lord Jesus, and Suffer the Little Children to Come unto Me, is best-known.

So far as America is concerned, there can be no doubt that many
portrait painters of the eighteenth and nineteenth centuries might
have produced excellent religious paintings, had there been occasion
for doing so. As it is, the peculiar position of the Puritans and the
Reformed churches in general with regard to church paintings has
done much to discourage artists. At the present time, however, the
building of more pretentious Lutheran churches may have a decided
influence upon the art, since it depends largely upon the encouragement of artistic ability whether these aids to the edification of the
congregation be installed.

CHAPTER 9.
History of Ecclesiastical Art: The Minor Arts.

All the minor arts which serve in the embellishing of a Christian
church are merely the handmaids of architecture and can justify
themselves only by loyal service to their mistress. In accordance with
the demand of this fundamental principle, we can devote only a short
chapter to windows, dinanderie, sacred vessels, furniture, bells, organs, sacred vestments, and paraments, though each of them in itself
is worthy of a description which might well reach the compass of
a book.

The *windows* of the early basilicas were situated, as a rule, in
the clerestory only, and were small in size. They were much more
frequent than a later taste and the change in cultus required and,
since many of them were open to air and light, the interior of the
churches was flooded with an illumination sufficient for all purposes.
In many churches, the small windows were provided with hinged

shutters of stone, as a protection against cold and rain. When the custom of closing the window-opening became general, a lattice-work of metal usually sufficed, or a thin plate of stone, marble, or alabaster was inserted, closely perforated with small openings composing an ornamental design or pattern. The small openings were often filled with clear or colored glass, but this practise was comparatively rare. The rays of the sun, having free ingress through the small apertures, assisted much in bringing out the effect of the interior mosaics. In the Byzantine churches, the windows, in many cases, became longer and narrower, but there was no attempt to change the former method of filling the opening. The windows of Hagia Sofia, as originally built, were exquisitely beautiful.

When the large churches and cathedrals of the Romanesque period were erected, the decoration of the windows received its share of attention. Since many churches of the Carolingian age had used tapestry for window curtains, the builders made use of the idea in inserting glass windows with tapestry patterns. The small Romanesque windows are therefore largely mosaics of colored glass, for the most part purely decorative. The drawing is still rude. The dominating colors are reds and blues, enlivened with yellow or toned down with green. Wherever the influence of the Cistercians was felt, colored windows were not permitted, but the builders succeeded in producing very beautiful effects in the so-called grisaille windows, in which the bulk of the glass was white, studded here and there with jewels of color. When properly executed, the alabaster-like glass acts as a splendid foil for the jeweled insets, producing a very rich impression. Figure windows also were not unknown in this period. In the dome at Augsburg there are five windows showing figures of prophets. A great artist was Wernher, of Tegernsee, which was a center for this kind of work. There are also fine examples at Hildesheim and in St. Remy, of Rheims.

But the "golden age" of art windows begins with the wide introduction of the Gothic style in France, Germany, and England. Since the heavy walls were no longer needed to carry the roof, the entire space between pilasters was available for windows. It was then that artists realized the possibilities of such large surfaces for elaborate ornamentation. From that time on, the windows of Gothic churches became a very prominent feature of these beautiful buildings. Every device was employed to make these windows works of the highest art in themselves and to have them serve for enhancing the total effect of the interior by proper gradations in color. During the early Gothic period the art windows were notable for their rich color, often of a barbaric splendor, in reds and blues, relieved by greens, yellows, and purples. The mosaic character is still prominent. There is an example at Canterbury, where there are over fifty pieces in a space of less than a square foot. There is vigorous line work in the brown enamel inherited from the Romanesque period, laid on with a brush in firm, expressive, beautiful strokes. The figure windows of this period show expositions of Christian doctrine, scenes of the human descent of Christ, especially the Tree of Jesse, the Virgin with Child, etc. Some of the best examples are at Canterbury (Jesse window), Lincoln (Salome before Herod), Sens (Prodigal Son), Chartres (Christ of the Apocalypse), Cologne, Strassburg, and Regensburg.

In the second Gothic period the full development was attained. The artists found that colored figure work could be combined with grisaille in the same window, and thus solved the problem of lighting. The heavy iron-work was replaced by stone tracery. The invention of silver stain aided much in securing splendid effects. The canopy in the upper part of the windows was developed. At the same time, the art of drawing was improved, becoming, however, somewhat affected. Green and yellow became more prominent than red and blue. The subjects remained the same, but were carried out much more elaborately. The best example is the window The Five Sisters at York, which has been called "a shimmering mass of pearl and silver." Other specimens are at Salisbury, Rheims, Westminster, Exeter, Gloucester, Cologne, Oppenheim, and Freiburg.

The third period shows the effect of the over-decorated, flamboyant style. The canopy was modified, the amount of silver stain increased. There was a more advanced style of drawing, but also the abandonment of the natural form in ornament. The immense height of the English perpendicular windows offered great possibilities, but also great temptations. At Exeter the great window is seventy-eight feet high. In many instances, there are indications of a gradual decay, as at Great Malvern. In France the limitations of the art were partly disregarded, the attempt being made to apply canvas painting to glass. During the age of the Renaissance, this tendency fitted in well with the general trend toward ornamentation for its own sake, and thus deterioration and decay followed. The costliness of the genuine potmetal glass caused its abandonment in favor of a lighter and cheaper grade of uncolored glass, painted or enameled so as to give approximately the effect of the colored glass formerly used. With the revival of interest in the magnificent windows of the early Gothic, it became imperative to revert to ancient methods and to employ a glass which would compare with that formerly used. Conspicuous among the leaders in the revival of stained glass work in Protestant countries were two Americans, Tiffany and La Farge, the latter being the discoverer of opal glass, which is unexcelled for art windows. Even now there are windows in many parts of the country which compare favorably with those of Europe, and the art is but in its infancy here. The possibilities, therefore, with proper instruction and direction, are unlimited.

Among the articles of use and adornment in a Christian church the *altar* has always occupied a prominent place, being almost indispensable where the requirements of the cultus are observed.[115)] At the time of the apostles, the congregations made use of simple tables for the celebration of Holy Communion, 1 Cor. 10, 21. In the catacombs, the stone slab beneath which the bones of the martyr lay, was used as the altar. In the basilicas, a similar form was in use, since the apse was often erected over the crypt of a saint. Their altars were commonly rectangular stone slabs, resting on columns, although cubic, circular, and semicircular altars have been found. The columns of the altar and even the space below were regarded as a place of refuge, as Synesius reports.[116)] The use of wooden altars, of much the same shape, is proved by early texts. In the sixth century, the practise of building a *confessio* below the altar, which permitted a view of the relics, became general. After that it did not take long before the bones of the saints were deposited under the altar, which was then enclosed on all four sides by plates of stone, thus becoming a mere chest for the preservation of relics.

In the first centuries, the gifts of the people were not deposited on the communion altar, but were laid on special tables of prothesis. Later on, not only the consecrated elements were placed on the altar, together with cup, paten, and linen cloth, but it was made the receptacle for all the treasures of the church, which were there exposed as on a silver chest. Plurality of altars is not found till the fifth century, when lateral altars were placed at the chancel arch, and afterwards in chapels. When the *lectorium* became prominent, a low or lay altar was often placed in the nave, as distinguished from the high altar in the apse. When the idea of consecration gained favor, portable altars were made, consisting, in many cases, only of a stone or bronze slab. Once consecrated, these altars could be used for mass in all places, also in mission work.[117)] So long as the altar had its position at the entrance to the apse and retained the characteristic table form, the position of the officiating priest was behind the altar, facing the people. But gradually a change was introduced, due, first of all, to the ciborium. The ciborium or baldachino was a canopy of

115) Kliefoth, *Die urspruengliche Gottesdienstordnung*, I, 362. 422.
116) Bond, *The Chancel of English Churches*, Chapter I.
117) Tavernor-Perry, *Dinanderie*, Chapter XIII; Kliefoth, III, 275.

masonry or precious metáls and drapery above the altar. It usually had the form of an inverted cup or an Egyptian water lily *(kiborion)*. "In the West, however, a steep conical or pyramidal roof seems to have been more common." [118]   The four supporting columns were set far enough from the altar to permit free access to the clergy. Between these columns, beautiful curtains or veils, called *tetravela,* were suspended, sheltering the sacred elements against dust and the profaning glances of non-members.[119]   According to ancient accounts, these veils were often of wonderful richness, white, crimson, or rose-colored silk, beautifully decorated.[120]   The ciborium was later replaced by the tabernacle, a notable example being that of St. Peter's. And finally it was reduced to the small tabernacle or *sacramentarium* placed on the altar, for housing the sacred host.   But the essential form of the ciborium is still found in many altars.   In the ninth century, the custom was inaugurated of placing the relics of saints on the altar in special shrines, which usually had the form of a coffin with a separate roof. A monument of this kind, too large even to permit its being placed upon the altar, is the shrine of St. Sebald, in Nuremberg, cast by the eminent artist Peter Vischer.   This custom, making an addition to the altar necessary, was provided for by the so-called *retabulum* or *superfrontale* (Altaraufsatz, reredos=ad retro dos or dorsum).   Like the *frontale* or front wall of the altar this rear wall, extending up over the mensa, was ornamented in various ways, being separated into compartments or niches for various vessels, crosses, and candelabra.   The reredoses of many high altars on the Continent as well as in England are works of art of the very highest order, as those of Winchester, Worcester, Durham, Lincoln.   Even when the relics were no longer placed in or on this *superfrontale,* about the fourteenth century, the reredos was retained.   It was at this time that the Gothic artists, especially of Germany and France, found opportunity for the most elaborate ornamentation, since both wood carving and oil painting could be placed in the service of the altar builder.   The three panels with their niches were no longer sufficient for decoration, but the niches were deepened and provided with simple or with folding doors.   Both the outside and the inside of these doors were decorated with statues or with figures in high relief, and thus different sections of the doors could be exhibited on the various festivals *(Fluegel-, Klappen-, Wandelaltaere).*   Only the smaller churches retained the simple triptychs.   The Renaissance exerted its influence also on the altar, producing, in many cases, such grotesque absurdities that the name altar could be applied to them only by

118) Lowrie, *Op. cit.,* 167.
119) Meurer, *Altarschmuck,* 31; *Kirchenbau,* 223.
120) Rock, *The Church of Our Fathers,* I, 154.

courtesy.[121])   When the Reformation began its triumphant march through Europe, the question of abolishing or retaining the altars was broached.   Carlstadt, Zwingli, and Calvin decided against their use, adopting a plain table for the celebration of the Holy Communion. But Luther, always conservative where there was nothing essentially wrong, merely insisted upon certain changes and modifications.   The plurality of altars was discontinued, since they had been in the service of the mass.   The shrines and tabernacles, as well as the lamps with the "eternal light," were removed.   Otherwise the altar with all its ornamentation was retained, and also the altar paintings, without the slightest suspicion, however, of idolatrous practises.[122])

Just as the ciborium was erected for the purpose of adding dignity to the sanctuary, so many churches had a row of four or six columns in the presbyterium, at first for ornamental reasons only.   They were not even designed for the support of curtains, much less to hide the altar from the gaze of the believers.   Yet from this ornamental feature arose the *iconostasis* of the Greek Church, the screen separating the sanctuary from the nave, adorned with various sacred pictures and pierced by a central door, as well as the rood-screen or *lectorium (Lettner)* of the Gothic churches.   It received its German name from the Latin, on account of the fact that the reading of the lessons usually took place from this screen.   It has now been replaced in most Western churches by the chancel railing, which, according to Durandus of Mende, "teacheth the separation of things celestial from things terrestrial."   From this railing, the entire sanctuary received the name chancel, which is often applied to it, especially in the Anglican Church.

The *pulpit* has an interesting history.   In the early basilicas the bishop usually delivered the sermon from his cathedra, which was an elevated chair at the eastern wall of the apse.   The reading of the lessons, however, took place from two ambons or pulpit-like platforms on either side of the choir.[123])   The northern ambon was used for the reading of the Gospel, and the southern ambon for the reciting of the Epistle.   The Epistle ambon had a special platform for the Graduale, from which the sermon was delivered as early as the fourth century.[124])   Later, the Epistle ambon was moved into the *lectorium,* the dividing wall between apse and nave, under the triumphal arch. It was then that the rood-screen became identified with the chancel railing and this ambon expressly called "Kanzel" in Germany.   In

121) Gradmann, 556; Meurer, *Der Kirchenbau*, 226.
122) Kliefoth, *Die urspruengliche Gottesdienstordnung*, IV, 134—137.
123) Kliefoth, I, 422.
124) Gradmann, 36; Meurer, *Der Kirchenbau*, 210.

Italy, the mendicant orders erected special preaching platforms or pulpits in the nave. In Germany and England, pulpits for preaching were rare, especially the fixed or stationary pulpits. At a time when the entire interest of the Church was centered upon the sacrificial act of the mass, it was barely to be expected that preaching would receive its due share of attention. Italy possesses some splendid monuments in altars, notably the pulpit of the Baptistery of Pisa, Germany only a few. Meurer mentions those of Wechselburg, Landshut, and Strassburg. The Reformation brought back the pulpit into the church as a preaching station, and it insisted upon giving to the pulpit the prominent position it deserves, because it is essential that the preacher be heard and seen from all parts of the church. The use of the lectern grew out of that of the Gospel ambon. There is one in Freudenstadt, dating from the twelfth century, whose desk rests upon four carved apostolic figures. The usual type in English churches is the eagle lectern, although many wooden lecterns were carved, without the eagle. Notable examples of bronze work are the lecterns of Notre Dame, at Tongres, and that of SS. Giovanni et Paolo, in Venice.

Baptismal fonts have been employed in the Christian Church almost from the beginning, though the usual method of administration was by immersion in the basins of the baptisteries. But when the baptism of adults became an unusual happening and the administration of the sacrament was no longer the bishop's prerogative, the baptisteries were united with the parish churches. Since the ninth century the baptismal font has been in general use. At first it was so large that the candidate for baptism could step down into it. Later its size was reduced, and it served for aspersion or pouring only. It was situated near the western entrance on a small platform within a chancel railing and received a cover which was highly ornamental, after the manner of tabernacles. The basin itself was commonly ornamented in rich geometrical and figure decorations, and rested upon animals, sometimes on twelve oxen after the model of the brazen sea in Solomon's temple. The brass fonts in dinanderie work are in part of high artistic merit, as those of Liege, of the Frauenkirche at Rostock, of Hildesheim, and of St. Sebald, of Nuremberg. During the Gothic period, the carved stone fonts came into general use. Those of England were, for the most part, conservative, but some of those on the Continent were carved in most elaborate designs. The font at Reutlingen shows the types of the seven sacraments, with late Gothic, realistic embellishments. The Reformers with iconoclastic tendencies discarded the baptismal fonts, but the Lutheran Church has kept them, with the exception of those that represented false doctrines.

So far as the other furniture of churches is concerned, the space of one short chapter is too limited for an extended discussion. For there were so many subsidiary vessels and structures that whole books have been devoted to their discussion. The pyxes were cylindrical boxes for the host, suspended over the altar. Many monstrances had the figure of the sun, with a crystal center. The reliquaries were enshrined in gold or silver. The censers also were commonly made of precious metals, as were the croziers, though in their case dinanderie work is often found. Of the same materials were holy water vats or stoups, book-covers, ewers, water vessels, sanctuary rings or knockers, and other accessories. Pews were not in general use before the Reformation. In the large cathedral and parish churches, the people crowded about the celebrating priest or gathered beneath the pulpit. Since the Reformation, the pews have gone through several periods, ostentation, utility, and ornamentation battling for supremacy at various times.

Church-bells in the modern sense of the word were unknown in the early Christian Church. The faithful were summoned, or special times and hours were announced, by other means. The Old Testament Church had used trumpets, Num. 10, 10, and the Christians, who in early times had made announcements of meetings by word of mouth only, after the formal recognition of the Christian religion devised ways and means of giving loud signals with metal instruments. In the monasteries of Egypt, trumpets were used, in others a hammer (malleus nocturnus). The Greek Church, especially of the sixth and seventh centuries, used a wooden instrument called *simantrum (semantron),* and one of iron, called *hagiosideron.* Bells were introduced at the end of the ninth century, becoming great favorites in the Russian Church, which still boasts the possession of the largest bell in the world, that standing beside the Ivan Tower in Moscow. In the West, the use of bells was adopted at the same time that the first towers were built. Very likely the Roman bishop Sabinianus (604—609) was the first one to use bells for the purpose of serving the cultus. The use of bells, suspended in special bell-towers (campaniles), spread very rapidly, as a number of edicts tend to show. Some of the largest bells in the Occident are those of Ollmuetz, of Vienna, the Maria gloriosa of Erfurt, of Cologne, the Dominica of Halberstadt, of Toulouse, of Paris, and of Milan. Unfortunately, a good deal of superstition and idolatry was connected with their so-called baptism, and this caused them to be discarded by the Reformed churches. The Lutheran Church discarded every appearance of luxury and tolerates no superstition or abuse, but has wisely retained the bells for the purpose of calling the people to services, striking the chief hours of prayer, and for announcing deaths in the congregation.[125])

The invention of the *organ* is generally ascribed to St. Cecilia, according to the legend. Tertullian names Archimedes, and Vitruvius and Pliny Ctesibius, as the inventor. Originally, it consisted of ten pipes pitched according to the tones of the diatonic scale. The organ was in use in the Church by the time of Augustine and Cassiodorus. Charlemagne introduced organs north of the Alps, and the art of building these instruments soon reached a very high degree of perfection, although they were unusually clumsy from the modern point of view. Wolstan gives an account of an organ which had 400 pipes and required seventy men to pump sufficient air. The keys were connected with the valves of the pipes by means of heavy ropes and were usually three inches wide and one and one-half inches thick. Since the mere pressure of the fingers would have had little effect upon such ponderous keys, it was necessary to strike them with the clenched fist in order to produce a tone. In the course of time, the improvements upon the organ were of such a nature as practically to change the entire instrument. By the sixteenth century the mere pressure of the fingers sufficed for playing. Splendid and costly instruments now became the order of the day. Such organs are at Danzig, Harlem, Rome (St. Peter's), Weingarten, Breslau, Leipzig, Sevilla, Birmingham. In America, the art of organ-building has reached a very high degree of perfection, and one can hardly compare the modern instruments, having thousands of pipes, complete orchestration, and pneumatic and electrical control for every part of the mechanism, with the organs of the Middle Ages.[126]) The largest organs of the world at this time are the following: that of Grace Church, New York City; of Yale University; of St. Paul's Church, Toronto, Can.; of Pilgrims' Church, Kevelaar, Germany; of the Cathedral of the Incarnation, Garden City, N. Y.; of Royal Albert Hall, London; of the Town Hall, Sidney, Australia; of the Cathedral, Liverpool, England; of St. Michael's Church, Hamburg, Germany; of Century Hall, Breslau, Germany; and of the Wanamaker Store, Philadelphia. The last-named organ was exhibited at the Festival Hall of the St. Louis Exposition, in 1904. Several years after, it was transported to Philadelphia, enlarged and rebuilt, and placed in the court of the Wanamaker Store. It is by far the largest organ in the world, having five manuals, 17,954 pipes, and 232 speaking stops.

Special *clerical vestments* have been in use in the Christian Church almost from the beginning. The example of the priestly

125) Alt, *Der kirchliche Gottesdienst*, 63—70; Kliefoth, II, 415. 416; III, 221; IV, 149.   126) Cp. Alt, 136—146.

garments of the Old Testament probably caused their adoption, and the classical dress of the first centuries of the Christian era determined their form. The *tunica talaris,* fashioned after the common tunic of the times, is represented as a bishop's or presbyter's dress in a second century fresco of S. Priscilla. This is also the garment in the case of the S. Hippolytus statue. The *dalmatica* was practically a variety of the ungirdled tunic. It was usually richly ornamented, and was worn over the tunic. The material might be either linen or wool, climatic factors probably deciding the choice. It soon became

THE VESTMENTS OF THE PRIEST AND THE HIGH PRIEST.

the distinctive garment of the deacons. The *paenula* or *casula* was originally a storm cloak of heavy woolen cloth, with a hole in the middle, through which the head was thrust. Its later form was round or elliptical and its color usually a chestnut-brown. The *pallium* scarf was derived from the pallium mantle. It was made of white wool and ornamented with crosses. In the East, as the *omophorion,* it was the badge common to all bishops. In the West, the wearing of the pallium was soon restricted to metropolitan bishops upon whom the pope conferred the distinction. The *stole* or *orarium (peritrache-lion, epitrachelion)* was of white wool or colored silk, properly a neck-cloth. The *maniple,* originally a napkin or towel used by deacons, later became a kind of handkerchief, used by all classes of the clergy.[127]) In the course of time, the clerical garments grew ever more elaborate and costly. Their ritualistic use was prescribed with the most explicit directions in the missals. The well-known liturgiologist Rock devotes a large part of his book "The Church of Our Fathers" to the discussion of clerical garments and ornaments. The *chasuble* was circular, with a hole in the middle only large enough to let the head of the wearer go through. It fell in folds all around the person, muffling his arms as well as his shoulders. The *dalmatic,* together with the *alb,* the sacrificial robe of the deacon, was a long loose tunic or frock, without any opening in front, but slit up below a little way on either side, and its wide sleeves reached almost as far as the wrist. The alb was of white linen or silk, with brightly tinted silken or golden border. The *tunicle* of the subdeacon was like the dalmatic, but smaller and less conspicuously adorned. The *offertory veil,* about ten feet in length and two and one-half inches broad, silk-hemmed and ornamented with gold lace, was worn by the sub-deacon during mass. The *stole,* a linen cloth, nine to ten feet long and two to three inches wide, was used by bishops and priests. It formerly hung straight down from the neck, but is now crossed over the breast. The *gremiale* or lap-cloth was either of linen or fine silk, flowered with gold. The *maniple* was a small towel worn or thrown over the left arm. The *subucula* was a vest of white linen, below the alb, reaching to the knees. The *amice* (orale, humerale, superhumerale) was a linen collar worn during mass. The *surplice* was a modified alb, lined with furs and reaching almost to the feet. It had no opening in front. The *rochet* was a modification of the surplice, practically a linen tunic. The *cassock* or *pelisse* was a cloak-like garment, usually black, only doctors of divinity wearing scarlet cassocks. The *cope* was made of silk in the color of the season, with hood for protection against bad weather. The *almuce* answered the purpose of a cap and tippet. The *pall* of the bishop was a long, straight band of white wool, marked with crosses. It was worn around the neck and crossed over the left shoulder, one end hanging in front and one behind.[128]) These vestments have been retained in the Roman Catholic Church from the Middle Ages to the present time, with slight variations and modifications.

The Reformation wrought a great change, so far as the Reformed churches are concerned. Zwingli declared that the garments used in the celebration of the mass were essentially wrong,[129]) and this view

127) Lowrie, *Monuments of the Early Church,* 389—413; Alt, *Der kirchliche Gottesdienst,* 126—128.
128) Rock, *The Church of Our Fathers,* I, 256—II, 104.
129) Kliefoth, IV, 305.

is held in most of the Reformed churches to-day. The Anglican Church, after the first turmoil had subsided, returned to the use of clerical vestments, modifying them to some extent. The Protestant Episcopal Church of America, in the section with high-church leanings, prescribes the cassock, cincture, and biretta for general official wear, the surplice for all services other than Holy Communion, and the amice, alb, girdle, stole, maniple, and chasuble, for the celebration of the Eucharist.[130]   Luther's position was a conservative one. In his *Formula missae* of 1523 he advocates the retention of the clerical vestments, but in such a way that luxury and ostentation be avoided.   In many parts of Germany and the Scandinavian countries, the ancient garments were retained, at least for the celebration of the Holy Communion, for several centuries, and the use of the casula may be traced down to recent times.   Gradually, however, the cassock, which Luther himself used for a preaching vestment on the 9th of October, 1524, for the first time, became the only garment used in the majority of the Lutheran churches.   The collar worn by the Scandinavian pastors and the bands used by the German pastors are probably a remnant of the ancient stole in the form of the *peritrachelion*.[131]

The *paraments* or liturgical vestments of the Old Testament Church were prescribed by God, both as to materials and colors, Ex. 28, 5.   The colors were gold, blue, violet, scarlet, and white, and the chief materials were linen or byssos and silk.[132]   The liturgical vestments of the New Testament Church do not go back to a special command of God, although the Mosaic cult has been cited in justification of their use.   Paraments have been employed in the Christian Church since the earliest times.   On account of the absence of monuments and exact descriptions, comparatively little is known of their materials and colors.   Veils, tapestries, and coverings are mentioned which were woven in the most elaborate and intricate patterns, often of rich silk, in white, crimson, or purple.   But the custom of having definite liturgical vestments did not find its ritualistic fixation till the twelfth century, when Innocentius III authorized the use of four colors: black, scarlet, white, and green, basing his regulations upon Ex. 28.   The white color was to be used for the feasts of martyrs and virgins, red for the festivals of apostles and martyrs, green for the common Sundays and festival days, and black on days of fasting (Ember Days) and mourning.   In a very short time the fifth color, violet, was added, which, according to the Roman Missal,

---

130) *St. Mark's Year Book*, Denver, *sub* Vestments.
131) Cp. *Lehre und Wehre*, Jan., 1918.
132) Cp. Baehr, *Symbolik des mosaischen Kultus*, I, 335—345.

was used only twice during the year, on Laetare and on the Feast of
the Innocents.   William Durandus, bishop of Mende, has a detailed
discussion of paraments in his *Rationale divinorum officiorum,* which
agrees almost exactly with the regulations of the *Missale Romanum*
of Pius V (1566—1572).   White, the color of innocence, was used for
the festivals of "virgines non martyres," on the festivals of angels,
of the Virgin, on All Saints, on the festival of John the Evangelist,
from the vigil of Christmas to the octave of Epiphany, on Maundy
Thursday, Easter, Ascension, and Dedication.   Red was the color for
the festivals of the apostles, the evangelists, and the martyrs, for the
Pentecostal season from the vigil to the following Saturday, for the
commemoration of the death of John the Baptist.   Black was used
for Good Friday, on Rogation Days, at masses for deceased, and for
penitential processions, in some cases also for Advent and Lent.
Green was prescribed for ferial services, also for the Sundays between
the octave of Epiphany and Septuagesima, and for the time between
Pentecost and Advent.   When violet had been accepted in all parishes,
it was used during Advent till the vigils of Christmas and during
Lent till Maundy Thursday.   There has been little change in the prescribed order to the present day.[133])   These colors were used not only
in the materials for the covering of the altar mensa, but also for the
antependium of altar, pulpit, and lectern, and for gremiale, palla,
and bursa.   The linen cloths, which have also been in use in the
Church for many centuries and are used during the entire year, are
the altar cloth for the plate of the mensa, the corporale, upon which
the sacred vessels are placed, the velum for covering the sacred vessels before and after use, and several smaller cloths, used principally
for hygienic purposes.[134])

Since the Reformation, only the Anglican Church and the Lutheran Church have retained the paraments, though individual congregations in other denominations make use of rich hangings and
tapestries, and occasionally of liturgical colors.   There are few Episcopal churches that do not possess a full set of paraments, white, red,
violet, black, green, and also the linens, fair linen, corporal, pall,
chalice veil, and burse.   In the Lutheran Church in America, their
use is not so general, some congregations having only one or two
colors; but the movement for correct liturgical appointments is gaining ground.

The earliest *Eucharistic vessels* were in thorough accord with
the simplicity of our Lord's institution.   Cups and plates made of
glass, of wood, and of the baser metals were in common use, as a re-

---

133) Strodach, *Liturgical Colors,* 9—12.
134) Reed, *Altar Linen,* 31—34.

mark by Jerome shows. At the same time, however, vessels of a more pretentious character were used, and soon became the rule. Even in ante-Nicean times, gold and silver vessels were mentioned among the possessions of many churches. Sometimes they were even adorned with gems. Gold leaf decoration upon glass being in great favor, the use of such vessels is found in some localities. The form of the early chalices was that of a two-handled vase. The patens or disks were shaped much like the antique libation dish, with two handles. They were often ornamented with appropriate symbols, such as a lamb or cross. Since it was the custom in this period for all members to partake of the Holy Communion, these vessels were necessarily much larger than the ones now commonly in use. At the time of Jerome, the bread was kept in a basket, but later a special vessel was designed, first, for receiving the consecrated bread that remained, and afterwards, as a receptacle for the wafers. This vessel received the name ciborium from the baldachino which had formerly sheltered the entire altar. According to Gregory of Tours, it usually had the shape of a dove and was suspended over the altar. From the time of Constantine to that of Justinian, the splendor and costliness of the Eucharistic vessels, especially for larger churches and cathedrals, defies all description. The *Liber Pontificalis* is therefore usually satisfied with giving the weight of the gold and silver, and the number of chalices and patens. When the great movement of church building during the Middle Ages set in, the Eucharistic vessels received their share of attention. The great decorated chalice of Ardagh, now in Dublin, dates from the tenth century. When the Romanesque movement was at its height, beautiful pontifical and distributing chalices were produced. The latter were provided with small tubes for the use of the communicants until the time when the full withdrawal of the chalice took place. The Romanesque cup had the round shape of the Roman *poculum,* with circular base and knob. Beautiful work in engraving, relief, and filigree has been preserved. This was true also of the paten, which now received the shape of a plate. The ciborium was shaped either like a dove or like a small chest. During the Gothic period, the paten remained virtually unchanged. The Gothic chalice is slenderer and more graceful, the hexagonal base rising gradually to the knob, which was ornamented with button-like projections. The shape of the cup was that of the hyperbola. The late Gothic artists provided the entire base, even to the holder of the cup, with cleverly modeled, but often excessive, ornamentation. And the Renaissance changed the chalice to a secular cup, often with wide flaring edges, entirely destitute of all churchly character. In recent years, a cup with an egg-shaped holder has been introduced in Germany. Eucharistic vessels in almost every style and form have been in use in American Lutheran churches, even such as have been modeled after antique classical types. In some churches, individual communion sets have been introduced for supposed reasons of hygiene.

In the ancient churches a large *cross,* usually of gold or silver, and set with precious stones, stood near the altar, or a smaller cross was suspended over it. After the fourth century, it was sometimes customary to have an engraving or a relief figure of the lamb on the cross. In the ninth century, the crucifix makes its appearance. It was used at first mainly for processional, benedictional, and devotional purposes, and only in the smaller size. With the general acceptance of reredoses, however, the crucifixes were used also on the altars. There are some beautiful examples of crucifixes, dating from the Romanesque period. The Gothic artists changed the lines of the cross decoration, without interfering with the corpus. In England, the crucifix was not introduced generally till the fourteenth century.

About the time of Gregory the Great, a large *candelabrum* with the so-called Paschal candle belonged to the equipment of most churches, being situated usually near one of the ambons. With the introduction of the crucifix on the altar, candlesticks were also adopted as a part of the equipment of the retabulum. The cross or crucifix being in the center, the two candlesticks formed with it a pyramid, which harmonized especially well with the Gothic triumphal arch. The Reformed churches have declared against both candelabra and crucifixes, although a resolution of the Council of Zurich (1524) still permitted their use. The Lutheran Church has retained both the candlesticks and the crucifix, defending their use against all attacks,[135] since there is no sin connected with having the figure of Christ on the cross, but only in using it for idolatrous purposes. There can be no denying the fact, however, that the plain crosses, as they are in use in the Protestant Episcopal Church, have a beautiful dignity, and that they certainly are nearer to the simplicity of the Canono-Catholic times than the crucifixes. In America, the Lutheran Church uses either the crucifix or the cross, and, in many cases, the seven-armed candelabra are in use during the celebration of the Eucharist, while the vesper candlesticks burn during every evening service.

---

135) Kliefoth, IV, 33. 146.

PART II.

The Practical Execution of the Lutheran Church Building and its Appointments.

CHAPTER 1.

Preliminary Considerations and the Choice of the Style of Architecture.

In spite of the fact that Ruskin and others have been ridiculed as foolish visionaries, if not as dangerous cranks, the principles enunciated by such art critics deserve a far wider application, especially in church building. They are really the ideas which are fundamental and should be thoroughly understood by architects, builders, and building committees. It is in devotional architecture more than in any other branch of the art that the factor of permanence must be considered a prominent and guiding principle. This will demand a spirit of sacrifice, as a matter of fact. A mere offering of surplus riches does not argue for a great and abiding love of the cause. It is the willingness of a greater effort than the customary, habitual giving which is required in the erection of a house of worship. Where the ardor of the first love is unabated, the willingness of the Israelites, Ex. 35, 21—29; 36, 4—6, or of the early Christians, Acts 4, 34—37, will be found. But in many cases, the spirit of worldliness has so far entered a congregation, that the attitude is almost like that of the Israelites after having returned from their captivity, which the Lord deemed it necessary to reprove, Hagg. 1, 2—8. "It is not the church we want, but the sacrifice; not the emotion of admiration, but the act of adoration; not the gift, but the giving." [136]

Where such a spirit of sacrifice is rife or can be aroused, it will also insist upon truth or honesty. Any violation of truth is out of harmony with the ideals of Christianity. Sham, disguise, deception, pretension, whether in materials or in workmanship, especially the covering-up of cheap and light construction with ornaments that suggest stability or strength, is out of place in a house of worship dedicated to God. "Readers of Ruskin are familiar with his 'Seven Lamps of Architecture' and the emphasis which he lays on the 'Lamp of Truth.' And surely, nowhere else is truth more essential than in the building of the church, founded as it must be on the foundations of truth. Materials that lack permanence or are made to appear what they are not; structural elements that are not simply adorned but

---

136) Ruskin, *Seven Lamps of Architecture*, 25.
Kretzmann, Christian Art.

concealed by ornament; or designs that falsify in their details the central theme, all darken the 'Lamp of Truth.' The stability, reserve in adornment, and unity of design which characterize the best type of architecture are expressive elements of truth that should enter into the building of every church. Moreover, to be true, the church must be churchly. A clubhouse or a classic temple cannot be a church in the proper sense. The clubhouse, at best, stands for worldly comfort and entertainment; while the church, however comfortable and joyous its worshipers may be, always represents an order of ideas that transcends all human conditions." [137])

That a church should be symbolical of power is a requirement which agrees well with the symbolism of the invisible Church. It may not be necessary to insist upon the severe and even mysterious majesty which Ruskin mentions, but dignity and sublimity will do much toward expressing the possession of that power which characterizes the church of God, Ps. 87, 1. 5; Matt. 16, 18. It is not merely the greatness of the actual dimensions which will create the required impression. As a matter of fact, many a village church furnishes a better example of the quality of strength than a metropolitan tabernacle. It is compactness and solidity which express power, not loose-jointed, sprawled greatness The whole building, or at least its principal lines, should be seen at one glance, and present the impression of unity and strength.

That beauty is demanded in a church building, is in full accord with the qualities of the Church of Christ, whose abode the house of worship is fashioned to be, Eph. 5, 27. This excludes all ostentation, every effort to place cheap and gaudy embellishments on walls or façade. It demands a complete harmony of all parts of the church, not a collection of disjointed members strewn over a certain amount of square feet. It eliminates, at once, most of the Baroque and all of the Rococo construction, as being out of harmony with natural forms. Simple lines, simple arches, simple ornaments that are in harmony with the central idea of the building, will make for dignified beauty. "The type of the Romanesque arch is always before us in that of the apparent vault of heaven, and the horizon of the earth. The cylindrical pillar is always beautiful, for God has so molded the stem of every tree that it is pleasant to the eyes. The pointed arch is beautiful; it is the termination of every leaf that shakes in summer wind." [138])

It may seem, at first glance, as though the requirement of life in a church building is an unreasonable or a purposeless demand. But one need only to visit a church where this principle has been disre-

---

137) *The Brick Church and Parish House*, 5. 6.
138) Ruskin, *Op. cit.*, 101.

TRINITY CHURCH, ST. LOUIS.
(Missouri Synod.)

garded, and the impression of chilliness, of death, will cause a feeling almost of repulsion. The Church of Christ is a healthy, living body, Eph. 2, 20—22, and every resemblance, even remote, to a corpse or dungeon, in a Christian church edifice, must be carefully avoided. If the architect causes a building to be erected which is a mere copy, or if he has not grasped the fundamental principles of the style in which he attempts to work, or if the execution is too delicate or over-refined, then this sensation is usually aroused in the visitor. Sometimes the colors of the windows or of the fresco-work cause the same impression. Church architecture, more than any other, must be healthy, brimming with life, full of vitality.

Even the lamp of memory cannot be said to be unessential in a Christian church. Since it is not a mausoleum, but a living record, it has an historical significance which often speaks to the descendants more plainly than the written document. The church that we build represents our love for our Church, our ambitions, aspirations, and hopes; its furniture and appointments speak a language which will tell later generations the entire situation as to our understanding of the essential requirements of church building. It will tell them, especially, whether we have penetrated into the uttermost secrets of the adopted style, or whether the style we created was an actual spontaneous expression of creative art in our midst. For obedience to the laws which have been discovered in the past and found to be immutable so long as this universe exists, without slavish subjugation so far as definite forms are concerned, is a necessary requirement in those who would erect a church. To become expert at adapting without adopting as a mere copyist, that is true obedience.

It is in full conformity with these principles that Kidder writes: "In the first place, a church is supposed to be a temple, erected by man to the glory of God and for the observance of religious services and the spreading of His Word. The aim of the architect and of the church body should therefore be to express this purpose as clearly and distinctly as may lie in their ability, while at the same time providing suitable arrangements for the church services and conveniences for such charitable and social work as the church may undertake. . . . When erecting a habitation for the Most High God, the church should not be niggardly in its expense, but should feel that nothing is too magnificent for an offering to the Lord, 1 Chron. 22, 5. . . . . The work should be entered upon in a spirit of reverence and love, and with a desire to build pleasing in the sight of God. No shams or subterfuges of construction should be permitted. The building, above all, should be honest, truthful, even if it must be plain." [139)]

---

139) *Churches and Chapels*, 11. 12.

A fundamental requirement, when a church building is contemplated, is this that the house, as planned, actually serve the purpose for which it is intended. Any accomplishment of talent or genius does not measure up to the standard, of a work of art unless this demand is complied with. "A Christian church building must express the idea of the Christian service and serve its purposes, as a whole as well as in all its parts." [140]   There are three purposes which a Chris-

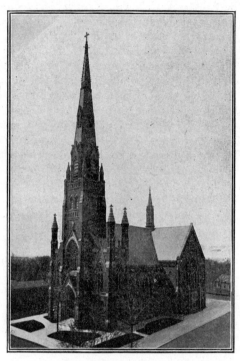

ST. PAUL'S CHURCH, FT. WAYNE, IND.
(Missouri Synod.)

tian, and especially a Lutheran, church is to serve. It is intended, first of all, as a house where the Gospel of Jesus Christ is to be preached. The Lutheran Church has every reason for the proud boast that she is the Church of the Word. The proclaiming of this Word marks the culmination of the service, Matt. 28, 19. 20; John 8, 47a. "Where the Word of God is not preached it is far better neither to sing nor to read nor to come together. The greatest and most important part of all service is to preach and teach God's Word." [141]

---

140) Meurer, *Der Kirchenbau*, 101.
141) Luther, quoted in Schultze, *Das evangelische Kirchengebaeude*, 23.

If a Lutheran church is built without keeping this demand in mind, it is neither a work of art nor a church, properly speaking. It may, under circumstances, serve to stimulate devotion by other means, but it has no reason for existing *as church*. Closely connected with this requirement is this that the Sacraments may be administered properly. They really represent the application of the spoken Word by visible elements, "the Sacrament itself being made and blessed and hallowed by the Word of God." The Word is thus brought to the attention of the congregation in the sermon, in the liturgical lessons, in the absolution, in the benediction, and in the sacraments. "The architect should therefore primarily keep in mind the majesty of the Word of God, as read from Scriptures, but then also the unconditional demand of the cultus of admonition and free exposition of the Word of God through the preacher, and therefore subordinate his thoughts absolutely under this conception of the divine Word. With his entire artistic ability he must vouch for the most perfect audibility of the divine Word." [142]) As these two requirements represent the sacramental acts of the cultus, so the third consideration expresses the sacrificial act of the service. For the church is also the place of prayer. Not with that emphasis, indeed, which Meurer places upon this factor with reference to Matt. 21, 12. The hearing of the Word of God in the sacramental part of the services comes first. But the congregation is also active, not merely by a silent participation in the liturgical prayers, but also by the singing of the beautiful Lutheran hymns, many of which are true votive offerings before the throne of grace. The Reformation has given the hymnbook into the hands of the Lutheran congregations, and the Lutheran Church proudly calls itself the "singing Church." Therefore this sacrificial part of the service must be borne in mind very carefully and provision made that it receive due consideration in the erection of every Lutheran church building.

But not only must the object of a church edifice in general, and that of a Lutheran church building in particular, be observed with such care, but there are also certain historical considerations which cannot be ignored. The Lutheran Church is a product of reformation, not revolution, and therefore its church buildings should continue conservative traditions, purging, whenever it seems necessary, but only of actual idolatrous and superstitious Roman Catholic customs. There is no reason for the attempted creation of a so-called new style, and all efforts to that effect deserve to be abortive. Luther and his colleagues, as well as the leaders of the Lutheran Church throughout Germany (when there was still a Lutheran Church in

142) Lechler, quoted in Schultze, 23.

Germany) had no hesitation about using the church buildings as they found them. Whether ecclesiastical architecture will ever succeed in evolving a new, perfect style, which will adequately express the ideas of the Lutheran cultus and all its demands, is a question which has not been solved as yet, in spite of sporadic outbursts of misguided enthusiasts. In no case may a Lutheran church be subjected to the arbitrary whims of an experimenting architect.[143] "The Christian character of a Lutheran church building demands the use

ST. PAULUS CHURCH, SAN FRANCISCO.
(Missouri Synod.)

of one of the historically developed Christian styles of architecture," says Mothes, in his notes on the Eisenach Regulative.[144]

It is necessary that the character of a Lutheran church edifice be expressed by every part of the building, both exterior and interior. "It should be distinguished from buildings for profane purposes, and also from the temples of other religious confessions. The chief form should witness that the building serves no small, but the greatest purpose, no passing end, but an eternal, no material use, but an ideal,

---

143) Schultze, *Das evangelische Kirchengebaeude*, 26.
144) Horn, *Lutheran Principles of Church Architecture*, 85.

no worldly aim, but a spiritual, no lowly purpose, but the very highest;
that it belongs to no person, but to the whole congregation, invites
the whole congregation to enter, take part in assembly, prayer, praise,
illumination through pure doctrine, in short, to the adoration of God
and exaltation to Him; but also that the chief principle of the worship celebrated in it in evangelical freedom is embraced in the notions
of congregational assembly, common hearing of the Word, thanksgiving for Christ's Word of redemption, reception of the gifts of
His grace, and therefore has nothing to do with processions, the sacrifice of the mass, and other mystical ceremonies, the worship of the
saints, etc. For such a witness the building needs, primarily, earnestness and dignity of appearance, great simple masses, even with mod-
est additions and wide organization of members, an ideal form,
aspiring relations, avoidance of forms which are subject to passing
fashion, declaration and awakening of assurance of long continuance
by means of solidity, external signification of inner sanctity by great
windows, and a broad entrance under a tower rising up towards
heaven. In all, in every particular, in every part, mass, and form,
the exterior should render the inner purpose, that inner organization
in ante-chamber, congregational space, and altar space, and their
unified combination, visible. On the room of the congregation should
be impressed the character of rest and quietness; on the altar space
of motion, of aspiration, without interfering with the artistic unity.
But everything that might remind one of a mystery, of the advance
of a procession, of the separation of the priesthood from the laity in
contradiction of the universal priesthood of the congregation, or of
adoration of the saints, is to be strictly avoided." [145]) Moreover, the
specifically Lutheran characteristics should appear in a Lutheran
church building. These requirements are stated by Horn as follows:
"A Lutheran church differs from a Roman Catholic church, 1. in having but one altar; 2. in making due provision for the preaching of
the Word; 3. in providing that the whole congregation may intelli-
gently take part in the whole service of worship; 4. in not making a
separation between a 'clergy' and a 'laity'; 5. in providing for the
communion of the people, instead of a celebration of the Sacrament;
6. in arranging for a service whose reality depends on the presence
and participation of the congregation. On the other hand, the sanctity of a Roman Catholic church is guaranteed by the supposed presence of Christ upon the altar, and the consecration of the church.
A Lutheran church differs from a non-Lutheran Protestant church
because in the former 1. Christ is present in His Word and Sacraments, through them speaks to us, and through them imparts Him-

---

145) Mothes, quoted in Horn, 109. 110.

self to us; 2. and the Holy Communion is not merely a mark of the confession and communion of the people, but is a Sacrament." [146]) There are other differences which fix the character of a Lutheran church very definitely, some of a doctrinal, some of a liturgical nature, most of which will be touched upon in subsequent paragraphs.

ST. MARCUS, MILWAUKEE.
(Wisconsin Synod.)

There are thus certain demands of history and historical tradition which cannot be ignored.

But if the proper historical considerations are to be observed, there is another factor which cannot be considered a matter of indifference, namely the orientation of a Lutheran church building in such a way that in the axis of the structure the altar is given its

146) *Lutheran Principles of Church Architecture*, 79. 80.

place in the east end, while the main portal is on the west end. It is a custom which has been observed in the Christian Church since about 420 A. D. It is not a remnant of pagan demonolatry, as a modern writer has asserted. The heathen temples, as a rule, had their main portals facing the rising sun. The same orientation was employed in the temple at Jerusalem. And it is also true that most Jesuit churches, at least in Germany, have their altars in the west end of the church. Why not, then, as a distinctive mark, follow the Canono-Catholic custom, which has such a fine symbolism? *Ex oriente lux!* Christ arose with the rising sun. Out of the East came the glory of the Gospel of the Savior to the entire West. Therefore the Christian congregation faces the East, where the heavenly Sun, the Sun of Righteousness, arose. There is also a practical reason for this orientation, since the chief service takes place in the morning, and again, that it is uplifting to look towards the East.[147] "The orientation of the church building, which has been fixed by tradition in such a way as to give to the altar its position at the east end of the axis, should not be abandoned without urgent reason. Small deviations (to southeast or northeast) do not interfere with the symbolical thought."[148] "The choir (apse) is type of the world of transfiguration toward which the pilgrimage of the congregation in the nave is directed. She has left the world, and through Baptism has entered the holy place; her face is turned to the East, and her progress is through time to eternity."[149] "We seek one to come," and "Not as though I had already attained," and "Set your affection on things above," and "The day-spring from on high hath visited us," are finely expressed in the proper orientation of a church.[150] Rietschel, indeed, with a cynical aloofness which is apparent in more than one instance, declares the question of orientation to be non-essential.[151] Granted that the custom is not essential for the Lutheran character of a church building and that circumstances may sometimes render it impossible to observe the orientation, it is also true that most other historical and practical considerations may be set aside and the structure still deserve the name of a Lutheran house of worship. Besides, the investigations of Lowrie have shown that actual deviations from the rule are extremely rare, the few actual cases being due to the influence of Constantine, who retained many traces of his earlier sun worship.[152] Since, in most cases, it will be merely a mat-

147) Horn, *Op. cit.*, 84. 88. 111.   148) Schultze, *Op. cit.*, 36.
149) Luthardt, quoted in Schultze, 26.
150) Cp. Meurer, *Der Kirchenbau*, 110. 111.
151) Rietschel, *Lehrbuch der Liturgik*, I, 124.
152) *Monuments of the Early Church*, 176—178.

ter of choice with the congregation, the ancient customs should not
be disregarded without urgent reasons.

The liturgical requirements of a Lutheran church have been

ST. JACOBI, MILWAUKEE.
(Wisconsin Synod.)

touched upon under historical considerations. But a few factors
should be emphasized more strongly. Church architecture cannot
feel fully satisfied with a building for worship, when the contractor
simply puts up four walls, covers the intervening space with a roof,

and provides seating capacity for a stated number of people, for the
rest following his own, often florid, imagination; but it demands a
church building which expresses the idea of Christian worship and
fully answers the purpose of the ritual, as a whole and in all its parts.
"In fixing the dimensions and proportions, in the disposing of the
individual parts, in the location of portals and windows, of aisles
and seats, in the designing and placing of pulpit, baptismal font, and
altar, in the ornamenting of walls and windows, in the ordering of
church equipment, paraments, and vestments, structural and aesthetic
reasons alone should not decide, but the demands of liturgics should
receive first consideration, in order that the place of the cultus, its
purpose in the ecclesiastical ministration, may not be misunderstood
and the visitor, as often happens, be reminded of the ball-room, the
concert-hall, and the theater." [153])   This criticism applies, in general,
to American Protestant church buildings.   When we enter and see
the arrangement of the auditorium, the gallery (and sometimes the
balcony) extending across the nave into the transepts and even into
the apse, with box seats and similar appurtenances; when one sees
the large platform with its elevated portion for the singers and the
monster organ in the front, searching in vain, at the same time, for
altar and pulpit, until one discovers an insignificant lectern and a
still less significant table, one is tempted to indulge in criticizing
levity and to inquire when the performance is scheduled to begin and
to wonder whether programs are furnished with box seats only.   The
Lutheran Church has retained the division of its church edifices into
nave and apse, not in order to make a distinction between clergy and
laity, as in the Roman Catholic Church, but in order to give expression to the division of the liturgy in the sacrificial and sacramental
parts of the service.   Everything that pertains to the office of redemption, the reading of the Scripture lessons, the pronouncing of the
benediction, the preaching of the Gospel, the administration of the
Sacraments, takes place in the apse; all acts of a sacrificial nature,
prayer and singing of the congregation and choir, confession of sins
and of the Creed, are performed by and with the assembled congregation in the nave.

    In order, then, to summarize all the requirements of an aesthetic
or artistic, an historical, and a liturgical nature, the following demands express sound Lutheran usage.   A Lutheran church building
should typify: *Christianity,* in a Christian style of architecture and,
in larger churches, the adoption of the cruciform ground-plan, as well
as the other symbols of Christianity; *unity,* — it should not have a
number of detached towers and additions, but the building must form

153) Meurer. *Der Kirchenbau.* 101. 102.

an harmonious whole; *simplicity,* — all ostentation in design and ornamentation must be avoided; *solidity* and *stability,* — all pretense and flimsiness is out of place in a church building; *strength and vitality,* — this can be shown in the arrangement of arches, in solid masonry, as well as in the free use of the lines of force where the architecture calls for such; *growth,* — by avoiding depressing ceil-

ST. MARK'S CHURCH, TOLEDO, OHIO.
(Ohio Synod.)

ings and shortness of outline, thus gaining the effect of height and free space. A Lutheran church building should express *liturgical and confessional usage.* The sermon, together with the Sacraments of grace, should be yielded the most prominent part of the church. The sanctuary and the space immediately before it should be used exclusively for this, the principal part of the service. Everything that will detract the devotion from the sacramental acts of the liturgy has no place before the congregation. Prayer, as the secondary part

of the service, must be given due consideration, inasmuch as nothing
in or near the apse should distract the attention or interfere with the
proper edification of a devout audience. The subordinate parts of the
Lutheran service are represented by the organ and choir. These are
auxiliary, ancillary factors, and, in spite of the importance accorded to
them, must never be given the same prominence as the means of grace.
Their position in the apse or in front of the congregation, especially
on a greatly elevated platform or loft, is liturgically wrong and may
also be construed as confessionally dangerous. In most Protestant
churches of America, the organ is the most conspicuous part of the
church equipment in the apse or on the large front platform, and the
names of the soloists are carefully printed in large type on the
"program," as well as the titles of the musical compositions that shall
delight and, perhaps, edify the congregation; but the pulpit occupies
a hidden corner, if it is present at all, and the sermon is regarded as
a somewhat superfluous adjunct. This arrangement is a confession
of doctrine which coordinates prayer and the means of grace, and
often subordinates the latter to the former. This matter is so important that it will be taken up at greater length below. The fact
must ever stand out with absolute clearness that the arrangement of
the parts of the building, as well as the placing of every part of the
equipment, must be governed by liturgical considerations, as established by confessional usage and hallowed by history and tradition.

The question as to the most appropriate style of architecture for
a Lutheran church has been answered, in a way, by the statement
above that a Lutheran church requires a Christian style. This excludes at once all heathen styles, whether they be Egyptian, or Persian, or Assyrian, or Greek, or Moorish, or whatever other style a
perverted fancy may suggest. The only styles that come into consideration at all are those which have been employed in the Christian
Church since the second century. There are people, of course, and
among them artists, who look upon every suggestion as to an established style as an insult to their intelligence and creative power. And
when men of the caliber of Rietschel defend an emancipated eclecticism as attempting to meet the needs of Evangelical worship,[154]) one
can hardly be surprised at the audacity of lesser minds. And when,
in addition, they bring the charge of a dead formalism and of dis-
couraging art, the question of church architecture seems destined to
be thrown into the forum of dispute, like imagist poetry and cubist
painting. But new styles, as Mothes points out, are not invented by
reflection, but are the fruit of an organic growth. A new style, if
there ever will be such a thing in the American Lutheran Church,

---

154) *Lehrbuch der Liturgik*, 125. 126.

will be spontaneous, and not the result of deliberate effort. Besides, there is a strong measure of doubt as to the feasibility of discarding all the principles enumerated above. So far as the accusation is concerned as though the employment of a definite style represents dead

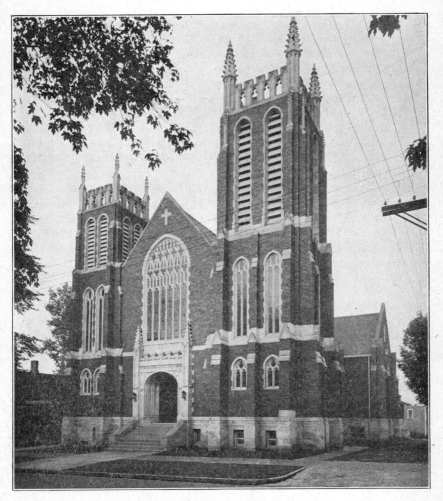

EMANUEL'S CHURCH, MARION, OHIO.
(Ohio Synod.)

formalism, the charge is more than ridiculous, it is absurd. No one has suggested the copying of a dead art. There is only one Cathedral of Amiens, or York, or Cologne, but the fundamental principles of Gothic art live forever. It is the same glorious fact which weaves enchantment around every art, lifting it out of the dreary rut of the commonplace, and causing it to become a lodestar for all times. There is only one Stradivarius, one Bach, one Praxiteles, one Apelles, one Shakespeare, and yet the inspiration of their wonderful achievements in the realm of their respective art has caused a thousand minds to seek the principles of their art and to emulate, at least in a measure, their glorious success. That is what every designer and every builder of a Lutheran church should keep in mind. A mere copying of outward forms or of ornament without understanding the principles of a style is no art. There is all the difference in the world between more or less slavish copying, even though genius may aid one to modify with pleasing effect, and gaining the original inspiration and allowing it to work out in its own new way. The latter is the ideal we are striving for. And in this sense we venture a critical discussion of such styles as have been in use or have been advocated for adoption since the Reformation.

So far as the construction of a Lutheran church in the Byzantine style is concerned, little need be said. The centralized building has fortunately never had any decided influence on architectural art in the Occident. It lives only in established, conventional forms, and its symbolism can be interpreted only as that of an effort which has expended itself, and can now merely portray the complete, the self-sufficient, and the dead. Besides, the domed Byzantine church is an inorganic, intentional, but unsuccessful amalgamation of Christian considerations with antique and Oriental ideas, as Schnaase says. One cannot escape the sense of depression in such a church building, so far as the Lutheran cultus is concerned.

The style of the early basilica is mentioned in the Eisenach Regulative. And it cannot be denied that the basilica possesses certain advantages which recommend it to a denomination that insists upon having "Predigtkirchen": it offers a great deal of floor-space and a large seating capacity for its dimensions, and it permits the introduction of galleries. The acoustics is also favorable, and the cost of construction relatively low. And yet the basilica cannot be said to meet the requirements of a Lutheran church. The specific Christian character is lacking, since there is too much that originated in secular architecture. And since the vertical lines are by far the more prominent, the building makes an impression of great heaviness, especially since the tower is lacking; it looks too much like a corpse sprawled along the ground. The vertical ceiling furthermore precludes all possibilities of height, thus conflicting with religious symbolism.[155]

---

155) Schultze, *Das evangelische Kirchengebaeude*, 28.

Although the German Renaissance is not summarily ruled out, as Mothes remarks, yet the style of church architecture of the Renaissance, especially that of the Jesuit era, can hardly come into consideration here. The cupola or dome in this style presents a grand appearance from the outside, but it really has no liturgical meaning from the standpoint of Christianity. The magnificence of the dome, in addition, cannot compensate for the lack of commensurate harmony in the rest of the building. And in either case, the dome, which was copied from antique styles, is the type of heaven brought down to men, but resting on the priests, who are represented by the massive columns supporting the dome. The classical pagan element is evident at every turn. Besides, this style has its birth-place in Italy, in the midst of thoroughly ultramontane influence. And it is,

LUTHERAN CHURCH, ST. SEBALD, IA.
(Iowa Synod.)

to this day, the only proper church building for Roman Catholic congregations, where the hierarchy, under the direct control of ultramontanism, has full sway. For basilica and Renaissance style, as well as the Classic Revival, it holds true that anything which savors of trabeated architecture is out of harmony with the spirit of the Lutheran cultus.

The only styles, then, that can be considered with any degree of seriousness, are the Romanesque and the Gothic. Both styles are preeminently ecclesiastical styles, grown out of the spirit of the Church and imbued with its symbolism. They are dissociated from the profane. They have brought forth magnificent structures of a noble art, and their fundamental principles are applicable to all requirements of a Lutheran church building. There is no denying, of course, that there are types of these styles that are not so suitable as others. The Norman style has been mentioned favorably, and there

are some fine monuments of parish churches in England. But the
Norman style shows too many features of trabeated architecture. Its
tower is so massive that it stamps the entire building with the character of a fortress, in a measure grim and forbidding. There is little
that is friendly and inviting. Here in America the Tudor style of
recent parish churches has found much favor. And it has much to
commend it, particularly in the case of smaller churches. Its vaulting has lost in height, and the factor of comparative cheapness of
construction is an important one. Its great fault, so far as the position of the choir is concerned, could be corrected, as Cram points
out.[156]   But there is a fundamental principle which is antagonistic
to Lutheran requirements. The Tudor style represents the decay of
the English Gothic and the preparation for the Renaissance. It is
not a style which stands for full vitality and power, so far as churches
are concerned. In secular architecture it has accomplished much,
because it proved unusually adaptable to large buildings, such as
schools and colleges. But the arches and the vaulting in the case of
churches exhibit retrogression, not progression.

There still remains a great latitude of choice in the French and
German Romanesque, in the Early and Middle Pointed periods of the
Gothic in France and Germany, and in the Decorated and Perpendicular styles of the Gothic in England. In many cases, the simple,
dignified Romanesque style may meet with all requirements. But it
cannot be doubted that the Gothic is the higher and more completely
developed style. The great favor it is finding in America may well
be explained if one considers its symbolism fully. And the words of
praise from various critics which have been recorded in the chapter
on Gothic Architecture, could be supplemented by many more. "The
religious devotion, the free uplifting of the soul to God must be
symbolized in the interior and exterior construction of the (Gothic)
church"; it shall "in its language, the language of architecture, express the *sursum corda*. The high vaultings, the airy spaces, the
tower shall speak this language, and everything up to the spire flower
that opens its petals in intense yearning toward heaven. Everything
that produces a depressing, narrowing, gloomy impression must be
avoided." [157]   "Although it is not style or ornament that makes a
structure Christian, but rather the manner in which the architectural
features are used, still it appears to be easier to give a religious impression to a building by means of the Gothic than by either of the
other styles (Renaissance and Romanesque). It is also a noticeable
fact that the larger proportion of the best examples of church architecture, both in this country and in England, are in the Gothic

---

156) *Church Building.* 19.   157) Schultze, *Op. cit.*, 25.

style. . . . In conclusion, it must be admitted, perhaps, that God can
be worshipped as truly in an amphitheatrical church as in a Gothic
cathedral, but it is nevertheless true that a church which speaks un-
mistakably of its mission and inculcates in the attendant a feeling
of reverence and faith in God adds greatly to the effect of the
service." [158])   "Gothic is the one style in which we can work." [159])

ST. PAUL'S CHURCH, S. ST. PAUL, MINN.
(Iowa Synod.)

Of course there are objections to both Romanesque and Gothic, as
Rietschel notes,[160]) if we should have the idea that the churches of
those periods should be copied. But all the factors which he mentions:
the high choir obstructing the view of the altar, the columns cutting
off the view of the pulpit, the poor acoustics, are non-essentials, and

158) Kidder, *Churches and Chapels*, 12. 14.
159) Cram, *Church Building*, Chapter II.
160) *Lehrbuch der Liturgik*, 126. 127.

the charges will not stand if the course suggested above is followed, namely, that of adaptation.

There are certain general suggestions as to the practical and technical execution of a church building which should be kept in mind at all times. The choice of material depends, to a great extent, not only on the purses of the builders, but also on the laws of the state, city, or town, and the availability of certain materials. The time may not be far distant when some of the richer congregations will be in a position to choose granite and even marble for church building. But for most congregations, a good building-stone, either lime-stone, or the best grade of sand-stone, is more likely to come into consideration. Then there are the various grades of brick in all shades and colors which are available in almost every part of our country. Cement blocks are frequently used for small church build-

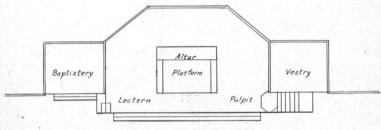

ARRANGEMENT OF APSE.

ings, the disadvantage connected with their use having been practically overcome. The use of common brick or hollow tile, with a facing of rubble or cement stucco, will greatly reduce the cost of a church building without detracting materially from its appearance. In a case of this kind, the cement must not be laid out in blocks to imitate stone or perhaps even rusticated masonry, since such a proceeding would be opposed to the principle of truth. Frame construction is often the only construction which can be considered in smaller congregations and in the country. It should not be employed, however, unless absolutely necessary, because frame construction is not monumental. Even for chapels, the demand of stability is a prime consideration.

Since, in the Romanesque style, the round arch is the governing principle and the arcs of this arch ought to be equal in height and width, and since also the diameters of the circles ought to correspond, there is little opportunity for variation from the square. The proportion of the length to the width is also governed by this consideration. The width ought not to be less than one-half and not more than four-fifths the length of the building. The width of the apse ought to be one-half the width of the church. The vestry (not an integral part of the church proper) ought to be south of the sanctuary. The corresponding room on the north may be used for the study of the pastor, or, better still, as baptistery, in which case the wall between the nave or transept and this room must be omitted. Small churches should be built in the rectangular form, large churches ought to be cruciform, the transept on either side extending one-eighth to one-fourth the width of the church. The main portal is in the west wall, at the end of the principal axis of the church, opposite the altar. In this way, the idea of length is fully retained. And it

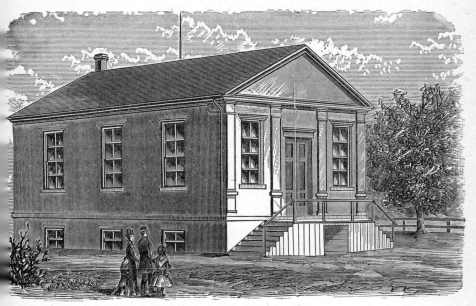

OLD SWEDISH CHURCH AT ANDOVER, ILL.
(Augustana Synod.)

makes no difference whether the church has a center tower or two side towers with narrow aisles leading diagonally from either tower entrance to the altar, the main or center aisle, symbolizing the direct, open way of every person to the grace of God, should never be omitted. It is also very practical in case of weddings and funerals. The structure of the windows is limited by the round arch, as indicated above, and the windows will be comparatively small. The vestibule may be either in the center tower room or under either side tower, or it may extend the width of the church building. This seems especially desirable in our days, when a retiring-room for women, particularly those with little children, must be arranged for off the vestibule.

The question of the balcony is usually very bothersome. The balcony opposite the apse, over the main portal, was originally intended as a choir or organ-loft, after the introduction of that splendid instrument. But reasons of economy and the necessity of having a "Predigtkirche" forced poorer congregations sometimes to extend the balcony around the sides of the church, into the transept, and even into the apse! And sometimes a gallery was added above the balcony! This was making utility the paramount principle with a vengeance, and Spener applauded. Every reason of art speaks against such an extension of the choir loft, besides the liturgical consideration that the hearer ought never to look down upon the preacher in the pulpit. The extended balcony is, in some cases, a necessary evil, in others, an absolute nuisance. It always injures the effect of freedom in a church, besides shutting off light and spoiling the harmony of the architecture, not to mention the difficulty which the speaker experiences in addressing two widely separated tiers of hearers. Let us hope that some day in the near future the balcony will again become that for which is was intended, the place for the choir, and especially in the Lutheran Church.

So far as the furniture for a church building in the Romanesque style is concerned, it must be remarked that the lines of the entire equipment of the building ought to conform to the style of architecture. The altar and pulpit above all must show the round arches corresponding to the barrel vaulting above. It need hardly be mentioned here that consistency in style, interior and exterior, is an absolute requirement. It is just as easy to preserve harmony as to build an architectural monstrosity. There is one warning that must be sounded in regard to the Romanesque style of church building. Too great a similarity to the ancient basilica is not commendable in this style. Christian characteristics must never be relegated to the background. And when the horizontal lines of the antique are followed too closely, the building makes the impression of a corpse lying sprawled on the ground.

Everything that has been said of materials and general shape applies also to church building in the Gothic style. It is dangerous to attempt a very small church or chapel in this style, unless the unessential factors, and especially the ornaments, are reduced to a minimum. "One constantly finds churches, seating perhaps less than two hundred, where the plan is cruciform, and there are aisles. clerestory, columns of iron or wood; insignificant towers, gables, belfries, and porches complete the already shapeless exterior; and the result is a scandal." 161) In larger churches, more of the Gothic fea-

---

161) Cram, *Church Building*, 16.

tures may be employed. The division of the auditorium into three
aisles is commonly observed in the Gothic style. Cram suggests that
the nave be 24 to 27 feet wide and 75 to 90 feet long, separated from

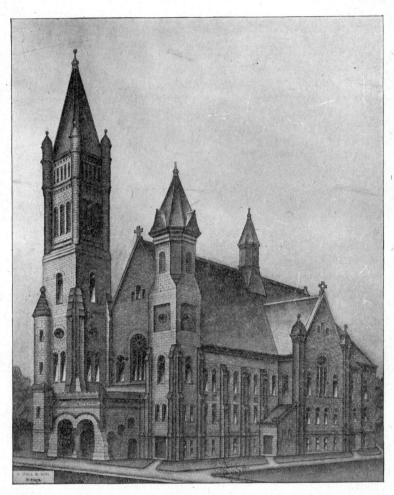

FIRST EV.-LUTH. CHURCH, JAMESTOWN, N. Y.
(Augustana Synod.)

aisles 13 to 15 feet wide by arcades of arches supported on stone
shafts 15 feet on centers.[162]) It may be possible, however, to reduce
the number of columns to a minimum or to approach the idea of the
German "Hallenkirchen" as being more in conformity with the re-

162) *Op. cit.*, 39.

quirements of a church for preaching, in which every one that attends may not only hear, but also see, the preacher. The general proportion of width to length should never go beyond one to two. The mathematical rule is that the height of the spire corresponds to the total length of the building, the height of the transept to the width of the nave, and that the built-out portion of the transept is one-fourth the width of this part. These are the proportions of the Cologne Cathedral, admittedly one of the finest examples of Gothic art in the world. Since, however, the harmony of the arc in the Gothic does not require proportionate measurements throughout the building, there is a much wider latitude for expression than in the Romanesque. The greater the radius of the arc of the vaulting, the greater will be the effect of height and distance. The walls can be built proportionately thinner, because the pilasters, braced by buttresses, easily carry the vaulted roof. The apse, which is usually one-half the width of the auditorium, and whose depth is one-half to two-thirds its width, can be made a beautiful niche, the triumphal arch rising in front and the octagonal or polygonal vaulting rising in a majestic curve to meet above the altar. The vaulting of the transept should be simple cross-vaulting to correspond to the cruciform plan of the church. Star- and fan-vaulting is inappropriate. The tower should rise in lighter and more graceful lines than in the Romanesque, receding, if possible, with each story, until the spire rises octagonally to a needle point. Flower and leaf ornamentation on decorative turrets and ridges should always have an upward tendency. The arches throughout the building, but especially in doors and windows, should have the same curve or arc. Christian symbolism may be observed by arranging the window openings (of which there should not be too many), especially in the transept, in series of three. The vestry should never be located behind the sanctuary, since the apse is the head of the church building, and any chapel or other subordinate room behind it will destroy the harmony of the building. The ambulatory may well be dispensed with. As for the balcony, the same demand holds true here as in the Romanesque, only, if possible, with still greater emphasis. Any horizontal lines here are in still greater contrast with the style, and cannot be tolerated, except where absolutely necessary, as in the case of the choir loft. The place for the choir is on this loft, opposite the altar. Chancel choirs have become fashionable, remarks Cram rather sarcastically, but the place for the organ and mixed choir is at the west end in a gallery. Any other place, with the exception, perhaps, of the north or south transept, is, liturgically speaking, impossible, especially in a Lutheran church. Coordination and subordination of the various parts of the Christian

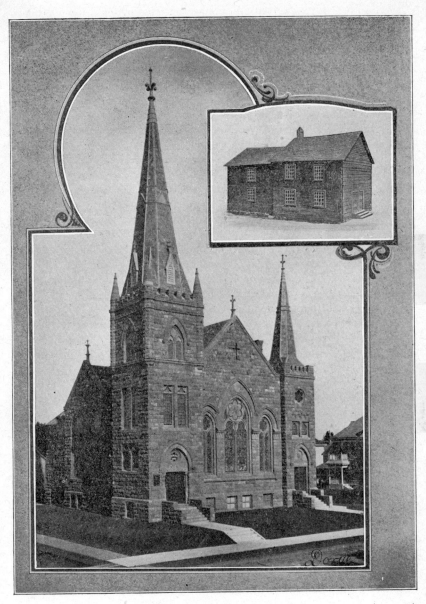

BETHLEHEM CHURCH, MINNEAPOLIS.
INSERT: MUSKEGO CHURCH.
(Norwegian.)

service must be apparent also in the arrangement of the house of worship. If the floor of the auditorium is inclined slightly, it will be of advantage to the audience, both for seeing and hearing. It will be well to have sound-proof flooring laid in the auditorium. Above all, it cannot be repeated too often that consistency must rule and harmony be preserved. Many a church which otherwise might have been beautiful, has been spoiled by the mixing of two or more styles, and the result is a disharmony, a discord which strikes even the casual visitor. This will appear even more when the several parts of the church building are discussed.

There are other preliminary considerations of a practical and technical nature which may not be ignored. It is manifestly impossible, in a country as large as ours, where so many different conditions obtain, to state more than general rules and requirements. It is also advisable to have some reference book, written from the purely technical side of the question, such as Price's "Practical Book of Architecture," as a guide to the understanding of legal and technical difficulties, always at hand. Most of these, however, will be avoided, if a congregation will observe Kidder's seven preliminary steps before beginning building operations. They are 1) Organize according to the laws of the state and the discipline of the church; 2) Secure the best possible site, with a clear title; 3) Provide the means to build without embarrassing debt; 4) Secure suitable plans prepared by a competent architect; 5) Let the building committee consist of competent men; 6) Insist upon the supervision by the architect; 7) Make no changes in the plans, and if such are found necessary, let every transaction be carefully recorded. These suggestions are plain and to the point.

The question of a suitable building site is of such importance that it should be considered most carefully. "The spot chosen for the building should be easy of access to all parts of the congregation." [163] This does not imply that the location must be in the geographical center of the congregation, but about in its center of population, removed, however, from a disagreeable neighborhood, not too near a railroad or directly on a street-car line or where the traffic is unusually noisy. An advantage which can be secured in a town or village, or in the country, oftener than in a city, is that the church be on an elevation, open on all sides or with a wide approach from the west. When a church is wedged in between other buildings, this often proves a disagreeable feature in more than one respect.

A very difficult question is usually that of the size of the church. Conditions vary so greatly in the various congregations that the de-

163) Mothes, quoted in Horn, 107.

termination of this factor depends almost upon the individual instance. In congregations which are growing rapidly only one limit can be set, and this is that the size of the flock should not be too great for one pastor's strength to minister to. The maximum number of souls in the care of one pastor should not exceed 1,000, the number of communicants 600. In old congregations the size is practically stable, and there the determination of dimensions for a new church will be an easier matter. Church attendance in various sections of the country and in different congregations also varies a great deal. There are places where a 90% attendance is not unusual, and others in which

ST. JOHN'S CHURCH, HAGERSTOWN, MD.
(General Synod, United Lutheran Church.)

a 30% attendance would be considered remarkable. As a rule, a 60 to 75% attendance is figured, and regular seating capacity provided for that number. The best authorities figure two-fifths to one-half a square yard of area for the church, including apse and vestibule, for every person attending. It seems safer, however, to place it at two-thirds to three-fourths of a square yard, allowing for the entire area of the church building.

It is always safe to investigate the subsoil of the proposed site down to bedrock. Water or quicksand may be present at a small depth and cause great expense and delay. It is almost self-evident that the footings of the foundation be heavy enough to carry the walls. There should be no settling in the foundation. Brick walls more than fourteen feet high above the water-tables, which are not braced by frequent buttresses, should be at least sixteen inches thick (without mortar), and no wall should be less than twelve inches (thirteen inches) thick. The floors should be built to carry a load of at least eighty pounds per square foot, and one hundred and twenty pounds in places that are likely to be crowded. The timbering of the roofs and the vaulting of the ceilings must conform with the style of the church. From forty to fifty pounds per square foot is usually allowed for wind pressure, but in places subject to heavy winds sixty to seventy pounds must be allowed. If the entire church is not made fireproof, provision should be made to have fireproof or slow-burning construction at least under the stairs and balconies. Much is gained if the roof can be covered with slate or tiling, and metal lath used throughout the building. Fortunately, the building laws in most states now provide for adequate safeguarding in public buildings.

Much more might be said with reference to various general considerations, but many of the questions will find an easy solution if a good architect has charge of the construction. But the problem of acoustics is so important that it seems to require some attention. Experiments that have been made within the last two decades have resulted in the following general rule: "Make the height of the rooms equal to one-half the width, plus the distance from the speaker's mouth to the floor, and the depth (measured from the position of the speaker) from one and one-half to twice the width, but not greater than ninety feet. The relation of height to width appears to be more important than that of width to length. . . . The formation of recesses, breaking up end walls, rounding and canting off angles, bringing the ceiling on the walls with a cove or cant, and breaking it up with groining, are all methods of avoiding the risk of acoustic failure." [164]   It is best for the station of the speaker to be against a flat wall. It will also be found to aid acoustics if the walls are left with a rough surface. In some buildings, extreme cases of resonance and reverberation have been remedied by furring the walls at certain places, or by drawing wires across the auditorium, or by suspending drapery or banners at definite intervals.

---

164) R. Smith, quoted in Kidder, *Churches and Chapels*, 120. 122.

CHAPTER 2.

The Architecture of the Various Parts in a Lutheran Church Building.

An architect that understands not only the practical, but also the historical and liturgical requirements of church buildings, is almost an exception. Many members of the craft pay almost no attention to this side of their work, and when consulted, attempt to carry off the matter with a bluff behavior. Others have informed themselves upon the special demands of Catholic and Anglican churches, but have disregarded the Lutheran point of view entirely. This may be due to the fact that the rules in the stronger ritualistic churches are more absolute, while the Lutheran liturgy permits of a wider latitude. Nevertheless, the proper understanding of the liturgical and confessional attitude of the Lutheran Church is essential for proper Lutheran architecture. The fault lies, to a great extent, with the Lutheran congregations and their pastors, who neglect to inform themselves as to what is appropriate for their own use. In some cases, also, a spirit of false liberalism is becoming manifest, which may eventually result in disastrous consequences to the thoughtless prater against "dead formalism." There is usually none so bigoted as he that apes every new fad and boasts of his eclecticism. The hideous nightmares which are compelled to serve as Lutheran houses of worship in some sections of our country are a florid example of such bigotry. It is for this reason that it may prove of benefit to those who would have all things done decently and in order that a brief discussion of the various parts in a Lutheran church building is here offered.

It has been stated above repeatedly, and it is here reiterated, for the sake of emphasis, that the Lutheran church is primarily a "Predigtkirche," that its chief function is to serve for the preaching of the Word. Luther's words in the Torgau Consecration Sermon, so often quoted, that in the worship of God nothing else takes place than that "our dear Lord speaks to us through His holy Word, and we, in reply, speak to Him in prayer and praise," have an enduring value. Accordingly, the auditorium demands· the most careful attention, whether it be a simple nave, or one with transept, whether one or both of these parts are one-aisled or three-aisled. The evident tendency in our days is toward the centralized form of auditorium. The nave is constructed shorter and wider in proportion than formerly. In many cases, the church proper is practically square, the gable alone indicating the position of the former transept. The principle of length, in a case of this kind, has been sacrificed entirely to utility. The other extreme is represented by the English Gothic, in which the idea of length is over-emphasized. So very prominent has this feature become in some instances, that the central aisle resembles a long corridor, at whose farther end, beyond the choir, is situated the altar, in the dim distance. It will be best to observe the golden mean in a Lutheran church. We gladly adopt the suggestion that a good church building should begin in simplicity, at the western entrance, and converge at the (high) altar. In other words, the idea of the nave (*navis*) ought to be expressed very plainly. The nave represents the ship of the Church sailing bravely out of the darkness of this world toward the eternal Light, beckoning onward to the glorious harbor above. It is not a ship according to the ideas of the medieval artist whose picture Luther so vividly describes, where the vessel contained the clergy only, but it is a ship which offers security and a safe passage to all who enter this nave and listen to the voice of the Great Pilot. For this reason, the width of the entire nave should not be less than one-half or more than four-fifths the length. If a transept is present in a larger church, it may extend one-eighth to one-fourth the width of the church building. This will mean not merely the observing of an ancient symbolism, but will yield a very decided advantage, so far as acoustics is concerned. The great majority of the hearers will then be able to sit in reasonable proximity to the speaker, a fact which will also add to the compactness of the audience, if the ushers possess that invaluable quality, skillful tact. The question whether three-aisled churches should be abandoned has been broached in all seriousness, the contention being that it is impossible to arrange the seats so that all the people present may hear well and also be able to see the preacher. As a matter of fact, the difficulty seems to have been exaggerated. Most of the larger Gothic churches in America have the three-aisled plan and do not seem to experience decided inconveniences on that account. On the other hand, if the suggestion as to the maximum size of individual congregations can be carried out, a one-aisled church with transept can be built without great expense, which will fully accommodate the maximum audience that may be expected, even upon festival occasions. A point which should not be forgotten in planning the floor of the auditorium, in case this is intended to be of the inclined variety, is this that only the actual portion containing seats should be constructed obliquely, the space in front of the apse, in front of any side doors, and in the vestibule always remaining level. In case a bowl-shaped floor is adopted, the semicircle in front of the sanctuary should be large enough to include also the pulpit.

The chancel (apse, sanctuary, altar space) is the head of the church, the eastern end of the axis which begins at the western portal and leads down the main aisle directly to the altar, without any dividing line or obstructing railing. The Greek or the Gothic rood-screen has no place in a Lutheran church, and the reason sometimes offered for their adoption, namely, to keep the dogs away from the altar, will hardly appeal to a modern congregation. While the low rail which was in use before Leo III, with a broad and always open entrance, may not be objectionable in itself, it nevertheless is a reminder of the strict dividing line between clergy and laity which obtains in the Catholic Church, and, to a large extent, in the Episcopal Church, and had better not be introduced, unless the congrega-

GRACE CHURCH, WADSWORTH, OHIO.
(General Synod, United Lutheran Church.)

tion from former days has been used to it. In this event, however, the Eucharist should never be distributed at this railing, but always at the altar. The altar space should be visible from every part of the church, with all that it contains, and should be so constructed and arranged that it is "the culmination and goal and completion of the place of the congregation and so announce that it is the place for communion with the Lord." [165] The apse should, for these reasons, be elevated, at least two, at the most five steps above the floor of the nave. This emphasizes the loftiness and dignity of the Eucharist,

165) Mothes, quoted in Horn, 108.

besides bringing the pastor, in the performance of his official acts, into the full view of the congregation. The shape of the apse is usually octagonal or polygonal. The English churches have the peculiarity of a square apse, which differs very radically from the original shell shape (concha) of the sanctuary and seems out of harmony with the rest of the building. It also makes the impression of too great a depth and a consequent removal of the altar from the people. If the shape of half a polygon is used, and the ceiling converges above the altar in graceful lines of force, the effect is a very beautiful one. The platform for the altar should be one step higher than the apse, and situated in its center. Four to six feet should be allowed behind the altar as a passage for the communicants in going from the north side to the south side, and as many feet in front of the altar, so that the confirmands, the bridal pair, and others that receive the blessing at the altar, may have sufficient room to step forward before kneeling down. This extra riser is also very practical for kneeling during the distribution of the Holy Communion. It makes a very fine impression if the altar is planned to fit the chancel in such a way as to make the distance from either side of the altar to the walls, and that of the highest ornament to the ceiling, the same. Everything that shows harmony is restful and quieting, conducive to receptivity for edification. This should be remarked also in regard to the lighting of the apse. In Catholic churches, the sanctuary is purposely kept dark, in order to enhance the impression of the great mystery of transubstantiation. In Anglican churches, also, it is suggested to keep the chancel "quite dark, for, by so doing, we increase the effect of length and size, adding, as well, a touch of that mystery that comes from shadow, — a quality that should be achieved in every church." [166]   On the other hand, Lutherans, in many cases, flooded the apse with a disproportionate amount of light, in order to obviate the suspicion of popery. The result was often seen in the placing of two large windows in the chancel, on either side of the altar, whose glaring light was very painful for the audience to face. The solution of the difficulty is obvious. If one window is placed behind the altar reredos in such a position that the direct light rays are cut off, the illumination of the chancel will be fully satisfactory for all purposes, and the audience will escape a distressing experience.

A suggestion which has been repeatedly made is to find some room, if possible one open to the auditorium and connected with the apse, which might be used for a baptistery or baptismal chapel. Many liturgists advocate the return to the method anciently used, when the administration of baptism was practically confined to adults,

166) Cram, *Church Building*, 19.

and separate baptisteries were no longer in general use. At that time, the baptismal font was placed near the western entrance. The first part of the sacred act took place at the doors. When the words: "The Lord preserve thy going out and thy coming in," etc., had been spoken, the baptismal candidate with the attendants followed the priest to the font, where baptism was administered. It is for the purpose of preserving this ancient custom that the plans of Episcopal churches show a baptismal chapel off the vestibule, on the north side. In Catholic churches, there is usually an alcove or a chancelled place not far from the main entrance, but inside the nave, which is set aside for a baptistery. In Lutheran churches this position is rare, though advocated by some for its alleged appropriate symbolism. Meurer also mentions the position of the font in the Minster of Ulm, where it is located near a pillar in the nave, surrounded by a chancel railing, and protected by a canopy.[167] But the symbolism has changed somewhat since the earliest Christian era. At that time, only the members in good standing were allowed to be present in the church proper during the *missa fidelium,* and even the *lugentes* or *hiemantes* were not admitted inside the main portals during the *missa catechu-menorum.* The symbolical meaning of the rite of Baptism (not its sacramental use) therefore was simply this that the baptized person was now outwardly admitted to the congregation and had the right to remain for the Eucharist. In our days, the exclusion is not so rigid, so far as presence at services is concerned. Any person may attend Lutheran services and also be present during the celebration of the Eucharist. But the apse, the place for the dispensing of the means of grace, is open to Lutherans, members and guests of the congregation only. A position for the font, therefore, which is liturgically correct, is that at the entrance to the apse, on the north side. By a proper dividing of the form of baptism, the symbolism of admission to the congregation may well be preserved. This may be done still better by using the space north of the chancel, which is now often utilized as a storeroom or for the organ, as a baptistery. If the wall toward the transept be omitted, the opening arched, and the floor raised to the same level as that of the chancel, this space would serve excellently well for a baptismal chapel, the form for the act being divided as in the early Church. Seats may be provided for the sponsors with the child near the entrance to the baptistery, where the pastor would meet them for the first part of the sacred act. In the baptistery, the Sacrament is then administered, whereupon the concluding prayer, which most liturgies call for, should be spoken at the altar. It is assumed, of course, that the Baptism will, as a rule, be

---

167) *Der Kirchenbau,* 219.
Kretzmann, Christian Art.   11

administered in the presence of the congregation. For, as the prayer-book of Edward VI very pertinently remarks, the assembled congregation should witness the receiving of the new members into its communion, and every Christian should thereby be reminded of his own Baptism and its wonderful blessings.

The question of the balcony in a Lutheran church was touched upon to some extent above. It is a case where utility and practical needs on the one side, and liturgical and artistic considerations on the other side, often render a decision very difficult. Some writers have considered balconies a characteristic feature of Protestant churches, but without sufficient reason. "They must rather, since they spoil the effect of a large, free space and remind of theaters and ball-rooms, be considered as an evil." [168] If this evil be necessary, then the balconies should be as unobtrusive as possible. They do not serve materially to reduce the cost of a church. Their only valid excuse for being is in a large congregation, where the great mass of hearers must be brought as near as possible to the apse. In that case, the balcony should not extend very far beyond the vestibule wall into the nave, nor beyond the side aisles into the center aisle of the nave. If there are transept balconies, they should never extend into the nave, or, as in some cases, to the side of the pulpit. It is far better for both speaker and audience if the assembly is situated in a compact body, where he may look directly at each hearer without straining the neck or resorting to other undue contortions. For such as feel that galleries are a necessary adjunct to a Lutheran church building, the words of Mothes may be comforting, when he writes: "Since galleries not only are necessary for the accommodation of a greater number and for economical reasons [?], but also contribute, in fairly large congregations, to a family-like gathering of the assembly around the speaker, in contrast with other auditoriums, and therefore are almost characteristic of Evangelical architecture, they must be arranged in connection with the pulpit in such a way that the preacher can be seen and heard equally well by those in the galleries and those under them, and so that the unity of the room is presented. Therefore the seats in the gallery must be so arranged that no straining of necks will be needed to see the altar, and so that those sitting in them will not have their attention diverted, and that those on the rear seats will not have the heads of those before them between them and the preacher." [169]

In spite of all this, symbolical and liturgical reasons are unfavorable to the large gallery. The unity of the congregation is spoiled by

168) Schultze, *Op. cit.*, 46.
169) Quoted in Horn, *Lutheran Principles of Church Architecture*, 103.

the two-story effect; those sitting beneath the gallery have no conception of the idea of height, and the hearers above either look down
upon the speaker, or, if the pulpit is elevated to a position near the
ceiling, those beneath the pulpit will endanger their cervical verte-
brae in the effort to look up at the preacher. The sanest and simplest
plan seems to be to have only the small balcony, known as the organ-
or choir-loft at the west end of the building, above the vestibule, op-

TRINITY CHURCH, LANCASTER, PA.
(General Council, United Lutheran Church.)

posite the altar. This is the proper position of the choir in a Lutheran church. For the choir is intended to sing with the congregation,
although occasionally it may represent the heavenly host in the *Gloria
in excelsis,* and sing the latter part of this hymn alone. It should
lead the assembly in the responses and hymns. And the sound of the
organ should flow in the same direction as the volume of praise, adoration, and supplication issuing from the mouths of the faithful. It
is a most unfortunate and deplorable circumstance that so many

Lutheran congregations have followed the so-called fashionable demand for a chancel choir, with the organ in full view of the audience. And a number were not satisfied with this achievement, but placed the organ-loft above and behind altar and pulpit, thus giving to it the most conspicuous place in the church and calmly ignoring all liturgical and historical considerations. "The organ and the choir of singers should be placed at the end of the church opposite the altar. The organ should not be placed behind the altar. This position is defended by those who hold that the whole service depends on the congregation, and deny the real presence in the Word and Sacraments, and by those who declare that, the service properly consisting of responsive interchange between the Christian people, it is part of the function of the choir to preach the truth. It is also urged that in this position the organ and the choir lead the singing of the congregation more efficiently. This is not the case. Their leadership lessens in power with the length of the church. It is most efficient when the music of the choir and organ proceeds in the same direction as the singing of the people; when coming from behind the congregation it is the background, and gathers up the singing and holds it together. Singing for entertainment and display is out of place in the church. The choir, as a part of the congregation, confesses the truth given by God through His Word. It does not dispense the Word. The Word, the division of the Word, the ministry of the Word, and the administration of the Word in the Holy Sacrament, must be distinguished as the sole source of the congregation's life and being. Neither should the organ or the choir be in the chancel nor to the side of it in view of the congregation. This custom is derived from the Protestant Episcopal Church, which teaches that there is a distinction between clergy and laity and does not hesitate to adopt the imitation of a priestly choir and to throw the choir between the people and the means of grace. In a Protestant Episcopal church, the worshipers may consist of clergy, choir, and people. In a Lutheran church, only the people are in the presence of God; the choir is a part of the congregation; the minister exercises the office of the Word, in which God speaks. There are the same practical objections to this position as to the position rejected in the preceding paragraph." [170] "In a Lutheran church the only proper place for organ and singers is at the end of the church opposite the altar. In Anglican and Episcopal churches it is perfectly consistent with their conception of the choir and its functions to place organ and singers between the altar and the congregation, inasmuch as they regard the

---

170) Horn, 81. 82. Cp. 92, § 11; 104, § 6; Meurer, *Der Kirchenbau,* 238. 286; Cram, *Church Building,* 19.

choir in the same light as the Old Testament choir of Levites, and as exercising semipriestly functions. But this is not the Lutheran idea. With us the choir should always be regarded as belonging to the universal priesthood of believers, whose proper function it is to lead and support the rest of the congregation, or to alternate with it in the responsive singing of the Psalms and Canticles, or to interpret to the congregation, in musical form, such parts of the liturgy as may be assigned to it, e. g. the Antiphons and Responsories." [171]) "If, in imitation of un-Lutheran custom, the organ is placed by the side of the altar space so as to face the congregation, it speaks of human

TRINITY CHURCH, BUFFALO, N. Y.
(General Council, United Lutheran Church.)

performance rather than of divine grace, and to the extent it does so mars, even as a decorative feature, the aim of the altar space to emphasize the grace of God. It is argued that, if the organ is in the rear of the congregation, people will turn around to look. Shall we, then, make looking easy by placing organ and choir in front? Many improprieties are avoided best by placing organ and choir where they properly belong." [172]) As for the last argument here mentioned, the great majority of the people in our congregations are fortunately so situated that it is not necessary for them to hear with their eyes, as a less fortunate minority of afflicted people. If pastors and teachers will only observe the proprieties, the other members will readily take the cue.

171) Dr. J. F. Ohl, in a letter of July 21, 1917.
172) Dr. C. Abbetmeyer, in *Lutheran Witness*, July 24, 1917.

The vestibule no longer has the significance of the early Christian Church as a *locus lugentium.* Nevertheless it serves a very practical purpose and should receive due consideration in planning a church. Some of the dark and draughty halls that have been honored with the name vestibule, are comparable only to similar places in our older public buildings. The entrance-hall to a house of worship should be planned in strict conformity with the dignity and sublimity of the house of the Lord. It must be large enough in proportion to the size of the church to serve as an easy passage-way in either direction, especially for egress. The fire-laws in most states will, of course, demand other exits, usually one or two in the rear, easy of access. But the main entrance leading from the vestibule will serve on all normal occasions, and therefore the vestibule must serve the average crowd. If the stairways are so situated that they obstruct the passage, or if the hall is so narrow that the streams of humanity meet in a swirling eddy which may result in disagreeable experiences, it is most unpleasant for the attendants. The vestibule may well have an area one-tenth to one-eighth as large as the auditorium. It should be cheerful, without the blatant, glaring ostentation of the theater foyer. To achieve this very desirable quality of cheerfulness, the lighting should be as ample as in the nave. A tympanum window is not sufficient, and in case it is used, it should be supplemented by smaller windows on either side of the entrance. The floor should be level, since the people are usually so crowded that they cannot watch their step. Sills should also be avoided as much as possible, since they are apt to cause stumbling. It is essential that the floor be made strong, with a carrying strength at least twice that of the auditorium floor. A fine plan is to make it fire-proof, if possible, or at least of slow-burning construction. The latter object can be attained by using metal lath on the ceiling beneath and placing steam-pipes, electric wires, etc., in fire-proof pipes or covering. An entire cement construction is considered fire-proof. It may be covered with a layer of cement smoothed down to a floor finish, or by terrazo, mosaic work, and other durable materials. No matter which material is used, the requirement of easy cleaning should not be overlooked. In very wet weather, both in summer and winter, a thorough cleaning of the vestibule, even between services, may be a matter of sanitary precaution. The vestibule will contain little ornamentation beside the tinting and frescoing of the walls. One thing, however, should be found in every vestibule, namely, a bulletin board for the congregation. In many congregations, the custom still obtains of having all announcements, even the most trivial, made by the pastor from the lectern and even from the pulpit. Any announcements outside of those pertain-

ing to the ministerial office, being connected with prayers, intercessions, and thanksgivings, such as churchings, funerals, births, mar-
riages, services, etc., are a desecration of the space reserved for the
means of grace. The pastor is not the town crier, and many of the
announcements made are altogether out of harmony with the dignity
of the church services. Let all notices of meetings, lost and found
articles, etc., etc., be posted on an appropriate bulletin board fastened
in a conspicuous place in the vestibule, so that every one that enters
may readily see and read, and our services will gain in beauty and
dignity by the omission of unchurchly announcements.

ST. JOHN'S CHURCH, CHARLESTON, S. C.
(United Synod South, United Lutheran Church.)

A tower should never be omitted in building a Lutheran church.
And if this is crowned with a spire, the symbolism of which has always been recognized, the effect will be all the greater. There is a
certain factor of incompleteness about a mere tower, even if surmounted by slender turrets, which somehow renders it incongruous.
The battlemented towers of many churches with Norman characteristics remind one more strongly of a castle or of a fortress than of a
church. A graceful spire rising from a strongly-built tower is always
a pleasing, and often an inspiring sight. The tower will, of course,
be an integral part of the church, although it will not be built flush

with the façade, but stand out one-fourth to one-half its width. "The tower, as a sign and summons, stands properly over the chief entrance, at the west. In spite of all attempts to find a proper position, as early as the seventh century, therefore long before Leo III, that over the west portal became the favorite and almost the rule. The few exceptions were due either to necessity or to the incompleteness of the building, or like the double towers at the choir, which were derived from Cluny and were of monkish origin. Therefore another position of the chief tower is to be allowed only to local necessities." [173]) An exception due to such a consideration may well be made in the case of a church which is not situated upon a large open site, but at a street-corner, with its principal view and approach from the corner diagonally opposite. In such a case the position of the tower and spire at the corner of the church may very well be justified, since it can fulfill its duty of guiding and summoning better in that case. In such an event, when the church is small, the corresponding corner on the other side of the church building receives a smaller tower or ornamental turret, to preserve the balance. In larger churches, two towers of equal height and identical construction are erected at the two western corners. If the work is properly done, the effect is most imposing. The cost, however, is an item which is apt to discourage many congregations, for towers and spires are very expensive. The entire tower must be buttressed very firmly, since in most cases it is intended to include the belfry and must bear the weight of the bells as well as that of the spire. The careful anchoring of the spire in the walls of the tower is an essential point, since the stress to which it is exposed, even in a mild wind, is one whose force is generally underestimated. The belfry of the tower, if it is to serve the purpose well, should be situated above the roof, in order that the sound of the pealing bell or bells may travel without hindrance in every direction. It is hardly necessary to add that the architecture of the tower must harmonize perfectly with that of the rest of the building. It will usually be a strong test of the architect's ability to plan the tower in such a way as to give it the appearance of an integral part of the church and also preserve its solidity and beauty. In case the tower is at the corner of the church which stands at the intersection of two streets, it is altogether permissible to have a side entrance, but not the main portal, here. But this should be the case in large churches only, and even then it would be preferable to have the main entrance as the only entrance in the west. If there is a basement entrance in the tower, it should be located below the level of the ground, in order not to disturb the harmony of the building.

---

173) Mothes, quoted in Horn, 112.

The vestry should never be planned as an integral part of the auditorium, though it should receive careful attention in the disposition of the various parts. It must never be located behind the apse, since the sanctuary is the head of the church, and its symbolism would be spoiled very decidedly by such an arrangement. Neither should it be a mere screened corner of the nave. Its purpose is such as to demand a separate room off the chancel, the southern room usually being chosen. Here there is direct communication with the altar space, and there may be direct communication also with the nave. The latter consideration should never be overlooked. It is often necessary for the deacons or other church officers, and sometimes for other members of the congregation, to speak to the pastor during services, and since it is not fitting for the altar space to be made a passageway, and since conditions of the weather often make it unpleasant to

FIRST LUTHERAN CHURCH, RICHMOND, VA.
(United Synod South, United Lutheran Church.)

go around outside, a door leading from the nave or transept to the vestry should be provided. The vestry, as its name indicates, is the room where the vestments of the pastor and also those of the altar and pulpit are kept, and where the pastor puts on his clerical garment. The room will therefore have a large wardrobe or closet for keeping all the vestments secure and clean. This is true of the pastor's gown and the bands as well as of the various paraments. The cabinets and drawers may easily be made moth-proof, a very important consideration when one reflects upon the costliness of the cloths. There may also be a cabinet, or preferably a safe, for storing the Eucharistic vessels. But all other things which are apt to accumulate in a church building should be kept out of the vestry. It is most distressing to find dilapidated crosses, broken statuary, remains of Christmas ornaments, Sunday-school pamphlets, catalogs, bric-a-brac, and what-not in the vestry, especially if this motley collection be covered with the dust of weeks, months, and even years. The saying:

"A church is no cleaner than its vestry," is one which often applies with peculiar force. The vestry will have, as a matter of course, a table for the pastor and several chairs, also a small bookcase for the various church and liturgical books. A wash-basin is by no means a superfluous addition, and a lavatory off the vestry is still better. It is hardly necessary to add that the vestry should be large enough for emergency meetings of the deacons or other church officers, though it should not be made the regular assembly room for such purposes.

A retiring-room for women, especially for such as have little children with them, should always be planned in building a Lutheran church. Unfortunately, the custom of frowning upon the presence of little children is growing in our congregations. But this is a matter to be deeply deplored. In many cases, it is impossible for a family to have a special nurse girl for the children, and most congregations have not yet provided a nurse or deaconess to have charge of the little ones in a room of the parish house during services. But both mother and father, with the rest of the family, should attend services. In many congregations in the country, where it is the custom for the whole family to attend, no one pays any attention to the little ones, unless their continued wailing or loud crying drowns out the speaker's voice. In such a case, the mother (or father) could very well take the baby to the retiring-room and perhaps in a few minutes succeed in restoring the Sabbath calm. So much the mothers, on their part, should be willing to observe. If the retiring-room is connected with the auditorium and also with the vestibule, the amount of disturbance will be reduced to a minimum.

So far as the exterior of the church is concerned, the elaborateness of the ornamentation will depend partly upon the style of architecture and partly upon the contemplated cost. The western façade will usually present the most attractive side of the building. In most cases, a rose window of proper proportions and beautiful design will do much to enhance the inviting appearance of the church. It must not be forgotten, however, that a rose window is a window placed into the wall for the purpose of admitting light. If it is hidden, on the inside, by the balcony or gallery joists, or by the ceiling trusses, it offends against the requirement of honesty and therefore has no "reason for being." The main portal in the center of the western wall may be a single large opening, in small churches, or a series of three doors, under one arch, in large churches. If the columns of the opening, the tympanum, and the spandrils receive the attention they deserve, for fine stone carving, the resulting effect will well repay the expenditure. The doors will rarely, under the present circumstances, be of cast bronze or decorated with the elaborate carving of the Middle Ages, but every congregation will try to have massive doors with appropriate hardware or artistic dinanderie. The addition of porches to serve as shelters for the main portals will aid in beautifying the façade only when they are planned in harmony with the rest of the church by the architect.

The basement of the churches has been treated with varying favor, according to the position of the congregation. If the Sunday-school could be accommodated in the parish house or in the rooms of the day-school, little attention was paid to the basement. But if this was of necessity used for Sunday-school purposes, as well as for meetings of a social nature in the course of the week, it was planned as carefully as the auditorium. In many cases, the greater part of the basement is now used for a hall or lecture room, smaller rooms being provided for kitchen and women's parlor, and for meetings of the various church societies. Just how much emphasis the individual congregation wishes to bestow upon the equipment of the basement, it must decide after its own circumstances. The number of exits will, in most cases, be fixed by the building laws of the respective state.

The foregoing considerations and suggestions agree, in many particulars, with the resolutions of the so-called Eisenach Regulative, of June 5, 1861, the Dresden Regulative of 1856, and the so-called Wiesbaden Program.[174)] There are a number of divergences, made necessary, in part, by the conditions and circumstances of the Lutheran Church in America, and partly by the fact that some progress has been made in the symbolical application of many requirements. The guiding principle was always to avoid the strictness of dead formalism, thus allowing the proper latitude for the application of the principles which are essentially distinctive of the Lutheran Church.

CHAPTER 3.

The Furniture of the Chancel and the Auditorium.

That the various parts of a Lutheran church building should be in perfect harmony with each other is an aesthetic requirement whose necessity appeals readily to most people. But incidentally, many church members forget that the factor of harmony in the interior furnishing and decorating of a church is just as essential. Even the most unobserving layman must feel the incongruity, when lines of various and diverse styles are brought together by application of a

---

174) Cp. Schultze, *Das evangelische Kirchengebaeude*, Anhang; Meurer, *Der Kirchenbau*, 116—118; Horn, *Lutheran Principles of Church Architecture*, 84—96.

rude force calculated to stifle their protest, but in reality causing the
clash to become more apparent. A little care in the planning of the
proper furniture or in the selection of the appointments of a Lutheran

A TUDOR GOTHIC ALTAR.
(Courtesy W. & E. Schmidt Co., Milwaukee.)

house of worship may make all the difference as to whether the harmony of all subsidiary factors will be conducive to restful edification
and meditation or to disquieting excitement. "Let all things be done
decently and in order," 1 Cor. 14, 26.

In naming the altar as the first piece of furniture in a Lutheran church, we do not wish to be understood as though the Lutheran Church appends a special intrinsic value to the altar. We have no formulas for anointing or dedicating altars after the manner of the Catholic Church. Neither do we ascribe to altars which are situated in dedicated churches any special merits which make them essentially different from other tables. On the other hand, the Lutheran Church does not accede to the iconoclastic tendencies of the majority of the Reformed churches which object to the very name "altar" and studiously avoid even the semblance of the Catholic sacramental table.

A SMALL GOTHIC ALTAR.
(Courtesy W. & E. Schmidt Co., Milwaukee.)

We reject the idea of transubstantiation, but do not go to the opposite extreme of rationalistic explanation. The altar of a Lutheran church is a confession of the real presence in the Sacrament. Therefore the altar does not make the Sacrament, as the Catholic idea has it, but the Sacrament makes the altar. This is the reason why we consider the altar a sanctified place in the church, even more so, in a way, than the pulpit, because the person of the minister is more prominent in preaching than in administering the Holy Communion. The altar is the Lord's table, where the great mystery of the communion of Christ's body and blood, in a sacramental manner, with the bread and wine, is celebrated, and, through the consecrated elements, His communion with His people. "Quid est altare nisi sedes et corporis et sanguinis Christi," writes Optatus of Mileve. And Ambrose calls it "locus, ubi Christus hostia est." [175]   The altar is thus primarily the Eucharistic table, the table of the Lord, but it is also the place of prayer and benediction, and thus has a sound "reason for being" in the liturgical sense. All the various sacrificial acts, the acts of prayer, which the pastor performs in the name of the congregation, are originally parts of the liturgy of the *missa catechumenorum et fidelium,* and therefore the general benediction, as well as the special forms of blessing used for confirmation, confession, marriage, ordination, etc., are closely connected with these and are spoken at the altar. Even the General Confession and the Great Prayer should not be made from the pulpit, as was the custom

ALTAR WITH CROSS AND CANDELABRA.
(Courtesy W. & E. Schmidt Co., Milwaukee.)

in parts of southern Germany, from where it was introduced into America, but from the altar.[176]   Rightly understood, then, the words of Cram apply also to a Lutheran church: "Unless the altar is treated with due regard, unless it has its proper relation to the rest of the fabric, then every effort to obtain a church that is a living thing, is vain and worse than vain." [177]   "The Supper is, in our conception, not merely a memorial-supper of believers among themselves, nor a memorial of Christ's offering and a thanksgiving for it, but a sacrament, a distribution of the gracious gift of the inmost union with the Lord in the new covenant sealed by that offering; and has its roots not in what we do, but in what the Lord does to us. Therefore the altar is primarily the table of the Lord; and not only this, but also the place of this inmost communion, of the thanksgiving, of the unspoken vow involved in such a communion of fidelity to this cove-

175) Kliefoth, *Die urspruengliche Gottesdienstordnung,* II, 226. 237.
176) Meurer, *Der Kirchenbau,* 227. 228.
177) *Church Building,* Chapter VII.

nant, and of further rites of iniation, and of vows of confirmandi, bridal pairs, ordinandi, etc., of benedictions, blessings for those who offer, celebrate, and vow; for the whole congregation, therefore, not as a place of offering in the heathen sense.   Both its form and material should be monumental, if possible of stone; although, because it is a table and is developed from a table, a solid and thorough construction of wood is not excluded.   It should be of a table form, should not be formed like a grave in reference to the Risen One; nor like a hearth, as the heathen and Jewish altars for burnt offerings were. . . It does not stand like a Catholic grave-altar or mass-altar or lay-altar or cross-altar, against the wall, but, like the old Christian table-

A SIMPLE BAPTISMAL FONT.
(Courtesy W. & E. Schmidt Co., Milwaukee.)

altar and the high-altar that grew out of this and afterwards was taken from the laity, it should stand free.   To put the altar against the wall is a return to Catholic ways, just as is its position before a windowless wall in a dark chancel." 178)   So far as materials are concerned, construction of sculptured stone or perhaps even of marble, inlaid with precious stones and gold, which some wealthy congregations can well afford, is out of the question for the majority of Lutheran parish churches.   In such a case, however, hard-wood altars which are appropriately carved and given a natural finish, will prove very satisfactory.   In this case the builders should guard against the effect of excessive somberness in the chancel, offsetting the darker color of the natural grain by a lighter wall color.   In many instances, even a hard-wood altar will be found too expensive, and one built of soft wood, painted or enameled white, with gold trimming, is alto-

---

178) Mothes, quoted in Horn, 105. 106.

gether permissible. For here the lamp of truth and honesty is not violated, since, as Ruskin says, "the gilding in architecture is no deceit, because it is therein not understood for gold," and so also the white enamel is not understood for marble. Besides, the effect of the pure white altar is eminently suitable for the sanctuary, and agrees well with the purity of the Lamb that was slain. No matter what material is chosen for the altar, a reredos, usually in triptych form, is always appropriate. It should be built so that its lower part includes a shelf for crucifix or cross and candelebra, since the mensa or plate of the altar is reserved for the service books and the Eucharistic vessels. If there is an altar painting or a statue, these should be placed high enough, in order not to interfere with the cross. As the frontale of the altar may be ornamented with carved or sculptured work (Last Supper, Lamb of God, vine, chalice, Alpha and Omega, etc.), so the super-frontale looks well with a certain amount of dignified decoration. The central panel may receive an altar painting, preferably one with special reference to the grace of Christ. Or it may be built in the form of a niche to hold the statue of Christ, in a posture of benediction or invitation. If texts are desired in the carving of the altar, the suggestion of Luther in regard to Ps. 111, 4 might well be remembered, or a simple Sanctus, Sanctus, Sanctus — Holy, Holy, Holy may be used. Other emblems, types, and symbols will be discussed below, in a special chapter.

The pulpit will agree with the altar in style, materials, and construction. The usual form of the pulpit is octagonal, very seldom round or square. Its diameter should not be less than a yard, and its (solid) balustrade may be four feet high, but no more. The pulpit rises from a single shaft or stem, which may be decorated as richly as the harmony will permit. The panels of the railing are often carved in very rich effects or constructed in the form of niches, with statues of the four evangelists or the four great prophets. If the requirements of acoustics have been properly observed, the sounding-board above the pulpit, which is often useless and still oftener disfiguring, may well be dispensed with. Where it is necessary, it should be constructed in perfect agreement with the rest of the furniture. The height of the pulpit, which in a measure will be governed by the construction of galleries, if such are demanded, should be as low as possible. Schultze gives the maximum height as four meters (about thirteen feet) from the floor of the church to the floor of the pulpit. With the more general introduction of inclined floors and the cutting-down of balconies to the irreducible minimum, the old swallow-nest type of pulpit is gradually becoming obsolete. It was actually a torture for the people in the front pews to crane their necks in the pitiful effort to see the speaker, no less than for the pastor with an inclination toward dizzy spells. A very practical advantage of the lower pulpit is this that the minister speaks up to the people, with his larynx free and unrestricted, instead of down to the audience, with that very necessary organ constricted and sorely hampered by the effort. A noted specialist has called attention to the fact that lawyers' chronic hoarseness is almost unknown, while "minister's sore throat" is a universal malady, and he ascribes this difference to the fact that the lawyer throws back his head in addressing the judge and jury, while the minister bends down, compressing his throat, in addressing his congregation. A suggestion has lately been made that the head of the minister, when he is standing on his pulpit, should be on the same level with that of a person sitting in the last row of the

WOOD LECTERN.
(Courtesy W. & E. Schmidt Co., Milwaukee.)

auditorium. The greatest difficulty has been experienced in finding the proper position for the pulpit. Some writers have urged with the greatest pertinacity that the altar, for theoretical, aesthetic, and practical reasons, ought to find its place exactly at the east end of the church axis. Referring to the practice of the early Church, some have advocated the return to the position behind the altar, corresponding to the bishop's cathedra. In that case, the reredos is to be omitted. But here the preacher is separated from his hearers by a great open space, instead of standing in the midst of his congregation. In many churches, the pulpit is above the altar, the central niche of the reredos, in some instances, being used as opening, and the platform being on a level with the mensa. In other churches, the pulpit or pulpit desk has been placed in front of the altar, at the opening of the apse, below the triumphal arch. Here it obstructs the view of the altar, and the concealment of the altar by the pulpit will always be offensive. Such an arrangement almost compels the erection of a second altar in front of the pulpit, for the liturgical service, which in turn savors of the high altar and low altar distinction. Besides, though the altar in the Lutheran Church has no inherent sanctity, yet any of the positions mentioned interferes materially with its dignity. So there is left for the pulpit only the position at the junction of the apse and the nave, on the south side of the triumphal arch, for practical reasons and for liturgical considerations, as Meurer points out. The speaker is nearer to his audience and, if he has a wall at his back, the acoustics should be excellent. He is also, as the witness of the Gospel, standing in their very midst. He is not a pulpit orator, separated from the members of the congregation by the special distinction of an anointed clergy, but the servant of Christ and witness to the congregation who, by their invitation and call, expounds to them the faith which binds all together. There need be no offense against architectural symmetry, if the pulpit is treated as a necessary, integral member of the building. There is an ancient tradition that the preacher should not make his appearance *quam deus ex machina,* mentioned by both Meurer and Mothes; therefore the steps leading to the pulpit should be at least partially visible.[179]) All these requirements may be met very easily by placing the pulpit as indicated in the accompanying figure (p. 148), with the steps leading up to it from the west door of the vestry. The symmetry may be preserved by having a platform for the lectern on the opposite side of the triumphal arch. This will give the additional advantage of leaving the view of the altar entirely unobstructed.

The baptismal font should have its definite, permanent position in the church. It is decidedly against all liturgical usage to have a movable font or, what is still worse, to place a basin on the altar, as required. The font must not be inside the sanctuary proper, for then it not only loses its significance, but also obstructs the view of the altar and often hinders the free movements of the communicants. It may be placed at the entrance to the apse, preferably on a small extension or platform. In this way, it readily signifies the preliminary step to the admission into the full communion of the congregation. The best position, however, is that discussed above, in a special baptistery or baptismal chapel, where every part of the symbolism may find its expression, and yet nothing interfere with the liturgical func-

---

179) Cp. Ziegeler, *Einfuehrung in die christliche Kirchenbaukunst,* 68; Meurer, 212—214; Schultze, *Das evangelische Kirchengebaeude,* 100; Horn, 90—92. 112. 113; Kliefoth, IV, 150.

tions. So far as the material is concerned from which the font is to be constructed, metal and especially stone are far preferable to wood. In former times, both in England and on the Continent, no one would have thought of a wooden font, as also the German name "Taufstein" indicates. Of all the fonts which Paley describes in his book there is none that is constructed of wood. We have accounts of a number of beautiful fonts cast in dinanderie. A requirement is that this indispensable piece of furniture be monumental, like the altar, as Cram demands. Some beautiful fonts are made of marble, with a cover of like material or of ebony-wood, with brass or gold ornament. They may now be purchased to suit every need, taste, and purse. Their form also varies considerably. The simplest one is that of a base with pedestal and basin holder. The sculpture work and inscriptions vary,

BRASS EAGLE LECTERN.
(Courtesy W. & E. Schmidt Co., Milwaukee.)

the verses "Suffer the little children to come unto Me," and "Feed My lambs," being used in many instances. Since Thorwaldsen sculptured his "Baptismal Angel," it has become a favorite, many churches having copies made for fonts. The warning of Meurer, that the sculpture work of the font, especially as to foliage, should not be too elaborate, may well be heeded in our days, when certain donors select very extravagant models in order to emphasize the donation.

The lectern is an almost indispensable piece of altar furniture, taking the place of the ancient ambon for the reading of the lessons. It is not in conformity with the dignity of the church to place a music rack at the entrance to the apse, nor should the baptismal font be used as a stand for that purpose. A special desk should be provided, harmonizing with the other furniture of the chancel. It enables the pastor to make the lesson readings more distinct and loud, since he is nearer to the congregation, and it permits him to rest the heavy Bible on a stand, thus relieving him of its unpleasant weight. By introducing the lectern and giving it a permanent position, the liturgy gains in vividness and therefore in effectiveness. There are many wooden reading desks in use at present which are very beautiful on account of their effective simplicity. Much more appropriate, however, are such as are carved from marble or cast in dinanderie. A favorite form for the reading desk of the lectern is that of an eagle, with wings partly extended. Others have the four evangelists forming the pedestal. More elaborate designs may be found in many churches of the Romanesque and Gothic periods. The lectern will, of course, be used by the lay reader, in the absence of the pastor, for the reading of the sermon. Where the old undignified custom still obtains of making announcements of every kind in the church, this should at least not be done from the pulpit or from the altar platform, but from the lectern.

The furniture proper for the altar space does not include a chair or a set of chairs for the clergy, as though they had a right to a seat apart during the entire service. The pastor should occupy the altar space only when he is officiating, "that the impression of God's gracious presence, which the altar space is intended to convey, may remain dominant." [180] If the pastor does not care to use the vestry during the pauses of his ministry, as a place for prayerful meditation, he may sit with the congregation, to which he belongs, or sedilia may be provided at the entrance to the apse.

While the mensa of the altar is reserved for the Bible, the liturgical books, and the Eucharistic vessels, the lowest shelf of the reredos, as noted above, is set aside for the purpose of holding the cross or crucifix and the candelabra. The cross will be the choice of all such as advocate the return to the purity of Canono-Catholic times. And there is no denying the fact that a simple cross with appropriate engraving (Alpha and Omega, Lamb of God, etc.) is very beautiful and effective, as it blazes out, in unadorned glory, from the altar wall. The corpus was hardly known before the ninth century, and even then was used almost entirely for processional crucifixes. At this time and also later, when the crucifix was used for the altar, there were many idolatrous and superstitious customs connected with it. In spite of the fact, therefore, that the Lutheran Church has defended the crucifix against iconoclastic tendencies, [181] the return to the plain cross may well be advocated. This consideration becomes all the more prominent when one examines the nature of the corpus in many

180) Dr. C. Abbetmeyer, in *Lutheran Witness*, July 24, 1917.
181) Kliefoth, IV, 146.

instances. Only in rare cases can the divine majesty of the suffering Son of God be expressed with becoming dignity in an unpretentious crucifix. And it certainly is not an aid to devotion to have either a sentimental effeminate figure or an excessively realistic figure on the cross before one's eyes. If the crucifix is used, the corpus should receive special attention. The face and figure should be ideal and not attract notice too extensively. It may be made of bronze, plated with silver, or carved from various kinds of wood, in which case the na-

ALTAR CROSS.
(Courtesy W. & E. Schmidt Co., Milwaukee.)

tural grain is retained. The cross of the crucifix may be of cast brass and gilded or plated with silver, or it may be carved from hardwood, which takes a high finish. If possible, only the best materials should be chosen, crucifixes of gold, silver, ivory, alabaster, and marble having a very rich effect. The candelabra, with one, three, five, or seven lights, should agree in style, materials, and construction with the cross or crucifix, as fine as the congregation can afford, so long as they are tasteful and harmonious. The same is true of the three-light vesper candlesticks, which are used at every evening service. In either case, the altar lights are now often connected with the gas or electric light system of the church. The candlesticks and candelabra should be arranged so as to form, with the cross in the center, a pyramid of regular rise. Beauty, simplicity, and dignity are the requirements which should be kept in mind.

It may be remarked, in passing, that the artificial flowers and plants which have found their place on the altar since the times of the Rococo, even if they are sheltered by a bell jar, have no excuse or "reason for being." They merely show the power of custom, no matter how ridiculous and purposeless it may be. On the other hand, a custom which should receive all encouragement is that of placing fresh, living flowers on the shelf of the altar every Sunday, and especially on festival days, Ps. 118, 27. Dead or artificial, imitated flowers symbolize death and decay, while living plants are in full accord with the life and growth of the Church and the beauty of its Gospel.

More emphasis even than upon the show pieces mentioned above should be placed upon the Eucharistic vessels. The Lutheran Church has not abrogated the use of precious metals as materials for communion goods, especially since gold and silver have been used for that purpose since the earliest periods of the Church. All vessels which are over-elaborate in design and execution or fashioned after secular models are not permissible for a Lutheran altar. So far as the chalice is concerned, the shape and design of the early Gothic period seems to be most satisfactory for practical use. The foot or stand should have a larger diameter than the top of the cup, since it must stand safely against shaking and top-heaviness. The chalice is rendered safe for serving by the knob on the stem, which enables the minister to obtain a firm hold on the vessel. The cup, finally, must be adapted for drinking without the danger of spilling. All these requirements are met in the chalice of this period. The Romanesque cup is too wide and shallow, the Renaissance cups often exhibit a flaring edge, which renders serving very difficult, and some modern designs in the egg-shape make it necessary for the pastor to tip the chalice to a dangerous angle. There are few old models which may be followed in the case of flagons. But excellent results have been obtained in the various styles. The flagons are not so large as the ancient vessels which archeologists describe, but hold only two quarts to a gallon. In this size, they are handled with the least inconvenience. An absolute necessity is that the opening be made large enough to permit a regular thorough cleaning of the interior. Profane styles are to be avoided even more carefully than in the case of the chalice, since the danger of introducing them is greater. The paten and ciborium should agree with chalice and flagon, as to material and style. The paten must not be too flat, since the wafers may then slide off the rim. The ciborium was often fashioned like a small tower rising on a stem from a large base, and having a cover like a steep roof. This more elaborate form is found less often than that of a small chest or box, whose cover bears a small lamb or cross. It should be large enough to hold all the wafers for every communion service. The basin of the baptismal font and the water pitcher are sometimes modeled after the same styles and, in fact, included in the same set with the communion vessels. Individual pieces as well as whole sets may be obtained at reasonable prices, as well in sterling silver, plated with gold, as in silver-plated brass and in the baser metals. The sym-

A SET OF EUCHARISTIC VESSELS.

bols on the communion set, either engraved, relief, or filigree work, should be such as have actual significance, as, for instance, grapevine and leaves, ears of wheat, various crosses, etc.[182]   A reminder which in many cases is anything but superfluous is this that the communion vessels should receive proper care, not only in being stored in a dust-proof place, but also in being cleaned regularly and thoroughly. Where individual communion sets have been introduced, in a few isolated instances, on account of the danger of offense, this warning is just as necessary as in the case of the common cup (which is not insanitary). It is almost self-evident that the pastor will carefully remove all moistness from touching the lips in giving the wafers by wiping on an antiseptic cloth, and that he will wipe the interior of

---

182) Cp. Kliefoth, III, 332; IV, 139; Meurer, *Der Kirchenbau*, 239—247; Schultze, *Das evangelische Kirchengebaeude*, 87—93.

the cup, after each serving to three or four, with a piece of antiseptic gauze or a clean cloth.

Since Lutheran churches are intended for preaching, the providing of proper seating facilities or pews is essential. Though the deliberations on this question will be governed, primarily, by the question of available funds, yet an excess of penurious tendencies in this one instance will be deplored more than foolish extravagance. It is far better to reduce in the expenditure for ornamentation than to provide benches, pews, or seats which are disharmonious, insubstantial, and uncomfortable. In most cases, pews will probably be the seats under consideration. And these are now, fortunately, made in more comfortable styles than the old straight-seat and straight-back instruments of torture, the sitting on which was often more of a penance than a privilege. In case pews are selected, care should be taken that the pew-backs are not too high, and that the decorative carving is confined to the pew-ends. Both seat and back should be fashioned according to the shape of the body, and there must be no sharp molding cutting into the back just below the shoulder-blades. Less conservative congregations nowadays are turning to auditorium chairs for seating purposes. And there are some reasons which commend this action very strongly. Where space is limited, the fact that chairs can be placed more closely together on account of the absence of heavy pew-back moldings and thus the seating capacity enlarged, is a weighty factor. Then, also, auditorium chairs in the same style and grade are far less expensive than pews, there is no disagreeable crowding together as in long pews, there is no crawling over the knees of the end people by late-comers, and last, but not least, churches with chairs are more easily cleaned. This is a factor even where a modern vacuum cleaner is used, and much more where the old mode of cleaning is still in vogue. And there is no danger of giving the church a profane or secular aspect by the use of auditorium chairs, because they are now made in styles which are fully as stately as the former heavy pews. Kidder preserves the golden mean by advocating the use of folding seat-pews, which have given great satisfaction wherever they have been tried. So far as the spacing of seats is concerned, the minimum distance from back to back should not be less than two feet, eight inches for pews, and two feet, six inches for chairs. Schultze would like to see the distance of at least one meter (39.37 in.) observed. The pews or chairs will, of course, agree with the style of the church and its interior furniture. In no case is the grotesque and bizarre admissible, nor should the pews be modeled too strongly after the ancient choir seats still found in Episcopal churches. In arranging the seating, care must be taken that both altar and pulpit may be seen from every part of the auditorium.

The organ, the "queen of musical instruments," is indispensable as soon as a congregation can afford a suitable one.   A plain reed organ cannot fill a church of any size.   A vocalion, if a really good instrument, will, in some respects, take the place of a pipe organ. But the final ambition of a congregation is usually a pipe organ of some kind, one whose volume will be just suitable for the size of the church auditorium, and which will beautify the services and serve

FLAGON.

for the edifying of the congregation, in accompanying the hymns. There is such a wide range of pipe organs, from the small one-manual organ to immense orchestrons or orchestrions, worth almost a king's ransom.   In no other line, perhaps, have builders of musical instruments in America attained to a higher level than in perfecting the organ, and the double-pneumatic, electrical connections enable the organist to control at will the softest pianissimo and the most thundering fortissimo.   It is best if the organ is built especially for the church that purchases it. "The organ case should not be shaped as a member of the building dependent on the other constructions, but as an independent instrument! The form of a building is to be avoided, and the ethereal character of music is to be suggested by a light ornamental style. The form should not be derived from the forms of constructions in stone, nor should it point to arrangements which indicate limitations caused by the necessities of the building;

CHALICE.

but it should have a complete space, arranged for it with due deliberation." [183] The place for the organ is in the choir loft above the main portal, opposite the altar. The correct position of the organ and the relation of this noble instrument to the services in the Lutheran Church cannot be emphasized too strongly, especially in America, where the danger of being influenced by the Reformed and extra-Christian congregations is unusually great. "The organ is intended, first of all, alone or supported by a choir of singers, or by

183) Mothes, quoted in Horn, 114.

other instruments, to open, accompany, and close the services in a clear, significant, but not obtrusive way, and especially to complete and dignify, lead and accompany, the unison singing of the congregation. A further employment for concerts, etc., must give place to this liturgical purpose and function." [184]) This is brought out by Kliefoth in his usual clear, emphatic way, basing his remarks upon various early Lutheran books on church polity. "Since the organ has merely an accompanying position," he writes, "it must be kept in this position. In the service of the congregation only such music is justified as aids and acts as bearer for the Word. The organ must not

PATEN.

presume to play an independent role, without congregational singing. Extensive pre-, inter-, and postludes must be discontinued; and above all the introducing of extemporaneous fugues and similar aberrations, which change the congregation assembled for services into a concert audience. When services are fully at an end, the organist may show his art and play a fugue or a similar composition." [185]) In accordance with these requirements, the organ will show its ancillary character throughout the services, and thus aid in the emphasis placed upon the Word. The preludes before the opening of services, and the postludes after the close, may be as pretentious as the skill of the organist permits. But during the service the organ has only one function, namely to intone and to accompany the singing. Short preludes

184) Mothes, quoted in Horn, 104.
185) *Die urspruengliche Gottesdienstordnung*, V, 357; IV, 280. 281.

may indicate the nature and suggest the melody of the following hymn, but the interludes should not exceed a few bars, and may often be omitted entirely, especially in the singing of the Creed.

The hymnboards or numberboards are, as Schultze puts it, indeed no decorative, but almost indispensable adjuncts in a Lutheran church. Between the announcing of the hymns by the pastor and the placing of their numbers upon the hymboard, the latter is surely the lesser evil. The hymnboard should properly agree with the altar and pulpit in style, design, and finish. It must of necessity be conspicuous, but should not carry its efforts in that direction too far. It would seem desirable to add one or two rows to the customary hymnboard, six rows being insufficient on special occasions. If there is harmony and consistency in all the furniture of the church, the effect of quiet restfulness will do much toward aiding in the beauty and effectiveness of the services.

CHAPTER 4.
Windows, Mosaics, Sculpture, Painting, Decorating.

The requirements which have been discussed till now may be considered primary needs. The Lutheran cultus demands most of them, and the church would be incomplete so long as they are missing. But there are also considerations which may be regarded as secondary or not essential in the same degree, which still are of such importance that they warrant a separate treatment. For in no other cases have the canons of art so often been disregarded and flagrantly violated as in those parts of the church in which the fine arts are represented. To say that a transgression of certain demands has resulted in the very epitome of ugliness and tastelessness is merely stating a fact which may be corroborated in numerous instances.

This is true, first of all, of the windows. It was natural for the first Lutherans in America to wish for colored windows, like those which they had seen so often in their former home beyond the ocean. And, their poverty forbidding the installation of elaborate and costly windows, they were often persuaded to resort to imitations, which served their purpose, in a way, but could never replace the genuine article. Even in our days, real art windows are the exception. One often sees windows of cheap colored glass, in the most impossible geometrical and ungeometrical designs, squares and polygons and diamonds and scrolls and lines of magnificence and curlicues all being employed to produce a hopelessly incongruent effect. At the same time, the selection and juxtaposition of colors is so inharmonious as to threaten the vision. And the interior of the church, bathed in multicolored radiance, often presents a ghastly effect. Yet the aim to possess colored windows of the right kind is a most laudable one. For, as Uhland says, "painted (art) windows seem to me essential for a Christian church, for the place is not closed so long as the eye can gaze through the windows into the wide heaven. It is a requirement of the church window that it does not permit a look or a thought to go out, but serves for the admission of all that is heavenly." [186]   There are three kinds and grades of glass which come into consideration. The common colored glass is cathedral glass. It is the ordinary crown glass to which simple pigments have been added. It is seldom that one finds a rich effect in this glass. A better glass with richer tones is the Venetian glass, which greatly resembles the Bohemian. But the best grade for art windows is the thick iridescent variety which is called opal or opalescent glass. It is in this glass that the most artistic results may be obtained. For it is the material which was produced owing to the revival of interest in the magnificent windows of the Middle Ages. Conspicuous among the leaders in the revival of stained glass work were two Americans, Tiffany and La Farge, the latter being the discoverer or inventor of opal glass. Opal glass is essentially fusible porcelain. Its peculiar beauty consists in this that it responds to various processes during its manufacture with the most surprising effects. According as the ingredients, and especially the pigments, are evenly or unevenly mixed in the melting pot, subjected to even or uneven pressure, corrugated or otherwise manipulated, the glass varies in texture, tone, and strength. One may see not only wave, cloud, and flame effects, but the most picturesque results, such as storm scenes, with masses of wind-swept twigs and branches in dark-brown, the emerald leaves torn from them filling the sky, which, with its irregular, flying clouds, was represented by a dark, grayish-blue foundation. With such material at his disposal, the artist in opal or opalescent glass has almost the latitude of the painter in oils. With patient care, he selects his color and tone harmony, building up light and shade from the detailed cartoon. After the first piecing together is finished, the task of backing up must eliminate all suggestions of crudity and mellow the picture into a rich harmonious whole. The glass of such a window therefore varies in thickness from a quarter of an inch to six or seven inches. And in the entire picture or pattern there is no painted surface, with the exception, perhaps, of the face and the flesh parts. And a recent improvement does away with the heavy leaded lines by welding the individual pieces together with copper strips into one harmonious unit. There are almost endless possibilities in stained

---

186) Quoted in Schulze, 114.

glass windows, especially if the artist tempers the bright southern light in a church with dark patterns and warms the cold northern light with bright and cheerful colors. For "windows depend not only upon the design, but also upon the ability of the worker to select such colors and thicknesses as will give the desired effect under the particular light to which it will be exposed." [187])

A building committee will, of course, insist upon receiving cartoons of the various windows in the correct colors. And the main factor to be considered, beside the appropriateness and the correctness of the design, will be the question of light and its effect upon the finished window. Above all, the considerations mentioned by Cram [188]) must be emphasized. Stained glass windows should be decorative, not pictorial. Each window is a piece of colored and translucent decoration and must therefore continue the structural wall perfectly. It must be flat, without perspective and modeling, for it is technically a mosaic of pieces of glass. Great sheets of glass modeled into folds of drapery are not permissible. In compound windows, it is best to take single figures for each opening, filling the space between two mullions. The upper portion of the window is filled with rich canopy work which should be the same for all openings, at least on the same side. The figures must be formal and conventional, not naturalistic, the backgrounds decorative, not descriptive, the clothing and vestments symbolic, not realistic. The number of Bible scenes which are suitable for church windows is almost endless. Christ in Gethsemane, the Crucifixion, the Resurrection, the Transfiguration, the Ascension, and others are especially good for triple windows. So far as medallions in plain art windows are concerned, a number of symbols will be found in a special chapter below.

The principles which govern the use of mosaic decorations are closely connected with those governing the windows. No matter whether wall mosaics or pavement mosaics are employed, they should be decorative, not pictorial; the idea of a flat surface must not be destroyed by an attempt to introduce perspective; and all figures must be formal and conventional. If wall mosaics are used, they will probably extend only as high as the usual wainscoting, except in the apse. The panels will usually bear a geometrical design, with a border of conventional flowers, especially ivy, passion flowers, lilies. If the border is set with terra-cotta tiling, the rich effect is greatly enhanced. Floor or pavement mosaics should be used, if possible, in the vestibule and in the main aisle, though one often finds main and wall aisles laid with rubber or cork composition, with mosaic border,

187) Kidder, *Churches and Chapels*, 59.
188) *Church Building*, Chapter VI.

on account of their ability to deaden the sound. In the vestibule, this requirement is not so prominent, and terrazo and mosaic flooring is much more frequently employed. Here the choice of designs is also limited. Thorns, thistles, and grasses may be represented, also lions, dragons, whales, animals of the deep, lizards, snakes, etc. (Ps. 91, 13; 148, 1—13), in the space before the altar also deer (Ps. 42, 2). Figures of saints, angels, etc., may not be used, for it is not proper to tread the holy things under foot. Usually, geometrical designs may be relied upon as being satisfactory. There are so many combinations of circles, squares, polygons, arcs, etc., possible, that there is no danger of lack of variety. So far as materials are concerned, tiling and terra-cotta are less expensive than marble, but are generally considered not quite so lasting and durable. Terrazo finish is fine and not beyond the reach of the average congregation. Cement molds are the least expensive, and will probably be satisfactory where the expense is a serious consideration.

The general sculpture of a Lutheran church, both around the windows and doors and in the frieze ornamentation and the capitals, depends upon the style of the building and must carry out the main idea consistently. As a general rule, classic patterns should be avoided, since they remind too strongly of pagan temples. There are so many beautiful and appropriate models from the Middle Ages, for capitals as well as for frieze and cornice work, that one need not go back beyond the Romanesque and the Gothic. Cheap imitations of marble sculpture carried out in stucco or plaster of Paris should not be tolerated. They have no place in a Christian church, where honesty and truthfulness should be leading traits. It will probably not occur very often that the elaborate portals of the Gothic cathedrals or the Norman doorways are used as models, but if such decoration is not beyond the aspiration and ability of the congregation, there is no reason why beautiful sculpture work should not adorn the tympanum, the spandrils, and the columns of the main entrance. The grotesque and bizarre effects of the Gothic builders had better not be imitated, however, either in the gargoyles or in the peculiar representations of legends, as pictured by the medieval mind. To place statues or reliefs of saints somewhere about the main entrance savors strongly of Romanism. A large church in the Renaissance style, in one of our large cities, has the twelve apostles in high relief on the arch above the main portal. Others are content with fancy carving which gradually breaks into leaf tracery and foliage and points upward to the cross which crowns the gable. If the church is built of brick with white sand-stone trimming, the effect of stone carving, if correctly carried out, is one of exquisite grace. Sculpture work in the interior of Lutheran churches will probably be confined to window tracery, the mullions, and the arches over the windows. The ivy, the passion flower, the palm, the lily, and even leaves of the local flora, may be chosen as models. More effective, perhaps, than such decorative work, is the providing of small niches on the side walls, especially at the corners of the transept, in which the statues of evangelists, apostles, or prophets may be placed. In this way, the very walls and stones will assist in proclaiming the Word. Of sculpture and carving on the panels of the pulpit and on the frontale and superfrontale of the altar we have spoken above. The statues of Moses and Elias, or of Moses and John, which are sometimes used, are inappropriate for the altar. However, Thorwaldsen's "Come Unto Me" or another Christ figure expressing the grace, mercy, and loving-kindness of the Savior in the central panel-niche of the altar is very fitting and correct.

The art of painting has not yet received the attention which it demanded in the later Middle Ages, when everything was placed at the disposal of the Church, and which it merits to-day on account of its beauty and impressiveness, if properly employed. But it is slowly coming into its own. There are, indeed, but few mural paintings in churches which are worthy of note, with the exception of an occasional symbolic panel. But there are some beautiful and elaborate examples of altar paintings, for this branch of the art has been cultivated with great success in America, a number of artists devoting their entire time to this work. In paintings of this kind, the use of perspective is fully permissible, all the highest attainments of the art being welcomed for the embellishment of the house of God. But realistic presentation is not acceptable, especially in pictures of the Christ, for they distract the devotion. The conception must be ideal, and the execution, especially as to clothing and vestments, symbolic. Even the work of Rubens transgresses this requirement. Among the Italians, the work of Rafael, da Vinci, and Corregio measures up to the ideal standard, and of the painters of the last century whose work is deservedly popular Hofmann, Plockhorst, Thoma, Carolsfeld, and others may be mentioned.

The mural decorating or frescoing of a church, as well as vitreous brick finishing in buff or tan, is so important that it might properly demand a chapter for itself. But the statement of certain fundamental principles will enable us to do justice to this branch of the art of painting and call attention to the necessity of their observance. First of all, a general color scheme must be chosen, depending upon the lighting of the building, both by day and by night. Then the character of the colors must be considered. Blue and white are cold colors and will rarely serve well for a base. Beginning with cream, and continuing through various shades of yellow, golden red, orange, and maroon, a rich and warm tone predominates. The various shades of green are also cheerful and inviting. So much depends upon the psychology of colors that the impression of an entire church building may be governed by their proper selection and application. At any rate, it is well worth while consulting a good interior decorator, one who is really a master in his line. He must understand, above all, the limits of his craft and guard very carefully against over-ornamentation. In some churches, the attempts at emphasizing art have resulted in hideous nightmares of garish wall-painting without a central thought or, in fact, any idea at all. If the purpose were to see how many different kinds of color can be applied to a given surface area, the solution might be found more easily by exploding cans of every pigment in the rainbow scale in the middle of the church, and then adding a few cubist touches. The dignity of a church building demands more than that. It requires the intelligent use of color harmony combined with the application of Christian symbolism, without any Catholic admixture. It is worth a church committee's while to work out, with the artist, a scheme of interior decoration which will preserve the style of the church, harmonize perfectly with its interior, and express the Christian idea. "Attention is directed to the fact that the frescoing of our churches very frequently is inartistic, and even when performed by good craftsmen, is often inappropriate or, at least, meaningless in a house of worship. We believe that these strictures are well taken. Too frequently we observe designs which materially detract from the beauty of otherwise fine, churchly interiors, either by reason of the garish tints employed, or on account of the amateurish execution, or because they are inartistic in choice of subject. It certainly is a mistake to accept an ambitious plan of wall treatment involving the representation of floating angels, the figure of the blessed Savior, of the evangelists, etc., and permitting unskilled hands to execute the sketches. It is a fact too often overlooked that even ordinary technical training is not sufficient for the successful treatment, especially of ceilings and the curved surface of altar niches. The representation of the human figure to be seen at such angles involves a knowledge of perspective very rarely found even in trained frescoers. When attempted by an ordinary painter, the effect is quite unsatisfactory, as those who have seen the result of such experimenting will testify. Here, as in the case of architects' sketches, one must be cautioned against trusting too much to a beautifully drawn and colored sketch of wall-treatment. Only a man of experience can be trusted to execute such designs in a way which will harmonize with the furniture of the church, and will 'stand up' under illumination at night as well as in the daytime. When a congregation is unable to employ the services of a trained fresco artist, it ought to permit the walls to remain white, or simply tinted, with stenciled borders. But no matter how simple these borders may be, they should always be churchly, should in some way indicate the purpose of the building. To employ such features in a design does not necessarily mean a great outlay of money. Even a very simple plan of wall-treatment, entailing the expenditure of only a few hundred dollars, may be made to comport with the architecture of the building and with its purpose as a house of worship. Aside from being artistically correct, — correct in drawing and coloring,— the decorations in our churches ought to be of a distinctive *Christian type*. The designs ought to bear a message, ought to be full of meaning. In the decorative scheme employed and in the various features within that scheme, the purpose of the church building as a house of divine worship ought to be embodied. There ought also to be a suggestion of that bond which unites those who worship with the church of all climes and ages. The cardinal truths of our religion, the hopes and aspirations of Christianity, its chosen task and mission, should stand forth in this decorative embellishment. All these purposes are served by employing *Christian symbolism* as a basis of interior decoration." [189])

CHAPTER 5.

Lighting, Heating, Ventilating, Bells, Hardware.

When a church is contemplated, the fine arts are not the only ones that come into consideration, the industrial arts playing a very important role. Just as in the erection of the church building itself structural engineering is employed in figuring load and wind stresses, on floors, stairways, choirloft, trusses, towers, spires, etc., so the science of mechanical and electrical engineering, especially that portion which refers to lighting and heating, is used in planning the interior. And very often these practical questions determine to a large extent the habitability and always the comfort of the church building in all its parts.

The proper lighting of a church is an important problem. If the church is fittingly orientated, the disposition of windows is easily arranged, particularly so if there are large transept windows. Windows directly behind the preacher are a nuisance and should be avoided, as it is very painful for an audience to face a window. For the same reason, the lighting of the apse should be provided for as

---

189) *Lutheran Witness*, Dec. 14, 1915.

described above, by windows located behind the superfrontale of the altar or on either side in such a way as not to throw any light rays into the eyes of the attendants at holy worship. The windows on the south of the building should not admit any direct light rays, being fitted with colored (art) glass which may be said to be between translucent and opaque. Those on the north side, however, being on the left of the congregation, may be so light as to be between translucent and transparent. The modern opalescent art glass allows for an almost infinite variety of combinations in the various shades of the same color scheme and pattern. And the rose window over the western portal will represent the mean between the two. A small parish church in the West selected a dark amber color for this window, and the afternoon and evening sun, sending its rays through the opal lights, floods the church with waves of liquid rose fire which is indescribably beautiful. The basement rooms should be provided with as many windows as possible, since frosted panes will usually be desirable, and these are merely translucent.

Since a modern church building is used in the evening just as much as during the day, the artificial illumination is a question for itself. In many country churches, evening services occur so seldom that almost no provision is made for them. The few oil lamps shed a dim luster in the feeble effort to penetrate the Stygian darkness, and there is a general effect of a more than religious light. Luckily, the Lutherans know a great many of their beautiful hymns from memory, and it is assumed that the pastor also knows his sermon, so the ultimate result is better than might be expected. But it is by no means an ideal state of affairs, and the efforts of such country churches as are installing adequate oil or acetylene gas illuminating systems are heartily to be commended. In cities (and in many country districts) the congregations will usually have the choice of gas or electricity, or both together. Even in small towns electricity is now produced, at least in the evening, and in country districts at a distance from an electric line small individual plants may be installed. Even if electricity is chosen in the city, it will always be a matter of good policy to have at least a few so-called combination fixtures, in order that a few gas lights may always be in commission and no confusion or even panic result in case the electric current is interrupted or turned off. Formerly the direct lighting system was generally used, but since the chandelier lights are usually glaring and affect the eyes, the indirect or semi-indirect system of lighting is used more and more for church auditoriums. There are a number of these systems now in use which are far past the experimental stage, and a congregation will do well to examine the several methods closely and decide according to circumstances. An excellent way of lighting the apse is by means of a row of lights set inside the triumphal arch and invisible to the audience. Some auditoriums have all the lights hidden in recesses just below the arch of the ceiling, while the ceiling itself is set with clusters of bulbs. Though the effect of this arrangement is very pretty, it does not seem so churchly as individual suspended fixtures. No matter what form of illumination is decided upon, it should never result in a mere "dim religious light," but should enable every attendant with normal eye-sight to read the hymns without straining his vision.

The question of heating is usually a serious and difficult one. In smaller parish churches, especially in the country, stoves are still in general use. Their placing often interferes with the view of altar and pulpit, and the long sections of stove-pipes are not exactly decorative features of the interior. They have the additional drawback that their neighborhood, at least on one side, presents a section of the torrid zone, while distant parts of the auditorium may be experiencing the rigors of an arctic winter. For these reasons, the stoves are gradually being replaced by furnaces. These are fully satisfactory, even for churches with a seating capacity of more than three hundred. It depends, of course, upon the way in which the registers are placed. Some furnace systems require many wall registers and are, therefore, more costly in proportion than such as require only two or three large floor registers. The furnace pipes, in many cases, render the use of the basement almost impossible. Hot water heating is employed in many church buildings which are in use every day. Many architects consider steam heating as the only satisfactory heating system for a church building, the argument being that a much cheaper grade of coal may be used and that the draining of the radiators, if these be correctly placed, can be done thoroughly and rapidly. The time may, of course, not be far distant when other systems will supersede the ones now in use, such as the individual gas steam radiator system, but at present electric heating and other systems are not beyond the trial stage. But where electricity is very cheap, it may well be employed for heating the smaller rooms of the church building, when the weather is not too excessively cold. The principal attention must be paid to the even distribution of heat, whichever system may be selected. The usual experience has been that the floor became so cold as to make it very uncomfortable in zero weather. Some congregations have therefore found it advantageous to run steam pipes along beneath the seats, thus keeping the feet warm. In one western church, the auditorium floor is built up in the tiers, with a few inches elevation for each successive one, and the ducts with the hot air open beneath the seats. This method is very effective, but may consume a great deal of fuel. If ordinary radiators are used, the plan of placing them in recesses of the wall, behind ornamental screens, seems to be gaining favor, and with good reason. A radiator is at best an unsightly addition to a room, and if it can be placed out of the way without interfering with the effectiveness of the heating plant, the plan should be adopted far more generally. A requirement which is often overlooked is this that the women's retiring room be kept warm. In some churches, it seems to be considered sufficient if a little warm air from the auditorium finds its way into this room. But when the door of this room is closed, the temperature may become dangerous for little children. It has been suggested that every congregation have one or more oil stoves for just such rooms which will often not receive their full complement of heat, such as the vestry. If the people are forced to resort to automobile and carriage foot warmers to keep from having chills, the congregation is not giving the necessary attention to an item which demands careful consideration.

Closely connected with the question of heating is that of proper ventilation. In the past, this factor was so sadly neglected that the foulness of "church air" became proverbial. It stands to reason that the respiration and perspiration of several hundred people, not to speak of modern perfumes, will quickly produce a vitiated atmosphere. It may be perfectly true, as the results of recent investigations have established, that carbonic acid gas may be inhaled in much larger quantities than was formerly supposed, since it is not in itself poisonous. But in a church where no ventilation is provided, the exhaled gas and the moisture from lung and skin will hang over the audience like a pall, replacing attentive alertness with sleepiness, and often with dizziness and faintness. In a church of that kind, a preacher of even more than average ability cannot succeed in arousing interest and holding the attention. Therefore the atmosphere in a church should be renewed continually by ventilation, the best plan being that of furnishing thirty cubic feet of pure air per minute for every person. This can, of course, be attained to a degree by keeping the air inside the building in motion. Electric fans not only enable the air to take up a greater amount of perspiration, but their action also draws air from outside through every crevice. If natural ventilation is the only method employed, it should at least be put into use regularly. If windows and doors are opened for a good airing, before and after each service, to permit all the foul air to escape, the pure air will be heated through all the more quickly. In many churches at least so much has been provided for that there is ventilation by aspiration. A double flue is built into the chimney and, as the warm air ascends on the one side with the smoke, the cold air sinks down on the other side. The outlet for the warm air is placed above, and the intake for the cold air below. Many churches have ventilators in the

window sills or just below them. They have the advantage that they
will not cause draughts. In many instances, the tower is used for
ventilation by aspiration, since the partition need not extend very
far. The most successful method of ventilation is the fan or power
system. The exhaust method in this case draws out the bad air, and
the plenum method forces in pure, fresh air. The exhaust method
may easily be installed by placing the fan in the east wall of the
tower. It would ordinarily be used between services, but, since it
runs noiselessly, it could also be in motion during services. The
plenum method provides pure washed air, but, unfortunately, it uses
a great deal of fuel, since in this case the fan blows the fresh, cold air
through the heating coils and along the ducts into the rooms. There
are no draughts in this case. The entire method should be recommended most emphatically to the attention of the congregations. In
this respect, at least, they may learn much from an inspection of
large halls, auditoriums, and theaters, provided these are modern.

Only in recent years has the importance of hardware for church
buildings received some recognition in Lutheran congregations. This
is of such consequence that there was every reason for the emphasis
placed upon dinanderie in the Middle Ages. In addition to the articles for ecclesiastical use made of copper and its alloys, brass and
bronze, there are the various instruments and ornaments made of
wrought iron which deserve the most careful attention. It is true, of
course, that a Lutheran church has no need of portable altars, nor of
pixes, monstrances, shrines, reliquaries, censers, croziers, holy water
vats or stoups, and sanctuary rings or knockers, but Eucharistic vessels, crosses, candlesticks, light holders, lecterns, book-covers, fonts,
ewers and water vessels, bronze doors, and bells are in use to-day and
should be made as fine as circumstances permit. Most of these articles have been discussed above, but there are several that have not
yet been considered, and do properly belong to hardware. So far as
lighting fixtures are concerned, chandeliers, semi-indirect and direct
units, and wall brackets are now made in every style, with a range of
prices fully accomodating every demand. In selecting them, care
must be taken that they are constructed so as to catch the least possible dust. In many bowl fixtures, this factor is not taken into account, and the resulting frequent cleaning is decidedly unpleasant.
The fixtures may be made to order after a special pattern. In one of
our northern cities, there is a church whose fixtures are modeled after
a medieval lantern, the effect being very quaint and interesting. Care
must be taken, however, that no secular models be introduced and the
churchly character be in any way interfered with. At least some of
the wall brackets should be combination fixtures, for reasons stated
above.

The registers and the radiator screens can be selected to harmonize with the other fixtures of the building, especially if these be elaborate. On all the doors, but notably those of the main portal, the door-knobs and plates, as well as the hinges, should be chosen with the same idea of harmony in mind. Stock fixtures do not draw the attention in a building devoted to secular uses, but in a church one involuntarily looks for signs on all sides, showing that the building has been set apart from ordinary use. If railings of metal are employed anywhere in the church, as for stair-way balustrades or the choir-loft (or, though not so fittingly, for the chancel), they should also be ordered with a view of preserving the restfulness of the interior. In many cases, the railings resemble poultry or rabbit netting more than appointments in the house of God. Moreover, they are often cheap and dingy-looking, and thus detract greatly from the effectiveness of the church. There is no excuse for such conditions. Far better omit subsidiary features of a church than to spoil an otherwise harmonious interior by such mistakes.

About bells nothing much need be added. The Lutheran church has retained them with a full understanding of their usefulness. With the removal of all superstition and idolatry, the bell is now an instrument whose "pealing, charming, clamorous sweetness" has an effect more potent and compelling than many another form of musical instrument. A church without a bell is almost like a person without a voice. No wonder that a bell with a pure, loud, far-reaching tone, calling the Christians to divine service, reminding them of the special hours of prayer, inviting the absent to join with the congregation in the Lord's Prayer, or announcing to them, with measured strokes, the death of a member of the congregation, has become an almost indispensable piece of church furniture. The number of bells is either one, or three, or a set of chimes.

CHAPTER 6.

Paraments and Clerical Vestments.

Although the Reformation had not interfered with paraments, so far as the Lutheran Church is concerned, and though the enlivening function of the altar and pulpit vestments was fully recognized, there arose in certain quarters, especially those under Reformed influence, a certain antipathy against their retention. In spite of this, they were maintained in most of the parishes of northern Germany. The age of Pietism and then that of Rationalism exerted a much more pronounced influence by creating a peculiar sort of apathy against the use of paraments which proved much more effectual in causing

their abandonment than open and pronounced opposition might have done. But there has been a healthy revival of interest in church vestments in the last half-century. Bock, Meurer, and Beck in Germany were among the leaders in reestablishing a sane and proper appreciation of Evangelical paramentics. In America also a healthy interest is becoming manifest. Professor Beck's book "Evangelische Paramentik" was hailed with joy by the reviewer in the "Lutheran Survey." And many a Ladies' Aid Society has deemed its members honored by providing proper paraments for the house of God. The fear as though the vestments are too costly is without foundation. The initial cost of an entire set is not so high as that of an altar, and though this may seem large for a single expenditure, it must be remembered that the several cloths may be purchased one at a time. Undoubtedly, also, it requires only a suggestion to have a special Altar Guild organized in a congregation, whose members would make the purchase and proper care of church vestments for all seasons their object, and incidentally have charge of the Eucharistic vessels. It is by no means a mere compliment on the part of Meurer, Beck, and others, if they laud the work of the women of the congregation or of such special organizations. With the proper instruction, such women will take pride in keeping the house of worship in its proper order, so far as the vestments are concerned. Wherever there is no interest for such embellishments, the fault lies, as a rule, not with the parishioners, but with the pastor.

So far as the altar vestments and the Eucharistic cloths are concerned, the white linen paraments are used at all seasons of the church year. They signify the unchanging doctrine of the Christian Church. There are mainly three white vestments to be considered, two others occurring only rarely in the Lutheran Church of America. The white cloth covering of the mensa should be of fine linen. It should fit the mensa perfectly and may even project beyond the edges for several inches. This part should receive neither embroidered nor drawn-work designs, but should extend in immaculate, undisturbed whiteness. This does not exclude a hemstitched border. That part of the cloth also which hangs over the sides may be left wider, from six to ten inches, and receive the full attention of a good needle artist in a geometrical drawn-work design. The representation of small plain crosses and chalices had better not be used, as Beck says, because the contrasted repetition is tedious. A border of lace is most appropriate, if made in a churchly design. Bone-lace, Cluny, Tulle, and Hardanger (not Battenberg or Valenciennes), in a width from three to ten inches, will serve very well. Instead of the open-work lace effect, it is still better to use the outline stitch or the stem stitch, with red or blue silk, to apply the designs. Even white satin-stitch work is not excluded from the border, but in this case it will be better to outline the figures in red or blue, since they will otherwise not show up well at a distance. If symbols are used in the lace border of the altar-cloth, the old Christian initials I H S, wheat-ears, grapes and grape-leaves, or passion flowers may be used. The patterns printed by Beck show very simple as well as very elaborate designs. If the altar is of stone, the altar-cloth may be protected against dampness by a chrismale, that is, a linen cloth stiffened by a wax bath, of the size of the altar, "over which should be laid a cloth of unbleached or stiff bleached linen of the same size, which is often omitted, though it contributes very much to the preservation of the other vestments." [190]) The same purpose is served by a heavy covering of felt, which just covers the mensa.

The Corporale is a square white linen cloth, to be placed under the Eucharistic vessels on the altar. It sometimes has a fringe of narrow Cluny or Hardanger lace. It may also be hemstitched and have a small cross or Christmonogram embroidered in each corner. No other embroidery or adornment is permissible for this cloth. Its size must be sufficient for all communion vessels, or two cloths may be used. Incidentally it may be said that the silver serving plate, upon which the Eucharistic vessels are carried to the altar, must never be used on the mensa, since the Corporale only is used for that purpose.

The embroidery of the Velum may be as pretentious as the needle artist desires. It is a linen or batiste cloth a little larger than the Corporale (30x30, 36x36 inches), to cover the Eucharistic vessels on the altar, especially the chalice and the flagon. If the number of vessels is such that one Velum will not suffice, a second one of the same size and design should be provided. Hem-stitching, and a narrow border of Cluny or Hardanger lace may always be employed. Ears of wheat and grapevines may be embroidered on the Velum, either in chain-stitch, or, still better, in outline-stitch. Solid embroidery should not be employed, since it interferes with the draping of the vestment and gives it an aspect of stiffness and heaviness. Beck has a beautiful pattern for a Velum, showing alternating grapevines and wheat-ears, with a monogram (Chi Rho, Alpha Omega) in the center, and small stars in the open space. The Purifical in use in some churches agrees with the foregoing in pattern and execution.

Besides these principal linen vestments, many altar sets now include also a Palla, or a number of palls, one for each vessel. They are made of linen (in preference to the custom, sometimes found, of using the colors of the season), and are folded or hemmed over a

---

190) Mothes, quoted in Horn, 116.

THE ALTAR BIBLE IN THE CHURCH OF
THE REDEEMER, JERUSALEM.

piece of cardboard. The embroidery may be like that of the Velum, especially where both chalice and paten are covered with palls. The Bursa is rarely used in the Lutheran Church. It is a pocket or reticule, sometimes of fine white linen, but oftener of silk, in the color

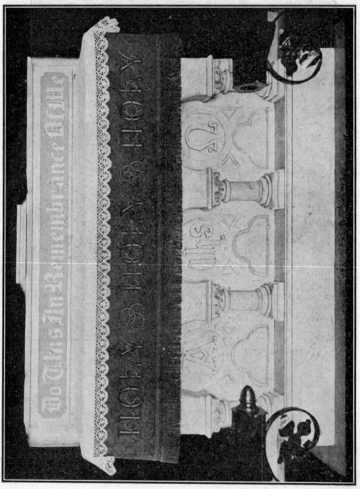

ALTAR COVERING (Red).

of the season. Its purpose is to serve as a holder for the Corporale, before and after administration.

Not ritually indispensable, but yet called for by the liturgy and aiding much in putting change, life, and significance into the services, is the decorative clothing of the altar in the colors of the season. There are altogether five liturgical colors: white, the color of

the angels and of all saints, as Luther calls it, symbolizing innocence
and holiness, majesty and glory; red, the majestic color of dominion,
of joy, of light-giving doctrine, of the fire of the Holy Ghost, of blood
and of martyrdom, symbolizing especially love, the love of the Bride,

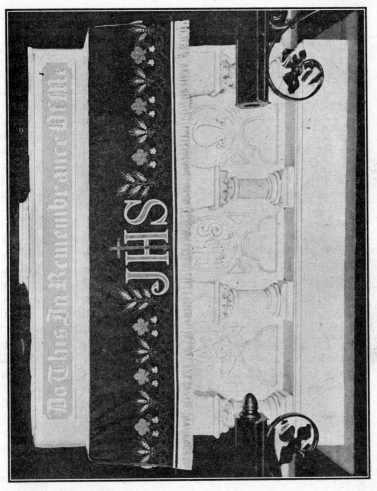

ALTAR COVERING (Green).

the Church, to Christ, the Bridegroom; green, the every-day color of
the earth, the restful and refreshing color of hope, of peace, and of
victory; violet (not purple, or lilac, or any shade of blue) the solemn,
earnest color of penitence and mourning, humility, concentration,
and prayerful selfcommunion; and black, the color of humiliation,
sadness, and deepest mourning. The liturgical seasons during which

the vestments in the respective colors are used, are these: white, for
the great Christ festivals, the times of the greatest majesty and glory
in the church-year, from Christmas Eve till the Epiphany octave, on
Easter and till Ascension; red, on the festivals next in rank, on
which also the love of the Church toward Christ is emphasized, on
Pentecost, Trinity, Michaelis, Reformation Festival, and Dedication
Day, all of which are a result of Whitsunday; green, during the time
when the life and growth of the Church are proclaimed, for the every-
day seasons of the Church, from the Epiphany octave till Quinquagesima, and on all Sundays after Trinity; violet, during the so-
called closed seasons, the times of prayerful meditation, during
Advent, during the Lenten season from Ash Wednesday till Palmarum,
also on Exaudi Sunday, as the day of preparation for Pentecost;
black, during Holy Week, on days of penitence, and when funeral
services are held in church. If, for various reasons, a congregation
cannot make it possible to get all five colors, at least three colors
ought to be provided: green, red, and black, red taking the place of
white, and black that of violet. But it will be found much more
satisfactory to have the complete set of colors.

A word of caution must be inserted in regard to the choice of
colors, especially red, green, and violet. They must be the full, solid,
fast colors, in each case, not rose-color, or light green, or robin's-egg
blue, neither orange, or bronze, or olive-green. In certain cases also,
the dyes are of such a nature as to react with the gold and silver cord
used in some parts of the embroidery. In most cases, it is not advisable to order through a local store, especially if the town is small,
but rather apply to a large house of noted integrity, which is able to
procure the correct shades. As for the kinds of material best adapted
for the colored vestments, they are the following: for white, silk
damask, brocade, or broad-cloth; for green, broad-cloth; for violet,
broad-cloth or silk damask; for black, broad-cloth or silk. In white
and violet, it may be possible to secure silk damask, in which the
pattern will show lions, dragons, or deer in gold thread on the white
background. There is a possibility that a sufficient demand for such
cloth will cause it to appear on the market. Reputable firms dealing
in church goods will gladly supply the necessary information.

It was stated above that the cost of the paraments is not such as
to cause hesitation on the part of the congregation in procuring the
same. As a matter of fact, there is such a great range in excellence
of paraments and therefore also in prices that congregations of every
size may be accommodated, broad-cloth with plain embroidered designs being within reach of even the poorest church. Velvet, especially cotton velvet, should not be chosen; it fades easily and becomes
shabby quickly. It is not absolutely necessary that the respective

vestment cover the mensa of the altar. As noted above, special linen
cloths or a thick piece of felt may be used for that purpose. And
the white linen altar covering must be on the mensa at all seasons of
the year, thus covering whatever cloth may be in use. For the altar,

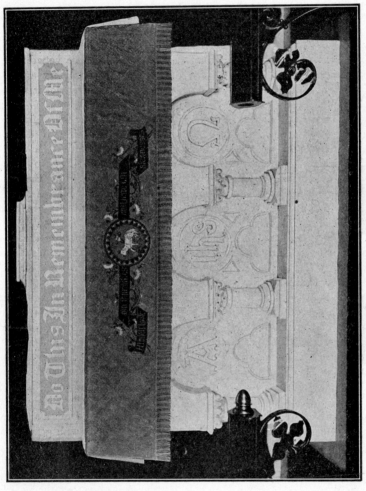

ALTAR COVERING (Violet).

a strip of the colored parament from eight to eighteen inches wide
as a minimum will be sufficient. Many are twenty-four inches wide
and richly embroidered. This strip may be fastened to the edge of
the mensa, beneath the border of the altar-cloth, by means of hooks
or snaps. The cloth for the altar reading-desk, if there is such a
piece of furniture, will rarely be more than eighteen to twenty-four

inches wide and two to three feet long. And the covering for the pulpit reading-desk will have about the same dimensions, as will that of the lectern, if a vestment is necessary there. The covering for the baptismal font has been replaced, almost universally, by a marble or metal lid. The pulpit railing should have no vestments. Like the baptismal font, it is no table, and should not have the covering of a desk. The only thing that might be done here would be to upholster the railing on the top with felt. All the material necessary for one complete set of colored vestments will be between two and two-thirds and three square yards. If the embroidery and the fringes are then chosen in a simple design, the cost will not be found excessive.

The proper fringes for the various vestments are: for white, red, and green — golden or pure yellow fringes, alternating, if desired, with fringes the color of the vestment, ten cords or pencils of the liturgical color alternating with five of the contrasting fringe; for violet and black, silver or white fringes, alternating with the color of the vestment in the same manner. In the case of violet paraments the golden alternative is permissible, and in the white, red in addition to the gold. If silver and gold fringes are used exclusively, the effect is not so beautiful. The corners of the paraments, on the altar as well as on the reading desks, may be fitted with tassels whose weight will tend to keep the cloth stretched evenly. Some liturgiologists advise against their use.

It is in the execution of the embroidery on the various vestments that the great difference in cost principally appears. It is understood, of course, that the designs and figures which are chosen for the paraments will harmonize thoroughly with the style and interior decoration of the church, especially with the altar and pulpit. Then, also, the limitations of the art of embroidery must be carefully observed. As Beck points out, it is a very ambiguous compliment if church needle-work is praised as looking "realistic," "with perfect perspective," "as though chased in gold," or "carved from alabaster," etc. The embroidery of paraments is decorative and symbolical, nothing more. Its effect is dependent entirely upon contrast of color, to distinguish principal and subsidiary parts of the figure. For it covers a flat surface, it is to serve as a cover or hanging, and should attempt nothing more. It is essential, also, that the various representations be united and enclosed by geometrical lines, to guard against the illusion of a drawing or painting. And so far as human and animal figures are concerned, all attempts to represent them in a natural, realistic manner is out of place in the church. This includes the accentuation of the trait for which a certain figure is

chosen. If the effort to obtain a certain effect in the expression of
the face or in the position of the body becomes too apparent, the result may become a ludicrous carricature.

A rather difficult question is the choice of color for the em-

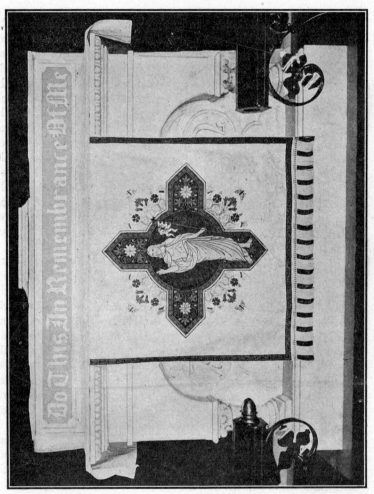

WHITE ALTAR ANTEPENDIUM.

broidery of the various vestments. Contrasts which are too striking
are just as absurd as the choice of the same color as the vestment,
which renders the design almost invisible, except at short distances.
For black paraments, the chief embroidery color is white. If the
lines of the design are carefully graded, the contrast will not be so
great as one might suppose. And if a certain heaviness in the em-

Kretzmann, Christian Art.   14

broidery cannot be avoided, it may be relieved by using blue, violet, and olive in some parts of the pattern, or by choosing gold or purple for all the work. Red and bright green must be avoided in embroidering black paraments. So far as the violet vestments are concerned, the same general rules apply, the only difference being that black is here employed as basic color. In green cloths, the basic colors of the figures may be black, blue, red, and golden-brown, with various darker and lighter shades of green, while the prominent lines will be golden, and outline stitches white. For red vestments, the artist should choose blue, olive-green, and shades of red for basic colors, while the principal lines are executed in gold and white. The most difficult color is white, since it requires the greatest contrast to bring out the embroidery well. In general, the choice of dark violet, green, and red shades has given the best results. The outlines may be golden yellow, to relieve the sharpness of the contrast. In many cases, the heaviness of the figure will not permit such a juxtaposition, however, and in that event it will be best to use white as the basic color in the design, with the outline stitches in darker colors. Some of the finest examples of such work in this country are found in Trinity Church of Reading, Pa., and in St. John's and in the Motherhouse of Deaconesses, Philadelphia.

In the actual execution of the design, the individual case must decide whether the embroidery may be applied directly to the cloth or must first be applied to a linen stiffening and then sewed to the goods. If the work is done by professional needle artists, they will have their own method. But with the attention that needle-work has received in the last few years, it is more than probable that some one from the congregation with real talent will volunteer to do the work. The stitches used are those commonly employed in work of this nature. The stem-stitch or outline-stitch, as its name implies, is used principally for outlines and stems of flowers and plants, though it may be applied to surface work. Where the chain-stitch is used, the outline-stitch is employed at least for the fine lines. If the design is such as to permit chain-stitch embroidery, the work can be done much faster, but there is much machine-work which has hurt its reputation to some extent. For large and even surface-work, the flat or satin-stitch and the overcasting or couching stitch have proved most serviceable. The latter stitch especially brings out the beauty of the silk in a very remarkable way, and, since it may be done on a frame, has other advantages which make it a favorite. Certain patterns may also be embroidered in cross-stitch work, but the execution is very difficult in the case of figures. For such as find it impossible to do embroidery of the finest kind, the plaited slav stitch has many advantages, since it does not require such continuous eye-strain.

To discuss the various appropriate designs and symbols for paraments almost calls for a special chapter, and most of them will be referred to below. It may suffice here to give just a few examples as to possible combinations, according to Beck. The white paraments are to proclaim Christ's work of redemption. A lamb in the center, treading upon a dragon, and surrounded by panels picturing the angels of Christmas and Easter, is very beautiful. The red paraments symbolize the work of Christ for redeemed mankind through His Church. An effective pattern shows the triumphant Lamb, surrounded by the figures of the four evangelists. Others give the monograms of Christ in various designs, surrounded by the emblems of the evangelists. The violet vestments deal with the types of Christ. Melchizedek and Aaron, the sacrifice of Isaac, and similar designs are used. The green paraments symbolize the life and growth of the Church, and therefore figures concerning the Lord's Supper, the Water of Life, the fountain in the wilderness, and others are eminently fitting. For the black paraments only such figures are chosen as deal with the suffering and death of Christ. The various monograms of Christ, the letters I H S, with or without cross, the Alpha and Omega in various combinations, the ancient Chi Rho ☧ in different designs, and others are always appropriate. The Bible verses selected for the antependium of the pulpit should always be short, and have reference to the special season, or to the work of redemption in general. "Hear ye Him," "God is Love," "Fear not!" and many others may readily be suggested.[191])

The carpets of the sanctuary and the space just in front of it are also usually discussed under the paraments. Their color should be neutral, in order that it may harmonize with any of the liturgical colors. So far as designs are concerned, the same principles apply as in the case of mosaics. Geometrical figures are to be commended, also figures of the lower animals, dragons, serpents, etc., but no representation of a person or thing which is regarded as sacred in the Church. The kneeling-stools of the altar must not be upholstered in the liturgical colors.

The Lutheran Church has retained only a part of the clerical vestments to the present day, although there is no doctrinal or liturgical objection to the use of as many vestments as, for instance, the Anglican and the Protestant Episcopal churches have kept. In most of the American Lutheran congregations, the cassock or pulpit robe is the only full garment worn as the distinctive vestment of the minister. It signifies that the wearer is engaged in the actual performance of his ministerial calling, in the proclamation of the

---

191) Cp. *Common Service Book and Hymnal*, 292.

Gospel. It is to be hoped, therefore, that it will be retained for this purpose and not be replaced by the unsightly, and often ugly, Prince Albert frock coat. But the gown or cassock should really have a meaning. Many of the gowns now in use may have been designed with good intentions, but the result is a nondescript garment, whose relation to clerical vestments is charitably assumed to be beyond challenge. The Lutheran cassock or pulpit gown is an academic

PULPIT GOWNS.
(Courtesy Cotrell & Leonard, Albany, N. Y.)

vestment and should adhere closely to this style. There are several good houses in this country which make a specialty of such garments and can provide everything that may be desired. The following regulations apply to academic gowns, and are therefore also generally accepted for pulpit gowns. "The gowns shall be of the patterns commonly used by colleges and universities. The long pointed sleeve indicates the Bachelor's degree; the long closed sleeve, with slit near

upper part of arm, indicates the Master's degree; and the round open
sleeve indicates the Doctor's degree.   The material for the Bachelor's
gown shall be worsted, for the Master's and Doctor's gowns, it shall
be either worsted or silk.   The color shall be black.   The Bachelor's
and Master's gowns shall be untrimmed.   The Doctor's gown shall
be faced down the front with black velvet, with bars of the same
across the sleeves; or the facings and cross bars may be of the same

PULPIT GOWNS.
(Courtesy Cotrell & Leonard, Albany, N. Y.)

color as the binding or edging of the hood, being indicative of the
degree." [192])   All graduates of a Lutheran theological seminary may
use a Bachelor's gown or one of the various forms of pulpit gown.
The Lutheran gown has round sleeves, a closed front, a yoke, and a
high neck, with collar so arranged as to permit the easy fastening of
the bands.   The Geneva form of gown is usually worn open in front,

---

192) *Minnesota Alumni Weekly*, XV, 31: 11.

though it may be designed to close in front or to be worn with a cassock front.

In addition to the cassock or pulpit gown, Lutheran clergymen have commonly worn either a ruffled collar or the so-called bands, in either case of a pure white color. The bands are each two inches wide and six inches long. They may be hem-stitched and have a small embroidered cross. There is a tendency in our days to discard the bands entirely. In a way this would be unfortunate. For if the bands are derived from the Greek *peritrachelium,* as adopted in the Roman *orarium stola* of presbyters and bishops, its significance would be that of a mark of rank, to distinguish between ordained ministers actually engaged in clerical work on the one hand, and students of theology, superannuated ministers, etc., on the other hand. If desired, the use of the bands for preaching might be discontinued, but it should be worn in the administration of the Sacraments, since at such times the pastor officiates in a very pronounced manner, by virtue of the power vested in him by the call.

CHAPTER 7.

The Symbolism of the Lutheran Church Building and Its Appointments.

In these days of scientific investigation and suspicious research it may be considered the very essence of unscientific procedure to devote a chapter to the symbolism of the church building and its appointments. Nevertheless, the summary here presented may be of some aid in understanding the externals of the Lutheran cultus, especially since an effort has been made to rule out all arbitrariness, such as has characterized similar discussions in the past.

The entire Lutheran church building and all its parts speaks a reverent and inspiring language to him who approaches with an open mind and proceeds to examine everything in an intelligent manner. The buttressed tower, rising like a castle wall, speaks of invincible strength, Ps. 46; Matt. 16, 18. The lofty spire points to the true home above, the goal of every Christian's desire and hope, Col. 3, 2; Phil. 3, 20. The main portal opens wide and inviting: "Come, for all things are now ready," Matt. 22, 4; Luke 14, 17; Matt. 25, 10. When there are three doors under one great arched portal, they refer to the mystery of the Triune God, as do all the windows which are grouped in series of three. The great rose window over the main entrance reminds the Christians of the fact that the desert of nations without Christ has bloomed like a rose, through the Gospel, Is. 35, 1. As the Christian enters the vestibule, he remembers the word of earnest admonition to make his service one of true devotion, Ex. 3, 5; Eccl. 5, 1; Ps. 26, 5. 6. The wide central aisle leading to the sanctuary is a type of the way of grace, which leads directly to the mercy of God, through the merits of Christ, Prov. 15, 24; Heb. 10, 20. The cruciform plan of the church represents the symbol of Christianity, the Cross of Christ. The same emblem occurs over the portals, on the spire, on the altar, and in many of the ornaments of the building, Gal. 6, 14; 1 Cor. 1, 18; 2, 2. If the form of the church is rectangular, the entire arrangement will nevertheless signify a striving forward toward the beauty and strength of the means of grace, Is. 60, 1; Ps. 42, 2. The organ with the choir is on the choir-loft, opposite the altar, to lead in the hymns, and especially in the antiphonal liturgy, Ps. 26, 12; Rev. 19, 5. The large figure windows will remind of some great deed of Christ, or represent Him in one of His parables. The emblems of other windows and on the frescoed walls will point to one or the other of the Sacraments or represent the beauty of some Christian virtue. The altar represents no hearth, no sacrificial altar, no sarcophagus, but a table for the celebration of the Lord's Supper, as the gracious Sacrament of His mercy, 1 Cor. 10, 21. Everything on and about the altar reminds, in some way, of the redeeming grace of Christ, as it is revealed and communicated in the Eucharist. The pulpit stands before the congregation and yet in their midst, because the pastor, when preaching the Gospel, it a witness of the faith which has been committed to the saints, Jude, v. 3. The baptismal font is at the entrance of the apse, or in a chapel adjoining it, because the child, by Baptism, is received into the communion of saints. The apse is elevated above the auditorium and yet belongs to it, since all believers have free access to the full mercy of God, Rom. 5, 2; Eph. 2, 18; 3, 12. For this reason no railing, no rood screen, or any other device shuts the apse off from the rest of the church. All the lines of the church are simple, but dignified and beautiful. Everything is designed to awaken and to foster a feeling of devotion and reverence.

This spirit of devout uplift will be strengthened still more by the inscriptions on the paraments, on the altar, pulpit, walls, etc. And it is well to remember here that the strictures of Meurer, Beck, and others, in which they criticize the prevailing custom of placing the names of the donors in conspicuous places on the gift, with the greatest severity, are well taken. "While the latter [the Roman Catholics] are satisfied with the condition that their names be remembered after their death in masses for their souls, our people, during their very life-time, have either their coat-of-arms or their name boastfully embroidered in that place where only the divine name and the symbols of divine power and grace belong. Not without reason did a visitor of a church in which the altar showed the embroidery of a golden crown of laurels, inside of which the equally golden name of 'Barnewitz' shone, ask, whether this was the altar of the unknown God, which St Paul had found in Athens." It shows a spirit of irreverence or at least a sad lack of taste and tact, when memorial windows, and altar cloths, and liturgical books, and Eucharistic vessels, and what-not, all blazon forth the names of the individual donors or of the societies that were kind enough to help the cause of the congregation and its house of worship along. If anywhere, the admonition that the left hand should not know what the right hand doeth, is applicable in the furnishing of the church. The work of men must be relegated to the background, the words and works of the Lord must stand out prominently, and alone. In order to carry out this intention, the inscriptions throughout the church must be selected with great care. If an inscription is desired over the northern arch, especially if this be the arch of the baptistery, the verse "He that believeth and is baptized shall be saved," Mark 16, 16; or, "Suffer the little children to come unto Me," Mark 10, 14; or, "Feed My lambs," John 21, 15, would be fitting. For the central arch a congregation might choose, "Lord, I have loved the habitation of Thy house," Ps. 26, 8; or, "Blessed are they that dwell in Thy house," Ps. 84, 4; or, "I am the Way, the Truth, and the Life," John 14, 5. 6. Over the south arch, where the pulpit is located, may appear the admonition, "He that is of God heareth God's Words," John 8, 47; or, "He that heareth you, heareth Me," Luke 10, 16; or, "Blessed are they that hear the Word of God, and keep it," Luke 11, 28. So far as the paraments are concerned, the inscriptions will have to fit the season of the church year for which they are used. For the white paraments, the verse "Fear not," Luke 2, 10; Matt. 28, 5 is very appropriate, or, "Immanuel," Is. 7, 14; or, "Wonderful, Counselor, the Mighty God, the Everlasting Father, the Prince of Peace," Is. 9, 6; or, "Blessing, and Honor, and Glory, and Power be unto Him," Rev. 5, 13. The red paraments might have the inscription "Holy, Holy, Holy," Is. 6, 3; or, "Peace I leave with you," John 14, 27; or, "Abide in Me," John 15, 4. The green paraments should receive general admonitions, such as "Come, for all things are now ready," Luke 14, 17; or, "O taste and see that the Lord is good," Ps. 34, 8; or, "The Son of Man is come to seek and save that which was lost," Luke 19, 10; or, "Continue ye in my love," John 15, 9. Appropriate verses for the violet coverings are, "Thou art a Priest forever, after the order of Melchizedek," Ps. 110, 4; or, "We love Him, because He first loved us," 1 John 4, 19; or, "God is Love," 1 John 4, 8. For the black paraments, verses from Is. 53 are most fitting, or simple crosses may be chosen.

The symbols which may be used for paraments, emblems, sculpture, and in part also for mosaics, etc., are so numerous that entire books have been devoted to their discussion, notably those of Smith,

Collins, Didron, and Geldart. Lack of space compels the summarizing of the best information on the subject. In the general symbols, the cross takes first place. It may be without the summit, in the shape of the capital T; with summit, but only one transverse bar, the usual Latin cross; with summit and two transverse bars, the upper to symbolize the superscription; with summit and three transverse bars, the third indicating the foot-rest; the Greek cross, having cross arms of equal length; the St. Andrew's cross, in the form of a multiplication sign; the Celtic cross, which is a Latin cross with a circle having its center in the middle of the cross-bars. The cross is also represented in connection with various flowers and plants, the thistle, roses, ears of wheat and grape-leaves, pomegranates, lilies, passion flowers, and clover leaves.

The names and monograms of Christ are always appropriate. Most of them have been derived from the Greek capital letters *ΙΗΣΟΥΣ ΧΡΙΣΤΟΣ*. The simplest abbreviation was made by taking the first, second, and last letter of each word, *ΙΗΣ* and *ΧΡΣ*, or, according to the uncial method, *IHC* and *XPC*. The meaning of these abbreviations soon became obscure, and so new meanings were devised: *Iesous hemon soter* for the Greek, Jesus hominum Salvator in the Latin, also In Hoc Salus, In Hoc Signo (vinces); *Jesus, Heiland, Seligmacher,* in the German. It is best to explain the meaning of this monogram to the congregation or else discard it entirely. The same is true of the beautiful Christogram or Chrisma Chi Rho (✳). Unless the people understand the symbol, it has no value. The monogram Alpha and Omega, in various combinations, is more easily explained, on account of the Scripture passages Rev. 1, 8. 11; 21, 6; 22, 13. Since the Alpha is developed from the triangle, and the Omega from the circle, a combination of the two will incidentally be a representation of the Trinity, of the Triune God.

The symbolism of animals is especially richly developed, the Physiologus furnishing the artists of all times sufficient material for all purposes. The ass was used to represent humility and patience, the beaver as a type separating himself from works of the flesh, the bear as a symbol of the devil, as also the fox. The elephant represented the continual fight against the dragon, the goat was a picture of Christ seeing dangers from afar. The hart represented the redemption of Jesus Christ, also the soul longing for God's mercy (Ps. 42, 1. 2.) Jonah and the whale represented the resurrection of Christ (Matt. 12, 39. 40; 16, 4; Luke 11, 29). The fish was in use since ancient times, since the Greek letters forming its name are the initial letters of the words *Iesous Christos Theou Hyios Soter,* Jesus Christ, Son of God, Savior. The wolf was a type of the hypocrite. The cock typified vigilance, but also human weakness and repentance, in connection with the fall of Peter. The devil was most often represented as a griffin and as a dragon and serpent (Rev. 12 and 13; 20, 2). Much oftener, however, than any of these the figure of the Lamb is in use (Is. 53, 7; John 1, 29; 1 Cor. 5, 7; 1 Pet. 1, 19; Rev. 5, 6; 6, 16). It is usually a type of the Savior, characterized by the cross or the cross-pennant, sometimes as the suffering Lamb, whose blood flows into the chalice, then again as the victorious Lamb, looking backwards upon the conquered enemies (Rev. 5, 12. 13). The Lamb is also pictured as fighting and conquering the dragon, as sitting enthroned upon the Book with the seven seals, as opening the Book. In the pictures of Christ as the Good Shepherd, the lambs, of course, represent the Christians. The picture of a ram is sometimes used as a type of Christ, with reference to Gen. 22, 13. Christ is also represented as the Lion out of the tribe of Judah (Rev. 5, 5), and the virtues of the ruler of the animal kingdom ascribed to Him (cf. Gen. 49, 9. 10). But the lion is also used as a type of the devil (1 Pet. 5, 8), and of all the evils which the Christians should conquer (Ps. 91, 13). A representation of sheep often referred also to the apostles gathered about the Good Shepherd.

Among the birds which were used for symbolic representations the dove is the most common. It is a type of the Holy Spirit (Luke 3, 22), of peace and the hope of eternal life (Gen. 8, 11), and of the Christians (Matt. 10, 16). The eagle represents the renewing of youth, which should characterize the Christians (Ps. 103, 5; Is. 40, 31). The legend has added the saying that an eagle may renew his youth by bathing in a miraculous fountain, and for that reason he also typifies resurrection. The same thought is connected with the phoenix, which was said to come forth in full vigor after a voluntary death by fire. The story is found as early as Clement (I Clement, Chapter XXV; cf. John 10, 18). The pelican, which was formerly said to tear open its breast in order to feed its young with its blood, at the same time healing them from a serpent's sting, is a picture of the love of Christ made manifest in His vicarious suffering and death. The hen gathering her chickens under her wings (Matt. 23, 37; Luke 13, 34) is a type of the searching love of Christ. One of the most peculiar pictures is that of the unicorn who was hunted down by four hounds, mercy, truth, righteousness, and peace, Ps. 85, 10, and found shelter in the bosom of the virgin Mary, thus typifying the Incarnation.[193]

The symbolism of flowers and plants is also very rich and may be extended by careful artists almost indefinitely. The picture of the vine and the branches is explained by Jesus Himself (John 15). The use of ears of wheat and grape-leaves with reference to the Lord's

193) Cp. *Zeitschrift fuer deutsches Altertum*, 2, 282.

Supper is also easily understood. Thorns and thistles are usually pictured in connection with the cross, the curse of God (Gen. 3, 18) and the redemption being thus represented together. If the cross is wound with roses, especially five roses with five petals each, it reminds of the love which endured five wounds for the sake of fallen humanity. The great gift of the Sacrament, earned through the suffering on the cross, is represented by a cross with wheat-ears and grape-leaves. If pomegranates are used in that connection, they refer to the life brought by the vicarious work of Christ, for this fruit represents the tree of life and the fulness of divine grace. If the cross is surrounded by lilies, it reminds of the innocence and holiness which is the result of the agony on the cross. If the cross is decorated with palm leaves, it points forward to the final victory of all those who enroll under this emblem. The passion flower and the clover leaf are also used in this connection. The lily (calla or Easter) is also used in other combinations, to represent purity and holiness. Palm branches are used to represent the victory of all the saints (Rev. 7, 9), as also the crown with a wreath of palm leaves or laurel (2 Tim. 4, 8; 1 Pet. 5, 4; Jas. 1, 12; Rev. 2, 10; 4, 10). The rose may be used alone, with reference to the rose of Sharon (Song of Sol., 2, 1). The water-lily, the blue bell, ivy, and oak leaves are also employed with excellent effect.

When symbols representing the Trinity or any person of the Godhead are used, the nimbus should be employed. This may take the shape of an elliptical aureole, of a circular, triangular, square, cruciform, or ray-cross nimbus, of luminous clusters, of a sun with seven or fourteen rays, etc. The aureole which surrounds the whole body is a characteristic of the divinity. God the Father was formerly often represented as an old man, the "Ancient of Days" (Dan. 7), and the Middle Ages did not hesitate to picture the entire Trinity as persons. Such realism interferes with a reverent conception of God. The presence of God the Father may be intimated by a hand extended from the clouds, either in benediction or clasping a crown, or the name of Jehovah may be inscribed within a radiating circle. Many of the figures used for Christ were mentioned above. The only ones that might be added are those of a pilgrim (Luke 24) and of an angel, the form in which the Old Testament represents Him. The Holy Ghost is shown either as a plain white dove, or one with six wings. The Trinity is represented by an equilateral triangle, by a triangle with the word Jehovah inside, by two triangles interlocking and forming a star, by an equilateral triangle inscribed in a circle, by three equal circles interlocking, sometimes with their centers joined and forming a triangle. Other representations of the Godhead are not to be recommended. The Old Testament types of Christ are used very generally, especially the figures of Isaac and of Melchizedek.

Symbols and types of a general nature are the anchor, signifying hope and firm reliance upon God; the star (Num. 24, 17); the sun (Mal. 4, 2) and the sunflower; a ship, as a type of the Church, sailing over the stormy seas of this world toward the eternal harbor; chalice and paten, to represent the Eucharist; a font, to remind of Baptism; the instruments used for torturing Christ, the spear, the nails, the crown of thorns; the armor of the Christians (Eph. 6); the open Bible, representing the Gospel; two tables, representing the Law; the flaming torch; the cross with the crown, and many others.

The symbols of the four evangelists are especially interesting, since they are based upon Ezek. 1 compared with Rev. 4. The four cherubs are distinguished as the man-cherub, the lion-cherub, the ox or calf-cherub, and the eagle-cherub. The first cherub was assigned to Matthew, since he places the emphasis upon the human descent of Christ. The second cherub was assigned to Mark, since he emphasizes the victorious power of Christ, by which He conquered sin and death. The third cherub was assigned to Luke, since he pictures the sacrificial act of Christ in giving His own body for the sins of the world. The fourth cherub was assigned to John, since he emphasizes the divine origin of Christ and His return to God. These symbols are usually arranged so that they form a cross, the lion on the left, the ox on the right, the man above, and the eagle below; or they form a rectangle, with the man and the eagle above, and the lion and the ox below, from left to right. The symbols must always be placed in connection with some symbol of the Godhead or, preferably, of Christ, the monograms making a very effective center for a group.

It will undoubtedly prove of great value if the parables of Christ and incidents from His ministry were employed oftener. The Nativity might be shown in the figure of the Christ-child, the Passion in the Ecce homo, the Resurrection in the figure of the Victorious Christ. The feeding of the multitude, the parable of the sower and the seed, of the draw-net cast into the sea, of the vineyard, and many others suggest symbols and figures which could very well be carried out in a conventional manner, both in the fresco-work of a church and in the embroidery of some of the paraments. Whatever figures are chosen, however, must either be intelligible or be made intelligible to the people, so that they may appreciate and enjoy their house of worship all the more. If other denominations find it useful to have even special descriptions of their churches and all the decorative features printed, the Lutherans should at least take time to study the beautiful appointments which are their heritage, and not suffocate any evidence of awakening understanding by a lack of interest.

CHAPTER 8.

The Parish House.

In the first centuries after the formal recognition of the Christian Church, the house of worship was not the only edifice which the congregation erected. It was merely the most prominent of a group which included the baptistery, chapels, a tower, and often hospices, hospitals, schools, baths, and the dwellings of the clergy.[194] In our days, many of these buildings are no longer erected in such close proximity to the churches, although many of them are still controlled, directly or indirectly, by individual church bodies. However, the clergyman's dwelling and the parish house are found also in America and deserve at least a brief mention, in order to round out the present discussion.

It is very unfortunate that the parish house, in many cases, shows no evidence of being set apart by the congregation for the direct or indirect service of the Lord. And yet, it is not intended for, and should not be looked upon, as a mere club house. The affairs that are carried on in its rooms are such as pertain to the work of the congregation; they are under its control and guided by the Word of God. It would be eminently fitting, therefore, if this fact were in some way indicated in the architecture and arrangement of the building. It would not be necessary to carry out an elaborate scheme. But if we remember that the guild-halls, the hôtels de ville, and many other public and semi-public buildings of southern Germany, northern France, and Belgium, were erected in the Romanesque and Gothic style, and that the Perpendicular and Tudor Gothic of England has its particular branch in the scholastic, academic, or collegiate style, it will be apparent that the difficulties of designing are not so great as might seem at first glance. The trouble is that too many congregations build in an entirely haphazard manner, without a definite plan. The fact that the church and the adjoining parish house belong together, and that the latter also serves the congregation, may well be expressed in the style of the building. There are a few fine examples in America to-day. And the laudable custom, which dates back to the time of the great abbey schools, of having the parish house connected with the church by means of a covered corridor or cloister is one that can be recommended most heartily. It is the same idea which was followed on a large scale in the missions of southern California, thus rendering the grouping of buildings a fine expression of the Christian community spirit.

It will hardly be necessary to discuss at any length the useful-

194) Lowrie, *Monuments of the Early Church*, 182—184.

ness of such a building and the services it may render the congregation in various ways. It will include rooms for the parish school, which, if possible, should not be a mere Saturday or Sunday or afternoon school. If it contains the rooms for the parish school, these must be arranged and equipped according to all the requirements of sound pedagogy and all the rules of hygiene. Dresslar's "American Schoolhouses," Bruce's series of Books on School Architecture, and other modern books will provide all the necessary information on this subject. The Sunday-school, if possible, and especially when it is a graded school, should not be housed in the basement of the church. The "Akron Plan" has been much recommended, according to which the Sunday-school auditorium is built semi-circular in form, with an added width equal to one-fourth the radius. The separate classrooms are provided for by means of alcoves surrounding the main auditorium. The latter receives light from clerestory windows. It would seem far more appropriate to have separate rooms for each department of the Sunday-school. The common meeting place of the children should be the church, where they should gather with the congregation for regular services. Where this is found impossible, the children might meet for opening exercises in the large hall of the parish house, and then proceed to their classrooms for the lessons. If Sunday-schools are a necessary evil, let them at least make the most of the very limited time, and let the school be managed and conducted like a real school, with a definite object and high ideals.

In most cases, the room for confirmands or catechumens will also be located in the parish house. In large classes, some of the regular school equipment is needed at that time. The ladies' parlors, work-room, and kitchen will also find their place in the parish house. A separate entrance should be provided, in order that any class in session may not be disturbed by the opening and closing of doors, etc. Whether there is a special men's club or not, one or two rooms may be set aside for their use, since there are many committee meetings which call for a certain amount of privacy. The choir should also have a meeting room, though the rehearsals may often take place in the hall or in the church. A church library may be combined with the room for the associations of the young people. If there are any other organizations in the congregation, it will be found possible to provide a meeting place for them also, since, in many cases, efficiency demands that all the rooms be in use a large part of the time. One room, however, ought to be provided and furnished for one special purpose, if the congregation will be found willing, and that is a nursery. Many mothers find it impossible to attend divine services with any degree of regularity, because they have small babies and have no one at home to take care of them. If the congregation would provide a nursery and engage a nurse for Sunday mornings, such mothers would have an opportunity to come to services regularly. It is here that deaconesses would find a most interesting branch of their work.

The need of a hall has been emphasized above. It would serve as a meeting place for the voters of the congregation or of any large organization. It could also be equipped with platform, stereopticon, curtain, etc., for lectures and entertainments. The building laws of the city or state will provide for the proper number of exits, fire escapes, etc.

If the parish house is thus equipped, it may be a feature of great moment in the life and work of the congregation, in order that our beloved Lutheran Church, in church, school, and general parish work, may be a power for good in every community, city, and state, to the glory of God and the temporal and eternal welfare of many souls.

BOOK II.

A HANDBOOK

OF

LITURGICS, HYMNOLOGY, AND HEORTOLOGY,

ESPECIALLY FROM THE STANDPOINT

OF THE

AMERICAN LUTHERAN CHURCH.

INTRODUCTION.

"The emancipation which the religion of Jesus Christ has brought to the spiritual life of man embraces the freedom from fixed forms of worship. The ceremonial statutes in Exodus, Leviticus, and Numbers, which were laid down for the Church of the Old Covenant, have no counterpart in the New Testament. The Church of the New Dispensation has no divinely prescribed liturgy and *agenda*. Still, the New Testament abounds in admonitions to the followers of Christ to engage in private and public individual and joint worship of God. 'The true worshipers shall worship the Father in spirit and in truth; for the Father seeketh such to worship Him' (John 4, 23), — this saying of Christ is the only regulation which the Author and Finisher of the faith that saves men has considered it necessary to human acts of worship offered to the true God. This regulation is comprehensive, but it relates to the inward motive and quality of the worshiper rather than to the external expression and features of his worship. Christ has taught men that God esteems the doer more than the deed, the devout heart more than an act of homage, which even a hypocrite may offer whose heart is far from the Lord and whose worship, accordingly, is vain and valueless. When men draw near to God with a true heart, in full assurance of faith, having their hearts sprinkled from an evil conscience, and their bodies washed with pure water (Heb. 10, 19—25), He condescends to join them in their public assemblies, and hallows by His presence, every form of worship which the character of the day and season suggests to their faith. His presence is conditioned on one thing only, viz., that they must meet in His name (Matt. 18, 20).

"Evangelical freedom from the old ceremonialism does not mean license or extreme individualism. There may be, especially in the joint public worship of Christians, things that are unbecoming (See 1 Cor. 11, 14; Col. 2, 16 ff.). The apostolic warning: 'Let all things be done decently and in order' (1 Cor. 14, 40), was uttered with reference to forms of public worship. In a similar connection the same apostle has declared: 'All things are lawful to me, but all things are not expedient; all things are lawful for me, but all things edify not' (1 Cor. 10, 23), and has urged the members of the church to 'follow after things wherewith one may edify another' (Rom. 14, 19)."

These paragraphs from the new "Liturgy and Agenda" (St. Louis, 1917) may fitly serve to give the reason for any extended liturgical discussion. It is gratifying in itself, of course, that a new interest in liturgics is becoming increasingly manifest in the Lutheran Church of America. But if the interest is confined to a few students and synodical committees whose starting-point may have been archeology or music or even the liturgical drama, one can expect neither intelligent cooperation nor reasonable application of liturgical knowledge, even with the best of apparatus. The position of a great many ministers in our day is very much like that of a philologist who, for the first time since his undergraduate days, is told to enter a well-equipped laboratory of physics, but not for the purpose of studying, but of teaching. In the words of the modern undergraduate, who is often more terse and epigrammatic than polished: It can't be done. To open the flood-gates of beautiful and historically correct liturgical forms and acts upon an unsuspecting and untrained multitude may result in a disappointing and even disastrous inundation instead of the beneficial irrigation which was proposed. It is necessary, nay, it is essential that the clergy as well as the laity receive the information and training which will enable all to appreciate properly and to use correctly the forms of service which are in use in the Lutheran Church. For we say it, not without a certain amount of pride and gratitude to the Giver of all good gifts, that our liturgy is the beautiful and pure heritage of the ages. And it is edifying in the best sense of the term. It gives proper attention to the sacramental as well as to the sacrificial side of worship, thus offering a true medium to awaken and foster devotion. And it is thoroughly doctrinal, it places the proper emphasis upon the great central doctrine of Christianity, of justification of the poor sinner by faith, through the merits of Jesus Christ the Savior.

In order, then, that the glorious heritage of the entire Christian era, which we have in the liturgy of our Church, may not suffer for want of proper appreciation or understanding, but that the average intelligent person may feel at home wherever its beautiful acts are in use, a short but comprehensive treatise on liturgics is here offered.

The scope of the discussion is indicated by the word liturgy itself and its outline by the order of worship and the sacred acts followed in the usual Church Book and Agenda. The etymology of the word liturgy has been investigated most carefully by Suicer,[195] Cremer,[196] and others. Luther, according to these scholars, was altogether right, when he maintained, over against the claims of the

---

195) *Thesaurus ecclesiasticus.*
196) *Biblisch-theologisches Woerterbuch.*

Roman Catholics that liturgy meant a sacrifice, the derivation from the public ministry in the Greek cities: "But we say that the word in no way means a sacrifice, but the administration of every office or service, whether it be secular or spiritual." [197) There is also an excellent discussion of the etymology of *leitourgia* in the Apologia Confessionis, Art. XXIV, De Missa, "De vocabulis missae." [198) In the ancient Athenian state the functions of *leitourgia* were principally those of publicum officium reipublicae praestare, and these functions often had a religious aspect in connection with the public spectacles (λεῖτος = λήϊος = δημόσιος; ΕΡΓΩ = ἐργάζομαι). For this reason, the verb *leitourgein* and the nouns *leitourgia* and *leitourgos* were used by the LXX to express the Hebrew Levitical terms *sheret, abad, abodah,* and *moshatet,* respectively (Ex. 29, 30; 30, 20; Num. 4, 37; Joel 1, 9. 13; Ezek. 45, 5; 46, 24). This use of the terms was familiar to the New Testament writers, and they employed them frequently, especially with reference to the temple service (Luke 1, 23; Heb. 9, 21; 10, 11; 8, 2. 6; Acts 13, 2), but also to denote any ministering which served spiritual needs (Phil. 2, 25. 30; Rom. 15, 16. 27) directly or indirectly. The Church Fathers made it a technical term to describe the special ministrations of the Christian cultus, embracing divine services and all sacred acts. Thus Clemens Romanus says that the Master "commanded us to celebrate sacrifices and services" *(prosphoras kai leitourgias),* and speaks of the "proper ministrations of the High Priest" *(idiai leitourgiai).* I Epistle to Corinthians, Chapter XL. The liturgy, then, properly speaking, is the sum total of all the fixed parts of public Christian worship and sacred acts.[199) The meaning of the word is often, however, restricted to the designation of a particular order of service, especially to the order of the communion service, as found in certain ancient rituals. The science of liturgics, therefore, deals with the established acts and orders of divine service in the Church, so far as they are the acts of the whole body, and, with the exception of the sermon, are performed in the name of the whole body. It is necessary that every pastor be a good liturgist and conduct the service, apply the liturgy, properly. And while not essential, it is highly desirable that the pastor be also a liturgiologist, in a measure at least conversant with the subject of liturgics as a science.

The scope of Lutheran liturgics and its task is determined by the sphere and object of the services for whose ministrations it is intended. The liturgy should express the consensus of the orthodox Church in all ages and places. In the prayers, Psalms, hymns, and

---

197) *Zwei Abhandlungen von der Liturgie,* 16, 1009.
198) Mueller, 266, §§ 78—87.
199) Fuerbringer, *Liturgik,* 1; Horn, *Outlines of Liturgics,* 8.

spiritual songs, we are united with the true believers of all times, for they are the visible and audible expression of the faith of the invisible Church. Since all the forms of Christian services make extensive use of Scriptural passages and expressions, their continual use will be conducive to the spread of the faith and its maintenance in the midst of adverse conditions, such as heretical teaching. It is necessary, also, that the liturgy express the doctrinal position of the church body employing it, although this use is limited, to some extent, by the considerations stated above. As a matter of fact, almost all liturgies of antiquity, and most of the modern orders, contain some expressions which will reveal, upon closer investigation, the viewpoint of the body in question with regard to some doctrine. The Monophysite churches of the far East as well as the Reformed churches of these latter days present evidence of their belief in the wording of their prayers. And the Lutheran liturgy will very properly emphasize the fundamental doctrines of Christianity, as they have been brought forth out of the darkness of the Papal errors. The liturgy should finally express, not individual devotion and worship, but the form of worship of the whole congregation, and preferably of the whole church body with which the congregation is united. In the liturgical part of the service, it is not the man whose individuality shall find expression, but the liturgist who is expressing a common faith, by reason of a common call, in a common, fixed form.

With these facts in mind, the task of a student of liturgics is readily defined. With a foundation of the historical development of the form of service he will make a careful study of the various parts of worship in their sequence and interrelation, trying every section by Holy Scripture and by history, and correct or amend such forms as are inconsistent with these principles and out of harmony with the doctrinal position of the Lutheran Church. He may at the same time become sufficiently interested to make a detailed study of various ancient liturgies or periods in the development of any individual order, or of some related subject, such as church architecture and ecclesiastical art, church music, heraldics, numismatics, sphragistics, and others.

It is manifestly impossible, within the bounds of a handbook, to offer more than a summary of liturgics, but in order that it may serve its purpose, the following outline will be followed. In the first part, a history of the liturgy will be given, showing the spread and the development of the order of services in the several countries. An outline of hymnology will next be offered, including the history of Christian church poetry from ancient times. A full part will be devoted to heortology, for a better understanding of the church year. Since the handbook is to serve principally the Lutheran Church in

America, a full section will be given over to the Lutheran services, and sacred forms. The great danger in presenting these subjects will lie in the tendency toward not maintaining a proper balance, since the many by-paths that interest the investigator offer alluring attractions, whose detailed descriptions may interrupt the sequence of thought. If a kind indulgence will overlook an occasional lapse from the path of consecutive narrative and condone a Lutheran's excusable pride in the treasures of his church, the study of the dissertation presented here may be as great a pleasure to the reader as it was a delight to the writer.

PART I.

History of the Liturgy.

CHAPTER 1.

The Old Testament Cultus.

There are several reasons why the study of the Old Testament cultus has a compelling interest for the student of liturgics. It is not merely the historical and archeological side of the question which beckons him on, which also, as in the case of Baehr *(Symbolik des mosaischen Kultus)* leads him on to an examination of heathen religious forms and customs, with conjectures and hypotheses as to their possible influence upon the cultus of the Jews. Of much greater interest is the study of the Old Testament cultus on account of the significance of its types from the standpoint of the fulfilment in the New Dispensation. To compare the account of the Old Testament ordinances with the fulfilment of the types as described in the Epistle to the Hebrews or in certain parts of the letters of St. Paul, is intensely interesting and remarkably illuminating. And, in addition to this, the present chapter will serve to show to what extent we may expect to find the New Testament church indebted to the Hebrew temple and synagog for liturgical expressions, forms, and customs.

The temple services, especially after the first temple had been completed, and also when the beautiful edifice of Herod had been erected, were elaborate and impressive. If one compares the account of the Talmud with the Old Testament injunctions and then reads the description of Edersheim, Kliefoth, and other scholars, a complete picture may be gained. When the first rosy streaks of dawn over the eastern hills heralded the breaking of the day, everything was made ready for the morning sacrifice. The priests on duty assembled in the Court of the Polished Stones, and it was determined by lot who was to officiate at the altar of incense and to whom the ministrations at the altar of burnt offerings were assigned. Blasts of the silver trumpets announced the opening of the temple gates. The officiating priests were attired in the gorgeous vestments of their office and hurried to their stations. The Levites also donned their ministerial garments and prepared to take part in the liturgy. Their simple white linen overdress was replaced, under Agrippa II, by the full priestly garments. The priests who were to cleanse the altar and prepare it for the sacrifices of the day, were told off first, then those who were to offer the sacrifices and officiate at the cleansing of the candlestick and the altar of incense. Then came the section of those

whose duty it was to burn incense in the Holy Place, an honor most
highly esteemed and most jealously sought and guarded. The last to
be chosen were the priests that officiated at the concluding rites, in
the offering of the sacrifices. Now, according to the account of
Edersheim, the morning prayer was offered, Deut. 26, 15; Neh. 11,
17. It had undoubtedly, at the time of the third temple, assumed a
definite liturgical form, including thanksgiving and eulogy, supplication, petition, and intercession, and closing with a great doxology.
By this time the first two divisions of priests had performed their
ministrations and, as the morning light "advanced as far as Hebron,"
the morning sacrifice was made, to which the blasts from the silver
trumpets had invited the people. The lamb was slain, and its blood
was sprinkled against the altar according to the prescribed ritual.
It was then cut up according to the rules, and the six priests who had
charge of this work for the day, made the sacrifice on the great altar.
Before the third division of priests went out to perform the rites
allotted to them, a prayer of preparation was offered and the ten
commandments and the *shema* repeated by the assembly. The incensing priest and his assistants then proceeded to their posts, and
after due preparation and the withdrawal of the helpers, the burning
of the incense took place amid the deep silence of the assembled multitudes, who prayed in the outer courts during the hour of incense.
After the work of the fourth lot had also been performed, the incensing priest or the high priest himself spoke the Aaronic blessing,
Num. 6, 24—26.

   This concluded the first part of the daily services. The next act
was the presenting of the high priest's daily meat-offering, followed
by the appropriate drink-offering. Then came the temple music,
which was undoubtedly the most impressive part of the liturgy. To
hear the well-trained voices of the Levites' chorus chant the three
sections of the Psalm of the day, accompanied by simple, but effective
orchestral music, a loud blast from the silver trumpets indicating the
division of the chant, must have been a memorable experience. On
the first day of the week Psalm 24 was chanted, on the second, Psalm
48, on the third, Psalm 82, on the fourth, Psalm 94, and the fifth,
Psalm 81, on the sixth, Psalm 93, and on the Sabbath, Psalm 92.
This closed the morning service. There were now more than four
hours left for the sacrifices and offerings which private Israelites might
bring. Often the bringing of such individual sacrifices continued
till near the time of the evening sacrifice.[200]

   The time for the evening sacrifice was from two and one-half to
three and one-half hours after high noon, excepting on the eve of the

   200) Cp. Edersheim, *The Temple*, Chapter VIII.

Passover, when it was offered an hour earlier. The order of services at the evening sacrifice resembled in all respects that of the morning, but only the incensing priest was determined by lot, who performed his work after the last pieces of sacrifices had been laid on the fire of the altar. In the evening, the Aaronic blessing was usually omitted.

On the Sabbath, the services took on a still more impressive character. A much larger multitude might be expected for the sacred assembly, Lev. 23, 3, and the ceremony of the weekly renewal of the show-bread had to be performed. On this day, also, two lambs were offered in addition to the usual sacrifices, Num. 28, 9, 10.

The daily sacrifices in the temple, the only place where the offering of sacrifices was permitted, were of various kinds. Edersheim makes the following classification. He distinguishes between sacrifices *in* communion with God, which include burnt and peace offerings, and offerings *for* communion with God, which come under the heading of sin and trespass offerings. He names the unbloody sacrifices, the meat and drink offering, the first sheaf at Passover, the two loaves at Pentecost, the show-bread. All others are included in the category of bloody offerings: oxen, sheep, goats, turtle-doves, and young pigeons. He finally characterizes as holy offerings certain meat offerings, all burnt, sin, and trespass sacrifices.[201])

The burnt offering (Lev. 1, 3—17; 6, 8—11; 7, 8; 9, 7; Num. 15, 1—12; 28, 2—13. 19—31; Ex. 29, 38—42) was the regular morning and evening sacrifice in the temple, made in the name of and for the entire congregation. It was also made by individuals, and in either case symbolized the entire surrender of the one who brought the offering, "with shedding of blood." The offering had to be a male without blemish, either a bullock from the cattle, or a sheep or goat from the herd, or turtle-doves or young pigeons of the fowls. The animal had to be led to the door of the tabernacle, later to the Holy Place. There the petitioner put his hand on the head of the offering to signify the transfer of sin and guilt. It was then accepted by the officiating priest and killed as an atonement. The blood was either sprinkled or poured out against the side of the altar. After the removal of the skin, the animal was divided according to the prescribed rules. The sinews of the thigh, the stomach, the entrails, etc., were removed. And then the pieces were burned, after they had been duly salted.

This bloody sacrifice had to be accompanied by the unbloody sacrifice of a *minchah,* Lev. 2, fine flour, upon which oil was poured, and frankincense added. After the priest had taken out his handful of the offering, the flour was burned as a sweet savor to the Lord.

---

201) *The Temple*, Chapter V.

The same kind of unbloody sacrifice was made at the time of all free-will offerings, except the praise-offering, and when vows were dedicated to the Lord. But the amount of flour, oil, and incense varied with the importance of the occasion and the size of the animal under consideration.

The sin-offering (Lev. 4, 1—35; 6, 12—30; Num. 5, 22—31) was made for sins committed through ignorance, including transgressions for want of knowledge, or unintentional, or out of weakness, or without realization of guilt. It was also offered in case of defilements of the body which are the result of the sinful condition of man. A priest was commanded to offer a young bullock, as also the whole congregation, a ruler brought a kid of the goats, a male without blemish, while the individual member of the congregation was ordered to bring a kid of the goats or a lamb, a female without blemish, two turtle-doves or two young pigeons. It was a sin-offering which was made by the high priest on the yearly Day of Atonement. The sacrifice had to be brought and killed in the same way as that of a burnt offering, but the emphasis was placed upon the method of dealing with the blood. If the offering was for a priest or for the whole congregation, the blood was sprinkled seven times before the Lord, before the veil of the sanctuary. Of the remainder, some was put upon the horns of the altar and the rest poured at the bottom of the altar of burnt offering. When the offender was a ruler or a layman, only the last-named rites were performed. In every case, the sin-offering was made for the purpose of an atonement for the sins which had been committed, that they might be forgiven. After the sprinkling of blood, all the fat in the abdomen, both connective tissue and fatty covering, the two kidneys, and the caul of the liver were burned upon the altar of burnt offering. The other parts of the animal were taken to a designated place outside of the camp or city and burned (Lev. 4, 11. 12. 21; 6, 30; 6, 27). There was no unbloody sacrifice connected with the sin-offering (Heb. 9, 22).

The trespass-offering (Lev. 6, 1—7; 7, 1—7; 5, 16. 18) was akin to the sin-offering, but implied greater guilt, since the offender was conscious of his transgression and committed the wrong in spite of better knowledge. This sacrifice was always a male animal, generally a ram without blemish, out of the flock. It is probable that the entire chapter Lev. 5 concerns an offering of this kind, and that the degree of the transgression was determined by the priests, who thus controlled the sin- and trespass-offerings. In some cases it may have been difficult to establish, with reasonable exactness, whether there was a doubtful or a certain trespass, and the confession of guilt was taken as evidence (Lev. 5, 15; 6, 2; 19, 20; 14, 12; Num. 6, 12). The treatment of the sacrifice in the first part of the rite was like that of

the other offerings, but the flesh was not burned, since the Lord had
commanded the priests to eat it in the Holy Place.

The peace-offerings (Lev. 3; 7, 11—21. 29—34; 22, 21—33) were
of three kinds, and all of them symbolized a happy fellowship with
the covenant God, and had the purpose of establishing the proper
relation, that of sons and daughters, toward a loving Father, between
the people and the Lord. The offering might be either male or female, a lamb or a goat. This bloody offering was made in the same
way as the sin-offering and the flesh eaten the same day it was offered. The sacrifices of thanksgiving (Lev. 7, 11—15; Ps. 107, 22;
116, 17) were made in praise of the goodness of the Lord (Lev. 9,
18—21; Deut. 27, 7; Josh. 8, 31; 1 Sam. 24, 5). These sacrifices were
accompanied by a *minchah* of unleavened cakes mingled with oil,
and unleavened wafers anointed with oil, and cakes mingled with oil,
of fine flour, fried (Lev. 2, 4—9; 1 Chron. 23, 29). The sacrifices of
vows were made whenever a person had vowed to give the Lord a
special gift or service and the supplication had been granted (Gen.
28, 20; Num. 21, 2; Judg. 11, 30; 1 Sam. 1, 11; 2 Sam. 15, 7. 8). The
purpose of the sacrifice therefore was to render praise and thanks to
the Lord for His goodness (Num. 6, 1—21; 1 Sam. 1, 21. 24; Ps. 22,
26; 56, 13). The sacrifice of voluntary offerings (Lev. 7, 11. 12. 16;
22, 18. 23), as its name implies, was made without any special direct
provocation or reason, whenever the devotion of the Israelite felt the
desire to enter into a closer and more harmonious relation with the
Lord (Judg. 20, 26; 21, 4; 1 Sam. 13, 9).

The offerings here named were the usual offerings, which concerned the entire people in their every-day relation toward God.
There were many other sacrifices for special classes of people and
special occasions of various kinds, all of which were governed by individual ordinances.[202] We shall discuss the rites and sacrifices of
the great Jewish festivals in a special chapter below.

The temple services were practically the only public services for
many centuries. But after the Jews returned from their exile, synagogs were gradually introduced into the cities of Palestine to supplement private worship in the homes. The members of a local congregation would convene in the synagog on the Sabbath to recite certain
prayers, also by means of responsive reading, to hear portions of the
Old Testament Scriptures, and to listen to a discourse upon the Law
by one or more of their rabbis or elders. Public worship in the synagog was opened with the *Shema* (Deut. 6, 4—9; 9, 13—21; Num. 15,
37—41). It was preceded in the morning and evening by two bene-

---

202) Cp. Edersheim, *The Temple*, Chap. V, VI, VIII; Baehr, *Symbolik
des mosaischen Kultus*, II, 189—453; Kliefoth, *Die urspruengliche Gottesdienstordnung*, I, 28—122.

dictions, and succeeded in the morning by one, and in the evening by two benedictions. The prayers before and after the *Shema* are contained in the *Mishnah,* and have remained practically unchanged to the present day. Then followed the prayers before the "ark" or scroll-chest at the end of the auditorium. They consisted of eighteen eulogies or benedictions, called *Tephillah.* The first three and the last three of these eulogies are very ancient and may well be said to have been in use in the time of the Lord. The prayers were spoken aloud by one man selected for the occasion, and the congregation responded with Amen. The liturgical part of the service was concluded with the Aaronic benediction, spoken by the descendants of Aaron, or by the leader of the devotions. After this followed the reading of the Law. Seven persons were called upon to read, and the lectionaries were arranged so that the Pentateuch would be read twice in seven years. On week-days, Mondays and Thursdays, only three persons were called upon to read the Law. After the Law came the reading of the Prophets. At the time of Christ, all the reading was accompanied by a translation into Aramaic by a *meturgeman* or interpreter.

After the reading of the Prophets came the sermon or address. When a very learned rabbi gave a theological discussion, it was not spoken to the people directly, but a speaker gave a popular transcription of the discussion transmitted to him. The more popular sermon of the local elder or rabbi was termed a *meamar,* a speech or talk, based, as a rule, upon a Scripture passage (Luke 4, 17). After the sermon, the services were closed. In the first centuries of the Christian era, some additions to the liturgical parts of the services were made, notably by the reading or chanting of Psalms and by choir music.[203] The order of services here given is also that described by Gwynne, who summarizes as follows: 1) Two prayers, 2) *Shema* (Deut. 6, 4—9; 11, 13—21; Num. 15, 37—41), 3) Prayer, 4) Eulogies and Benedictions (Lifting up of hands and Num. 6, 23—26), 5) Last Eulogy, 6) Reading of Law and Prophets, 7) Sermon, 8) Short Prayer.[204] This order is also given by Mercer,[205] who adds as a summary of the temple service 1) The daily offering of a sacrifice with meal and wine, 2) Daily offering of incense, 3) Special Psalms, 4) Special services on feast days.

Opinions differ as to the amount of influence which must be conceded to the Jewish liturgy in the development of the Christian order of worship. Many writers, especially those of the Anglican

203) Cp. Edersheim, *In the Days of Christ,* Chapter XVII; Dembitz, *Jewish Services in Synagog and Home,* Book II, Chapter I.
204) *Primitive Worship and the Prayer Book,* Chapter II.
205) *The Ethiopic Liturgy,* 29.

Church, would base the *Missa catechumenorum* directly upon the synagog service, and the *Missa fidelium* directly upon the temple service. It seems safer, with Cabrol [206]) and Kliefoth [207]) to assume influence from both, but in such a way that the probability of copying is precluded at the very outset. A careful examination of the early liturgies will show that the injunctions contained in the writings of the apostles exercised a greater influence in the molding of the primitive liturgies than any other factor. Whether the selection of an order of worship which reminds one strongly of that of the synagog was intentional or not, will always remain a mooted question. And as for the supposition as though the Eucharistic service were based upon the temple worship, it can hardly be said to have gained credence before the third century, when the more elaborate priestly garments were generally introduced and the hierarchical distinctions were being urged as existing by divine right. The history of the primitive liturgies substantiates this most abundantly, if one will but strip them of the excrescences and accretions, and attempt to establish the liturgy as it existed in the time of the apostles and their disciples.

CHAPTER 2.

The Liturgy of the Early Christian Church.

When our Lord instituted the Lord's Supper in the upper room of the house at Jerusalem where He ate the Passover lamb with His disciples (Mark 14, 15; Luke 22, 12), He undoubtedly followed the order which was observed by all Jews upon this solemn occasion, with the recital of the Hallel Psalms in the intervals (Ps. 113—118). But His command: "This do," referred to the Eucharist only and to the celebration according to His institution. He fixed no form of ceremonial outside of the words of institution. Even the giving of thanks over the elements was not made obligatory by His order and institution. In much the same way, Christ permitted a very wide latitude in other services. He commanded that preaching should be done, but fixed neither the day, nor the place, nor the hour, nor the form. He commanded that all nations should be discipled by Baptism, but left only the form: "In the name of the Father, and of the Son, and of the Holy Ghost."

This does not imply, of course, that the elements of Christian worship were a matter of entire indifference to Him. In His various discourses, He named a number of parts or elements of worship which

---

206) *Monumenta ecclesiae liturgica*, 1, xix.
207) *Die urspruengliche Gottesdienstordnung*, I, 174. 175.

were well-pleasing to Him: 1) Assembly in His name, Matt. 18, 20;
2) Prayer in His name, John 16, 23. 24; 3) Common prayer, Matt.
18, 19; 4) A form of prayer, Matt. 6, 9—13; 5) The Holy Supper was
instituted and its observance commanded, Matt. 26; 6) The office
of the ministry of teaching the Gospel and administering the Sacraments was established, Matt. 28, 18; 18, 18; Luke 24, 47. 48; John
15, 27; 20, 21—23; 7) The use of the Holy Scriptures was enjoined,
John 5, 39; 8, 31; Luke 16, 31; Matt. 4, 4—10.[208]) In no way did the
Lord reestablish the ceremonial law of the Old Testament nor burden
the believers with new injunctions concerning sacrifices, feast days,
forms of worship, or any liturgy. He expresses this very plainly in
His conversation with the Samaritan woman, when He makes the
statement: "The hour cometh, when ye shall neither in this mountain, nor yet at Jerusalem, worship the Father. . . The hour cometh,
and now is, when the true worshipers shall worship the Father in
spirit and in truth," John 4, 21. 23. The apostles followed in the
footsteps of their great Master and did not attempt to put a yoke
upon the neck of the disciples. St. Paul calls the regulations of the
ceremonial law "weak and beggarly elements, whereunto ye desire
again to be in bondage," Gal. 4, 9. He declares that the believers of
the New Testament are no longer subject to ordinances concerning
outward forms of liturgy, Col. 2, 16—20.

And yet, neither St. Paul nor any other disciple was in favor of
a disorderly worship, still less did they favor iconoclastic proceedings
which were not preceded by careful instruction, Acts 15 and 16;
1 Cor. 10—14. He states the position of the New Testament church
very clearly, when he says: "Let all things be done unto edifying. . .
God is not the author of confusion, but of peace. . . Let all things be
done decently and in order," 1 Cor. 14, 26. 33. 40. It was in accordance with this principle that the apostles had the congregations establish orders of worship, and it is very probable that they themselves
introduced liturgies, at least in some of the cities where they labored.
There are certain indications of this even in the writings of the New
Testament. We are told that the first Christians in Jerusalem "continued steadfastly in the apostles' doctrine and fellowship, and in
breaking of bread, and in prayers," Acts 2, 42. Their preaching
services in the early days were held in the temple, Acts 5, 12, but the
celebration of the Eucharist took place in the midst of the house
congregations, v. 46. There is no need for assuming, upon the assertion of some liberal critics, that the "breaking of bread" (klasis tou
artou) might not have been the Holy Supper.[209]) Scholars like Klie-

208) Horn, *Outlines of Liturgics*, 91. 92.
209) Cp. *Memoirs*, VI; 4.

foth, Graebner, and recently Gwynne have shown conclusively that the ancient interpretation is perfectly safe (Cf. Acts 20, 7. 11; 1 Cor. 10, 16). The hours of prayer were observed at least by the Jewish Christians, Acts 3, 1; 10, 3. 9. 30; 16, 25; 22, 17. St. Paul speaks of psalms, and hymns, and spiritual songs in a perfectly matter-of-fact way, indicating that they were well-known to the disciples at his time, Eph. 5, 19; Col. 3, 16. It was not long before certain rules were drawn up for the celebration of the Holy Supper, 1 Cor. 11—14. The reading of the apostles' letters was introduced as a regular part of the liturgy, 1 Thess. 5, 27; Col. 4, 16; 2 Pet. 3, 15. 16. The "kiss of peace," which is mentioned several times in the New Testament, 1 Thess. 5, 26; 1 Cor. 16, 20; 2 Cor. 13, 12; 1 Pet. 5, 14, was also made a part of the liturgical service. The practise of bringing gifts for the poor, 1 Cor. 16, 1. 2; 2 Cor. 8 and 9, became an established custom. Even in the time of Paul, the "oblation of gifts," of bread and wine, was in existence, since he is called upon to regulate the custom and the feast connected with it, 1 Cor. 11, 20. 21.[210]

Nor is this all. There is plain evidence in Scriptures that liturgical forms were by no means unknown, and the fact that many of the quotations of this nature cannot be traced to Old Testament sources or synagog prayers makes it all the more likely that fixed prayers, doxologies, eulogies, etc., were incorporated into the liturgy at a very early date. Some of the most notable instances of liturgical quotations are the following: 1 Cor. 15, 45. 55—57; Eph. 5, 14; 1 Tim. 1, 15; 3, 1; 4, 8. 9; 2 Tim. 2, 11—13. 19; Titus 3, 5—8.[211] The most complete list of such quotations is that given by Cabrol.[212] The most interesting passage of this group is 1 Cor. 2, 9, of which Lightfoot and Neale have thought that it certainly was of apostolic origin, since the reference Is. 64, 3 is evidently not a source, and the words in the Invocation of the Anaphora in the Post-Sanctus of St. James agree with the passage exactly.[213] Most of the modern scholars reject the idea, though some of them are willing to concede that the nucleus of some of the later prayers may have been of apostolic origin.[214]

If we take all facts together, as we find them in the New Testament writings, we are enabled to form a picture of the services in the time of the apostles. They included in their order reading of

---

210) Mercer, *The Ethiopic Liturgy*, 39; Kliefoth, *Die urspruengliche Gottesdienstordnung*, I, 236. 237.
211) Neale, *Essays on Liturgiology*, XV. Cp. Srawley, *The Early History of the Liturgy*, Chapter I.
212) *Monumenta ecclesiae liturgica*, Vol. I.
213) *Ante-Nicene Christian Library*, XXIV, 30; Brightman, *Liturgies, Eastern and Western*, I, 53.
214) Cp. *International Critical Commentary, sub voce*.

Scriptures (at first of Old Testament, later of apostles' letters), preaching, prayer, singing, Lord's Supper,[215]) or, as Kliefoth puts it, after his long discussion of the various features of apostolic worship: "There was preaching, prayer (also in the form of hymns), and gifts were offered and communion celebrated in connection with a common meal." [216]) It is possible, of course, and may perhaps be said to be probable, that the services were even at that time elaborately arranged, but in the absence of documentary evidence it is better to assume too little than too much.

Toward the end of the first century, when most of the apostles had died or been martyred, their work was carried on by their disciples and then by the so-called apostolic fathers. It was at this time that the liturgy began to assume the form into which it was definitely molded after the beginning of the fourth century. Recent writers on the liturgy, following the example of Harnack, have greatly stressed the distinction between the order of worship in the Jewish-Christian congregations and those composed largely of Gentile Christians. The emphasis has probably been too great. There can be no doubt, of course, that the converted Jews, especially in Jerusalem, continued to observe such Jewish customs as did not clash with the freedom of the Gospel. But the sequence of events in the Book of Acts, culminating in the attack of the fanatical Jews upon Paul (Acts 21— 24) shows conclusively that the difference between the old and the new church became more apparent as time went on. The efforts of Judaizing teachers were opposed with the greatest firmness by Paul and the congregations at Jerusalem and Antioch, both of which were incidentally bi-lingual. It is probable that only the small remnant of the Jerusalem congregation that fled to Pella before the destruction of the capital city retained the Jewish characteristics, all the others yielding to Hellenistic influence almost from the start. There is every reason to believe that the following order of service was general in the last half of the first century. There were daily services with teaching of the Word and prayer, in which all such as wished to become acquainted with the Christian doctrine were made welcome. And there were special services for the celebration of the Eucharist, usually on Sunday evenings, with preaching of the Word, offering of prayer, oblation of gifts, common meal, and the Holy Supper, in which the whole congregation took part, none but members being admitted, 1 Cor. 16, 1. 2; Acts 20, 17; Rev. 1, 10.[217]) Jacobs [218]) gives the order as follows: 1) Psalm; 2) Teaching;

---

215) Richards-Painter, *Christian Worship*, Chapter I; Memoirs, VI: 4.
216) *Op. cit.*, I, 237.   217) Kliefoth, I, 250.
218) Memoirs, VI: 4.

3) Prophecy; 4) Tongues and their Interpretation; — meeting of Lord's Supper: common meal or *agape,* followed by Eucharist.

There is sufficient evidence from the end of the first and the larger part of the second century to afford a very good picture of the form of worship at that time. The earliest testimony is that of Clemens Romanus in his First Epistle to the Corinthians, which probably dates from the year 96 A. D. He writes: "We ought to do in order all things which the Master commanded us to perform at appointed times. He commanded us to celebrate sacrifices and services, and that it should not be thoughtlessly and disorderly, but at fixed times and hours. . . . So then those who offer their oblations at the appointed seasons are acceptable and blessed, for they follow the laws of the Master and do not sin. For to the High Priest his proper ministrations are allotted, and to the priests the proper place has been appointed, and on the Levites their proper services have been imposed. The layman is bound by the ordinances for the laity." [219] While Clement here does not state the order of worship, he plainly indicates that such an order was in general use, and that every member of the congregation should submit to this order. In the course of the same Epistle, Clement has many other passages which bear a pronounced liturgical mark. His prayers, especially, bear evidence of a fixed rite, and have been thought by many scholars to be sections from the liturgy of Rome at the end of the first century (Chap. LIX —LXI). The argument of Clement, briefly stated, is this: The whole congregation, being a congregation of priests, brings the sacrifice of prayers and gifts through its High Priest, Christ. For this purpose she is in need of a ministry, a *leitourgia.* And this ministry is fitly in the hands of the presbyters and deacons, according to the apostolic example. The presbyter led in prayer, but the congregation prayed with him; the congregation offered gifts, and the presbyter spoke prayers of thanksgiving over them, thus recommending them to the blessing of the Lord.[220]

The next witness for the form of service in sub-apostolic times is one to whose testimony a peculiar interest attaches, since he reports entirely from the standpoint of the outsider. It is Gaius Plinius Caecilius Secundus, commonly called Pliny the Younger, who, in his capacity as procurator of the province of Bithynia-Pontus, found it necessary to address some letters concerning the Christians to the Emperor Trajan, which, together with the answers, have been preserved. It appears from these letters, whose date may safely be put at ca. 103 instead of 112, as commonly given, that the Christians

219) Lake, *The Apostolic Fathers,* I, 76. 78, Chapter XL.
220) Kliefoth, I, 271—273.

had the habit of meeting on a certain day before sunrise, to sing a hymn to Christ as God, antiphonally or by some form of alternation; that they met again later in the day for a common meal (quod essent soliti stato die ante lucem convenire carmenque Christo quasi deo dicere secum invicem. . . quibus peractis morem sibi discedendi fuisse, rursusque ad capiendum cibum, promiscuum tamen et innoxium.[221]) An added remark seems to indicate, as Kliefoth shows, that the Christians were ready, at that time, to drop the *agape* as a feature of the celebration of the Eucharist.[222]) It seems, according to this testimony, that the daily meetings of the congregations for the purpose of instruction in the Scriptures had been discontinued. The early service on Sunday morning was evidently a song and praise service, perhaps with the recital of the Ten Commandments or of some form of creed or discipline. The evening service was devoted to the Lord's Supper preceded by the *agape,* which was falling into desuetude at about that time, and probably by a sermon or some form of teaching.

The discovery of the *Didache* or Teaching of the Twelve Apostles by Byrennios in 1875, in the Patriarchal Library of Jerusalem at Constantinople, added another witness to the post-apostolic writings. According to recent investigators, its date may safely be placed between 120 and 160 A. D. This interesting document is devoted largely to the history of the polity and worship of the Church at the beginning of the second century. It designates Wednesday and Friday as days of fasting, and recommends that the Lord's Prayer be said three times a day (Chap. VIII). It names the prayers over the cup and the bread in the Eucharist, the prayer in chapter X being in the nature of a Preface, ending with "Hosanna to the Lord of David." In chapter XIV, the Sunday worship is briefly described: "On the Lord's day of the Lord come together, break bread, and hold the Eucharist, after confessing your transgressions, that your offering may be pure; but let none who has a quarrel with his fellow join in your meeting until they be reconciled, that your sacrifice be not defiled." And in chapter XV a final admonition for the liturgy is given: "But your prayers and alms and all your acts perform as ye find in the Gospel of our Lord." [223]) In this account special note should be taken of the thanksgiving over the cup: "We give thanks to thee, our Father, for the Holy Vine of David thy child, which thou didst make known to us through Jesus thy Child," since this may be a Christianized form of the Jewish benediction over the wine: "Blessed be thou who hast created the fruit of the vine," as Mercer

---

221) *Epistularum,* Ed. Lipsiae 1886, XCVI, 231.
222) I, 278. 279.   223) Lake, *The Apostolic Fathers,* 321—331.

suggests.[224] Whether the other prayers were also derived from, or in any way dependent upon, the Jewish ritual, is not so evident. The following liturgical elements were known to the compiler of the Didache: the prayers over the bread and cup, and the thanksgiving after the reception, which is more in the nature of the present prefaces. "There is evidence also that the author was acquainted with the custom of allowing only the baptized to communicate, and with the use of the liturgical Amen. The direction concerning the prophets, who are to 'give thanks as much as they will,' throws an interesting light upon the nature of prayer-forms, all of which had not yet become stereotyped, but were often extemporaneous." [225]

In the epistles of Ignatius of Antioch, which may be said to date from the time of Trajan, there are only a few references to the liturgy, since he seems to have been interested far more in church government than in forms of service. However, he emphasizes the conception of the Eucharist as the common feast (Philadelphians, Chap. IV) and speaks of the need of receiving it and of making use of prayer (Smyrnaeans, Chap. VII).[226]

Far more satisfactory for our purposes is the report of Justin Martyr, about the middle of the second century, in his First Apology, addressed to Antoninus Pius. He not only gives an account of Baptism (Chap. 61), but also describes the services of the Christians at great length (Chap. 65—67).[227] Justin's object was to obviate the suspicion of secrecy and the charge of unlawful practises. So he draws a parallel between the initiation into the pagan mysteries and the admission to the Christian congregation, placing special emphasis upon the two Sacraments, Baptism and the Eucharist. His argument is substantially this that only such persons as have confessed their faith may be received into the congregation by Baptism and thereby also be admitted to the Holy Supper. It is in this connection that he describes the various parts of the regular Sunday service, as it existed in his days. These parts were: 1) Lessons, "memoirs of the apostles or writings of the prophets"; 2) Sermon by the bishop or president; 3) Common Prayer for all men; 4) Kiss of Peace; 5) Presentation to the president of bread and a cup of wine and water by the deacons; 6) Thanksgiving Prayer of the bishop; 7) Consecration; 8) Intercession for the people; 9) Amen by the people; 10) Administration of bread and wine to members present and conveying of same to those absent by the deacons. At some time during the services

---

224) *Op. cit.*, 40.   225) Mercer, *The Ethiopic Liturgy*, 41. 42.
226) *Apostolic Fathers*, I, 243. 259.
227) St. Louis Ed. 1882, 71—74; Kliefoth, *Die urspruengliche Gottesdienstordnung*, I, 280—283.

there was also a collection of alms for the poor.[228]) Outside of the facts pertaining to the actual order of services, these witnesses present enough material to show 1) that the right of active participation in the service — praying, prophesying, exhorting, speaking with tongues, was gradually delegated to the office-bearers; 2) that the separation of the agape or common meal from the Eucharist was carried out generally; 3) that the former morning and evening services were consolidated into one.[229])

There is one other witness toward the end of the second century that describes the liturgical customs of his time with sufficient accuracy to permit of a reconstruction of his order of service. This is Irenaeus, bishop of Lyons in Gaul (d. 180 A. D.), in his book Adversus haereses. His references show the following parts: 1) An offering of the firstfruits of the creatures, bread and wine, the wine being mixed with the water; 2) A thanksgiving pronounced over them; 3) An invocation of God over the elements, the so-called Epiklesis.[230])

There is one more document, in regard to whose date there is much uncertainty, namely the second book of the Apostolic Constitutions. Some writers assert quite definitely that this book, with the rest of the first seven, is based in its entirety upon the Didascalia written in the fourth century, with sources reaching into the third century. Others believe that the sources extend back to the second century. Since the order of services as given in the second book is so much simpler than the Clementine Liturgy from Hippolytus in the eighth book, we shall give an outline of the order of services, assuming that its chief parts have an antiquity taking them back at least to the end of the third or the beginning of the fourth century. The order was: 1) Reading of Old Testament (Moses, Joshua, Judges, Kings, Chronicles, books written after the captivity, Job, Solomon, Prophets) two lessons, responded to by the people at the close of a Psalm of David, the congregation joining at the conclusion of the verses; 2) Reading of Acts and Epistles of Paul; 3) Reading of Gospels, the people standing; 4) The exhortations or sermons; 5) General prayer; 6) Oblation of the Eucharist; 7) Kiss of peace; 8) Great intercessory prayer; 9) Benediction; 10) Distribution.[231]) We are all the more justified in placing this order at this point, with omission of the rubrics, as even Brightman (p. xviii) places the Didascalia in

---

228) Cp. Mercer, 43; Srawley, *The Early History of the Liturgy*, Chapter II; Horn, *Outline of Liturgics*, 96.

229) Jacobs, *Christian Worship in the Apostolic Age*, Memoirs, VI: 4.

230) Cp. Mercer, *Op. cit.*, 44; Srawley, Chapter II.

231) *Ante-Nicene Library*, XVII, 83—86; Brightman, *Liturgies Eastern and Western*, I, 28—30; Kliefoth, I, 464—473.

the first half of the third century, and since both Tertullian and
Cyprian, commonly placed ahead of this document, present a stage
of development beyond that of the document here presented. It is in
Tertullian (first quarter of the third century) that we first find the
division into *missa catechumenorum* and *missa fidelium.* He speaks
of the Eucharistic service as a mystery and has reference to a fixed
Sanctus in the Proanaphora.[232])   And Cyprian, bishop of Carthage
from 248 to 258 A. D., went even beyond his master.   He represents
the Eucharist as a sacrifice.   The catechumens, the penitents, the
energumens, the lapsi, and even the heathen and infidels took part in
the *missa catechumenorum,* in the service of the Word, but the
Eucharistic service was guarded more jealously than the pagan mysteries and surrounded with the deepest and darkest veil of secrecy.
Cyprian also placed so much stress upon the General Church Prayer
that he really acknowledges only this as having full value.   The kiss
of peace, which formerly denoted the end of the intercessions, was
now made a part of the Eucharistic service.   The oblation of gifts
was also added to the communion service, thus rendering its sacrificial character more prominent.   There are evidences that miraculous
powers were ascribed to the consecrated elements.[233])

From the entire discussion, which has purposely been confined to
the form of a summary, it is evident that the liturgy, in spite of the
fact that it was still fluid and subject to change in detail, had, by the
end of the third century, "assumed the general form which it later
had in all great liturgies, that is, with two important parts, 1) a preparatory service, called the 'service of the Word', and 2) the main
service, later called the Anaphora; and, in addition, special stress
had come to be laid upon the idea of an invocation, whereby the
change in the elements was considered to be accomplished." [234])   It
is even possible, as Alt has done, to construct a composite liturgy, in
order to have a fairly correct idea of the order of service at the end
of the third or the beginning of the fourth century.   The order, in a
brief summary, is as follows: A. *Mass of the Catechumens.* 1) Private
confession of sins; 2) Chanting of Psalms, commonly twelve, beginning with Psalm 63, and closing with the Gloria Patri; 3) The Lessons, introduced with Salutation and Response "Pax vobiscum";
4) The Halleluja-Psalm, commonly Psalm 150; 5) The Gospel, to which
the congregation responded with Deo gratias or Laus tibi Christe;
6) The Sermon, introduced with the Apostolic Greeting; 7) Dismissal of unbelievers; 8) Prayers for Catechumens, Energumens *(ener-
goumenoi),* Enlightened *(photizomenoi),* and Penitents, and the Dis-

232) Horn, *Outlines of Liturgics,* 98. 99.
233) Kliefoth, I, 423—441.   234) Mercer, *The Ethiopic Liturgy,* 45.

missal of each group in order. B. *Mass of the Faithful.* 1) Private
Devotion; 2) The General Prayer in the form of a Litany, the congregation responding to each section with the Kyrie; 3) The Collect;
4) The Offertorium or Oblation of bread and wine, oil and frank-
incense; 5) The Pax and Kiss of Peace; 6) The Preface: Salutation
and Response, Sursum corda, Proper Preface, Sanctus, sung by
congregation; 7) Consecration with words of institution; 8) General
Intercessory Prayer; 9) Prayer post oblata; 10) Lord's Prayer (with
Sancta sanctis and Gloria in excelsis); 11) The Communion (with
Videte et gaudete Psalm); 12) Post Communion, with Prayer of
Thanksgiving, Benediction, and *poreuesthe en irene,* Ite in pace.
The reciting or chanting of the Creed was not introduced into the
liturgy until 471 A. D., by Petrus Fullo, bishop of Antioch.[235])

It is evident that up to this time the sacrificial and the sacramental elements were fairly well distributed and balanced in the
liturgy. The services consisted in the transmission of the grace of
God in Word and Sacrament to the congregation, which received
these assurances of the mercy of God in and through Christ with
prayers of supplication, praise, and thanksgiving. After the Council
of Nicaea, however, the sacramental element receded more and more
into a hazy background, while the sacrificial character of the liturgy
became more and more prominent, as will be shown presently.

CHAPTER 3.

The Divergent Orders from the Beginning of the Fourth Century.

From all the evidence which is at hand concerning the form of
Christian worship in the first three centuries, there does not seem to
have been a written liturgy in sub-apostolic and ante-Nicean times.
This does not imply, of course, that the sources of some of the later
liturgies may not extend much farther back, that their nuclei, in fact,
may have existed in apostolic times. As the discussion in the last
chapter showed, there were also certain fixed forms, prayers, responses,
etc., which showed little variation in the various countries to which
the missionary efforts of the Church had been extended. But these
forms had evidently not yet been codified, or there would probably be
some contemporary reference to such a document.

With the fourth century, however, when the Christian religion
was no longer merely tolerated, but became the acknowledged religion,
the state church of the Roman Empire, the forms of service which

235) Alt, *Der kirchliche Gottesdienst,* 184—201; Schuette, *Propositions
on Liturgics,* 96. 97.

had been handed down by tradition were written down in the various countries, and many manuscripts of such early liturgies have been preserved, thus enabling us to follow the development of the worship in each country. There are different methods of classifying these early forms of worship. If one wishes to go back as far as possible and trace all the various excrescences and branches, the division into four great groups or parent liturgies is usually adopted: the Jerusalem, the Ephesine, the Alexandrian, and the Roman. Some liturgiologists think this outline too narrow and distinguish the Jerusalem, the Antioch, the Persian, the Constantinopolitan, the Alexandrian (including the Coptic or Sahidic and the Ethiopic), the North African, the Roman, the Ambrosian, the Gallican, and the Mozarabic liturgies. For our purposes, it will probably be best to assume that there were five great nuclei for the forms of worship found in the various Eastern and Western countries, from the fourth to the tenth centuries, and existing, in part, to this day. These great centers of ecclesiastical life were Jerusalem, Antioch, Ephesus, Alexandria, and Rome, with Constantinople as a sixth, after the end of the fifth century.

It is possible, and perhaps even probable, that the nuclei of both the Palestinian and the Syrian liturgies may be found in the source of the order given in Book VIII of the Apostolic Constitutions. Modern scholarship is not yet agreed upon the time of this order. Since it bears a great resemblance to the Constitutions of Hippolytus, the Canones Hippolyti, it has been said to have been derived from them, which would place it between 350 and 400 A. D.[236] Brightman refers to the discussions by Funk, Harnack, and Achelis (p. xix). Mercer says of this order: "The Apostolic Constitutions is a fourth century pseudo-apostolic collection consisting of eight books; . . . the Constitutions of Hippolytus are thought to be an epitome or else a shortened form of a first draft of A. C. VIII." [237] If one concedes that the order, as at present preserved, is a late fourth century product, one may, nevertheless, with Probst, Bunsen, and others, assume that the liturgy itself, or at least the nucleus of the liturgy, may have been in existence before the Council of Nicaea, and perhaps even in the middle of the third century.[238]

The order of worship of this book, known as the *Clementine Liturgy,* after Clement of Antioch, includes the following parts: I. *Missa Catechumenorum:* Fourfold Lections, Law, Prophets, Epistles

---

236) Cp. Srawley, *The Early History of the Liturgy,* Chapter IV; Schaff-Herzog *Encyclopedia, sub voce.*
237) *The Ethiopic Liturgy,* 48. 49.
238) Cp. Palmer, *Liturgicae Origines,* I, Chapter I; *Ante-Nicene Library,* XVII, Part II: 3; Horn, *Liturgics,* 101.

and Acts, Gospels; Salutation and Response; Sermon; Dismissals,
1) Unbelievers, 2) Catechumens after prayer for them, 3) Energumens after prayer, 4) Photizomens after prayer, 5) Penitents after
prayer; General Prayer. II. *Missa Fidelium*. General Prayers, intercessory; Kiss of Peace; Oblation or Offertory; Anaphora (Thanksgiving — Apostolic Greeting, Sursum, Preface, Sanctus —, Prayer
with Words of Institution, Invocation, Intercession, Blessing, Inclination, Elevation — with Sancta Sanctis and Gloria in excelsis —,
Communion); Postcommunion with Thanksgiving and Prayer of
Dismissal; *apolyesthe en irene*.[239]) The resemblance between this
order and that gained from Justin Martyr is very striking, as Palmer
points out. There are other documents of this period which may be
consulted to round out the history of liturgical origins in the Orient.
Among these are the Apostolic Canons appended to Book VIII of the
Apostolic Constitutions, the Didascalia, the Testament of Our Lord,
the Egyptian Heptateuch, the Ethiopic Statutes, the Verona Latin
Fragments, the Canons of Hippolytus, and the Constitutions of Hippolytus, all of which are discussed by Mercer in connection with the
earliest church orders in the East.[240])

The liturgy which has exerted the most profound and lasting influence upon the development of the order of worship in the East, is
that of Jerusalem, commonly known as the *Liturgy of St. James*.
Modern critics will not concede to this order a greater antiquity than
the beginning of the fourth century, but Neale is very emphatic in
declaring that the most important parts have descended unchanged
from the apostolic authors and that the liturgy may have been written down before 200 A. D.[241]) It is marked by the increasing length
of the prayers and the attention paid to the dramatic element. There
are also special prayers preceding the service proper, those of the
Prothesis, the Parastasis, and the Enarxis. The preparation for the
entrance to the Holy Place is attended by a special prayer, prayers
are said at the entrance and during the passage to the altar. Then
the Mass of the Catechumens begins: Salutation and Response; Bid-
ding Prayer; Trisagion by the singers; Lections; Prayer with answering Kyrie by people; Gospel; Dismissal of Catechumens. The Mass
of the Faithful is also characterized by very long prayers: General
Intercessory Prayers; Great Entrance; Creed; Kiss of Peace; Inclination; Offertory Prayers; Anaphora (Salutation and Response,
Thanksgiving, Sursum, Praefatio, Sanctus, Invocation, Intercession,
Lord's Prayer, Inclination, Blessing, Manual Acts, — Sancta Sanc-

---

239) Brightman, *Liturgies Eastern and Western*, I, 3—27; *Ante-Nicene
Library*, XVII, Part II: 212—237; Horn, *Liturgies*, 101—103.
240) *The Ethiopic Liturgy*, 46—50.   241) *Early Liturgies*, 4.

tis —, Communion); Thanksgiving; Inclination; Dismissal; Closing Prayer in sacristy.[242]

There are other documents which are important in the discussion of the liturgy of Palestine. Among these are the Mystagogic Catecheses of Cyril of Jerusalem, Nos. 19—23, A. D. 348, containing instructions on Baptism, confirmation, and the Eucharist. According to his outline, the Anaphora contained the following parts: 1) Washing of hands (Ps. 26, 6); 2) Kiss of Peace; 3) Sursum corda; 4) Sanctus; 5) Invocation; 6) Intercessions; 7) Lord's Prayer, the people responding with Amen; 8) Sancta Sanctis; 9) Communion (with singing of Ps. 35, 9); 10) Final Thanksgiving.[243] Some information is also contained in Eusebius (about 339 A. D.), in Jerome, who was at Bethlehem from 386 to 420, and in the Pilgrimage of Etheria, about the end of the fourth century. It appears that there was a night office at cock-crow in the Church of the Anastasis, and at day-break a gathering at the greater basilica on Golgotha, with sermons by the presbyters and bishop. The *missa fidelium* was held at a smaller church.[244]

The Liturgy of St. James was used in the churches of Judea, Samaria, Mesopotamia, Syria, and the adjacent provinces of Asia Minor, that used by the Orthodox section of the Eastern Church being in Greek. It is used in that language to this day in Jerusalem, but only on one day in the year, namely on the festival of St. James. But the theological discussions between the councils of Nicaea and Chalcedon (325—451 A. D.) had their effect also upon the liturgy. The Nestorians did not hesitate to compose a liturgy in Syriac, which shows some dependence upon that of St. James. Neither did they refuse to translate their liturgy into the language of any people with whom they came in contact. Their order of worship was used in the language of Arabia, of Turkey, of Persia, and of India. The liturgy of India is that of Malabar or the "Mass of the Ancient Thomas Christians in the Mountains of Malabar in Eastern India," which was recast at the end of the 16th century to conform with the doctrine of the Roman Catholic Church, whose missionaries had at that time penetrated to this far country. Liturgiologists distinguish three orders of the Nestorians or Chaldean Christians: 1) The Liturgy of S. Adaeus and S. Maris, which Neale thought so important that he assigned to it an independent position among the Eastern liturgies, whence it is sometimes called the Persian Liturgy or the Liturgy of Edessa; 2) The Liturgy of Theodorus; 3) The Liturgy of Nestorius.

---

242) Brightman, *Op. cit.*, I, 31—68; 494—501; *Early Liturgies*, 11—45.
243) Mercer, 52; Brightman, 464—467.
244) Srawley, *Early History of the Liturgy*, Chapter IV.

The Nestorian or Persian rite, as now in use, with the Anaphora of SS. Addai and Mari, is so overlaid with later material that the reconstruction of the original form has not yet been carried out successfully. According to Brightman, the following parts are included in the service: Enarxis (Gloria in excelsis, Lord's Prayer, Trisagion, Prayer, Psalms, Anthem of Sanctuary, Prayer, Washing of Hands); Mass of the Catechumens (Sursum, Sanctus, Lections, Anthem of Praise, Prayer, Apostle, Prayer before Gospel, Gospel, Anthem of the Gospel); Mass of the Faithful (Prayers with answering Kyrie of the people, Inclination, Offertory, Anthem of the Mysteries, Creed, Preparation for Anaphora, Diptychs, Kiss of Peace, Anaphora — Prayer of Incense, Thanksgiving, Sursum, Preface, Sanctus, Words of Institution, Intercession, Invocation, Fraction and Consignation, Blessing, Comminution, Lord's Prayer, Elevation, Communion, — Thanksgiving, Dismissal, Eulogia, Prayers.[245])

The Monophysites of Syria, usually called the Syrian Jacobites, also adopted a liturgy in their own language, and chose the Liturgy of St. James.[246]) Its general order is the same as that of the Greek text, only a few parts being amplified largely. The rite is characterized by the prayers of dreadfulness: "Behold a time of fear and behold an hour full of trembling . . . Tremble, ye ministers of the church for that ye administer a living fire and the power which ye wield surpasseth seraphim's . . . How dreadful is this hour and how terrible this moment. It is the moment when the spirit of life and holiness comes down to the sacrifice of the altar and sanctifies it. Pray with fear and trembling!"[247])

In the meantime, the western provinces of Asia Minor were developing their order of services. So far as the region of Laodicea is concerned, the Canons of that church of ca. 363 show that the order of worship was substantially that of Syria and Jerusalem: 1) Old and New Testament Lessons, with a Psalm between each two Lessons; 2) Sermon; 3) Prayer for Catechumens and Dismissal; 4) Prayer for Penitents and Dismissal; 5) Three Prayers for the Faithful; 6) Kiss of Peace; 7) Communion.[248])

The liturgy of the Cappadocian church may be summarized from the references of Firmilian of Caesarea, Gregory Thaumatourgos of Cappadocia, both of the third century; of Gregory of Nazianzus, Gregory of Nyssa, and especially of Basil the Great, of the fourth century; and from the canons of several councils. While the liturgy

245) *Liturgies Eastern and Western,* I, 247—305. 490—494. Cp. Summary in Alt, *Der kirchliche Gottesdienst,* 372. 373, of the liturgy of India; *Early Liturgies,* 77—92.
246) Alt, II, 282—292.   247) Brightman, I, 69—110; Alt, 374.
248) Mercer, *The Ethiopic Liturgy,* 55; Brightman, 518. 519.

ascribed to Basil may not be his work in the present form, it is generally conceded that its nucleus is based upon his liturgical writings,
in other words, he codified the form of worship which he found.   The
general outline of the liturgy in the church of Cappadocia was the
following: 1) Lessons from Old and New Testaments with Psalms;
2) Sermon, preceded by Salutation of Peace; 3) Prayers for and
Dismissal of *akroomenoi,* catechumens, energumens, *cheimazomenoi,*
kneelers, *hypopiptontes;* 4) Prayers of the Faithful; 5) Kiss of Peace;
6) Offerings; 7) Oblations brought to Altar; 8) Sanctus; 9) Institution; 10) Invocation; 11) Fraction and Communion; 12) Blessing.[249]
Since the patriarchate of Caesarea extended from the Hellespont in
the west to the Euphrates in the east, including all of Asia Minor but
proconsular Asia, Phrygia, and the southern maritime provinces, the
liturgy of Basil obtained a wide use.   When the patriarchate of Caesarea came under the jurisdiction of Constantinople, in the middle
of the fifth century, the liturgy of Basil was accepted for the entire
exarchate.   The best text of this rite is therefore known as the Constantinopolitan, while that of Cappadocia is a Syrian text.   This
order has also been thought to have been the basis of the Alexandrian,
or at least to have influenced it at the time of Cyril.

Armenia had been Christianized in the third and fourth centuries, chiefly through the labors of Gregorius Illuminator.   In the
fifth century the persecutions on the part of the Persian kings interfered with the free spread of Christianity, and in the sixth century
the Monophysite errors were accepted, the Synod of Twin (595 A. D.)
declaring its adoption of that heresy, whereby the separation from
the Orthodox Church was carried into effect.   The liturgy, which was
at first that of Basil, has received additions from the Jacobites of
Syria, from Constantinople, and from other sources.   The order of
worship in the simplest form is the following: 1) Psalm; 2) Lessons
from Prophets, Epistles, Gospels; 3) Dismissal of Catechumens, etc.;
4) Anaphora (Kiss of Peace, Benediction, Sursum corda, Thanksgiving, Tersanctus, Continuation of Thanksgiving, Institution,
Verbal Oblation, Invocation of Holy Ghost, Prayers for the Church,
for all Men and all Things, Lord's Prayer and Benediction of People,
Sancta Sanctis, Breaking of Bread, Communion); 5) Postcommunion
with Thanksgiving.[250]

Byzantium, the new capital of Constantine the Great, was by
him elevated to the dignity of a metropolitan, patriarchal center.   The
second general Council of Constantinople, in 381 A. D., raised the

---

249) Srawley, *Early History of the Liturgy,* Chapter V; Mercer, 55.
56; Brightman, 521—526.
250) Brightman, I, 412—457; Palmer, *Liturgieae Origines,* I, Appen-
dix; Alt, *Das Kirchenjahr,* 221.

bishop to a position of power second only to that of the bishop of
Rome. The patriarchate acquired the jurisdiction of Thrace, and in
the middle of the next century also that of the patriarchates of Ephesus and Caesarea. Beside the liturgy of Basil, these churches have,
from very early times, made use of a liturgy bearing the name of
Chrysostom.[251]) His early life at Antioch had brought him in touch
with the best liturgical traditions of the East. It was a time of a
growing fixity of liturgical forms, and Chrysostom undoubtedly made
use of the traditions of Basil, as transmitted by his predecessor in
the patriarchate, Gregory Nazianzen. The outline of his liturgy, in
its original form, may be given as follows: *Missa Catechumenorum:*
Salutation, Lessons (Prophets, Epistles or Acts, Gospel), Sermon,
prefaced by Salutation and followed by Dismissal of Catechumens,
etc.; *Missa Fidelium:* Deacon's Litany (Salutation and Blessing, Offering of Bread and Wine), Kiss of Peace, Anaphora (Salutation,
Preface, Sursum corda, Dignum, Sanctus, Institution, Invocation,
Intercession for Living and Dead, responded to by Amen, Fraction,
Distribution), Postcommunion (Thanksgiving, Dismissal with "Go
in Peace." [252]) Out of this liturgy, in the course of time, grew the
order of worship which is at present used in the Greek and Russian
churches. This will be discussed in greater detail below.

Recent writers on liturgies devote very little space to the discussion of the *Ephesine Liturgy,* chiefly, perhaps, because there is no
part of the order extant, and also because the matter is again touched
upon in the history of the developed permanent liturgies. There are
two reasons for assuming the presence of a liturgy in Ephesus at the
end of the first and during the second century. The church at Lug-
dunum or Lyons, in southern Gaul, had a liturgy different from that
of Rome, and it was founded by missionaries from the exarchate of
Ephesus, Irenaeus, the second bishop, having been a disciple of bishop
Polycarp of Smyrna. And the Council of Laodicea (348—381), which
was attended by bishops from the provinces of Asia and Phrygia, in
its 19th canon regulated the order of worship, thus signifying that a
different order had previously been used. The exarchate of Ephesus
at that time extended over the provinces of Hellespontum, Phrygia,
Asia, Lycaonia, Pamphylia, and the maritime territory included
within their boundaries. It is very probable, as tradition has it, that
the first order of service in Ephesus was introduced by St. Paul, and
later amplified by St. John. Since the founding of the church at
Lyons must have taken place about the beginning of the second cen-

---

251) Palmer, I, Chapter IV.
252) Brightman, I, 527—551; Srawley, *Early History of the Liturgy,*
Chapter IV; Mercer, *The Ethiopic Liturgy,* 56.

tury, the supposition is that these missionaries introduced the original
Ephesine liturgy in the congregation which was presently organized.
The order of services which was thus established in southern France
became the nucleus from which the Gallican liturgy was developed,
from the third to the sixth century. Hilary of Poictiers (d. 368) is
credited by Jerome as having been the first to codify the Gallican
Liturgy. He was followed by Claudianus Mamercus, bishop of Vienna (ca. 450) and Musaeus of Marseilles (ca. 458). Of Sidonius
Apollinaris, bishop of Auvergne (473—494), Gregory of Tours relates
that he could recite Mass without a book. A little later, the Council
of Vannes (465) and the Concilium Epaonense (517) fixed the liturgy
by a decree. At the time of Gregory the Great, the Gallican Liturgy
was still in general use, although there are indications of Roman influence. This form of worship at that time extended throughout the
Frankish empire. The Roman rites were first generally introduced
in place of the Gallican by Pipin, and Charlemagne enforced the
legislation introducing the Roman Liturgy. There are several of the
Gallican service books accessible in good editions, the latest one being
the Missale Gothicum in the Henry Bradshaw Society publications.
The order of worship in the fully developed Gallican Liturgy was the
following: Anthem, Gloria Patri, Salutation and Response, Trisagion, Kyrie, Benedictus and Collecta post prophetiam, Lesson from
Old Testament, Epistle, Benedicite or Hymn of Three Children,
Gospel, Anthem by Choir, Sermon, Prayers, Collecta post precem,
Dismissal of Catechumens; Praefatio, Prayer, Oblations, Offertory,
Invocation of God on gifts (in later times only), Diptychs, Collecta
post nomina, Salutation and Kiss of Peace, Collecta ad pacem; Anaphora began with Preface and Canon (Sursum corda, Thanksgiving
called Contestatio or Immolatio, Tersanctus), Post sanctus, Institu-
tion, Collecta; Post mysterium or Post secreta (with verbal oblation
of bread and wine and invocation to Holy Spirit), Breaking of Bread,
Lord's Prayer, Benediction and Amen, Communion, Collect of
Thanksgiving.[253])

Closely related to the Gallican Liturgy is the *Mozarabic Rite*,
thought by most liturgiologists to be an offshoot of the Gallican,
though one might assume that the nucleus of the Ephesine liturgy
was brought to Spain by St. Paul and his disciples after him, since
a number of authorities agree that he visited Hispania. But no matter what the first beginnings were, it seems reasonably sure to state
that the Goths, when they overran Spain, were using the Greek-

---

253) Palmer, *Liturgicae Origines*, I, Chapter IX; Kliefoth, *Die urspruengliche Gottesdienstordnung*, II, 324—462; Daniel, *Codex liturgicus*,
I, 49—113.

Oriental liturgy. This was translated before 563 by Martin of Braza.
Subsequently, several leaders in the Spanish Church visited the
Orient, bringing back further material. And finally, Isidor of Sevilla
codified the parts of the liturgy and prevailed upon the Council of
Toledo (633) to establish the decree for the entire country of Spain
and Narbonensis, "ut unus ordo psallendi conservetur." Further additions were made by Ildefons of Toledo (ca. 660) and by Julianus
of Toledo (d. 728). At the Mohammedan invasion the name Mozarabic was applied to the liturgy (Arab Arabe, Arab Most-Arabe — an
Arab by adoption, softened into Mozarabic). It was approved by
John X about 920 A. D.[254]) Its further history will be discussed below when the order of service will be examined.

When the churches of Gaul had been established with some degree of firmness, they immediately sent out missionaries to other
countries. It was in this manner that the *Gallican Rite* was spread
through Germany, especially in the parts directly under Frankish influence. It was in this way, also, that the Gallican Liturgy was introduced into Great Britain, for we have records showing that bishops
from England (Britannia) were in attendance at the synods of Gaul
as early as the fourth century. It is for this reason that English
liturgiologists emphasize the Ephesine origin of the early liturgy of
their country. The history of this development is so important and
interesting that it will be referred to at length in a chapter on the
liturgy of Great Britain.

The civil diocese of Africa embraced the provinces of Africa
Proconsularis, Numidia, Byzacium, Tripoli, and the two Mauretanias.
The written liturgy of this formerly flourishing country of congregations has disappeared, and only by comparing the writings of Tertullian (d. 235), Cyprian (d. 258), Optatus (ca. 363), and Augustine
(ca. 395) are we enabled to gain a connected picture of the order of
service at the end of the fourth century and in the fifth century.
Neale and other students believe that the liturgy of North Africa
was developed from the Ephesine nucleus, missionaries from the
province of Asia having been the founders of the first African congregations.[255]) Others are equally positive that the North African
rite was based upon that of Rome. Certain it is that the Invocation
or Epiklesis points to the Orient, while other parts of the liturgy remind one strongly of the early Roman. Probably there was only the
Ephesine nucleus, the other elements being received from Rome. The
full order was the following: 1) Salutation; 2) Lessons from Old
and New Testaments, with Psalms; 3) Sermon; 4) Dismissal of Cate-

254) Baeumer, *Geschichte des Breviers;* Neale, *Essays on Liturgiology,*
V; Kliefoth, II, 255—324.
255) *Essays on Liturgiology,* V.

chumens; 5) Prayer of the Faithful; 6) Offertory and Psalms; 7) Sursum corda; 8) Intercessions and Commemorations; 9) Consecration; 10) Fraction; 11) Lord's Prayer; 12) Salutation; 13) Kiss of Peace; 14) Blessing; 15) Communion, with Psalm; 16) Thanksgiving.[256] The position of the kiss of peace after the consecration is characteristic of the North African rite.[257]

The liturgy of the church of Northern Italy, commonly known as the *Ambrosian Liturgy,* has also been traced to Ephesine sources. Neale says that it is a branch of the Ephesine family, molded by contact with the Petrine liturgy.[258] There seems to be a general consensus of opinion that the Milanese office was derived directly from the Orient, its first two bishops having been disciples of Barnabas. When Ambrose became bishop, in 374, he not only opposed the heretics and pagans, but also worked for the Church in a practical way by developing the liturgy, the so-called Ambrosian Chant being introduced by him. After his death, in 397, the Milanese liturgy gradually assumed completeness, and the Ambrosian office was probably perfected in its most important parts by 493. By 568, the lesser hymns and lections appear to have formed themselves. From 568 to 739 there occurred the Aquileian schism, during which the character of the Ambrosian liturgy was fully established.[259] Its earliest form may be determined by the treatise De Sacramentis, formerly ascribed to Pope Innocent I, and from the writings of Ambrose himself. The following order has been suggested: 1) Lessons from Old and New Testaments, with Psalms; 2) Sermon; 3) Dismissal of Catechumens; 4) Prayers of the Faithful; 5) Offering; 6) Sanctus; 7) Intercession; 8) Institution; 9) Invocation; 10) Amen after Consecration; 11) Kiss of Peace; 12) Postcommunion Prayer and Communion Chant; 13) Benediction.[260] The form of the sixth century is given by Palmer: Anthem "Ingressu," Kyrie eleison, Gloria in excelsis, Collect, Prophet, Psalm, Epistle, Alleluia, Gospel, Sermon, Prayer "super sindonem," Oblations of people, Prayer "super oblata," Preface and Canon (without second oblation), Fraction, Kiss of Peace, Communion, Prayer "post communionem." [261] Some of the passages in the Ambrosian liturgy point to the strong development of the sacrificial idea, as the expressions "Quod figura est corporis et sanguinis," "incruenta hostia," etc., tend to show.[262] Altogether, the Ambrosian liturgy had neither the pregnant brevity of the Roman, nor the richness and fulness of the Mozarabic.[263]

---

256) Mercer, 57.   257) Srawley, Chapter VI.
258) *Essays on Liturgiology,* VI.
259) Neale, *Essays on Liturgiology,* VI.
260) Mercer, 58.   261) *Liturgicae Origines,* I, Chapter 7.
262) Srawley, Chapter VII.
263) Richards-Painter, *Christian Worship,* Chapter IV.

The center of the early Christian Church in Egypt was Alexandria. Tradition has it that the patriarchate of Alexandria was founded by St. Mark, to whom also the ancient liturgy of Alexandria is ascribed. When the Monophysite disturbances extended to Egypt, the result, after the Council of Chalcedon, was a schism, which influenced also the liturgy. The orthodox Melchites came under the jurisdiction of Constantinople, finally adopting the liturgy of that church. By referring to the writings of Athanasius (d. 373), Peter (d. 311), Sozomen (d. 448), Cyril (d. 444), Timothy (ca. 460), Theophilus (ca. 412), and Synesius (d. 414), and comparing passages in their writings with the Ethiopic Church Order, the Latin Verona Fragments, the Testament of Our Lord, the Sahidic Ecclesiastical Canon 64, the Sacramentary of Serapion, bishop of Thmuis (ca. 350—356), and the Papyrus of Dêr Balyzeh (end of fourth century), the following composite liturgy is suggested by Mercer: Proanaphora — 1) Reading from the Old Testament, Gospels, and Epistles, preceded by the attendamus lectioni; 2) Sermon; 3) Prayers, which developed into Diptychs; 4) Prayer of the Faithful; 5) Kiss of Peace; 6) Offertory; Anaphora — 1) Thanksgiving, introduced by responses, with Sursum corda and Preface; 2) Invocation; 3) Institution; 4) Anamnesis; 5) Oblation and Invocation; 6) Invitation to Communion; 7) Communion; 8) Oil, water, and cheese offered after the liturgy.[264]

"The Greek liturgy of Alexandria was probably completed under the influence of St. Cyril, bishop of Alexandria, about the beginning of the fifth century, and it appears under the name of both St. Cyril and St. Mark. It may be considered a direct development of the liturgy first used at Alexandria, and as such it is the direct parent of the Coptic St. Cyril and of the Ethiopic liturgies, and also the source of the more characteristic features of Coptic Basil and Gregory."[265] This parent liturgy of the Egyptian Church is given by Brightman,[266] and has been reconstructed by Mercer in its probable fifth century form.[267] It contains the following principal parts: The Little Entrance, Lections, Prayers; Mass of the Faithful — Prayer, Salutation, Kiss of Peace, Anaphora (Thanksgiving with Sursum corda and Preface, Sanctus, Invocation, Intercession, Lord's Prayer, Inclination, Manual Acts, Communion), Thanksgiving, Inclination, Dismissal. This order agrees also in all main parts with the Ethiopic Twelve Apostles, St. Cyril, and St. Basil.[268]

---

264) *The Ethiopic Liturgy*, 64; Brightman, I, 504—509; Srawley, Chapter III.
265) Mercer, 79.
266) *Liturgies Eastern and Western*, I, 113—143.
267) *Op. cit.*, 116—137.
268) Mercer, *The Ethiopic Liturgy*, 88—90.

After the Council of Chalcedon (451), the Copts allied themselves with the Syrian Jacobites and adopted liturgies translated from the Greek, which are now known as the Coptic or Sahidic Liturgy. There are three Anaphoras in use, namely that of St. Cyril, of St. Basil, and of St. Gregory Nazianzen, with a common Proanaphora, that of St. Mark. The liturgy of Basil became the normal liturgy of the Coptic Monophysites, Gregory being used in Lent, and Cyril on festivals.[269]

The Church of Abyssinia was founded either in the first or the early second century, various traditions naming Queen Candace's eunuch, St. Matthew, and Frumentius of Tyre as the founders. The latter was made bishop of the Ethiopians about 340 A. D. The Abyssinian Church was always closely connected with that of Lower Egypt, and when Monophysitism spread in the valley of the Nile, it was introduced also into Ethiopia, about 480 A. D. The original liturgy of the Abyssinian Church was that of St. Mark, or the Alexandrian, an outline of which was given above. After 480, the liturgy was translated into the vernacular, and it may be safely asserted that "the liturgy of the Ethiopic Church in Abyssinia, from the beginning of the sixth century on, existed and was said in the Ethiopic language." [270] From that time forward, also, the two liturgies, the Coptic and the Ethiopic, have gradually grown apart in details, though not in general outline, as a further examination will show.

There remains now only the discussion of the early *Roman Rite*. And here the absence of documents and early references make the silence oppressive. Tradition says that the liturgy was introduced by St. Peter and is based upon apostolic sources. But even Baeumer does not go beyond this statement. Since, however, the church at Rome was founded in the first century, it is undoubtedly safe to assume, with Srawley, that the order of service was mainly Greek in character. The casual references of Jerome give little information as to its development after the middle of the second century. The next document which is extant, is the letter to Decentius, ascribed to Pope Innocent I (416 A. D.). It gives evidence of some liturgical customs in Rome: the kiss of peace at the beginning of the Canon, the announcement of names after offerings as commended to God, and the fact that the consecrated Eucharist was sent from the bishop's church to all the churches in the city.[271] The order of the Roman liturgy at the beginning of the fifth century, as given by Palmer, is the following: Collect, Lessons preceded by Anthem or Psalm, Sermon, Dismissal of Catechumens; Silent Prayers, Oblation and Offer-

---

269) Mercer, 79. 80.   270) Mercer, 142.
271) Srawley, *Early History of the Liturgy*, Chapter VII.

tory, Secreta or Super'oblata, Preface with Sursum corda, Tersanctus, Prayers and Commemoration of Living, Prayer over Elements — "he made to us the body and blood of Jesus Christ our Lord God" —, Institution, Oblation of Sacraments, Commemoration of Departed and Prayer for Communion with them, Bread Broken for Distribution, Lord's Prayer, Kiss of Peace, Distribution, Conclusion with Prayer.[272])

In concluding this chapter, we offer the following chart, on the

The Development of the Christian Liturgy.

Great Oriental.	Alexandrian.	Ephesine-Gallican.	Roman.
(St. James: Jerusalem and Antioch)	(St. Mark: Alexandria)	(St. Paul and St. John: Ephesus)	(St. Peter: Rome)
St. Basil (371) Syriac of St. James	St. Cyril	Gallican (Lyons)	
Chrysostom (398) Nestorian	Coptic or Sahidic Ethiopic or Abyssinian	Spanish or Mozarabic	North African Leo (451)
Present Greek-Russian India			Ambrosian (Milan) Gelasius (492)
Armenian		British Celtic Irish ·	Gregory (590)
			Present Roman (1570–1634)
		St. Augustine of Canterbury (601)	
		St. Osmund of Salisbury (1087)	
		York, Hereford, etc.	
		Anglican	
		Scotch-American Irish	
		American Lutheran Common Service	

THE DEVELOPMENT OF THE CHRISTIAN LITURGY.

basis of Gwynne, which serves both for orientation so far as the preceding discussion is concerned, and prepares for the better understanding of the subsequent history of the liturgy.

272) *Liturgicae Origines*, I, Chapter 6.

The Development of the Roman Liturgy to its Present Form.

The history of the Roman liturgy, strictly speaking, does not go back beyond the fifth century. Whatever statements are made with regard to the first centuries are either conjectures based upon uncertain traditions or deductions from limited references, those of Clemens Romanus, the Shepherd of Hermas, Justin Martyr, Jerome, and possibly Hippolytus. It is not known which bishop of Rome codified the liturgical forms then in use to become the nucleus of the present Roman Mass. Probst is evidently wrong in referring this work to Damasus I (336—384). The letter of Innocent I to bishop Decentius (ca. 416) shows that the kiss of peace had been transferred from its position at the beginning of the Canon to its end, after the consecration, and just before the communion. Drews, in the Schaff-Herzog Encyclopedia, gives the following order of the Roman Liturgy in the fifth century: I. *Mass of the Catechumens.* 1) Epistle; 2) Gradual and Hallelujah; 3) Gospel; 4) Sermon; 5) Dismissal; 6) Mediatory Prayer. II. *Mass of the Faithful.* 1) Offertory; 2) Secreta; 3) Preface with Sanctus; 4) Prayer introductory to the Words of Institution; 5) Words of Institution; 6) Anamnesis; 7) Epiklesis — it is doubtful whether this feature was still found in the fifth century —; 8) Prayer of Intercession with Reading of the Diptychs; 9) Kiss of Peace; 10) Communion; 11) Lord's Prayer; 12) Postcommunion; 13) Blessing; 14) Dismissal: "Ite, missa est." *(Sub voce* Mass).

The following popes, especially Celestine I (422—432), Leo I (440—461), after whom the Missale Leonianum is named, Gelasius I (492—496), whose Ordo et Canon Missae is the first complete church order of Rome, and Symmachus (498—514), who ordered the daily use of the Gloria in excelsis, were concerned more or less about the liturgy. It seems certain that the fifth century saw the discontinuance of the disciplina arcani, thus abolishing the distinction between the Missa catechumenorum and the Missa fidelium. The idea of an actual sacrifice in the Eucharist became more prominent: corpus Christi est in altari. By the end of the fifth century the Ordo et Canon Missae embraced the following parts: Salutation and Response, Sursum corda, Preface with Commemoration of Saints and Words of Institution, Lord's Prayer, Communion, Postcommunion with fourteen collects "ad libitum," Benedictions, Fourteen Collects.[273]

The next period of the Roman Liturgy is that in which the name of Gregory the Great (590—604) stands out prominently. His biographer, John the Deacon, summarized his work in this field in the

---

273) Daniel, *Codex liturgicus,* I, 13—21.

one brief sentence: "Taking many things from the ceremonies of the Mass in the Gelasian Codex, changing a few, and adding some for the better explanation of the Gospel lections, he comprised the whole in one volume." [274] His chief aim was the rich development of the liturgy with reference to the heortology of the church. At the same time, Gregory insisted upon a pregnant brevity in collects and prefaces, a feature which added greatly to the effectiveness of the services. He was greatly concerned about the proper singing or chanting of the service and introduced the mode of recitative chanting which bears his name to this day. The order of worship for the service of the Mass, according to the Ordo et Canon Missae Gregorianus, is the following: Introitus, Kyrie eleison, Gloria in excelsis, Oratio, Apostolum, Gradalis seu Alleluia, Evangelium, Offertorium or Oratio super oblata, Salutatio, Sursum corda, Vere dignum, Prayers for Living and Dead, Words of Institution, Lord's Prayer, Pax, Agnus Dei, Communion, Antiphona ad communionem, Postcommunio de tempore, Ite missa est.[275]

There are several points that should be noted carefully in connection with the Roman Liturgy, as established by Gregory. The Lord's Prayer was transferred to the place just before the Fraction which preceded the Communion of the priests, instead of following it as heretofore. The difference between the Roman and Greek rites became more prominent: 1) The "moment of consecration" in the former was not definitely fixed as in the latter; 2) The Roman contains no intercession for various classes of persons, which is so noticeable in the Greek; 3) The "corpus et sanguis Christi" marks the advance upon the Greek "figura corporis et sanguinis Christi"; 4) The conception of the sacrifice in the prayers is mainly Eucharistic; 5) The prophetic lesson disappeared at Rome in the fifth century; 6) The Invocation or Epiklesis, which may have been in use in the first centuries, was omitted at an early date.[276] On the doctrinal side, the following features are expressed very strongly in the Roman Liturgy: 1) That the priest is the mediator between God and the people; 2) That he has power to transubstantiate, though the word was not coined till somewhat later; 3) That he offers a sacrifice in the Mass; 4) That he has the power to forgive sins according to his discretion. Thus the sacerdotal idea triumphed, and the church showed ever more plainly a false position with regard to the Eucharist and the way to salvation.[277]

---

274) Quoted in Horn, *Outlines of Liturgies*, 106.
275) Daniel, I, 12—20; Kliefoth, *Die urspruengliche Gottesdienstordnung*, II, Anhang; Cp. 213—217.
276) Cf. Srawley, *Early History of the Liturgy*, Chapter VII.
277) Cp. Richards-Painter, *Christian Worship*, Chapter IV; *Memoirs of Lutheran Liturgical Association*, V: 1.

Although Gregory himself did not insist very strongly upon it, but advised a conservative course, the Roman Liturgy about this time began to supersede other rites which had been in use in the West, just as the Gallican Liturgy had influenced that of Rome and brought about some minor changes in the Leonine Sacramentary. When Gregory sent Augustine to England in 597, he was probably not aware of the strength of the scattered bands of Christians in the hills nor of the tenacity with which they clung to their Gallican Rite. Augustine did not enforce the Roman Rite, and Theodore of Tarsus, himself a Greek, made many concessions. And the Scottish and Celtic rites were used in many parts of the country till 1200, although the Council of Clovesho in 747 prescribed the Roman Ritual for all England.

In Ireland the case was similar. Palladius and Patrick, who had been ordained by Celestine (422—432), probably brought the Roman Ritual to Ireland. But there were many varieties of worship, due to native usages which had probably come from Gaul. The Synod of Tara in 692 decreed that such usages should be discontinued, and an extant Missal of the eighth century shows some similarity to the Roman Liturgy. But not till the 12th century were the Roman forms definitely established, when the Synod of Kells, in 1152, and the Synod of Cashel, in 1172, again passed the resolutions.

So far as Gaul is concerned, the Roman Sacramentary made its way there as early as the sixth century, the two rites thus exerting a mutual influence. In the next centuries, the monasteries were the chief factors in promoting the Roman forms, the Benedictines being especially zealous in this respect. It is also related of Chrodegang, bishop of Metz, that he introduced "Romana cantilena" after his return from Rome. But the real change came at the end of the eighth century. Pipin made a law abolishing the Gallican Liturgy, and Charlemagne, at the instigation of Pope Stephen (816—817), carried the order out most effectively. He introduced the Cantus Romanus in all churches of Gaul and wherever the Gallican order was used, and made it the duty of the clergy to become thoroughly familiar with the Roman Rite, "as our father Pipin of revered memory earnestly commanded, when he abolished the Gallican Form." According to imperial orders as early as 789 and 805, every candidate for the priesthood was obliged to be familiar, not only with the Ordinary of the Mass, but with the offices for all the festival days, according to the Roman Rite.[278]

In Spain much the same method of procedure was adopted. Alexander II introduced the Roman Liturgy into Aragon (1068—

---

278) Baeumer, *Geschichte des Breviers*, 231.

1071), and King Alfonso VI secured its adoption in Castille. Gregory VII induced the Synod of Burgos in 1085 to declare the Roman Liturgy valid for all Spain. An effort to restore the Mozarabic Liturgy in 1436 failed. Its subsequent history will be touched upon below. Thus, by the 12th century, the Roman Liturgy had superseded or supplanted the rites previously in use in Spain, France, Germany, England, Scotland, Ireland, and Italy with the exception of the archbishopric of Milan. This fact was of great advantage in more than one respect, especially for the Roman See. It produced a uniformity in the order of worship which made it possible for a person from any part of the Church to take part in the worship of any congregation, in whose midst he might find himself. And it abolished the abuse of the many local festival days dedicated to some particular saint of the community.

Partly as a result of this move, and partly in consequence of the change in the church's doctrine concerning the Eucharist, there was a change in the variety and number of the service books. As long as the various members of the clergy were regularly employed in the service, the lector reading the lections, the choir taking the chants, either responsorially or antiphonally, the deacon reading or chanting some of the prayers, the priest having charge of the Eucharist, there were various service books, each one for a special function. The Ordo contained the rubrics, the Sacramentarium the sacerdotal prayers, the Antiphonarium the chants, the Psalterium the Psalms, the Comes the lections. Other service books were the Lectionarium, the Martyrologium, the Hymnarium, the Homiliarium, the Passionarium, the Legenda, the Graduale, the Troparium, the Prosarium, the Ordinale, the Consuetudinarium, the Processionale, the Manuale, and many more. About the eleventh century, when private masses were celebrated with increasing frequency, the various liturgical books were united in a single service book, called the Missal.[279]) At present, the complete Missal includes three parts: 1) Proprium missarum de tempore, with the services for each day from Advent to the Great Sabbath, the Ordo Missae, the Proper Prefaces, the Canon Missae, and the services from Easter to the end of the church year; 2) Proprium missarum de sanctis, with the services for saints' days and extraordinary festivals, from January to December; 3) Commune sanctorum, with the common Mass for saints' days having no Mass of their own and various votive masses. In a similar way the material, chiefly from the Legenda, Antiphonarium, and Psalterium was collected, with special reference to the Horae canonicae, and issued in the form of the Breviary. The Breviary is usually divided into four

---

279) Kliefoth, III, 284.

sections or books, one for each quarter of the year, each section containing six parts: 1) Calendar, Rubrics, and Tables; 2) Psalms, Versicles, and Responses of the Ferial Office; 3) Proprium de tempore: Collects and lections for Sundays and weeks in that part of the year; 4) Proprium de sanctis: the same for the festivals of the saints which occur in that period; 5) Commune sanctorum: Lections, collects, hymns, etc., common to all saints for whom no particular office is appointed; 6) Offices for anniversaries, for the dead, etc.[280]

The liturgical work of Gregory practically determined the Roman Rite during the Middle Ages, there being no great changes recorded until the 16th century. There were some minor additions, especially the elaborate preparation of the priests in the sacristy, the insertion of the Creed after the Gospel, and the reading of the Prolog of the Gospel of St. John at the end of the Postcommunion. An interesting bit of liturgical history is that of the Breviary of Quignon, in the 16th century. It appears that Clement VII requested Cardinal Quignon to prepare a new Breviary. Whether the Reformation was directly responsible or not, the cardinal omitted the greater part of the legendary and apocryphal material in the lections and emphasized the necessity of reading more of the canonical Scriptures. The first draft appeared in 1535, and the Breviary was completed in 1539. From the first, there was a strong opposition to its introduction, and even to-day the judgment is that it is too one-sided.[281] The Council of Trent went on record as favoring the ancient forms, but it omitted some of the most patently apocryphal readings. The Breviary of Pius V in 1568 kept only the lections for the nocturn services from Quignon and absolutely abrogated all other service books for the two centuries preceding. But even this Breviary did not meet with universal approval. In 1604 Clement VIII issued a new Roman service book, thoroughly revised by a commission appointed for that purpose. The final revision of the Roman Rite was made under Urban VIII, and appeared in 1634. This is the form which is now used in the Roman Catholic Church. It may be said to be a recasting of the Gregorian Liturgy, the framework and much of the liturgical material having been retained.

The Canon Missae or the order of services in the celebration of the Mass in the Roman Church at present is the following:

1) *Initium missae solennis.* After making the sign of the cross on forehead and chest and saying: In nomine Patris et Filii et Spiritus Sancti, the priest prays the Introibo-Psalm, 43, antiphonally with his assistants. The Psalm is followed by the Gloria Patri.

---

280) Neale, *Essays on Liturgiology*, I.
281) Baeumer, *Geschichte des Breviers*, 392.

2) *Confiteor.* The priest kneels and makes a confession of his sins to "Almighty God, to the blessed Virgin Mary, the blessed arch-angel Michael, the blessed John the Baptist, the holy apostles Peter and Paul," etc. When the priest, in the course of his confession, utters the words: Mea culpa, the bell is struck and the entire con-gregation falls down upon the knees. The absolution is then said by the assistants, whereupon they confess and are absolved. Then fol-low the Thanksgiving Antiphons and the Collect for Purity.

3) *Introitus.* Only the opening words of the Psalm for the day are prayed, a different one being used every Sunday. The answering versicle is the Gloria Patri.

4) *Kyrie.* Alternating Kyrie, eleison, Christe eleison, Kyrie eleison, sung nine times, the assistants answering. This Kyrie is thought by Palmer, Kliefoth, and others to be a remnant of the Litany, transferred to this place when the General Prayer lost its place in the service.

5) The *Gloria in Excelsis.* It is intoned by the priest and taken up by the choir. When there is full orchestral accompaniment, the rendition of this hymn may be made unusually effective. It is omit-ted during Advent, and from Septuagesima till Easter.

6) *Collecta.* It is introduced with the Salutation and Response, and marks the opening of the second part of the service, the service of the Word. On great festival days, several collects may be used.

7) *Epistola.* The lesson from the Prophets disappeared at Rome at a very early date. The Comes prescribes the Lectio continua of the Prophets in the ferial services at certain seasons of the year.

8) *Graduale* or Hallelujah. At this point, in the early Church, the lector left the Epistle ambo or lectern and walked to the other (north) side and usually up the steps to the Gospel lectern. The Hallelujah of early days was superseded by a short hymn, called gradual, or by a prose, trope, or sequence, consisting of a recitative strophe or antiphonal chanting. From the Easter tropes of the Mid-dle Ages the Easter play arose and thus the modern drama was born.

9) *Evangelium.* The Gospel is preceded by the Munda cor meum, the Benediction, and the Salutation. The Gospel was for-merly sung by the officiating priest. The assistants respond with Laus tibi, Christe.

10) *Credo Nicaenum.* The Creed is intoned by the priest and taken up by the choir. If the proper accompaniment is used, the solemn orchestral music is most effective.

11) *Offertorium.* In the primitive Church, the offering of bread and wine took place at this point. At present, it is used to present the bread and the wine mixed with water, as an offering to God, the

priest meanwhile praying for his own sins and for those of all Christians. There is a short Invocation, followed by the Lavabo (Ps. 26, 6—12) and the offering of the oblation.

12) *Secreta.* One or more prayers are murmured, varying with the day, and the priest's voice does not become audible until the final words: Per omnia saecula saeculorum.

13) *Praefatio.* It opens with the Salutation, Sursum corda, and continues the Vere dignum with the Proper Preface, the choir responding with the Sanctus.

14) *Canon Missae.* In secret prayer, the priest makes an offering of the unbloody sacrifice on the altar, adds the commemoration for the living and the dead, the Pro defunctis being spoken after the Institution or Consecration, and after the Elevation and Adoration of both the bread and the cup. By this time the choir has usually finished the Sanctus.

15) *Praeparatio ad Communionem.* The priest chants the Lord's Prayer, and adds, to the seventh petition, a prayer urging the intercession of the saints. He breaks the wafer over the cup at the words: Per eundem. Again breaking one of the pieces, he throws the particle in the cup and says a secret prayer (Immissio in calicem).

16) *Preces ante Communionem.* These consist of the Agnus Dei and several collects.

17) *Sumtio.* The priest takes bread and wine himself and then administers the bread, if there are communicants, with the words: Corpus Domini custodiat. . .

18) *Communio.* The reading of Video caelos apertos or some other verse, a remnant of the Psalm which was formerly sung during the distribution.

19) *Postcommunio.* Salutation, followed by a collect, and the Ite, missa est.

20) *Finis Missae.* A secret prayer of the priest: Placeat tibi, sancta Trinitas, obsequium servitutis meae. . . .

21) *Benedictio.* Benedicat vos omnipotens Deus, Pater, Filius, et Spiritus Sanctus.

22) *Evangelium.* John 1, 1—14, upon which the assistants answer: Deo gratias.[282]

---

282) Lochner, *Der Hauptgottesdienst,* 14. 15; Daniel, *Codex liturgicus,* I, 48—112; Kliefoth, *Die urspruengliche Gottesdienstordnung,* III, 296—442; Alt, *Der kirchliche Gottesdienst,* 239—257; Horn, *Liturgics,* 109—119.

CHAPTER 5.

Ancient Liturgies of Various Branches of the Church in Use at the Present Time.

We have, in chapter III, followed the history and development of the various Eastern and Western liturgies, beginning with the nuclei or parent orders, and tracing the subsequent changes and their influence under various conditions to the beginning of the medieval period. Since, however, many of these orders are in use at the present time, a short summary of their more recent history and of the structure of their principal service may aid in the proper orientation and also in the appreciation of their relative importance.

Turning our attention first to the East, we find that circumstances have rendered the Constantinopolitan rites sole possessors of the Orthodox churches, not only in Greece and Russia, but also in Asia Minor and in Egypt. As the Liturgy of St. Basil was a recast of that of St. James, so the Liturgy of St. Chrysostom is an abbreviation and new edition of St. Basil's. In the ninth century, they were still both in use and had the following parts in common: Prothesis with *proskomide,* Enarxis; *Mass of the Catechumens:* The Little Entrance, Lections, Prayers, Dismissals; *Mass of the Faithful:* Prayers of the Faithful, the Great Entrance, Kiss of Peace, Creed, Anaphora — Thanksgiving (Salutation, Sursum, Preface, Trisagion), Secreta, with Words of Institution, Invocation, Intercession, Blessing, Lord's Prayer, Inclination, Communion, Thanksgiving, Dismissal, Final Prayer in Sacristy.[283]) A close examination reveals that there is little actual difference between the two liturgies, excepting that the form of Basil is longer, the Intercession being the only part in which Chrysostom has a longer prayer. It will be noted, also, that the ancient division of the service into the Missa Catechumenorum and Missa Fidelium is still observed. But this division is not marked much more emphatically than that of the Proanaphora and the Anaphora, the former ending with the Kiss of Peace and the Creed, just before the Sanctus.

So far as the present Orthodox Oriental Liturgy is concerned, the Liturgy of St. Basil is said on all Sundays in Lent except Palm Sunday, also on Maundy Thursday, Easter Eve, the vigils of Christmas and Epiphany, and the Feast of St. Basil (Jan. 1). The Liturgy of St. Chrysostom is prescribed for every other day in the year. The latter thus holds the position of greater importance. It has been enriched especially by the addition of rubrics which give to the chief service the character of a great symbolico-liturgical drama, repre-

---

283) Brightman, *Liturgies Eastern and Western,* I, 309—344.

senting the entire work of redemption. If one takes up the Vesper
service of the Vigils and continues his examination to the end of the
Eucharistic service, he will be able to witness the entire story of the
salvation of mankind, from the creation of the world to the ascension
of Christ. A full description of the Eucharistic service is evidently
impossible within the limits of a short chapter, but the following
summary includes the chief parts: *The Preparation of the Ministers*.
This consists of a number of prayers, including the Trisagion and
the Lord's Prayer, the Kyrie eleison and the Gloria Patri. The vesting of the bishop at the thysiasterion or ambon is accompanied by
a running comment of Scriptural references. After the ceremony of
the Lavabo (Ps. 26) the Prothesis takes place, with commemoration
of saints. The Censing introduces the Enarxis, with intercessory
prayers and a litany, Ps. 103, and a doxology. *Mass of the Catechumens*. In the Little Entrance the book of the Gospel is brought forth
from the holy place to the nave of the church with appropriate prayers. The Lections include the Apostle, to which the choir responds
with Alleluia, and the Gospel, which is read by the deacon. This is
followed by Prayers in the form of a litany, and then come the Dismissals. They no longer actually dismiss any attendants, but serve
to remind all those present of the necessity of true faith. *Mass of
the Faithful*. Prayers of the Faithful for peace, responded to with
a Kyrie eleison by the choir, one for each petition; the Great Entrance with the Eucharistic elements, followed by a prayer for acceptance; Kiss of Peace; Nicene Creed; Anaphora: Thanksgiving
(Salutation, *ano schomen, axion kai dikaion,* Trisagion); Invocation,
with secret prayer; Intercession, with diptychs for dead and living;
Lord's Prayer by choir or people; Inclination, Elevation; Manual
Acts and Communion, first of the priests, then of the people; Thanksgiving, Dismissal, with antiphonal singing and a prayer of blessing
by the priest; Eulogia or Benedicamus; Dismissal of Ministers.[284]

So far as the present Armeno-Gregorian Rite or the Armenian
Liturgy is concerned, it sprang from the Liturgy of St. Basil. It is
used in Armenia almost exclusively, and since this church is at
variance with the Eastern Orthodox Church, having been separated
from the latter since 595 on account of Monophysite errors, their own
account refers the liturgy to Gregorius Illuminator. Mass is read
only on Sunday, Thursday, and Saturday, these being the days upon
which fasting is not permitted. The language is no longer understood by all the people, but only by such as have studied the Old
Armenian church language. Neale states that the Armenian Church

---

284) Brightman, I, 352—399; Alt, *Der kirchliche Gottesdienst,* 203—
237.

has borrowed much from Rome, a fact which appears especially in the ferial services at terce, sext, and none. The office of the Prothesis and Eucharistic service has the following parts: A. *Officium tes protheseos:* The Vesting, during which the choir sings the hymn of the vesting; Lavabo (Ps. 26, 6) at the foot of the altar steps, in the middle of the church, responded to with the Gloria Patri; Confiteor and Absolution; Psalm 100 antiphonally, with Gloria Patri; Collect; Psalm 44 with Gloria Patri; Prayers to the Holy Ghost; Prothesis of wafer and wine; Hymn of the church: Rejoice greatly, O Zion; Enarxis with Collect and Blessing; Psalm and Hymn of the Day; Collect of the Entrance; B. *Missa Catechumenorum:* The Little Entrance; Trisagion; Prayer for Peace; Lections of Prophet, Apostle, responded to with Alleluia, and Gospel, with Glory be to Thee, O Lord our God; C. *Missa Fidelium:* Nicene Creed, Litany Prayers; Inclination, with Prayer for Peace; Great Entrance; Sanctus while priest and deacon say Psalm 24; Prayer, Kiss of Peace; Anaphora (Thanksgiving, Sursum, Preface, Trisagion, Words of Institution); Invocation, Intercession; Blessing; Lord's Prayer; Inclination; Fraction, Commixture and Communion, during which hymn is sung; Postcommunion with Thanksgiving; Descent from altar; Gospel, John 1, 1—14; Dismissal; Eulogia.[285])

The Nestorian liturgies are usually placed into the Great Oriental group, all of which are derived from the Rite of St. James, but Neale has ascribed to them a separate origin and development, with a Liturgy of St. Thaddeus of Edessa as basis. Its history up to the Middle Ages has been traced above. So far as the present use is concerned, the normal form of worship is the Liturgy of the Apostles Adaeus and Maris. The Office of Theodore the Interpreter is, as Neale thinks, a modification of this, which may fairly be attributed to that voluminous author. "It is used from the first Sunday of the Annunciation, which corresponds to our first Sunday in Advent, to Palm Sunday, and therefore for more than a third part of the year. The Liturgy of Nestorius is a graft of the Constantinopolitan on the old Eastern rite, undoubtedly composed by some Nestorian refugee after the Council of Ephesus. It is used on the Epiphany, Easter, the Vigils of St. John the Baptist, and of the Greek Doctors; and on the Wednesday of the week called the Supplication of Nineveh." [286]) The present liturgy of the Nestorians, including the Anaphora of SS. Adai and Maris, includes the following principal parts: *The Preparation of the Oblation:* The making of the loaves, censing, etc., Prothesis of bread and wine with Trisagion and various Prayers. Order of the Apostles: Enarxis (In the name of the Father, Gloria

285) Alt, 366—373; Brightman, I, 412—457; Daniel, IV, 451—481.
286) Neale, *General Introduction*, III, 317—335.

in excelsis, Lord's Prayer, Prayer of the Anthem, Anthem of the Sanctuary, Lavabo, Gloria Patri, Prayer); *Mass of the Catechumens:* Lift up your voice, Prayer, Lections of Old Testament, Acts, two Prayers before the Apostle, Apostle, Gospel introduced with Hallelujah and Prayer, Anthem of the Gospel; *Mass of the Faithful:* Prayers in the form of a Litany, Inclination, Offertory, Anthem of the Mysteries with Gloria Patri, Creed, Preparation for the Anaphora with Secreta of priest, Diptychs, Kiss of Peace, Anaphora (Thanksgiving with Sursum, Dignum, Trisagion, Institution, Intercession, Invocation, Fraction and Consignation, Blessing "The grace of our Lord," Comminution, Lord's Prayer, Elevation, Communion); Postcommunion with Thanksgiving, Dismissal, Eulogia, and Prayers.[287])

The Syrian Jacobites came into existence after the Council of Chalcedon (451 A. D.), when the Eutychians were excommunicated. They are Monophysites, and are placed on the same level with the members of the Egyptian Church. There have been few changes in their liturgy, so far as structure is concerned, but many of the prayers have been lengthened very much. Their complete liturgy, including the Anaphora of St. James, as now in use, contains the following parts: Preparation of the Celebrant with Psalm 51, Vesting, Preparation of the Altar by placing paten and chalice, lighting taper, etc., Prothesis closing service of penitence with Lord's Prayer; Second Service of Kurbono: Gloria Patri, Offertory, Prayers with Psalm 93 and Commemoration Prayer; *Mass of the Catechumens:* Censing, Lections of Old Testament, Apostles, responded to with Hallelujah, Prayer before Gospel, Gospel, Salutation; *Mass of the Faithful:* Prayers, Creed, Lavatory, Kiss of Peace, Inclination, Prayer of the Veil, Anaphora (Thanksgiving with Salutation, Sursum, Preface, Trisagion, Institution; Invocation, Intercession for Living and Dead, Blessing, Fraction and Consignation, Lord's Prayer, Inclination, Elevation, Communion, the priest taking the Eucharist first, giving the wine with a spoon); Postcommunion with Thanksgiving, Inclination, Dismissal; Ablutions, Eulogia.[288])

When the attempt was made, in the sixth and seventh centuries, to effect a compromise between the orthodox doctrine and that of the Monophysites, the result was another sect, that of the Monothelites, who rallied around Johannes Maron whom they revere as their first patriarch, and after whom they are called Maronites. They were excommunicated at the sixth Ecumenic Council in Constantinople (680 A. D.). They are practically confined to the region of the Lebanon and, to a degree, enjoy political independence. Their li-

---

287) Brightman, *Liturgies Eastern and Western*, I, 247—305; Daniel, *Codex liturgicus*, IV, 171—193; Alt, *Der kirchliche Gottesdienst*, 372. 373.
288) Brightman, I, 69—110.

turgy, which resembles the Coptic, is in Syriac, but the readings from the Gospels are in Arabic, the tongue which is now spoken by them.

The Liturgy of the Egyptian Church, as stated above, is divided into two rites, the Coptic or Sahidic and the Abyssinian or Ethiopic. Both churches are Monophysite in doctrine and have lost a great deal of the vigor in doctrine and practise which characterizes a live orthodoxy. Alt states that the Coptic clergy use a small instrument on the order of a drum, which is beaten during the services with increasing vigor and loudness, while the attendants stamp upon the ground and raise their voices ever higher, until the singing ends in a burst of hideous noise.[289] The Liturgy of the Coptic Jacobites, including the Anaphora of St. Mark and St. Cyril, as modified according to the Sahidic Ecclesiastical Canon, is represented by the following summary: the Prothesis, in which the bread is referred to as the Lamb, the choir singing Psalm 74 and Psalm 116; Enarxis with Salutation, Prayer, also over the Oblation, Absolution; *Mass of the Catechumens;* Censing during secret prayers; Lections of Apostle Paul, followed by Prayer, Catholic Epistle (of James) and Prayer after the Catholicon, Acts of the Apostles; Trisagion, Gospel, preceded by Prayer, and followed by Alleluia and Prayer, Sermon; *Mass of the Faithful:* Prayer of the Veil, the Prayers in form of a Litany, Creed, Kiss of Peace; Anaphora (Thanksgiving with Salutation, *ano, axion,* Preface; Intercession, very long, with response Kyrie eleison; Thanksgiving continued with Words of Institution; Invocation; Consignation; Fraction and Lord's Prayer; Inclination; Elevation; Consignation and Commixture; Communion); Postcommunion with Thanksgiving, Inclination, and Dismissal with Prayer of Imposition of Hands.[290]

The Liturgy of the Abyssinian Jacobites, commonly known as the Ethiopic Liturgy, does not differ greatly from that of Northern Egypt. Schermann has shown that the influence of the Syrian Church, between the fourth and sixth centuries, determined some changes in the liturgy which eventually caused the difference between the Sahidic and Ethiopic rites, especially in the prayers.[291] According to Mercer, the present Ethiopic Liturgy may be summarized in the following form: *Preparation of the Ministers.* Prayer of Penitence, Psalm of David (25, 61, 102, 103, 130, 131), Antiphon and Hallelujah; Prayer for cleansing, Prayer before withdrawing the veil with Doxology, Prayer of Basil; Prayer over all the vessels of the church, Prayer of John, Prayer over the Paten; Vesting with Prayer

289) *Der kirchliche Gottesdienst,* 373.
290) Brightman, I, 144—188.
291) *Aegyptische Abendmahlsliturgieen des ersten Jahrtausends.*

of vesting; long Prayer addressed to communicants with reference to Institution, Prayer after withdrawal of veil before Oblation, Hallelujah; Prayer over the Masob (ciborium) with sign of cross; Prayer at the tabot, Pouring of Wine into Chalice, Prayer over Paten, Prayer over Chalice; Salutations and Responses, concluded with Doxology and Hallelujah; *Enarxis.* Salutation, Prayer of Thanksgiving, Prayer in behalf of those that bring oblations; Salutation, Prayer of the Anaphora; Admonition of the Apostles, Covering of the Bread; Absolution of the Son; Litany; *Little Entrance.* Censing, introduced with short Prayers to the three persons of the Trinity and interspersed with Prayers; Salutation, Lections, including Epistle of St. Paul, Catholic Epistle, Acts of the Apostles, all introduced and responded to with the proper Prayers; Incense and Trisagion, with casting of incense and ascription, Prayer, Hail, Trisagion, Hail Mary, Blessing and final Ascription; Gospel, introduced with a series of Salutations, Prayer to Christ, and other Rites, and special responses after each section of the reading, Dismissal; *Mass of the Faithful.* Salutation, Prayers for the Faithful, responded to with Kyrie; Preparation for Creed; Lavabo with Prayers; Kiss of Peace; Nicene Creed (without the filioque); Anaphora: Thanksgiving (Salutation, Sursum), Intercession, Sanctus, Institution, Invocation, Inclination, Manual Acts, Consignation and Communion; Thanksgiving, Inclination with imposition of hands, Dismissal, Eulogia.[292])

As to other liturgies which belong to the Oriental group, they are of little importance, none of them having had a separate origin or a conspicuous development. The so-called Malabar Liturgy, used in Malabar and Ceylon, was a branch of the Chaldean or Nestorian family. When the Thomas Christians were won for Rome in the 16th century, Menezes, in 1599, reformed their liturgy to conform with the Roman Rite. But in the latter part of the 17th century, the influence of the Jacobite patriarchs of Antioch again gained the ascendency, and the Thomas Christians have returned to the use of Nestorian rites. The influence of the Roman Liturgy upon that of the Jacobites, whom Eugene IV won over in 1441, and upon the United Armenians in Turkey, Russia, and Austria is plainly noticeable in certain additions, but not so prominent as might have been expected. The Maronites have nominally been under the jurisdiction of Rome since 1445, but with the express proviso that doctrine and cultus should not be affected by the union.[293])

Of the early liturgies in the West, only two remain, the Ambrosian and the Mozarabic. An interesting story is told for the retention of the Ambrosian Rite. When Charlemagne was engaged in in-

---

292) Mercer, *The Ethiopic Liturgy*, 151—373; Brightman, I, 194—244.
293) Alt, *Das christliche Kirchenjahr*, 180. 181.

troducing the Roman forms into France, he was very anxious to have also Milan make the change. But as the bishops whose counsel was sought in this matter were unable to decide, they determined to leave the judgment to God. Accordingly, they sealed the service books of both rites and left them on the altar of St. Peter, determining to use the one which would be found open. When the appointed day came, both books opened in a mysterious manner, and the bishops came to the conclusion that both rites must be equally acceptable to God and that therefore the Ambrosian might be retained in Milan, while the rest of the Occident should adopt the Roman use. However credible the account of Landulph may be otherwise, it is much more probable that pious veneration of the name and work of Ambrosius determined the Milanese church in the retention of the ancient rite. When the Roman Rite was being revised, during the period of the Tridentinum, the question again confronted the hierarchy of the patriarchate, but the Synod of the Diocese of Milan in 1568 decided to keep the ancient form of worship. A revised Psalterium was issued in 1574, the other service books appearing later. In 1575 the rite was extended to those parishes of the diocese where it had not yet been in use.[294] The last revisions have very naturally been influenced very strongly by the Roman Rite, so that one may say that only the nucleus or core of the present Milanese use is Ambrosian. It will therefore be sufficient merely to point out the principal points of difference between the two orders of the Mass. The Ambrosian begins with the Psalm "Miserere mei, Deus" in place of the "In nomine." The first part of the Introibo is omitted, but the Judica me is included, also the Confiteor. The Adjutorium follows the Absolution instead of preceding it. The Ingressam of Milan agrees with the Introitus of Rome. The Gloria in excelsis is preceded by Salutation and Oratio super populum, and after it comes the Kyrie. There is a Prophetic Lection with Psalm, then Epistola with Hallelujah and Versus, but not the long Tractus and Antiphons of Rome. The Munda cor introducing the Gospel is short. It is followed by Kyrie and an Antiphona post evangelium. Instead of the Creed we next have Salutation, and then Oratio super sindonem, followed by a Prothesis of the bread and the chalice as an oblation. Then the Offerenda are said and after that the Creed. There is an agreement of the two rites again at the Orationes super oblata, Preface, Tersanctus, Canon with Commemoratio pro vivis, Institutio, and Commemoratio pro defunctis. Instead of the Elevatio there is a Fractio with the Antiphon called Confractorium. In the Pater noster, the Pax, the Agnus Dei, and the Distribution, the

---

294) Baeumer, *Geschichte des Breviers*, 532. 533.

two rites agree, in most cases verbally. Instead of the Video caelos apertos, the Ambrosian has the Antiphona Transitorium. The Post-communion is the same, but the Milanese form of Dismissal is Pro-cedamus in pace. The lesson John 1, 1—14 is used as in the Roman Rite.[295])

As for the Mozarabic Liturgy, the events of the eleventh century did not determine its fate for all time. It had been declared orthodox at Mantua in 1064, a few years before it was abolished in Aragon, and there were always some members of the clergy that were acquain-ted with it and to whom the sonorous fulness of its prayers appealed. An effort to restore its use in 1436 failed, but Cardinal Ximenes of Toledo did not rest until he had been granted permission to use the Mozarabic rites in Toledo and Salamanca. That was in 1500 to 1502. The permission still holds for the cathedral, the Ximenian chapel, and several oratories of Toledo, and one each at Salamanca and Val-ladolid. Migne has reprinted the entire liturgy.[296]) The order of the Mass seems to have been influenced to a great extent by the Ro-man Rite, as an examination of the chief parts shows. The opening of the service in the two rites is the same till after the Absolution. At this point the Mozarabic has a rubric directing the priest to kiss the altar and the cross upon it with the words: Salve crux pretiosa..., upon which follow four Collects. After the Introit comes the Gloria in excelsis. The Lections include the Prophet with following Psalm, the Epistle, and the Gospel, without the usual liturgical embellish-ments. After the Gospel, the Salutation introduces the Prayer of Oblation with the Manual Acts, and the choir sings the Sacrificium, whereupon the Missa Catechumenorum ends with a Prayer of Incli-nation. The Missa proprie sic dicta opens with the Salutation and Prayer de Tempore, upon which the choir sings the Trisagion. There are a number of Antiphons, referring to the oblation and commemo-ration, followed by the Collectio post nomina. There is a section devoted to the Kiss of Peace. The Illatio is a long Praefatio, at whose conclusion the Tersanctus is sung. The Canon Missae is very short, containing mainly the words of Institution, an Oratio post pridie, the Nicene Creed, the Lord's Prayer, and the Sancta Sanctis. Instead of the Agnus Dei the Mozarabic has Benedictio. During Communion the choir sings the Gustate et videte, and at the conclu-sion Refecti Christi corpore. The Postcommunio is introduced with the words Sollemnia completa sunt or Ite, missa est. . . . The Salve regina. . . . and the Concede nos famulos tuos close the service.[297])

---

295) Daniel, *Codex liturgicus*, I, 48—112; Alt, *Der kirchliche Gottes-dienst*, 374—376.
296) *Patrologia latina*, 84. 85. 86.
297) Palmer, *Liturgicae Origines*, I, Chapter 10; Alt, 376—380; Daniel, I, 49—113.

CHAPTER 6.

The Effect of the Reformation on the Liturgy.

"Our people are wrongfully accused of having abolished the Mass. For this is evident (speaking without self-glorification) that Mass is held with us with greater devotion and earnestness than with our adversaries. . . . . Thus also in the public ceremonies of the Mass no notable change has been made, but that in a few places German hymns (for the purpose of teaching the people and giving them practise) are sung in addition to the Latin anthems, since all ceremonies should mainly serve for the purpose that the people may learn what they ought to know in regard to Christ." [298]) It would be hard to find two sentences which in so few words express the principle of the Reformation with regard to its outer form than this passage from the 24th Article of the Augsburg Confession. In them the purpose of Luther and his coworkers to go about in a conservative and constructive manner in the Reformation of the Church is clearly crystallized. Luther had no intention of tearing down and destroying without regard to history and custom, but aimed to edify and build up. He insisted upon correcting the abuses that were based upon false doctrines, but he never used iconoclastic measures, preferring the method of instructing the people as to the reason for the change and then going about the proposed alteration in a quiet manner. And whenever there was a reason for retaining a good ceremony, or one which was not in itself sinful or dangerous, Luther gave his reasons for such retention. This fact redounds all the more to the credit of Luther, since he was by nature quick to think, speak, and act.

As a matter of fact, even the word Mass, so far as Luther was concerned, savored of Romanism and false doctrine. In one passage he derives it from the Hebrew word *mausim,* Dan. 11, 38, and gives the following explanation: "Missa or Mass comes from the Hebrew word *maosim,* which means gathered alms, contribution, or tax, for the sake of the priests or the poor people." [299]) In another passage he writes: "In my Hebrew language I find that *mas* means percentage or tax which is annually given to the government, as Gen. 49, 15: Isachar became a servant unto tribute. And in the books of the Kings it is often stated that countries and peoples were compelled to pay tribute to the children of Israel; for which reason Moses in one place, Deut. 16, 10, calls Missa not the sacrifice, as Dr. Carlstadt dreams, but the first-fruits, which they should willingly bring to the

---

298) Mueller, *Symbolische Buecher,* 51.
299) St. Louis Ed., 22, 1007.

priests on the day of Pentecost as an annual tax, and there before the Lord by their offering confess and thank that they had received such fruits and land from the Lord, as He teaches them in a fine way Deut. 26, 10. 13." [300])   And in the Lutheran Confessions we read: "Missa and liturgia do not mean sacrifices.   Missa in Hebrew means a collected tax.   For this was probably the manner that the Christians brought meat and drink for the benefit of the poor into the meeting. And this custom was derived from the Jews, who were obliged to bring such a tax to their festivals: this they called missa.   Thus also liturgia in Greek really means an office in which one serves the congregation; which agrees well with our doctrine that the priest serves as a common minister of those that wish to go to Communion and gives them the Holy Sacrament. . .   Some believe that missa is not derived from the Hebrew, but means as much as remissio, forgiveness of sins.   For when communion was celebrated, the final words were, Ite, missa est; Go in peace, you have remission of sins." [301])   "Quorsum opus est procul quaerere etymologiam, quum exstet nomen missa, Deut. 16, 10, ubi significat collationes seu munera populi, non oblationem sacerdotis.   Debebant enim singuli venientes ad celebrationem paschae aliquod munus quasi symbolum afferre.   Hunc morem initio retinuerunt et Christiani.   Convenientes offerebant panes, vinum et alia, ut testantur canones apostolorum.   Inde sumebatur pars, quae consecraretur; reliquum distribuebatur pauperibus.   Cum hoc more retinuerunt et nomen collationum missa." [302])   In spite of the fact that many liturgiologists, going back to the Peregrinatio Sylviae and the fourth century, make the unmodified assertion that the word Missa is derived from the formula of dismissal in the chief service, the etymology which Luther and Melanchthon defend has by no means been disproved.   For it was just at the time when the idea of a sacrifice offered in the Eucharist was being broached that the word Missa crept into the language of the Church.   In spite of the fact that Luther has such a strong antipathy against the word Mass, however, and although he cordially wished that he might return to the ancient designation "Communion," he retained the name "Missa," thus signifying that "in the external form of service he did not wish to establish anything new, but merely had the intention of leading back to the old, correct form of worship." [303])

This fact is also established beyond a doubt by a careful comparison of his writings in which he treats of the Mass and its form in some manner.   For Luther had soon gained the conviction that

---

300) 20, 176.   301) Apologia, Art. 24. Mueller, 267.
302) P. 266, Nos. 85. 86.
303) Lochner, *Der Hauptgottesdienst*, 10.

the false doctrines of the pope in regard to the Mass found expression in the Canon of the Mass, and had therefore, in his "Sermon of the New Testament, that is, of the Holy Mass" of Aug. 3, 1520, and in his "Exposition Concerning the Abuse of the Mass," which he wrote in November, 1521, but did not publish till 1522, condemned both doctrine and canon, wherever they did not agree with Scriptures. Another monograph of this period which served to throw light upon the dangers of the Mass, was his "Book of the Babylonian Captivity of the Church," of Oct. 6, 1520. Luther's object in issuing these books was to lay bare the foundation of false doctrine and ambiguity upon which the Mass rests, in order that the people might be able to judge for themselves and thus be prepared for changes in the external forms of worship.

But while Luther was thus working in a quiet manner and paving the way, by thorough instruction, for the abolishment of the anti-Scriptural ritual of the Mass, his colleague Carlstadt, who at that time was incidentally archdeacon of the dome-church, proved himself a man without judgment, whose rashness greatly interfered with the quiet spread of the Reformation. While Luther was at the Wartburg, on Dec. 22, 1521, he declared in a public sermon that he would, on the coming day of Circumcision, celebrate Mass according to Christ's institution. He carried out his intention even sooner, namely on Christmas Day. He celebrated Mass after the sermon, omitting everything that referred to the sacrifice and also the elevation, and finally giving the people bread and wine with the words of institution, but without previous confession, each communicant taking the elements with his own hands. Since Luther was not in Wittenberg, Carlstadt met with no serious opposition and acted according to his own good pleasure. A scant month later, on Jan. 24, 1522, the Council and the University of Wittenberg adopted the church order proposed by him. In this order, the form of the Mass is given as follows: "Let them sing introitum, kyrieleison, gloria in excelsis, et in terra, collecta or preces, Epistle, gradual without sequence, Gospel, credo, offertorium, praefatio, sanctus without canonem majorem and minorem, since they are not according to Scripture. Then begins the Evangelical meal; if there be communicants, the priest consecrates; if there be none, he consecrates and communes, if his devotion tends thereto; thereafter he concludes with the collecta, without Ite, missa est." [304) Here Carlstadt shows plainly that he has not the faintest understanding of either the correlation or the meaning of the ancient services. For that the Preface with the Sanctus should be sung and

---

304) Sehling, *Die evangelischen Kirchenordnungen des 16. Jahrhunderts*, I, 698; Kliefoth, *Die urspruengliche Gottesdienstordnung*, IV, 21. 22.

the consecration take place, even if no communion was to be celebrated, renders the liturgy meaningless. It is here that the reformers showed the proper intuition in their structure of the liturgy, for it is essential that the Distribution follow the Consecration, to complete the Communion. They amended the Augustinian maxim: Accedat verbum ad elementum, et fit sacramentum, by adding; Et distribuantur ambo. Fortunately, Luther arrived in Wittenberg on March 7, 1522, and his coming terminated the reign of license and lawlessness which Carlstadt and his coworkers had instigated. Through his well-known eight sermons against the iconoclasts Luther restored peace in Wittenberg and in a measure corrected the wrong impression which the "heavenly prophets" had produced in many minds. Luther's judgment in regard to Carlstadt's entire method of procedure is contained in one sentence: "It was done in a criminal outrage, without any order, with offense of the neighbor."

As matters now stood in Wittenberg, it would not have been advisable to return to the former Roman Mass, but Luther advised the most conservative progress in the matter of liturgical reform: to celebrate Mass in the accustomed vestments, with chanting and all the traditional ceremonies, and in the Latin language; to expunge all words in the Canon and in the prayers which have any reference to the sacrifice; to abolish private masses, but not the daily Mass, gradually reducing their number, however, until Eucharist be celebrated only on Sundays or when communicants are present. In the meantime, Luther advised the clergy to preach diligently concerning Holy Communion and to teach the people, in order that the way might be paved for further and more radical changes.

Luther himself did not remain inactive in this matter, although he made no public move with regard to the practical amelioration of existing conditions until the next year. The Council and the congregation of Leissnig prompted him to carry out the intention which he had had for several years, that of publishing a full order of worship, from which the objectionable features of the Roman Mass should be eliminated. The people of Leissnig sent their representatives to Luther on Jan. 25, 1523, expressing, in the accompanying credentials, the earnest hope and petition that Luther would collate for them "an order to sing and pray and read." To this petition Luther promised to accede, as he states in his answer of Jan. 29. Shortly after Easter, in accordance with this promise, there appeared his short monograph "Of the Order of Divine Service in the Congregation." [305] His position is still very conservative, but he wants the daily Masses abol-

---

305) 10, 220—225; Daniel, *Codex liturgicus*, II, 75—80; Kliefoth, IV, 27.

ished entirely and the liturgy purified of papal leaven. Above all, however, he enunciates the principle which he insisted upon ever afterwards with the greatest emphasis: "To abrogate these abuses, it is necessary first to know that the Christian congregation should never meet unless God's Word is there preached and prayed, even if it be very brief. . . . Therefore, when God's Word is not preached, it is better neither to sing nor to read nor to assemble."

In the course of the summer Luther found occasion to write to the Chapter of Wittenberg, under date of August 19, 1523, with reference to the services held in the dome.[306]) This he followed up, on October 12 of the same year, with a letter to Spalatin, in which he discussed the abolition of the Roman Masses and ceremonies in the church of Wittenberg.[307]) The very next month, November, 1523, he published his Formula missae et communionis pro ecclesia Wittenbergensi.[308]) It is addressed to Nicolaus Hausmann in Zwickau, who had been especially importunate in urging Luther to finish its collation. It is interesting to see here how carefully and tactfully the Reformer distinguishes and chooses. All the parts that were not anti-Scriptural, he retained; whatever he expunged, he omitted with good reasons, clearly stated. The changes which he advocated were equally well founded. His order of service contained the following parts: Introitus (quamquam psalmos mallemus, unde sumpti sunt); Kyrie eleison (ut hactenus celebratum est) with following Gloria in excelsis; Oratio seu Collecta (modo sit pia, ut fere sunt quae dominicis diebus habentur); Lectio epistolae; Graduale (duorum versuum simul cum Alleluia); Lectio evangelii (ube nec candelas neque thurificationem prohibemus, sed nec exigimus); Symbolum Nicaenum; Sermo (either in this place or before the Introit). In the first part of the service, therefore, Luther had omitted the Initium missae with the Confiteor and also the Sequences or Proses, the former, because it could not be retained in its form, as then obtaining in the Roman use, the latter in order to shorten the services somewhat. At the same time, Luther was anxious to have the sequences retained for the vesper services, either in Latin or in a good German transcription.

While Luther, then, in the first part, had admitted almost every part of the Roman ordo, he attacked the second part, with the Canon missae, with drastic zeal. He called this section an abomination and stated, in his characteristic manner: Abhinc omnia fere sonant ac olent oblationem. He deleted the Offertorium, the Secreta, and the entire Canon missae. He also changed the text in numerous places in order to remove every suspicion of false doctrine from the Collects. The following parts remained after he had finished his recension:

---

306) 19, 1184—1189.   307) 19, 1188—1191.
308) 10, 2230—2255; Daniel, II, 80—97.

Praefatio with Salutation, Sursum, Dignum; Verba institutionis (in
eo tono vocis. . . ., ut a circumstantibus possit audiri); Oratio dominica and Pax domini, preceded by Sanctus; Communion, during
which Agnus Dei sung; Postcommunio with Oratio, Salutatio, Benedicamus Domino, Benedictio (Num. 6, 24—26)." [309])

Much as had been accomplished by these changes, Luther was
not yet satisfied. The longer he studied the question, the more he
was filled with horror on account of the private masses, votive masses,
and masses for the dead, with their complete annihilation of the
Holy Eucharist. During the year 1524 he therefore issued his book
"Of the Abomination of the Private Mass which is Called the Canon,"
directing his invective principally against the portion called the
Secreta, with its false doctrine of the unbloody sacrifice.[310]) On the
17th of November of the same year he again directed a letter to the
Chapter at Wittenberg, begging them to celebrate the Eucharist sub
utraque and to omit the impious ceremonies. The result was that a
new order was introduced at Wittenberg on December 24, which
abolished all masses but those on Sundays. If no communicants had
been announced, Mass should not be said. In that case, the order of
service was to be: Introitus, Kyrie eleison, Et in terra, etc., Collects
de tempore, Credo, Patrem, Pater noster, Agnus Dei, and the order
of Luther of 1523 should be followed.[311])

In the year 1525 the Reformer succeeded in completing his first
draft for a German order of services. In regard to this order, he
wrote to John Lang and the other minister at Erfurt, on October 28:
"We had indeed drawn up an outline and have sent it to our Prince,
and now the form will, by his order, be completed and tried tomorrow,
on Sunday, in the name of Christ, in a public trial. But it will be
a German Mass for the lay people." [312]) He refers also to the printed
copies which might soon be expected. Thus the first German Mass
at Wittenberg was celebrated on the 29th of October, 1525, this being
the 20th Sunday after Trinity. The musician John Walther wrote
the music for the liturgy under Luther's direction, and with his help.
It is characteristic of Luther that he on that day, after the sermon,
once more briefly explained to the assembled people for what reason
and with what intention the change was made, in order to avoid offense.[313]) The public trial of the Mass in the vernacular having met
with approval, it was, at the following Christmas, permanently introduced into worship at Wittenberg.[314])

---

309) Lochner, *Der Hauptgottesdienst*, 15—17; Alt, *Der kirchliche
Gottesdienst*, 263. 264; Sehling, *Op. cit.*, 4—6.   310) 19, 1198—1214.
311) 19, 1196. 1197.   312) 21a, 797.   313) 11, 1786.
314) Cp. Kliefoth, Sehling, De Wette, Horn, Richards-Painter, etc.

Only a short time later, in the first months of the year 1526, there followed the printed edition "German Mass and Order of Services." [315]) Luther expressly states that this order in the vernacular was not intended to supersede or change the Formula missae. And there are, in the parts which he retained, only few additions. His substitutions were not so happy as they might have been, especially in the case of the German Sanctus and the substitution of the Paraphrasis for the Praefatio. The following parts are included in the full order of services: At the beginning an anthem or German Psalm; then Kyrieleison, three times, not nine times; then the priest reads a Collect; then the Epistle; after the Epistle is sung a German hymn: Now we do pray the Holy Ghost, or some other, and that with the whole choir; then the priest reads the Gospel; after the Gospel the whole congregation sings the Creed: We all believe in one true God; then follows the Sermon upon the Gospel of the Sunday or holiday. After the Sermon there shall follow a public Paraphrase of the Lord's Prayer and an Admonition to those that intend to partake of Holy Communion. Then follows the Office and Consecration: Words of Institution, the German Sanctus or the hymn, Now God be praised, or, Jesus Christ our Blessed Savior, and the German Agnus Dei during the Distribution. Then the Thanksgiving, Collect, and the Aaronic Benediction.[316]) Although the responsive liturgy had been reduced by Luther to a minimum, his order was, on the whole, liturgically correct, and the fact that it was in the vernacular appealed to the people very strongly. Bugenhagen soon made provision for the chief service, without the celebration of the Eucharist, by directing that the first part of the service should be held as usual. After the sermon, in the usual vestments of the Mass, shall be sung the Preface, Sanctus, the German Pater Noster, O Christ thou Lamb of God, a German Collect, and the Blessing.[317])

Luther's work was not only followed with great interest in Wittenberg and elsewhere, but it also had the warmest approbation and the most cordial coöperation of his colleagues and friends. Bugenhagen, Melanchthon, and Spalatin especially worked in the spirit and after the manner of Luther. Other men were not influenced so directly by Luther, but they took their inspiration from him and followed the fundamental principles for public worship as enunciated by him. The various countries of the German Empire soon published extensive church regulations (Kirchenordnungen), which contained the outlines, rules and regulations of all services and liturgical acts

315) 10, 226—257; Daniel, 97—112.
316) Cp. Alt, *Der kirchliche Gottesdienst*, 266—271.
317) Alt, 270, nota.

as they appeared in special service books, known as Cantionales and
Agenda. These church books have been preserved and edited mainly
by Richter and Sehling, and afford a most interesting study. They
are generally divided into three groups. The first group includes the
forms that were most conservative and carefully followed the traditional uses. The most notable are the Brandenburg (arranged by
Stratner of Ansbach and Buchholtzer of Berlin, in 1540), the Pfalz-
Neuburg of 1543, based upon the preceding, and the Austrian of 1571
(arranged by Chytraeus), which has marked Romanizing tendencies.
To the second group belong all the church orders of the Saxon-Luthe-
ran type, based upon the Formula missae and the Deutsche Messe.
Some of the best-known are the Prussian, 1525, Brunswick, 1528,
Hamburg, 1529, Minden and Goettingen, 1530, Luebeck, 1531, Soest,
1532, Bremen, 1534, Pomeranian, 1535, all of which appeared under
the direction of Bugenhagen; the Brandenburg-Nuernberg, 1533 (by
Osiander and Brenz), for Duke Henry of Saxony, 1539 (by Justus
Jonas), and others by Urbanus Rhegius, Chemnitz, and Andreae.
The third group presents the so-called mediating type between the
Lutheran and the Reformed service. Some church orders of this
group are those of Strassburg, Wuertemberg, the Palatine, of Baden,
Worms, and others. The beginning of this type was made by Bucer,
Capito, Hedio, and others, in 1525. The orders of Brenz, the Schwae-
bisch-Hall, of 1526, and especially the New Schwaebisch-Hall, of
1543, and the Great Wuertemberg, of 1553, show less of this peculiarity.[318]

It is most interesting to find the principles enunciated by the
great reformers laid down so distinctly in the Lutheran Confessions,
the principal passages being the Augsburg Confession, Articles XV
and XXVIII, the Apologia Confessionis, Article XXIV, the Articuli
Smalcaldici, Pars II, Art. II, and the Formula Concordiae, Art. X,
30. 31.[319]

Thus the reformers worked with all energy at the gigantic task,
producing scores of service books which were free from Roman doctrine and superstition and gave the people the opportunity to take an
intelligent part in services which were, for the most part, conducted
in the vernacular. Luther had good reason for writing, in 1533:
"God be praised, in our churches we can show a Christian a right
Christian Mass according to the order and institution of Christ, and
according to the true meaning of Christ and the church. There our
pastor, bishop, or servant in the ministry, correctly and truly and

318) Cp. Horn, *Liturgics*, 123; Richards-Painter, *Christian Worship*.
Chapter IX; *Memoirs*, IV: 1.
319) Mueller, 42. 62. 257—262. 301—305. 703.

openly called, who was consecrated, anointed, and born to be a priest
of Christ in Baptism, steps before the altar; he sings publicly and
plainly the order of Christ, instituted in the Lord's Supper, takes
bread and wine, gives thanks, distributes and gives it by the power
of the word of Christ: This is my body, this is my blood, this do, etc.,
to us, who are there and wish to receive it, and we, especially those
intending to partake of the Sacrament, kneel down beside, behind,
and around him, man, woman, young, old, master, servant, mistress,
maid, parents, children, as the Lord brings us together there, all true,
holy copriests, sanctified through the blood of Christ and anointed
and consecrated through the Holy Ghost in Baptism. . . That is our
Mass and the right Mass, of which we are no longer in want." [320])

CHAPTER 7.

The Liturgical Deterioration of the Latter Seventeenth and the Eighteenth Century.

"It is a lugubrious, heartrending chapter out of the history of
the Lutheran Church and of the Christian Church in general, this
chapter before us!" These words of Kliefoth [321]) may well be placed
at the head of this chapter. To turn from the beauty and glory of
the 16th century, where every pulse in the body of the renovated
Church was quivering and throbbing with vigor and energy, when
the ancient doctrine of justification was again proclaimed in all its
purity, and the service of the Church was once more fashioned after
the simplicity of the earliest times, — to leave this, and come upon
a scene of ruin and destruction, with only a few oases remaining in
a vast desert of blackened tombs, is very depressing and disheartening.
Just when the canker first appeared is not difficult to find. It may
be, of course, that the pressure which was brought to bear upon certain Lutheran communities at the time of the two Interims, the
Augustanum and the Lipsiense, and by Reformed influences in other
parts of Germany, determined, in a measure, their aspect of doctrinal
and liturgical questions. To such influences, for example, might be
traced the Austrian Church Order of 1571, on the one hand, and
some of the later ones of southwestern Germany on the other. It
may also be, as has been suggested, that the fire of the first love had
spent itself after a century of brightest burning. But the main reason for the liturgical deterioration, which began in the second half
of the 17th century and lasted well into the 19th, must be sought, as

---

320) *Von der Winkelmesse und Pfaffenweihe,* 19, 1279, 1280.
321) *Die urspruengliche Gottesdienstordnung,* V, 207.

Kliefoth shows, in the period of restoration, which had its beginning after the close of the Thirty Years' War, and extended to the first decenniums of the 18th century.[322])

The task which confronted the ecclesiastical authorities of Germany at the end of the Thirty Years' War was little short of Herculean. Not only single villages or cities, but entire provinces had been rendered desolate. The congregations in most states had been decimated, many of them had been reduced to a scant percentage of survivors. The churches and school-houses had been desecrated, burned, devastated, the sacred vessels and vestments had been taken as welcome plunder. Many parishes had neither pastor nor schoolmaster to maintain records and, in many cases, the records were lost entirely. The men, for the most part, were drafted for some form of military service, the boys joined the regular armies or the bands of guerillas for the sake of adventure. The education and training of the young was, of necessity, neglected. The few pastors that remained did their best to stem the tide of godless living and desecration of everything holy which rushed in the wake of the armies, but could do little to maintain Christian order and discipline. With the coming of peace, the leaders of the Evangelical Church in Germany intended to work order out of chaos. It was not a problem of reformation and renovation, but of restoration; "not the work of purifying the Church's faith and practise, which had already been done, but the much more difficult task of again bringing the purified faith and practise into the consciousness and life of a people demoralized by war, having no real hunger and thirst for the Gospel, and therefore not responsive to it as the masses of the preceding century had been." [323])

The leaders of the Church were bent upon a quick and thorough restoration of the status quo ante. Instead of depending upon the slow and laborious method of educating the people and gradually making them accustomed to decency, order, and a Christian life, they determined to set in again just where the war had interrupted the work of the Church. One of their first steps was the publication or re-issue of the old Church Orders, many of which had been destroyed during the war, and none of which were longer in operation. They added numerous provisions, instituted regular visitations, fixed the income of the parishes, regulated the circumstances of the congregational activities, restored the jurisdiction of the consistories, and sought, by legalistic means, to bring order into the cultus.[324]) It cannot be doubted that this method may have been demanded by the conditions. There is also no reason for assuming that the men who

322) Kliefoth, V, 210.
323) Ohl, *The Liturgical Deterioration, Memoirs*, IV: 6.
324) Cp. Alt, *Der kirchliche Gottesdienst*, 317.

instigated the restoration were not sincere and sought anything but the welfare of their charges. They were bred in the orthodox faith and filled with love and desire to work for the Master.

But the fatal defect of the revised Church Orders was their legalistic, bureaucratic character. "The conceptions underlying many of their new provisions were legalistic and often dogmatically unsound; obedience was to be effected not solely by the power of evangelical truth, as in the 16th century, but rather by threats of punishment for disobedience; and the result was that the very idea of the Church and its purpose became externalized, grades and hierarchical tendencies began to manifest themselves in its ministry, and, when at last the Church became a mere department of the civil government, the latter undertook to regulate not only the more external parochial affairs, but even to prescribe what liturgies, hymnbooks, and doctrinal standards should be used." [325])

The resulting deterioration came about in such a gradual manner that its insidiousness was hardly noticed at first. No doubt an important factor in giving impetus to the decay was the position of the rulers of Prussia, whose unionistic propensities were favorable to indifference in dogmatic and ritualistic position. The admiration for the doctrinal vigor and the liturgical beauty of the Reformation period remained, the intention of returning to the purity of the previous century was often proclaimed, but the vitality for concerted action was lacking. Since the congregations were not able to perform, as their part of the services, what the Church Orders of the 16th century demanded of them, and since the bureaucratic clergy felt no incentive to instruct their charges in a proper manner, the demands were simply reduced to the ability of the people. The last remnant of Latin chanting was omitted, and instead of rendering the parts of the service into German, the responsories of that kind were abolished. The more difficult anthems, involving antiphonal singing, followed, and before long the only participation of the congregation in the service was the singing of the chorals. The result was that the classic art of choral music fell into desuetude. In many cases, even the singing of the chorals was reduced to a minimum and all responsive chanting delegated to the choir and the cantor.[326])

Toward the end of the 17th century it became apparent that the Church of Germany had submitted to a dead orthodoxy with its consequent formalism. The pendulum was therefore bound to swing to the other extreme. The detached, uninterested objectivity was followed by an excessive subjectivity, which was bound to overshoot the mark in the opposite direction. The reaction crystallized in the

325) Ohl, *L. c.*, 68.   326) Kliefoth, V, 223.

Pietistic movement, as it was fully developed in the first part of the
18th century. The chief exponent of the movement was Spener.
Acting upon his suggestion, the public meetings of the congregation,
public communion, and private confession, were supplemented by
private religious meetings in the home (collegia pietatis), private
communion, and private religious conversation in the pastor's study.
But the revival of spiritual life, for which the early Pietism had
hoped, soon brought about methods and caused sentiments which were
destructive to the cultus of the Church. The subjective conception
of service and the idea of secret communion with God which the
closet exercises had generated reacted upon the form of service.
A critical attitude toward the content of the sermon became evident;
it was stated that the truth of the preacher's discourse depended upon
the attitude of his heart, whether he were truly regenerated. The
public sermon was no longer regarded as the most essential part of
the minister's work, but rather the individual pastoral cura. The
idea of fixed parts in the liturgy became increasingly distasteful to
the Pietists. "Extempore prayer was substituted for the church
prayer; the objective church hymn gave way to hymns descriptive of
the soul's changing conditions, experiences, and feelings; the hymnbooks were arranged according to the order of salvation instead of
the church year; new melodies suited to the emotional character of
the new hymns displaced the vigorous old church tunes; the sentimental aria and strains patterned after the prevailing style in opera
completely crowded out the noble polyphonic choir music of the early
masters; . . . in a word, what Pietism set out to do finally resulted
not in bringing about again a proper union between the objective and
the subjective, but in the overthrow of the former and the triumph
of the latter. The sacramental and the sacrificial were divorced, and
the sacrificial alone remained." [327]

In what manner Pietism brought about the gradual deterioration
of the old Lutheran form of service, is shown by the example of the
litany, adduced by Kliefoth. The litany, having a fixed form, could
hardly keep the approval of the new ideas. So its removal was effected in the following manner. The revised Church Order of Mecklenburg permitted the change between the litany and the church
prayer, so the prayer was given the preference, and the litany used
only for prayer meetings and rogation days. Then the antiphonal
singing was abolished, and the minister ordered to read the parts or
the congregation to sing them. And finally, its use was entirely abrogated. At the same time, the fixed church prayer was permitted to
be replaced by an extemporaneous effort, and the desired result thus
finally obtained.

---

327) Ohl, 70.

THE LITURGICAL DETERIORATION. 287

Pietism, culminating in a shallow subjectivism, had either destroyed a large part of the Lutheran liturgy or robbed it of its meaning And, in so doing, it had unfortunately prepared the way for the destructive activity of Rationalism. Rationalism, as Kliefoth states, is not a movement in the Church or of the Church, but a product of science, and that a science which is emancipated from the Gospel and the Christian faith. During its reign of almost a century, reason sat enthroned as a tyrant, obtruding its hypotheses and theories upon the congregations and making the divinely inspired Word an object of its blasphemous experiments. The Rationalists rejected both the form and the content of the historic church service. "What sort of appreciation for the church year could a theology have that based its belief, not on the great historic facts of redemption, but on its own speculations? How could such a religion of reason permit the service on its sacramental side to remain what it originally was in the Lutheran Church, — a real communication of divine grace through the audible and visible Word? What spiritual pleasure could it find in the hymns and prayers and liturgical formularies in which the living faith, begotten by Word and Sacrament, was once wont to bring its sacrifice of thanksgiving and praise? Or how could it even understand the meaning of a cultus with whose history it did not care to become familiar, and that stood for a past to which it was absolutely indifferent?" [328])

The result of such principles was a most disastrous one for the remnants of the ancient Lutheran service. The church became a mere lecture hall, not only in Germany, but in all countries where the germs of Rationalism were disseminated. The sermon became a discourse consisting of rhetorical platitudes, and even shallow, bombastic nonsense, with a slightly moral tinge. Fixed prayers were no longer recognized, not even those whose text is found in Scriptures; the old Lutheran hymns were mutilated beyond recognition. A service, however, which offered to the congregations nothing but insipid hymns, dry and bombastic prayers, and a tedious sermon which was often a mere twaddle concerning matters of the daily civil and domestic life, which edified none and, at best, had little practical value, was bound to make the churches empty.

Such were the factors which were instrumental in causing the deterioration and, in many cases, the total destruction of the ancient Lutheran liturgy. At the beginning of the last century, matters had come to such a pass that the order for the chief service had been pared down to the bare name, the minor services had practically disappeared, the ancient church calendar was no longer observed, and

328) Ohl, *L. c.*, 71.

the forms for sacred acts had been reduced to a conglomerate of bombastic phrases. The old liturgical parts, the Introits, Kyries, Credo, Prefaces, Agnus Dei, Litany and Te Deum, Magnificat, Benedictus, Nunc pacem, etc., which are either Scripture passages or almost as ancient as the Christian liturgy, were consigned to oblivion. In a few cases, the one or the other was still found in the order of worship, but either in the wrong position, or with the wrong mode of execution. For the glorious, uplifting Prefaces the new orders had insipid substitutes, such as: "Let every one of us according to his ability lift up mind, heart, and spirit to the invisible world, etc." [329] In the matter of collects, the greatest license began to rule. The pithy, sententious collects of the Reformation period were exchanged for verbose, diluted, subjective formulas. Even the Words of Institution, of Distribution, the Lord's Prayer, and the Benediction were recast. Of the Lord's Prayer, a great number of rhymed and unrhymed paraphrases appeared, and not in the language of Scriptures, but in the poetical imagery of the preacher, and Alt relates of one, that he had even succeeded in expressing the grand prayer in the form of a neat distych. One of the so-called ministers of this period opened the service of Easter Sunday with a morning hymn, read a prayer at the altar composed by himself in which he praised among the benefits of the Christian religion that it liberated man from error and superstition. There followed a hymn on the dread of ghosts and a sermon on the same topic.[330]

In this rarefied atmosphere, orders of services and agendas were notable for their attenuated tendencies. The private attempts of Seiler, Gutlin, Sintenis, Zollikofer, and others, as well as the unionistic measures of Frederick I, were full of sentimental subjectivism and without any idea of the demands of churchliness. The service as fixed by the last-named monarch included an opening hymn, prayer at the altar, sermon hymn, sermon, intercessions, thanksgivings, and proclamations, the general confession, Lord's Prayer, and benediction (without sign of cross), reading of words of institution, communion at table.[331] According to Kliefoth, one might construct a composite liturgy for the communion service of the latter half of the 18th and the beginning of the 19th century as follows. The Introit, Kyrie, and Gloria have been abandoned, their place being taken by an introductory hymn. Then follows Salutation, Collect, Epistle, Hymn, Sermon, the Creed being sung in a few places before the Sermon. The reading of the Gospel had been abolished. The Hallelujah, Sequences, Graduals, and the beautiful liturgical responses were con-

329) Lochner, 206.   330) Alt, *Der kirchliche Gottesdienst*, 320.
331) Alt, 316.

signed to oblivion. In that part of the service which was devoted to the Eucharist still less remained. The General Prayer was superseded by a short prayer formula. The Preface was no longer found. The Exhortation had been retained in a few places, as also the Consecration and Communion, but the congregation did not respond, and the Agnus Dei was soon unknown. Even in the Postcommunion the responses of the congregation were dropped, and the Nunc dimittis was replaced by a convenient verse. Often the Lord's Prayer was spoken by the minister in conclusion.

The saddest fact in connection with the general deterioration of the liturgy, however, was the corruption of the text in the ancient, venerable forms. One is inclined to mistrust his own eyes when reading sections from the Agenda of Schleswig-Holstein, by Adler, 1797.[332]) The sentimental shallowness of the Address and Prayer before Communion is actually revolting to anyone familiar with the corresponding passages of the 16th century orders. The Thanksgiving of the Postcommunion has the following form: "God, how happy are we, and what thanks we owe to Thee, our Father and Benefactor, that Thou through Thy Son, Jesus Christ, hast led us to the understanding of Thy heavenly truth and to the enjoyment of the benefits in which we, as Christians, find our delight. For all that we have in Him, as our Teacher, Redeemer, and Savior, for all the hope in suffering which we find in Him and in remembrance of Him, for all the comfort when our conscience torments us, we praise Thy fatherly love to-day. Let our thanks be well-pleasing to Thee! But awaken us now also to the proper use of the benefits which Thou hast given us! Keep us in Thy truth; confirm our faith; strengthen our love toward Thee and to our brethren; teach us to be of a like mind as Jesus Christ was, and imprint it deeply in our souls that He died for all, in order that we might not live to us, Father, but Thee, and to Him who for love to us went into death. Hear our prayer for the sake of Thy mercy." This paraphrase is at least unobjectionable from the doctrinal standpoint with all its verbosity. But the transcription of the Benediction is decidedly out of place: "The Lord bless you and keep you! The Lord, who forgives sin and transgression, be gracious to you! The Lord, who has called you to salvation, give you His peace!" [333])

Some instances of liturgical aberration are quoted also by Dr. Ohl,[334]) from which the following extracts may suffice. In an Exhortation, the sentences occur: "At this table, consecrated to the Lord,

---

332) Daniel, *Codex liturgicus*, II, 162—184.   333) P. 172.
334) *The Liturgical Deterioration*, 73—78.

let all eat and drink with profoundest emotion! Let this bread and
wine typify to you the death of Jesus on the cross; and let the eating
of this bread and the drinking of this wine symbolize the participation in all the blessings of His death! May you be deeply moved by
the surpassing greatness and beauty of soul of which this Divine One
gave evidence when for your salvation He permitted His body to be
broken and His blood to be shed, and died upon the cross! Come to
Him, then, as it is natural for good people to do, with ardent gratitude. . . ." The Words of Institution are treated thus: "Let all hear
the invitation of Jesus Himself to His Supper! After this manner
spake the Lord when He took bread, brake it praying, and distributed
it: Take, eat, this is My Body, which shall soon be offered for your
benefit. Repeat this in remembrance of Me! Thus spake the Lord
when He afterward also prayerfully passed the cup around: Take,
drink, this is My Blood; which shall soon be shed for your benefit!"
A Form of Distribution reads: "Use this bread in remembrance of
Jesus Christ; he that hungereth after pure and noble virtue shall be
filled. — Drink a little wine; he that thirsteth after pure and noble
virtue shall not long for it in vain!" The Lord's Prayer was mutilated thus: "Most High Father: Let it be our supreme purpose to
glorify Thee; Let truth thrive among us; Let virtue already dwell
here as it does in heaven; Reward our industry with bread, And our
forgiving disposition with grace; From severe conflicts preserve us;
And finally let all evil cease; That Thou art powerful, wise, and good
over all — let this forever be our confidence."

Some of the other examples quoted are still more incredible and
astounding. And the humiliating fact in connection with this review
is this, that in spite of all reconstruction across the sea some of the
Pietistic and Rationalistic leaven still clings to the Lutheran services
in many parts of our country. It is only by continued effort and
patient education that the last remnants of this sad period in the
history of our Church may be removed.

CHAPTER 8.

The Book of Common Prayer.

There can be no reasonable doubt, as eminent English liturgiologists have shown, that the ancient liturgy of England was derived
from Ephesine or Gallican sources, reaching England in the last part
of the second or in the third century by way of Lyons. This supposition is supported by a greater mass of evidence than that of any
other derivation. It is certain that there was constant and lively
intercourse between Cornwall, Wales, and Britain, on the one hand,
and Gaul, on the other. And the resemblances to the Gallican Rite

which are found in the English Rite are of a nature to preclude almost the possibility of any other influence. The second revision of the Vulgate was used, the same Paschal cycle appears, the proper prefaces are undoubtedly of the same origin as in the Gallican Rite. Then, also, the position of the benediction is significant, the prayers for the departed exhibit a striking similarity, the use in the ritual anciently of only two liturgical colors, white and violet, the wording of the rubrics "shall say" or "let him say": all these features stamp the use of England as one which is most assuredly related closely to the Gallican form.[335])

In 449 occurred the Anglo-Saxon invasion under the leadership of Hengist and Horsa. Although the purpose of the invaders was primarily the conquest of the country, yet they, together with the West Saxons which followed them toward the end of the century, directed their enmity also against the religious faith of the inhabitants. "The rage of the English," says Green, "seems to have burned fiercest against the clergy. The priests were slain at the altar, the churches fired, the peasants driven by the flames to fling themselves on a ring of pitiless steel." The greater part of Britain was thoroughly anglicized and the Christian Britons either reduced to slavery, killed, or driven to the mountains and fastnesses of Cornwall and Wales. Nevertheless, a remnant clung to their faith in spite of persecution and death.

Since the greater part of what is now England was now again under pagan dominion, it became necessary to win the country for the second time. The opportunity came when Aethelberht, king of Kent, and overlord over the southern and southeastern part of the island, married Bertha, the daughter of the Frankish king, Charibert of Paris, who was a Christian, like her Frankish kinsfolk. "A Christian bishop accompanied her from Gaul to Canterbury, the royal city of the kingdom of Kent, and a ruined Christian church, the church of St. Martin, was given them for their worship." [336]) This gave Gregory the Great, at that time pope, an opportunity to send missionaries to England. He despatched the monk Augustine, who landed in 597 and was soon made archbishop of Canterbury. According to the account of Bede, he was soon made aware of the fact that the old British or Celtic Church had persisted in spite of the oppressors and intended to keep its ancient rites. Gregory, who was prudent as well as energetic, gave Augustine the right to collect into a sort of bundle the best usages of Rome, of Gaul, or of other churches. In spite of this concession, however, Augustine did not succeed in winning the Britons over to the Roman rule. It was not until 668,

335) Cp. Gwynne, *Primitive Worship and the Prayer Book*, Chapter VII. 336) Green, *History of the English People*, 17.

when Theodore of Tarsus was made archbishop of Canterbury, that much progress was made. Although Theodore, to some extent, treated the British Christians in a high-handed way, he was also wise enough to make concessions, and thus gained many friends. During the next centuries papal rule gradually, but surely, won acknowledgment. The Anglo-Saxon Church went into complete vassalage to the papal see, and the state was subjected to ecclesiastical dominion.

In spite of all these changes, however, the Celtic and the Scotch Liturgy continued in use beside the Roman, and many of the remote dioceses retained their ancient organization. The Scottish Rite persisted till the eleventh century, and that of the Church of Wales even to the year 1200. In the mean time, the Norman conquest materially changed the situation in England. The pressure brought to bear upon isolated dioceses and parishes retaining the ancient forms was becoming increasingly burdensome. It was then that St. Osmund, of Salisbury, about 1085, revised the liturgy into national uniformity. Working upon the basis of the Use of Rouen, he nevertheless included certain features of the ancient Gallican Rite in his revision, in certain prayers and lections, in the form of the marriage ceremony, etc. Thus the Use of Sarum came into existence (ca. 1087). Other bishops did the same for their dioceses, in much the same manner. We therefore find uses of York, of Hereford, of Bangor, of Lincoln. Some of these have been published by the Henry Bradshaw Society, that of York by the Surtees Society. The complete Roman Rite was used in the monasteries throughout the country. Thus matters stood until the beginning of the 16th century.

In 1516, the prelude to the great anthem of the Reformation was sounded when the ancient Use of Sarum was amended and revised. This recasting was based upon the Leonian, the Gelasian, and the Gregorian forms, but still showed very strongly the influence of the Gallican Rite. In 1541, after the movement of the Reformation had found its adherents throughout England, a second revision of the Salisbury Rite was undertaken, following a reprint of the earlier liturgy, in 1531, and a revision of the Missal, in 1533. By 1548, the new movement had become so strong that Cranmer and other English scholars, who had directed their attention to liturgical and doctrinal formulas, with a decided Lutheran tendency, were ordered to prepare a short form for the Communion, in English. Meanwhile a committee to amend the service books had been appointed, in 1543, and in 1544 the Litany, done into English by Cranmer, had been published. Bishop Shaxton, of Salisbury, was chairman of the committee for an English liturgy, being succeeded by Cranmer of Canterbury. The books whose revision became the task of the committee were: Portiforium, Legenda, Antiphonarium, Graduale, Psalterium, Troparium,

Ordinale, Sacramentarium, Missale, Manuale, Pontificale, and others. The ritual which was finally adopted was indebted chiefly to the Reformation of Cologne, 1543. The Simplex et Pia Deliberatio had been drawn up for Hermann, Archbishop and Elector of Cologne, by Bucer, and revised by Melanchthon. The subject-matter is derived chiefly from the Brandenburg-Nuernberg Church Order of 1533, the Order of Herzog Heinrich, drawn up by Justus Jonas, 1536—1539, and the Hesse-Cassel Order of 1539. These were, in turn, influenced strongly by Luther's German Mass of 1526. The Latin form of the Cologne Ritual appeared in 1545, and it was translated and published in London in 1547. The committee undoubtedly made use of a great deal of other material, also. The Sarum Use, for one, which had been made obligatory by the Convocation of 1541, was used extensively, as was the Breviary of Quignon, 1535—1537. The various Primers, Marshall's of 1535, Hilsey's of 1539, and the King's of 1545, were also consulted. The result of these liturgical labors appeared as "The Book of the Common Prayer and Administration of the Sacramentes, and Other Rites and Ceremonies of the Churche: after the Use of the Churche of England," being ratified by Parliament in January, 1549, and placed in use since June 9 of that year.

The order for the chief service, that of the Communion, according to the Prayer Book of 1549 was the following: 1) Collect for Purity (from Sarum Missal), 2) Kyrie, 3) Gloria in excelsis, 4) Salutation and Response, 5) Collect for the day, 6) Epistle, 7) Gospel, 8) Nicene Creed, 9) Exhortation (based on Volprecht's of Nuernberg, 10) Passages of Scripture, instead of Offertory, 11) Salutation and Response, 12) Sursum Corda, 13) Preface, 14) Sanctus, 15) Prayer of Consecration and Words of Institution (based on Sarum, Cassel, and Cologne), closing with Lord's Prayer, 16) Pax, 17) Christ, our Paschal Lamb, is offered up, etc., 18) Invitation, 19) Confession (based on Cologne), 20) Absolution (based on Cologne), 21) Comfortable Words (Cologne), 22) Prayer of Humble Access (Roman), 23) Distribution (during which Agnus Dei is sung), 24) Scripture Passage after Communion, 25) Salutation, 26) Prayer of Thanksgiving (Brandenburg-Nuernberg).[337]

The First Prayer Book of Edward VI, as it is now called, did not receive the unqualified endorsement of the English clergy. Some found it too Lutheran, others pronounced it too Roman. It was regarded either very irreverently or not at all by a great portion of the clergy. The Council found it necessary to address a letter to Bonner, Bishop of London, July 23, 1549, admonishing him to redress the neglect and contempt of the Book of Common Prayer. Moreover, the

---

337) Cp. Jacobs, *The Lutheran Movement in England*, Chapter XIX.

old service books were abolished in 1550. Nevertheless, it was deemed expedient to publish a Second Book of Common Prayer, in 1552, in the faint, but what afterwards proved the vain, hope of conciliating certain radicals. By this time, Calvinistic influences were becoming apparent in England, and there are evidences of this in the new service book. The title of the Communion Service, which had been "The Supper of the Lord and the Holy Communion, commonly called the Mass," was changed to read "The Order for the Administration of the Lord's Supper, or Holy Communion." The Ten Commandments were inserted, the Lord's Prayer was transferred to the Post-communion service, the Gloria in excelsis to a position after the Thanksgiving Collect, the Invocation of the Holy Ghost was omitted, the vestments of the ministers were simplified.[338]) In 1553, upon the accession of Mary, the book was suppressed.

Fortunately, the reign of Mary lasted but five years, long enough, indeed, to work a great deal of harm. With the accession of Elizabeth, the old Latin form of the Catholic Church, which had been restored in 1554, was abolished, and preparations made for the publication of a service book in English. The work was based largely upon the Prayer Books of Edward VI, and the result represents a skilful compromise between the two. The revised book of 1552 had savored strongly of Calvin's order, since it was prepared by Bucer, Martyr, Cranmer, and others, all of whom had developed Calvinistic tendencies. In the Prayer Book of Elizabeth the vestments were reintroduced at the option of the priests, the Introits and Antiphons were omitted, also the metrical hymns. The Book had a better fortune than its predecessors. It was almost universally accepted by both clergy and laity, only 189 out of a total of 9400 clergy refusing to subscribe a declaration that the book was in accordance with the true Word of God.[339]) In 1560 the Prayer Book was published in Latin, for the use of the clergy, the universities, and the public schools (the preparatory schools for the universities). In the same year, the Irish Parliament passed the Act of Uniformity, authorizing exclusively the newly revised Prayer Book of Elizabeth, and allowing the use of the Latin language. A translation for the use of the Irish people was made by Nicholas Walsh, in 1571.

There were no alterations in the Book which was now acknowledged to be the Common Prayer Book till the next century. The Conference of Hampton Court, held on Jan. 14, 1604, and the following days, made only slight alterations in the text. After that, there was quiet for more than fifty years, so far as questions regarding the liturgy are concerned.

---

338) Jacobs, Chapter XIX; Humphrey, *On Book of Common Prayer*, Chapter III.   339) Humphrey, Chapter III.

Meanwhile the Reformation had made progress also in Scotland, and the question of a liturgy had strongly agitated the minds. The Order of Geneva, drawn up by John Knox in 1562, was authorized by the General Assembly in 1564. But it met with such determined resistance that it never obtained general currency, and soon fell into disuse. A revision of the Prayer Book for Scotland, by Maxwell and Wedderburn, usually ascribed to Laud, was authorized by a royal proclamation in 1636, and first used in July, 1637. The riots which followed were so serious that its general introduction was abandoned. There was, at the same time, an increasing number of people in England, with pronounced Calvinistic views, that were not satisfied with the liturgy. In order to effect a compromise, if possible, the Convocations of Canterbury and York were empowered by royal license to make a revision of the Prayer Book. The result appeared in 1662 and was approved by Parliament. A few concessions had been made to the Presbyterians, so far as externals were concerned, the Epistles and Gospels were given according to the Authorized Version of 1611, and a new Preface and Calendar of Proper Lessons was prefixed. In spite of the efforts to conciliate the Non-Conformists, the Book was a failure in this respect. As a consequence, about two thousand Independent, Baptist, and Presbyterian ministers were obliged to leave their benefices and go forth.[340] The Irish Church formally adopted the revised Prayer Book in 1666. A proposal to revise the liturgy in England, in 1689, never matured, and the Book of 1662 is in use to the present day, though there is a Ritual Commission in existence since 1867.

The Scottish Book of 1637 was revised in 1764 and has been in use ever since. Upon this Rite is based the American Book, which was adopted in 1789, as the ritual of the Protestant Episcopal Church in the United States of America. In 1877, the Prayer Book in Ireland was revised, the new book serving the Ancient Catholic and Apostolic Church of Ireland.[341]

The order of the chief service in the Anglican Church is the following: Lord's Prayer; Collect for Purity; Ten Commandments, read in their longest form, and responded to by the people with a Kyrie; Collect for the King; Collect of the Day; Epistle, the congregation seated; Gospel, the congregation standing; Nicene Creed; Announcements; Psalm sung by Congregation; Sermon; — Sentences read at altar with reference to offering then taken (Matt. 5, 16; 6, 19. 20; 7, 12. 21; Luke 19, 8; 1 Cor. 9, 7. 11; 13. 14; 2 Cor. 9, 6. 7, etc.); General Prayer; Exhortation and Invitation; Confession and Absolution; Comfortable Words (Matt. 11, 28; John 3, 16; 1 Tim. 1, 15;

---

340) Gwynne, *Primitive Worship and the Prayer Book*, Chapter XI.
341) Cp. Humphrey, Chapter III; Gwynne, Chapter XII.

1 John 2, 1); Preface, with Sursum corda and Proper Preface; Prayer of Humble Access; Prayer of Consecration, with Words of Institution; Communion of Priests and Distribution; Prayers of Oblation and Thanksgiving: Lord's Prayer, Prayer of Memorial or Oblation, Thanksgiving, Gloria in excelsis; Blessing (Phil. 4, 7); Final Rubrics.342)

The minor services and occasional acts of the Anglican Church are especially interesting from a Lutheran standpoint, because so many parts may be traced back to Lutheran sources.343) The Matins or Early Morning Service combines the former Matins, Lauds, and Prime of the canonical hours, and the Evensong includes the Vespers and Compline. Luther's proposal concerning the Morning Prayer had been included in his "Deutsche Messe und Ordnung des Gottesdienstes, 1526." He suggested that a few Psalms be sung, followed by a sermon on the Epistle of the day; then an Antiphon and the Te Deum Laudamus or Benedictus antiphonally, with the Lord's Prayer, a Collect, and Benedicamus Domino.344) This simple service is almost exactly that of the Prayer Book of 1549, the number of Lections agreeing with the number of Psalms, but the sermon being omitted. A similar agreement may be noted with regard to the Evening Services or Vespers. In Lections, the English reformers followed Luther's "Register of Epistles and Gospels." So far as the order of Baptism is concerned, the form of the English Church was borrowed principally from the Lutherans. The opening Exhortation is condensed from Luther's original formula; the Prayer follows Luther closely; the Sign of the Cross is taken from the Reformation of Cologne; the Collect is that which was adapted for infant baptism by Luther; the Exorcism contained the substance of Luther's vigorous formula; the Gospel Lesson Mark 10 was taken from Luther; the Collect is taken verbally from a Lutheran Order; and the rest of the form follows Luther's very closely. The Address to the Sponsors is based on the Brandenburg-Nuernberg Order of 1533, which was patterned after Osiander's of 1524. The order of Confirmation may likewise be traced to Lutheran influence, notably that of Cologne. At present the idea seems to be held as a principle that confirmation in olden times was restricted to the apostles and bishops, and that therefore its present use should recognize the same limitations. As for the Marriage Ceremony of the Book of Common Prayer, it is derived from the ancient English form, through the Use of Sarum, with additions from Lutheran orders. The Exhortation, the Ring

342) Blunt, *Annotated Book of Common Prayer*, 315—406; Alt, *Der kirchliche Gottesdienst*, 295—302; Gwynne, Chapters XIII—XXVI.
343) Cp. Jacobs, *The Lutheran Movement in England*, Chapters XX—XXII.   344) 10, 233.

Ceremony, and the Formula of Marriage were modeled after Luther's Traubuechlein of 1529. In regard to the formula of the Visitation of the Sick, the compilers of the English book adopted the order of the Reformation of Cologne, originally found in the Saxon Order of 1539.

It is most unfortunate, from the standpoint of Biblical truth and unity of the Church, that the influence of Luther and his work upon England was not more lasting. From 1520 to 1553 his books were eagerly studied, as Jacobs shows,[345] and their leavening power can plainly be recognized, not only in the English Bible translations, but also in the Ten Articles and even in the Thirty-nine Articles, beside the Book of Common Prayer. But the two churches now no longer have anything in common. There was some opportunity for a revision upon a Biblical basis, when the Episcopal Church of the United States issued the Book Annexed, in 1886, since the alterations pointed in the direction of the First Prayer Book of Edward VI and therefore were more Lutheran in type, but no approach resulted, nor is there one likely to come about. It appears rather that a word of warning to Lutherans may be in place not to pattern the liturgical part of their services after the order or in the manner of the Anglican Church. The liturgy is a confession, and its standing as such should be maintained.

CHAPTER 9.
Revival of Liturgical Interest in Germany.

It is a matter of thankful consideration and congratulation that Rationalism did not succeed in abolishing all liturgical feeling in Germany and the other countries where it held sway for about a century. The learned Gerbert defended the traditional form of worship with considerable skill, although from the Catholic standpoint. And there were always some pastors whose feeling of liturgical tact and doctrinal requirement prompted them to retain the ancient Lutheran form of service or to salvage at least some of the parts out of the wreckage. But the large mass of the people knew little but the shallow, subjective forms of an attenuated, emaciated liturgy, to which the description "without form and void" could most fitly be applied.

The awakening came at the beginning of the last century. Marheinecke, in his Homiletics, published in 1811, once more aroused an interest in the Lutheran cultus. Three years later, on Sept. 14, 1814, the Publicandum of the King of Prussia was issued. Although the reigning house was heart and soul for the Union, and the last steps for unionizing the state church were even then being taken, the effort

---

345) Chapters I—XVII.

at restoration of the liturgy is worthy of notice. The following statement of the Publicandum is significant: "The liturgies are in part
so incomplete and in part so dissimilar and imperfect that many
things are left to the arbitrariness of the single ministers, and that
the uniformity of ecclesiastical customs, which is one of the main
conditions for its beneficent effects, is lost almost entirely." [346]   "In
1816 appeared the Liturgy for the Court Church of Potsdam and the
Garrison Church at Berlin, and in 1822 the Kirchen-Agenda for the
Court- and Dome-Church in Berlin, whose principal author was King
Frederick William III. It was revised 1823 and 1826. This was an
epoch-making work, for it went back to the old Agendas and gave an
impulse to renewed liturgical study." [347]   According to this Agenda,
the Sunday service contains the following parts: I. *The Liturgical
Part:* 1) Opening Hymn; In the name. . ., Our help is in the name. . .;
2) Confiteor, with prayer for mercy and the confession of sins;
3) Verse after Confession, corresponding to the Introitus; 4) Gloria
Patri; 5) Kyrie eleison, three times; 6) Gloria in excelsis, with the
addition from the ancient forms for festivals; 7) Salutation and Response; 8) Collect; 9) Epistle, with Versicle or Hallelujah in response;
10) Gospel, with Praise be to Thee, O Christ, in response; 11) Creed;
12) Versicle after Creed, in place of the ancient Psalm; 13) Preface,
with Sursum, Dignum, and Sanctus; 14) General Prayer; 15) Lord's
Prayer. II. *The Didactic Part:* 1) Hymn of the Sermon; 2) Sermon,
preceded by apostolic greeting; 3) Publicanda; 4) Blessing from pulpit. III. *The Communion:* 1) Exhortation to Communicants; 2) Collect for spiritual strength; 3) Consecration with Words of Institution; 4) Pax; 5) Distribution, during which Agnus Dei or other
hymns are sung (formula of distribution: Our Lord and Savior
Jesus Christ says: This is my body . . . This is my blood); 6) Thanksgiving of Postcommunion; 7) Benediction and concluding Hymn or
Doxology.[348]   Where this order seems too long for the liturgical
ability of the congregation, the briefer alternative was offered:
1) Morning Hymn and, In the name . . .; 2) Confession; 3) Kyrie in
German; 4) Gloria in excelsis, short form; 5) Salutation; 6) Collect;
7) Lection; 8) Creed; 9) General Prayer and Lord's Prayer; 10)
Hymn; 11) Prayer, followed by Intercessions, Thanksgivings, Publicanda, etc.; 12) Benediction and final verse of Hymn.

  The first result of the publication of this Agenda was a flood of
writings both for and against its use and the vindication of its
authorship. Augusti wrote his "Criticism of the Prussian Church
Agenda," 1823, which was attacked by Schleiermacher in his book

---

346). Alt, *Der kirchliche Gottesdienst,* 321.
347) Horn, *Liturgies,* 143.
348) Alt, *Op. cit.,* 324—327; Richards-Painter, Chapter XIV.

"Regarding the Liturgical Right of Evangelical Princes," 1824, but defended by Marheinecke in the answer "Regarding the True Position of the Liturgical Right," 1825. Other men that became involved in the controversy were Nietsch, Schultz, and Gerlach. The King answered upon the criticism in a Publicandum of May 28, 1825, in which he reminded the critics that he merely wished to protect his evangelical subjects against the dangers and abuses of an arbitrariness which engendered doubt and indifferentism. But neither this nor a ministerial rescript of July 4, 1825, had the desired effect, and so King Frederick William issued, in 1827, his "Luther in Relation to the Prussian Agenda of the Year 1822." By the year 1830 opposition had gradually ceased, and the Agenda was in common use in the Kingdom of Prussia.

The way now being opened, the work of restoration was begun in earnest. Bunsen issued his revised Capitoline Liturgy to supplement the Prussian. And before long, the liturgical restoration and reformation was undertaken in other parts of Germany, in Wuerttemberg, Bavaria, Baden, and Saxony. In the last-named country, the work of the Dresden Conference is worthy of special mention. More recently, the Agenda of Boeckh is notable for its excellence.

Our summary would not be complete, however, without a reference to certain scholars who undertook the difficult task of delving in the tomes of half-forgotten liturgical lore and related branches of archeology for the purpose of making a critical survey and restoring a proper appreciation of the beautiful and dignified forms of the ante-Nicaean and the Reformation Period. Augusti led the way in this research work with his archeological studies. He was followed by Hoefling, whose thoroughness is most delightfully refreshing. His Sacrament of Baptism, 1846—48, can hardly be said to have been superseded, even at this late day. Close after him followed Alt with his Christian Cultus, 1851 and 1858. Seldom had so much material pertaining to the entire Christian cultus and all its phases been collected in the space of such few pages, and so excellently arranged, as in the case of Alt's book. About the same time, Loehe of Neuendettelsau published his Agenda for Christian Congregations of the Lutheran Confession, 1853, which was followed, after a few years, by his Haus-, Schul- und Kirchenbuch. His was a rare liturgical understanding, coupled with a fine tact which make it easy to forgive even his Romanizing tendencies. Other names that stand out prominently in this connection are those of Gass, Funk, Claus Harms, Schweizer, Vetter, Goldmann, Ehrenfeuchter, Klopper, Ebrard, Gaupp, Grueneisen, Koestlin, Gottschick, Rietschel, Sinend, Schoeberlein, Jacoby, Henkl, Steinmeyer, and others.[349]

---

349) Cp. Horn, *Liturgies*, 146—155.

A few words ought to be said yet in regard to Kliefoth, since he, together with Loehe, has exerted a large measure of influence upon a part of the Lutheran Church in this country. He demanded a return to the best liturgies of the 16th century, to such as were consistent with liturgical harmony. He was especially fortunate in being able to point to the work of Layritz, Hommel, Hoffmann v. Fallersleben, Wackernagel, and others, who had republished old liturgical texts and contrasted their beauty and the richness of their content with the diluted rituals of Pietism and Rationalism. He was especially insistent upon a living, practical, correct understanding and use of liturgical forms instead of a dead copying of ancient rites. To meet with this requirement, it is essential that the congregation be instructed in the meaning of the ritual, and above all that the congregation actually be present and take part in the services. But his greatest concern was for the proper restoration of the Communion Service. He insisted that the Lutheran Church has always demanded, on the one hand that the chief service never take place without communion, and on the other hand that there should always be a hunger and thirst after the Sacrament which warrants such a frequent celebration. The true Lutheran type of service, he asserts, always has the Communion as its culmination. In case there were no Communion, the conclusion of the service should always include an Admonition or Exhortation which should be a part of the liturgy, in order to maintain its strictly objective character. Kliefoth's insistence upon some of these points was so strenuous as to put him under the suspicion of Romanizing tendencies. The same is true of Loehe, on account of his well-known and unfortunate preface to the first edition of his Agenda. The idea which he enunciated at that time, as though the Sermon and the Eucharist were twin mountain peaks, he emphasized even more strongly in the second edition, where he made the celebration of Holy Communion the center and the object, in which the entire service culminated, and wanted to have the altar to be the ruling architectural feature. On the other hand, men like Alt exhibited a strong tendency toward unionistic ideas, and therefore were always in danger of making concessions to the Reformed Church. As matters stand at present, the liturgy of the Prussian Union or State Church is used in the congregations existing under its government,[350] while the various Free Lutheran Churches and Synods have their own ritual, which varies with the doctrinal position and the liturgical tendency of the body.

---

350) The separation of church and state does not seem to have been consistently carried out in the new German Republic.

CHAPTER 10.

The Liturgy in the Lutheran Church of America.

The Lutheran Church of America is recruited from many nationalities, the chief exponents being the Swedish, the Norwegian, the Danish, the German, the Finnish, the Esthonian and Lithuanian, the Polish, and last, but not least, the English Lutherans. The great diversity of tongues made for a great diversity of rites and ceremonies. Nowhere is the Lutheran principle of freedom in nonessentials, of liberty in adiaphora, so plainly exemplified as in the liturgy. Though many of the forms had originally been based upon, or influenced by, the forms of Luther or some of the other 16th century leaders, the vicissitudes of the intervening centuries had left their mark upon them, and there was indeed, in many cases, a wide divergence. But in one thing all the orders were agreed: the teaching of the Word must be the most prominent feature of the service. A short survey of the Lutheran liturgical history in America will lead to a warmer appreciation of the present situation.

The liturgy of the Lutheran Church in Norway had been influenced largely by the liturgical publications of Luther and Bugenhagen, the occasional offices being based upon the Enchiridion of 1538 and the Communion service upon the Manual of 1539. In 1688, the Book of Service of Bishop Bagger appeared. When the successive movements of Pietism and Rationalism spread from Germany, they caused also the Lutheran service of Norway to become meager. Bastholm states that the chants, creeds, and blessings were omitted, and a rescript of 1802 abolished also the Kyrie. The Creed and the Gloria were thereafter used on alternate Sundays, and the Gospel was not read at the altar, but the Sermon was made very prominent. This Order was in force till 1877, when a reaction set in, followed by a return to older Lutheran forms.

The first Norwegian Order in America evidently took into account the external circumstances of the poor settlers, for it contained only the following parts: Opening Prayer, Hymn, Collect, Epistle, Hymn, Sermon, General Prayer, Blessing, Hymn, Collect, Hymn, Closing Prayer. The influence of Hauge is seen in the absence of responsive liturgical parts. The Landstad and Lindeman Hymnal was used. Later a revised Book of Service was adopted, based mainly on the Order of the Bavarian Church. It has the following parts: Opening Prayer, Opening Hymn, Confession of Sin, Kyrie, Gloria, Salutation and Collect of the Day, Epistle, Short Hymn, Gospel, Apostle's Creed, Hymn, Sermon preceded by Prayer from pulpit and closed with Gloria Patri, General Prayer, Hymn, Preface (Salutation, Sursum corda, Gratias agamus, Vere dignum), Sanctus, Exhortation,

Lord's Prayer, Words of Institution, Distribution, Hymn of Thanksgiving, Thanksgiving Collect, Salutation and Aaronic Blessing,
Closing Hymn, Closing Prayer.[351])

The history of the liturgy in Denmark is identical with that of
Norway for several centuries, since Norway then belonged to Denmark. After Bugenhagen's visit the Ordinance of Christian III was
adopted by the Diet in Odensee, June 14, 1539. The Enchiridion of
Palladius appeared in 1538, the Manual of Vormordsen in 1539, and
the new edition of the Altar Book, in 1556, was based upon these
earlier publications, just as these had been drawn from Luther. The
Chief Service or Hoeimesse formerly was composed of the following
parts: Confiteor after Adjutorium, Introitus, Kyrie, Gloria in excelsis, Responsory and Collect, Psalm, Epistle and Hallelujah, Danish
Hymn or Sequence, Gospel and Response, Credo (hymn), Sermon,
Holy Communion (Admonition to Communicants, Lord's Prayer,
Words of Institution, Collect, Benediction, Hymn during Distribution), Sanctus, Agnus Dei, etc., Aaronic Blessing. The revised Order
of 1895 has simplified the Eucharistic service: Address to Communicants, Lord's Prayer, Words of Institution, Distribution, Collect,
Aaronic Benediction.[352])

The Lutheran Church in Iceland is only small, and its members
in this country are not numerous, but they have their liturgy and are
guarding their cultus carefully. Since Iceland was a dependency of
Denmark, any movement in the home country was apt to reach the
island in a short time. Thus the Reformation was introduced in the
latter part of the 16th century, after some opposition. In 1589 the
first Hymnbook was published, later the Graduale, which saw nine-
teen editions between 1594 and 1779. The service of the Malmo-Book
was much like that of the ancient Danish Church: Danish Hymn
(Adjutorium), Confiteor, Absolution, Introitus (Hymn), Kyrie
(Hymn), Gloria in excelsis, Salutation and Collect, Epistle, Hallelujah, Gospel, Credo and Hymn, Sermon, Hymn, Luther's Paraphrase,
Sanctus, Institution (Agnus Dei, Exhortation, Distribution, Thanksgiving), Salutation and Luther's Collect from Deutsche Messe, Benediction, Ten Commandments. Sometimes the Praefatio and the Sursum corda were sung before the Lord's Supper. The influence of the
Postil of Veit Dietrich, 1549, is apparent. The theological and liturgical defects of Rationalism affected also the Icelandic ritual, causing
the beautiful liturgical parts, the Introitus, the Kyrie, the Gloria,
the Credo, the Praefatio, the Sanctus, the Agnus Dei to disappear,
while the General Prayer was much shortened. In 1869, there was

---

351) Cp. E. K. Johnsen, in *Memoirs*, VII: 4.
352) Cp. E. Belfour, in *Memoirs*, II: 6.

a new revision of the Manual, introducing many Collects from the German. The Icelandic Synod in America has already introduced into its services the Gloria in excelsis, Gloria Patri, Kyrie, Hallelujah, and Pro Offertorio, and more changes may be looked for.[353])

The Lutheran Church of Sweden was likewise indebted to Luther and his colleagues for liturgical material, though the influence was not so direct as in other cases. The Handbook of 1529 was the first Swedish Lutheran Church Manual. It has the title "Baptism and Other Things." The Swedish Mass was published in 1531, according to the form in which it was then conducted at Stockholm, though it had been celebrated in the vernacular for about six years then. Its parts include: Allocution to the Congregation, Confession of Sins, Introitus and Kyrie with Gloria in excelsis, Salutation, Collects, Epistle, Graduale (Hymn or Ten Commandments), Gospel, Apostles' or Nicene Creed, [Sermon], Preface (no Offertorium, but Salutation, Sursum corda, etc.), Consecration (Words of Institution), Sanctus, Lord's Prayer, Pax, Agnus Dei, Communion (Admonition and Distribution), Swedish Hymn or Nunc dimittis, Salutation, Benedicamus, Benediction. The dependence of this order upon Luther's Formula Missae of 1523 is plainly seen. Some changes were inaugurated by subsequent revisions, especially by the Mass in Swedish, Upsala, 1541. In 1576 there was an attempt made to restore the Roman ritual: Liturgia Swecanae Ecclesiae Catholicae. In 1614, a revised Church Book appeared, according to which the chief service contains: Allocution; Confession of Sins; Kyrie and Gloria; Salutation and Collects; Epistle and Gospel (with Swedish Hymn as Graduale): Creed (Apostolic or Nicene); Swedish Hymn; Sermon; Confession of Sins; Salutations, Prefaces, Consecration, Sanctus, Lord's Prayer; Admonition to Communicants, Pax; Distribution with Agnus Dei; Salutation, Collect of Thanksgiving, Salutation with Response, Benedicamus, Benediction, Swedish Hymn pro exitu. New editions of the Church Book appeared in 1811 and in 1894, the latter being especially important. In the Augustana Synod, the congregation reads the Creed before the Sermon, and the Lord's Prayer after. A feature is the rhetorical address: Holy, Holy, Holy, at the beginning of the service.[354])

The forms which the German immigrants adopted for use in the Lutheran congregations were usually those of the country or district from which they came, with such modifications as occasion seemed to warrant. The Missouri Synod chose the Saxon models and introduced a chief service with the following parts: Opening Hymn; German

---

353) Cp. F. J. Bergmann, in *Memoirs,* IV: 9.
354) Cp. N. Forsander, in *Memoirs,* II: 3.

Kyrie in rhymes; Gloria in excelsis (Allein Gott in der Hoeh, All
Ehr und Lob); Salutation and Response, Collect; Epistle; Hymn;
Gospel; Creed (Wir glauben all); Sermon; Confession and Absolution; General Prayer, Intercessions, Thanksgivings, Lord's Prayer,
Votum; Create in me; Preface with Sanctus; Lord's Prayer; Consecration; Agnus Dei; Communion; Collect of Thanksgiving; Benediction; Gott sei gelobet, or some other concluding stanza. In many
mission congregations the services were much abbreviated, often becoming so meager, in fact, as to remind strongly of the most attenuated forms of Rationalism. The new Liturgy and Agenda, entirely in
English, puts the Common Service, which had been previously used
by the English District, in first place, and a translation of the Saxon
Order in second place. The Committee of Synod deserves the full
measure of appreciation for the completeness and thoroughness of the
orders and formulas here offered, for the excellent collection of Collects, and the mass of Agenda material which it has brought together.
The liturgy of the Evangelical Lutheran Joint Synod of Wisconsin,
Minnesota, etc., contains the chief parts of the ancient Lutheran service, but many of the parts are abbreviated. The form of service
used by the Iowa Synod is based upon the work of Loehe, and therefore contains the principal parts of the Common Lutheran Service.
The Buffalo Synod based its liturgy upon the ancient Agenda of
Pommerania and Saxony, thus obtaining a fairly complete order of
services. It includes the following parts: Opening Hymn (if possible, closing with Gloria Patri); Kyrie (in rhymed form); Gloria in
excelsis; Salutation and Response; Antiphon; Collect; Epistle; Hymn;
Gospel preceded by Salutation and Glory be to Thee, O Lord; Creed;
Sermon, introduced with Apostolic Greeting and Prayer; Lord's
Prayer; Publicanda; Confession and Absolution (with Retention);
General Prayer, with Intercessions and Thanksgivings; Hymn; Antiphon and Collect; Benediction. For the Lord's Supper, the following order was prescribed: Hymn Create in me; Salutation and Re-
sponse; Sursum; Preface; Sanctus; Admonition; Lord's Prayer;
Words of Institution; Agnus Dei and other hymns during Distribu-
tion; Salutation and Response; Antiphon and Thanksgiving Collect;
Benediction; Closing Stanza.[355])

    The antecedent history of the liturgy as now used in the United
Lutheran Church in America goes back to the time of Muehlenberg.
It was he who, with the assistance of Brunholtz and Handschuh, in
1748, prepared the first American Lutheran Liturgy, taking as the
basis of their work the Liturgy of the Savoy Congregation of London.
The Book of 1748 contained the following forms: 1) Manner of Pub-

355) *Agende*, Luth. Synode von Buffalo. 1888.

lic Worship; 2) Baptism; 3) Bans; 4) Confession and Holy Communion; 5) Burial.[356] The Morning Service included the following parts: Hymn; Confession; Gloria in excelsis; Collect with Salutation and Response; Epistle; Hymn; Gospel; Creed (metrical); General Prayer; Proclamations and Announcements; Votum; Hymn; Collection of Alms; Closing Collect with Salutation and Response; Benediction; Closing Verse. The Order of the Lord's Supper was complete: Preface with Salutation, Sursum corda, and Sanctus; Exhortation; Consecration; Invitation; Distribution; Benediction; Benedicamus; Thanksgiving Collect; Benediction; Closing Collect. It was patterned after Saxon and North German models. In 1782 the resolution was passed to have the Muehlenberg Liturgy published. This resolution was carried out in 1786, but the form was altered, the rubrics, the Gloria in excelsis, the Creed, and other parts being omitted. In 1795, Dr. Kunze of New York published a translation of the Liturgy of 1786, and in 1797, Rev. Strebeck followed this up with a Collection of Evangelical Hymns. In 1806, Rev. Williston brought out a Book of Hymns and Liturgy of the Lutheran Church. His work proved to be an adaptation of that of 1786, with the addition of parts taken from Book of Common Prayer. It was the first instance of the introduction of foreign liturgical material into the Lutheran liturgy in America. In 1817, the New York Synod took the initiative, the Drs. Quitman and Wackerhagen publishing, at its instance, a Hymbook and Enlarged Liturgy. Unfortunately, the poison of Rationalism had penetrated into that section of the Church, the result being a rationalistic, liberal, and un-Lutheran production. From that time, the decline was rapid. In 1818, the Ministerium of Pennsylvania brought out an Agenda with almost no vestige of responsive service. All the forms offered, especially that of the Lord's Supper, are departures from the chaste and ancient forms of the 16th century.

These books, however, did not meet with universal approval, and a reaction was slowly preparing. The Tennessee Synod, indeed, in 1833 resolved the publication of a liturgy, which resulted in a book based on that of 1786. It appeared in 1843 as the Liturgy or Book of Forms, the Rev. S. Henkel being the compiler. The responsive liturgy was omitted. In 1834 the New York Ministerium published a liturgy which was approved by the Pennsylvania Synod in 1835, and by the General Synod in 1837. This effort was again short-lived, for in 1839 the Pennsylvania Synod appointed a committee for a new edition of the Liturgy. This action was seconded by the New York Ministerium and by the Synod of Ohio. The new book appeared in 1842. In 1847,

---

356) Jacobs, *History of the Lutheran Church*, 269—275.

an English Liturgy appeared which was based on this. It included no responsive liturgy, the minister doing all the work. A turn for the better came in 1850, when the Pennsylvania Synod took the initiative in the preparation of a new liturgy, which was published in 1855. It had responses and all the essential features of the Lutheran service. A further improvement was made in 1860, when the English liturgy amended and altered the forms then in use, securing stricter conformity to ancient Lutheran liturgies. It was the precursor of the Church Book.[357]) The Order of Public Worship, as fixed by the General Synod Book of 1870, approached very closely to the ideal Lutheran form. The Chief Service included the following parts: Opening Sentences (In the name . . . ., The Lord is in His Holy Temple . . . ., From the rising of the sun . . . . etc.); Gloria Patri; Confession of Sin (without Absolution); Kyrie; Apostles' Creed; Gloria in excelsis; Reading of Scriptures; Hymn; Prayer; Hymn; Collection; Sermon; Brief Prayer and Lord's Prayer; Hymn; Benediction.[358]) The Kirchenbuch of the General Council, which appeared in 1877, has practically all the parts of the Common Service as now in use, with certain alternatives which gave a measure of latitude to the congregations. It places the Intercessions and Thanksgivings on the pulpit after the Sermon, with the alternative of including them in the General Prayer. The insertion of Hear us, O Lord God after the several paragraphs in the General Prayer gave to it the character of the Litany. In 1888 there appeared the order of service, which has since been known as The Common Service for Evangelical Lutheran Congregations. It was "compiled by a joint committee appointed by the General Synod, the General Council, and the United Synod in the South." The principle which governed the work of securing a Common Service was the desire to present the "common consent of the Lutheran liturgies of the sixteenth century." It went out at Whitsuntide, 1888, and has been in use not only in the three bodies represented by the joint committee, but also in the Ohio Synod, and in the Missouri Synod, the latter making it the first order of services since the publication of the new Liturgy and Agenda. The newly-formed United Lutheran Church in America has recently issued the Common Service Book of the Lutheran Church, which represents the combined labor of some of the foremost liturgiologists of the country. A full discussion of the Communion service according to this Common Book will be offered in a special chapter below.

_____

357) Cp. D. M. Kemerer, in *Memoirs*, IV: 8.
358) *Book of Worship*, 1870.

CHAPTER 11.

The Liturgy of the Reformed Churches in America.

When Luther at Marburg, in 1529, uttered the memorable words: "Yours is a different spirit from ours," he had reference mainly to the doctrine. But his words receive their application also in externals, in the cultus and in life. The Lutheran Church developed the science of theology, the Reformed that of morals. The Lutheran Church emphasized the justification of a poor sinner out of free grace, the Reformed Church placed the Law into the foreground. The Lutheran Church gave prominence to the sacramental part of the service, the Reformed Church was equally insistent upon the sacrificial element. Or, as Alt and Painter prefer to express it, the objective character of the services is emphasized by the Lutheran Church, the subjective by the Reformed Church. A sacramental act or ceremony, as Melanchthon explains in the Apologia Confessionis, is every act or ceremony, by and in which God grants to us what the promise of the act offers. A sacrificial act or ceremony is one in which the worshiper serves God. All that God offers in the means of grace, the Word and the Sacraments, is sacramental. Everything that the worshiper offers to God, in prayers, anthems, offerings, commemorations, etc., is sacrificial.

In the Lutheran service the sacramental idea preponderates. The Absolution is an announcement of an act of mercy on God's part, the Lections are strictly objective because fixed in the Pericopes, the Sermon largely doctrinal, the exposition of the Word taking precedence over the admonitory application, the celebration of the Lord's Supper is the visible Gospel, the application of the grace of God to the individual Christian. In the Reformed Church, the reverse holds true. The prayers are mainly extemporaneous and therefore subjective, the hymns, in many cases, were composed with special reference to a certain admonition, in the sermon the text is selected from the standpoint of a special object which the minister may have in view, exhortation takes precedence over objective doctrinal presentation, the Eucharist is a memorial service whose value depends only upon the devotion of the individual, the extent to which a believer can sink his very essence into the love of Calvary.

This difference became apparent as early as the time of Zwingli. The provisory liturgy which he compiled in 1523 still had a strong resemblance to Luther's Formuia missae of the same year. It contained the following parts: A. Introit, Kyrie, Gloria in excelsis, Collect, Epistle, Hallelujah with Sequence, Gospel, Sermon, Confession of Faith, General Prayer; B. Preface with Sanctus, Consecration, Distribution, Prayer of Thanksgiving, Nunc dimittis, Benedic-

tion.[359])   But Zwingli's service deteriorated with his theology.   In
his Fidei Ratio of 1530 he did not hesitate to assert that the sacraments not only do not give grace, but cannot even transmit the same,
that the visible sacraments do not bear the Spirit in themselves, that
the sacraments are merely given for a public testimony of the mercy,
which is previously present for every one.   In his effort to oppose the
doctrine of the opus operatum in the Catholic Church, Zwingli permitted the pendulum to swing to the other extreme of the arc, thus robbing
the Lord's Supper of its real value and reducing the act of celebration
to a mere service of commemoration without any transmitted spiritual
advantage but the intensifying of the devotion, due to the ability of
the individual to yield to the influence of the story in a subjective
way.   In a similar manner, Calvin was not in sympathy with anything that savored of the Roman liturgy.   His idea was to ignore the
intervening centuries and go back to apostolic simplicity in his order
of services.   His Order of 1536, in accordance with these ideas, had
the following form: Opening with Our help is in the name, Confession, Singing of Psalm, Free Prayer (for profitable hearing of the
Word), Text and Sermon, Exhortation to Prayer, followed by long
Free Prayer with Lord's Prayer, Apostles' Creed, Benediction; Prayer
of Invocation, Apostles' Creed, 1 Cor. 11, 23—29, Exhortation to Self-
Examination, Consecration, Distribution, while Psalms were sung or
Scripture read, Thanksgiving Collect and Prayer for proper acceptance, Nunc dimittis, Benediction.[360])

In Scotland, the form and content of the liturgy was largely determined by the labors of John Knox.   During his continental exile
at Geneva and at Frankfort-on-the-Main, he had come under the influence of Calvin, and his Order of Services shows the extent of the
Reformed sphere of power.   It contained the following parts: Confession, Scripture Lessons, Singing of Psalm, Prayer to Holy Spirit,
Sermon, General Prayer embodying Lord's Prayer and Apostles'
Creed, Singing of Psalm, Benediction; at Eucharist: Preface, Exhortation, Thanksgiving, Distribution, Prayer and Thanksgiving,
Singing of 103d Psalm etc., Benediction.   Even this simple form was
condemned by many as being too complicated and too complex.   The
tendency has been to shorten and simplify the services.   For the sake
of comparison, let us take before us a later liturgy of the Reformed
Church, that of Hugues (Celle, 1846).   In it are found the following
parts: Prelude, Hymn, Apostolic Greeting (Our beginning. . . or
Grace be. . .), Salutation, Prayer, Lections, Apostolic Blessing, Hymn,

---

359) Richards-Painter, *Christian Worship*, Chapter XIII; Alt, *Der
christliche Gottesdienst*, 273.
360) Cp. Schuette, *Before the Altar*, 147. 148; Richards-Painter,
Chapter XIII; Alt, 273.

Text and Sermon, General Prayer with Thanksgivings and Intercessions, Lord's Prayer, Hymn (Closing stanzas), Benediction, Postlude.[361])

The Puritans showed a decided tendency to simplify the services
to the point of omitting the liturgy entirely, especially when they
came to America and had the usual difficulties of frontier life to con-
tend with. Congregationalism began to spread in America about the
middle of the 17th century. About the same time, also, the Baptists
appeared as a separate denomination, having received toleration by
the Declaration of Indulgence (1687) and religious liberty under
William III (1688—1702). Somewhat later, before the middle of the
18th century, Methodism arose, soon extending its activity outside of
England, and growing in influence in the American colonies very
rapidly.

The liturgy of the Baptists is very simple. There is a Prelude
and a Hymn. The Lections are selected from either the Old or the
New Testament, usually with reference to the character of the sermon. Then follows a Prayer and another short Hymn. The Sermon
is not based upon a system of Pericopes, but upon a text after the free
choice of the pastor. The service closes with Prayer, Benediction,
and a short Closing Hymn.

The liturgy of the Presbyterian Church in America, according to
the Constitution (Philadelphia, 1907), is not much more complete
than the Baptist, although a wide latitude is granted, and many congregations have introduced features from liturgical denominations,
especially from the Anglican Church. According to the Directory of
Worship, the public reading of Holy Scriptures and the singing of
Psalms and Hymns are to be the main features of the Sunday services. The service of Public Prayer is opened with a short Prayer.
Then follows a Psalm or Hymn, then a full and comprehensive Prayer.
In regard to the Sermon it is stated that this should not be so long
as to exclude the other and more important duties of prayer and
praise. After the Sermon comes a Prayer with reference to the Sermon. The Offerings are considered a separate and specific act of
worship. The service closes with a Hymn and the Benediction. In
some churches, a choir has charge of the responses and versicles in
various parts of the service.

The worship of Congregationalism prescribes an Order of Public
Worship which also shows all the ear-marks of Puritan simplicity.
The order includes the following: 1) Invocation (concluded with the
chanting of the Lord's Prayer), 2) Singing, 3) Reading of Scriptures
(Old Testament, Gloria Patri, New Testament), 4) Principal Prayer,

---

361) Daniel, *Codex liturgicus*, III, 74—78.

5) Singing, 6) Sermon, 7) Singing, 8) Prayer, 9) Benediction.[362]
This order, though usually adhered to, is not rigidly followed, the
freedom of choosing a form of service to suit the circumstances being
stoutly maintained in all conferences.

The Public Worship of the Methodist Episcopal Church, according to the Doctrine and Discipline of the Methodist Episcopal
Church,[363] contains more liturgical material than that of any of the
last named denominations. The influence of the Anglican Church
seems to have been persistent enough to effect this and also a certain
amount of hierarchical structure in the polity. The Sunday Worship, after the Silent Prayer, contains the following parts: 1) Voluntary (instrumental or vocal), 2) Singing from Common Hymnal
(standing), 3) Apostles' Creed, 4) Prayer, concluded with Lord's
Prayer, 5) Anthem or Voluntary, 6) Lesson from Old Testament,
7) Gloria Patri, 8) Lesson from New Testament, 9) Notices, followed
by Collection with Offertory, 10) Singing from Common Hymnal,
11) Sermon, 12) Prayer (the people kneeling), 13) Singing from
Common Hymnal, 14) Doxology and Apostolic Benediction.

So far as the other Protestant denominations are concerned, it
is hardly possible to speak of a prescribed liturgy of any kind. Depending upon the minister or evangelist in charge, either the prayers
or the readings and the sermon are emphasized, and the order varies
with the object which is to be attained. In most evangelistic services,
a sentimental climax is carefully worked out, and the exhorters, choir
leaders, and various other officers and assistants are carefully drilled
in their role, in order that everything may reach the culmination
according to the prearranged plan. The service in such cases is entirely subjective, and the liturgy, in the proper sense, is wanting entirely. In general, however, there seems to be a tendency to make the
services more beautiful by introducing liturgical material, though
the execution of liturgical parts is usually left to a paid choir.

362) Dexter, *A Handbook of Congregationalism*, 84. 85.
363) Ed. by Bishop Andrews. 1904.

PART II.
Hymnology.

CHAPTER 1.
The Old Testament Psalms.

The first Canticles or Psalms of the Old Testament were composed by Moses. The first one was sung after the drowning of Pharao with all his host in the Red Sea, Ex. 15, 1—19. The second one was his swan song, composed at the end of his life, setting forth the perfections of God, Deut. 32, 1—43. In addition to that, we have the stately verses of Psalm 90, which is ascribed to Moses, the man of God. Another Canticle of the early days of Israel is Hannah's song of thankfulness, 1 Sam. 2, 1—10. In spite of these early evidences of poetical activity in the Jewish people (cp. Judg. 5), there is no indication that Psalms or Canticles were used in the service of the tabernacle before the time of David. The services of the tabernacle were probably, at that time, restricted to sacrifices and the work connected with their preparation.

When the ark of the covenant was brought up to Mount Zion, 2 Sam. 6, 12—19, the arrangement of the liturgy and its music was very simple. The three chief singers, Asaph the Gersonite, Heman the Kohathite, and Ethan or Jeduthun the Merarite, played the cymbals or leading instruments, while the fourteen musicians who were their assistants were divided into sections, eight playing the nabla and six the cither, 1 Chron. 15, 17—29. On special occasions, other musical instruments were used, as when the ark was brought up, "David and all the house of Israel played before the Lord on all manner of instruments made of fir wood, even on harps, on psalteries, and on timbrels, and on cornets, and on cymbals," 2 Sam. 6, 5. Asaph remained with the ark in the tent on Mount Zion, the other chief singers with their choirs were sent to Gibeon, where the tabernacle was then still standing. This was the beginning of the liturgical service which accompanied the sacrificial worship.

Later David organized the sacred music in a most elaborate manner for the temple service. He divided the musicians and singers by lot into twenty-four orders (1 Chron. 25), in conformity with the twenty-four orders of the priests in the regular work of the temple. Each division with its head contained twelve men, making a total of 288 men, singers and musicians. They were on duty for both the morning and the evening sacrifice, 1 Chron. 23, 30. During the entire service, the temple orchestra accompanied the singing, and at the end of each Psalm, when a pause occurred in the singing, the priests sounded the silver trumpets, and the people prayed. This order of David was continued during the Golden Age of the Jews. The liturgy at the dedication of Solomon's temple must have been especially impressive, for "the singers, all of them, of Asaph, of Heman, of Jeduthun, with their sons and their brethren, being arrayed in white linen, having cymbals and psalteries and harps, stood at the east end of the altar, and with them an hundred and twenty priests sounding with trumpets: it came even to pass, as the trumpeters and singers were as one, to make one sound to be heard in praising and thanking the Lord; and when they lifted up their voice with the trumpets and cymbals and instruments of music, and praised the Lord," 2 Chron. 5, 12. 13; 7, 6.

After the time of Solomon, the manner and extent of the worship depended, to a large measure, upon the reigning king, whether he did what was good and right in the sight of the Lord his God, or whether he walked after the manner of the pagan kings that remained for an offense to Israel. The kings that feared the Lord retained or restored the temple service. Thus we are told of Hezekiah that "he set the Levites in the house of the Lord, with cymbals, with psalteries, and with harps, according to the commandment of David, and of Gad the king's seer, and Nathan the prophet. . . . And all the congregation worshiped, and the singers sang, and the trumpets sounded: and all this continued until the burnt offering was finished," 2 Chron. 29, 25—28. During the reign of Josiah, also, there was a return to the full service, 2 Chron. 35, 2—6.

After the Babylonian captivity, Ezra and Nehemiah restored the ancient worship, Ezra 6, 16—22; Neh. 8, 9—18, but it is doubtful whether the full liturgical services were then attempted. With the Maccabean victories, however, and the prosperity which followed the Roman occupation of Judea, the ancient form of worship was restored fully. It was then that the temple service reached the elaborate, but dead, beauty of which the Jewish writers speak. The splendor and glory of the morning and evening sacrifice in the temple of Herod, as well as the still more impressive services on the great festivals, can hardly be conceived of in our days.

The Psalms were the anthems of the Jewish Church, their chanting forming the main feature of the liturgical temple service. The Psalms which were used in the regular week-day services were the following: on the first day, Psalm 24, on the second, Psalm 48, on the third, Psalm 82, on the fourth, Psalm 94, on the fifth, Psalm 81, on the sixth, Psalm 93, and on the Sabbath, Psalm 92. During the special sacrifice, which was offered on the Sabbath in addition to the

daily (Num. 28, 9. 10), the Song of Moses, Deut. 32, was sung, being
divided equally among six successive Sabbaths, and in the evening of
the Sabbath the Song of Praise (Ex. 15, 1—19. Cp. Rev. 15, 3). On
the Festival of Trumpets the morning Psalm was Psalm 81, and that
of the evening Psalm 29.

Upon the Passover Festival the great Hallel was sung, the hymn
which the Lord also used at His celebration with His disciples,
Matt. 26, 30; Mark 14, 26. It consisted in the chanting of Psalms
113—118, not all at one time, but in sections. They were sung not
only on the Day of Preparation in the temple, but also while the meal
was in progress. The Talmud mentions another great Hallel, which
occasionally was sung after the Passover meal, probably Psalm 136.
The first Hallel was called the common or Egyptian, in memory of
the deliverance from the slavery of Egypt. The great Hallel was
sung altogether on eighteen days and in one night: at the Passover,
as just mentioned, at Pentecost, on the eight days of the Feast of
Tabernacles, and on the eight days of the Feast of the Dedication,
both at the morning and at the evening sacrifice. During the Feast
of Tabernacles there were special sacrifices, Num. 29, 12 ff., and these
were followed by special Psalms. On the first day Psalm 105 was
sung, on the second Psalm 29, on the third Psalm 50, 1—16, on the
fourth Psalm 94, 1—16, on the fifth Psalm 94, 1—8, on the sixth
Psalm 81, 1—6, on the seventh Psalm 82, 1—5.

In addition to this arrangement, we have the superscription or
dedication of many Psalms, which gives us a clear statement as to
their intended use. All those which were headed "To the chief musician" were undoubtedly dedicated or transmitted to him for use in
the temple. Then, also, whenever the name of a singer or musician
is found at the head of a Psalm, as Asaph (Ps. 50; Ps. 73—83), or
Jeduthun (Ps. 39, 62, 77), or Heman (Ps. 88) and Ethan (Ps. 89),
the Levites, or the children of Korah, which was a whole family or
band of singers (2 Chron. 20, 19), it seems to indicate immediate
public use of the Psalm. We may add the so-called Psalmi graduum,
the Psalms of Degrees (Ps. 120—134). These Psalms were sung or
chanted either on the fifteen steps leading from the Court of Women
to the Court of Israel in the temple, upon the Feast of Tabernacles,
in commemoration of the return from Babylon to Jerusalem, or they
were used by the festival pilgrims, being sung by them on their way
to the capital city. A recent hypothesis surmises the following stations for the use of the various Psalms in this list: Psalm 120 upon
leaving the home town, Psalm 121 upon beholding the hills of the
Holy Land, Psalm 132 at the last stopping-place before reaching
Jerusalem, Psalm 133 during the entry into the city, Psalm 134 when
entering the temple gates. The remaining Psalms which tell of the

fall and rebuilding of Jerusalem and the temple, were sung on the way.[364]

According to all accounts, the people took little or no part in the liturgical services, with the exception of an answering Amen or Hallelujah at certain places of the service. This is substantiated by the practical consideration of ability, since the form of the Hebrew chant or cantillation, being more or less melodious although entirely subordinate to the poetry, required special training, which the Levites received through their skilled musicians. This becomes all the more evident if one remembers that the Psalms are not written in meter with definite rhyme-schemes and caesura, but are constructed upon the parallelism of members, leaving the widest latitude with relation to feet and accent. It was probably necessary, therefore, to practise the cantillation of each Psalm separately, a feat which was virtually impossible even for the members of the Jewish Church living in Jerusalem, and entirely out of the question for those outside of the city. So the liturgical service, as the Jewish accounts state, was confined to the Levitical choir, which consisted of selected Levites and their sons and, at least in certain periods of Jewish history, also of female voices. Ezra speaks of two hundred men and singing women, Ezra 2, 65, and Nehemiah mentions two hundred forty and five singing men and singing women, Neh. 7, 67; Cp. 1 Chron. 16, 36; Jer. 33, 11; Ps. 26, 12; 68, 26; Rev. 14, 1—5.

The manner of rendering the Psalms in the service was probably similar to that of the Gregorian Chant, which may have been suggested by, or taken from, the temple chant. As the later Christian chant, so also the temple chant was executed antiphonally, two choirs alternating, as the forms of certain Psalms indicate (Ps. 136; 118, 2—4; 147, 7). The melody seems to have been sung in one voice (2 Chron. 5, 13). When the melodies were no longer transmitted by oral tradition, a form of notation was devised for the chants. The reading of the Holy Scriptures was thus done by cantillation, which was not a melodious anthem, but carefully modulated declamation, certain accents denoting the inflection or intonation of the voice. This mode of declamation is referred to in the Talmud, and may accordingly have been in use in the early centuries of the Christian era.[365]

The melodies according to which the Psalms were rendered, are indicated in the superscription of a few of them. Psalm 22 was to be chanted according to the melody Aijeleth Shahar, which Luther renders "Hind which is hunted early," Psalm 45 has the melody "A song

364) Cp. Loehe-Hommel, *Haus-, Schul- und Kirchenbuch*, III, 203. 204.
365) Loehe, 202. 203.

of loves," Psalm 59 Altaschith, "A golden jewel," etc. These melodies were well-known to the singers, probably being taken from secular songs or folk-songs, as the words indicate. These melodies were lost with the temple, and even those which the people knew, as the Psalmi graduum and the Hallel, did not preserve their melody.

The instruments which were used by the temple orchestra presented a wide variety. For the number of instrumental performers was not limited, nor yet confined to the Levites, some of the distinguished families which had intermarried with the priests being admitted to this service. The rabbis enumerate thirty-six different instruments, fifteen of which are mentioned in the Bible, five in the Pentateuch. The principal musical instruments were the following. The *kinnor* of David was a small lyre or harp. The *ugab* was either a single tube-like flute or oboe or a connected series like Pan's pipes or the syrinx. The *toph* was a hand-drum or tambourine, the *shophar* a curved tube of metal or ram's horn, the *hazozerah* a long silver tube or trumpet, the *nebel* a harp or guitar, the *chalil* a pipe, oboe, or flageolet, and the *magrephah* a form of organ used in the temple, but whether merely for signals or for accompanying, is not known. David is named as the inventor of the ten-stringed *nevel* or lute. The flute was played upon the occasion of the twelve special festivities, on the first and second Passover, the first day of Unleavened Bread, Pentecost, the eight days of the Feast of Tabernacles, also for the Psalms of Degrees or Ascent by the pilgrims, at marriage feasts, and at funerals. Cp. Gen. 4, 21; 31, 27; Ex. 19; Josh. 6; Num. 10, 2—8; 2 Chron. 5, 12. 13; 29, 26—28; 13, 12—14; 1 Sam. 10, 5; 2 Sam. 6, 5. 14. 15; 1 Chron. 16, 5. 6; 23, 5; 2 Chron. 5, 12—14; Ezra 3, 10. 11.[366] The word Selah, which occurs so often in the Psalms, indicated either an instrumental interlude or flourish or the fact that at this point the people bowed in prayer.[367]

The description which Edersheim gives of the regular service with Psalm singing gives a good idea of the beautiful and impressive mode of worship. "Upon this the temple music began. It was the duty of the priests, who stood on the right and left of the marble table on which the fat of the sacrifices was laid, at the proper time to blow the blasts on their silver trumpets. There might not be less than two nor more than 120 in this service; the former in accordance with the original institution, Num. 10, 2, the latter not to exceed the number at the dedication of the first temple, 2 Chron. 5, 12. The priests faced the people, looking eastwards, while the Levites, who

---

366) Dickinson, *Music in the History of the Western Church*, Chapter I; Edersheim, *The Temple*, Chapter III.
367) Dickinson, 32.

crowded the fifteen steps which led from the Court of Israel to that of the Priests, turned westwards to the sanctuary. On a signal given by the president, the priests moved forward to either side of him who struck the cymbals. Immediately the choir of the Levites, accompanied by instrumental music, began the Psalm of the day. It was sustained by not less than twelve voices, with which mixed the delicious treble, from selected voices of young sons of the Levites, who, standing by their fathers, might take part in this service alone . . . The Psalm of the day was always sung in three sections. At the close of each the priests drew three blasts from their silver trumpets, and the people bowed down and worshiped. This closed the morning service." [368])

<hr />

CHAPTER 2.

Hymns in the Apostolic and Ante-Nicean Church.

The New Testament contains some of the most beautiful canticles of the entire Scriptures. Therefore the praise service of the early Church had a splendid mass of material to select from. All the canticles of the Old Testament, not only those of Moses, Hannah, and Deborah, but the collection of Psalms and the glorious poetry of the prophets had been codified and was in common use in the Jewish Church, to which all the twelve apostles belonged, as well as Paul, the great teacher of the Gentiles. And not only that, but the inspired hymns of the New Testament were written at an early date in the books of the Christian Church, and were probably known in wide circles even before the apostles and evangelists committed them to paper. The Magnificat of Mary, Luke 1, 46—55, the Benedictus of Zacharias, Luke 1, 68—79, the Gloria in excelsis, Luke 2, 14, and the Nunc dimittis of Simeon, Luke 2, 29—32, belong to this list. They were bound to receive special reverence and regard in the eyes of the Christians, because they were so closely connected with the story of the Savior. Both facts may therefore be assumed: in the first place that the early Christians received much from the Jewish ritual, with the inference that the Hebrew melodies were borrowed at the same time; and in the second place that there was soon evident a dependence upon Greek influence, introduced with the wider acceptance of that language.

The latter fact is supported by evidence from the epistles of St. Paul. Eph. 5, 19 he writes: "Speaking to yourselves in psalms, and hymns, and spiritual songs," and he repeats the same phrase Col.

<hr />

368) *The Temple,* 171. 172.

3, 16. The Psalms are, of course, those from the book of that name. The hymns may easily be identified with the canticles which were enumerated above. And as for the odes, there is no reason for rejecting the assertion that the spiritual songs were composed, not only by Mary and Zacharias and Simeon, but by many other members of the early Church as well. Surely where the charisma of glossolalia was common, the inspiration to write odes containing the praises of God and the Savior could not have been lacking (Cp. Acts 16, 25). Says Dr. Stoeckhardt in his commentary on Ephesians: "It does not seem so unsuitable if we, with reference to the word *psalmoi,* think of the Biblical Psalms, which were surely sung at an early date in the services of the Christians; with relation to *hymnoi* of the anthems of prayer and praise which were composed by Christian hymn-writers, which, corresponding to our chorals, were mainly intended for the public services; and, with reference to *odai pneumatikai,* of all the spiritual beautiful songs, 'spiritual' as distinguished from secular, which were sung in the homes of the Christians," p. 236.

As a matter of fact, we have evidence that hymns and spiritual songs were in general use in the time of the apostles. The singing of a hymn "with one accord," Acts 4, 24—30, certainly points in that direction. Other passages which are decidedly liturgical in appearance and may well be portions of ancient hymns are Eph. 5, 14; 1 Tim. 3, 16; 6, 15. 16; 2 Tim. 2, 11—13; Rev. 1, 4—8; 5, 9—14; 21, 10—14; 22, 17. Other liturgical quotations were discussed above, Part I, Chapter II. If one considers, also, that the verb *psallein* is freely used in the New Testament for the singing of Psalms and hymns, Eph. 5, 19; Rom. 15, 9 (Ps. 18, 50); 1 Cor. 15, 15; Jas. 5, 13, the evidence becomes all the stronger. It is safe, then, to say that at the end of the first century there were not only many spiritual songs and newly-composed hymns in general use in the Church, but there were also definite liturgical chants or canticles, whose use was practically universal. They were the following: 1) The Lesser Doxology or the Gloria Patri, 2) The Greater Doxology or the Gloria in excelsis, 3) Tersanctus, 4) Hallelujah, 5) Evening Hymn, with Nunc dimittis, 6) Benedicite or Song of the Three Children, 7) Magnificat, 8) Te Deum.[369] There may be some doubt as to the last, because some students do not wish to drop the Ambrosian authorship, but the list otherwise is safe enough. We might even add the Amen, 1 Cor. 14, 16, the Kyrie, Luke 18, 38, the Pax, John 20, 21, the Pater Noster, and others.

Progress was rapid in the second century. Ignatius of Antioch (beginning of second century) is said to have introduced antiphonal

---

369) Cp. Daniel, *Thesaurus hymnologicus,* II, 289.

chanting. So there was, at that time, both choir singing and alternate or responsive singing. This is corroborated also by the Younger Pliny, who, in the letter quoted above, records that the Christians were accustomed to sing responsively a hymn to Christ as God. In the time of Tertullian the Church must have had a wealth of hymns and spiritual songs, since he speaks of them repeatedly.[370] The oldest Christian hymn extant, at least in the East, was the Greek composition found in the works of Clement of Alexandria (170—220), and ascribed to him. It is a turgid, lifeless *Panegyris tou logou*. The Apostolic Constitutions speak of a singer or precentor [371] and hypophonic Psalm-singing. Eusebius also refers to hymns, which he styles "modern productions of modern men" in a most matter-of-fact way, showing that the composing of hymns and the use of hymns in those days was nothing new or unusual.

The first great era or golden age of Christian hymn-writing in the early Church is found in Syria. Bardesanes (154—222) and his son Honorius tried to spread their Gnostic speculations by means of hymns. Ephraem the Syrian knew of a collection of 150 psalms which Bardesanes had composed after the analogy of the Psalms of David. The hymns of the so-called Acts of Thomas have also been ascribed to Bardesanes. Certain it is that he and his son exerted a tremendous influence upon the hymn-writing of his time, and there is every reason to call them the creators of the Syriac church hymn. Others followed in their foot-steps, and it became a favorite method of the heretics to gain adherents for their views by means of hymns. For the common people accepted the hymns and sang their way ever more deeply into dualism. A mere prohibition of their use would have availed little. The rhythm and the melody had impressed these compositions so deeply upon the minds and hearts that the people could not be deflected by a peremptory order. Therefore Ephraem Syrus (4th century, died 378) determined to meet the evil influence with orthodox hymns. It is for this activity that he was celebrated in the ancient Church, such titles as "Lyre of the Holy Ghost" and "Prophet of the Syrians" being given to him. He attained his object not only in his day and age, but his hymns had so much intrinsic merit that they have been retained in the Orient in part to the present day. Many of them are alternating songs. The Syrians ascribed to him a total of 12,000 songs, and the Copts even 14,000, but it should be remembered that all the songs of his school, as well as the hymns of many lesser poets have been credited to him. His best-known hymn is the poem On the Nativity of Our Lord, with the opening stanza: "Into his arms, with tender love, Did Joseph take

370) Horn, *Outlines of Liturgies*, 80.   371) Book VIII, § 69.

his only son." A hymn is also cited by Basil (died 379), which has the opening line *Phos hilaron hagias doxes,* "Hail, gladdening Light," which was used by Longfellow. Clement of Alexandria quotes a poem from an earlier author (about 200 A. D.), which we now know as "Shepherd of Tender Youth." Other hymns from the third and the beginning of the fourth century are: *Echos,* "We who have risen from our sleep," and *Psyche mou,* "O soul of mine." As the earliest hymn of all Duffield quotes, not that of Clement, but a very short stanza to the Trinity:

> "My hope is God,
> My refuge is the Lord,
> My shelter is the Holy Ghost;
> Be Thou, O Holy Three, adored!" [372]

So far as antiphonal singing is concerned, its development in the fourth century had reached the following stage. There were, according to Baeumer, four varieties of chanting and responsive singing: 1) Cantus responsorius, in which the lector chanted a Psalm by paragraphs and the congregation repeated each section; 2) Cantus antiphonus, in which two choirs alternated in chanting the Psalms of David; 3) Cantus tractus, in which the Psalm was sung without interval or division from beginning to end; 4) Cantus directaneus, in which all those present or the choirs together sang the entire Psalms without pause or interlude tamquam ex uno ore.[373]

CHAPTER 3.
The Canono-Catholic and Roman Catholic Periods.

When the Gnostic and Arian heresies were spread by means of hymns, the orthodox party, as we have seen, met them on their own ground, offering to the people such anthems as coincided in every respect with the requirements of pure Christianity. It was for this reason, also, that the Council of Laodicea (343—381), in its 13th canon, appointed singers for the churches. These choristers had the special duty to recast the secular melodies they desired to transplant, using them mainly for the Psalms and canticles. The same council, however, recognizing the danger from heterodox hymns, in its 59th canon made the rule that no *psalmoi idiotikoi* were to be used in church services.[374] The contrast which is included in the expression of the council makes it evident that it is not so much the Psalms of

---

372) Duffield, *The Latin Hymn-Writers and their Hymns,* Chapter I.
373) *Geschichte des Breviers,* 118 ff.
374) Alt, *Der kirchliche Gottesdienst,* 426, nota.

David which should be used to the exclusion of all others, but that no one had the right to palm off inventions of his own, without sound Scriptural basis, on the Church, under the guise of church hymns.

These resolutions acted as a great stimulus, not only upon Ephraem Syrus, as shown above, but also upon other teachers of the Church. There is a hymn at the lighting of the lamps extant from this period, with the opening lines: "O gladsome light Of the Father immortal." Gregory of Nazianz combined theological learning with poetical ability, and his hymns have been classed with the best products of classical times. The Syrian poet Synesius also wrote a number of poems, of which ten are still extant. But they were lacking in the appealing simplicity which would have made them acceptable to the great mass of the people, and never enjoyed great popularity. The second period of Eastern hymn poetry, which began in the second quarter of the eighth century and lasted for about a century, produced a number of poets whose compositions were far from mediocre. Among these Cosmas, Bishop of Majuma, Andrew, Bishop of Crete, Germanus, Patriarch of Constantinople, Johannes Damascenus, Theophanes, Metropolitan of Nicea, and Joseph, Deacon of Constantinople, furnished the best hymns. They were especially prolific in furnishing hymns to Mary and the saints, whose cult was definitely established at that period and whose festival days required a large number of songs. In general, their hymns present a fine narrative style and objectivity, thus meeting the principal demand of the popular hymn. They were praised, accordingly, not only by their grateful contemporaries, but their importance is recognized even at this late day.

Before we continue our survey of the development of hymnology in the Western Church, it may be well to devote a few paragraphs to the Psalms and hymns of the Canonical Hours, which grew out of the hours of prayer in the primitive Church and were finally regulated by Benedict of Nursia, at Monte Cassino, between Rome and Naples, in the first half of the sixth century. The third, sixth, and ninth hours were observed by the apostles and first disciples, Acts 3, 1; 10, 9. The first hours for daily service of prayers which were fixed by rule were Lauds and Vespers. The Apostolic Constitutions name the third, sixth, and ninth hours of the morning, the evening, and at cock-crowing.[375] The Horae canonicae, as fixed by Benedict of Nursia, included the following hours: Vigils, at 2.00 A. M., Matins, at dawn (incipiente luce), Prime, at 6.00 A. M., Terce, at 9.00 A. M., Sext, at 12.00 M., Nones, at 3.00 P. M., Vespers, at 6.00 P. M., Com-

375) Book VIII, Chapter 34.

pline, at 9.00 P. M.[376]) Baeumer gives the following list: Matins,
Lauds, Prime, Terce, Sext, None, Vesper, Compline, — and Nocturn
(Book I). In this case, the service of Lauds, which was frequently
joined with Matins, is given a separate service, in order to keep the
eight hours of prayer. The Matin service on certain days is divided
into three parts, called Nocturns, but on all ordinary festivals, as
well as in ferial services, there is but one Nocturn.

Matins is now celebrated just before dawn. Its Invitatory is
Psalm 95. A number of Psalms, averaging about twelve, are then
chanted, with Antiphon or Hallelujah after each Psalm or part of
Psalms. There is also a hymn, a lection, the Te Deum, and the Can-
ticum de evangelio, followed by the Litany and the Lord's Prayer.
Lauds are held at dawn. Their purpose is the praise of God for the
creation and regeneration. A feature of this service is the Canticle
Benedictus. The services of the four smaller hours, Prime, Terce,
Sext, and None, are much alike: Antiphon, Hymn, three Psalms
with Gloria Patri after each one, Lection, Antiphon, and Litany. At
Vespers, the purpose is to look back upon the blessings of the day
with a grateful heart, and praise God's providence and grace. There
were four Psalms with Antiphons, a Lection with Responsorium, the
Canticum de evangelio (Magnificat), the Litany, and the Lord's
Prayer. In the service of Compline, the faithful looked back once
more, and then forward to the lowering night. He admonished his
soul to be vigilant and commended his spirit into the hands of his
Lord. There were three Psalms without Antiphons, a Hymn, a Lection with Antiphon, the Litany, and the Benediction. Later the
Canticle Nunc dimittis was introduced as being the most perfect and
all-embracing prayer of commendation. Every week the Psalter was
thus chanted complete. And the hymns for the Horae canonicae, of
which Daniel, Wackernagel, and Milchsack publish a great many,
were often of great beauty. The Antiphons, the Responsoria, the
Te Deum, the Litany, and the Canticles all served to enhance the impressiveness of these services of prayer.[377])

So far as the general liturgical service of this period is concerned,
the names of Ambrose, Leo, Gelasius, and especially Gregory the
Great, stand out most prominently. The antiphonal chanting at
Milan was due to Oriental influence, through the agency of Ambrose.
Augustine says of it: "How abundantly did I weep to hear those
hymns and canticles of thine, being touched to the very quick by the
voices of thy sweet church song. . . . At this time was it here first

376) *Memoirs*, II: 5; Kliefoth, *Die urspruengliche Gottesdienstordnung*, III, 186.
377) Kliefoth, *L. c.*, 186—190; Loehe-Hommel, *Der Psalter*, 205—209.
Kretzmann, Christian Art.   21

instituted, after the manner of the Eastern churches, that hymns and Psalms should be sung. . . ., which custom being retained from that day to this." [378] Ambrosius was the inventor or introducer of four scales in the church music, the Dorian, the Phrygian, the Aeolian, and the Myxolydian. The Ambrosian chants which were sung in these melodies, were varied by ebullitions of melody. The simple Plain Song melodies were largely syllabic, but some of the ornate chants were exceedingly florid. Antiphonal psalmody was introduced in Rome by Celestine (422—432), and Leo I (died 461) established the first community of monks for canonical hours' service, which was later regulated by Benedict. In the meantime, the Ambrosian chants deteriorated rapidly, losing their original simplicity and purity. Gregory the Great (590—604) undertook the great work of reforming the music of the liturgy. He extended the scales introduced by Ambrose to double the original number, he freed the Church from the fetters of Greek prosody, he collected the existing chants and issued an Antiphonary. He became the inventor of the Gregorian Plain Song Chant, which has not lost its influence upon church music since that time. The plagal scales invented by Gregory were later enriched by the addition of four further scales, making a total of twelve scales used for church songs and liturgical music: the Dorian, in d; the Hypodorian, in a; the Phrygian, in e; the Hypophrygian, in b; the Aeolian, in f; the Hypoaeolian, in c; the Mixolydian, in g; the Hypomixolydian, in d; the Lydian, in a; the Hypolydian, in e; the Ionian, in c; the Hypoionian, in g.[379] To secure the dignified simplicity which he deemed necessary for church music, Gregory insisted upon a certain definite melody for each text, which differed from the metrical, rhythmic singing of the Ambrosians. Regardless of the meter, the Plain Song marched on in stately grandeur, the entire choir singing one voice, whence it was also designated as Cantus choralis. Gregory founded a large school in which promising boys were instructed in chanting, and it became a rule that all priests must be well versed in church music.

The Gregorian Chant was soon brought to England, finding an eager reception throughout the Church of Britain, the Council of Cloveshoven (747) retaining it unchanged in all the churches. Charlemagne introduced the Gregorian Chant into Germany. Through the agency of the music schools at Metz, Orleans, Sens, Toul, Lyon, Cambray, Dijon, and Paris, the Frankish kingdom was soon flooded with men who were trained in the new chant. Charles the Great also encouraged Rhabanus Maurus in his work at Fulda, which resulted in further schools at Reichenau, Corvey, Mainz, and Trier.[380]

---

378) *Confessions*, Book IX, Chapters VI and VIII.
379) Alt, *Der kirchliche Gottesdienst*, 393. 394.   380) Alt, 396.

The choice of the scale for the various chants is controlled largely by the significance of the scale or its special meaning in musical notation. According to Bona, Antony, and Loehe, the following symbolism is generally accepted. The Dorian expresses gentle seriousness, dignified joy, and may be used upon all general occasions. The Hypodorian expresses longing, sorrow, mourning. The Phrygian is used when lively, strong emotion, eagerness and determination, decided commanding and threatening are to be brought out. The Hypophrygian indicates gentle sensations, it begs for sympathy and compassion, and disarms passionate outbursts. The Lydian expresses joy, jubilation, triumph. The Hypolydian signifies dignified joy, a peaceful, quiet, devoted condition, humble devotion, sympathy. The Mixolydian expresses stately, majestic gravity, a joy which is too deep for levity. The Hypomixolydian may represent the various sensations of sweetness, charm, and grace.[381])

The hymn-writers of the Western Church have left so many gems of Christian hymnody that it is often difficult to make a proper selection. Their great choir is opened by Hilary of Poitiers (died ca. 367), whose Liber Hymnorum is lost. Yet the hymns which are ascribed to him show a poetical force which have caused their retention in the Church to this day. Among these Lucis largitor splendide (Thou splendid Giver of the light) is the best-known, but Deus, Pater ingenite (Eternal Father, God), Beata nobis gaudia (What blessed joys are ours), and Jam meta noctis transiit (The limit of the night is passed) are also of high merit. At about the same time Pope Damasus in Rome introduced rhymed and accented poetry. He composed the hymn Martyris ecce dies Agathae (Fair as the morn in the deep-blushing East).

Much more important and influential, however, were the Ambrosian hymns, which found their earliest recognition in Spain, but were soon accepted in every part of the Western Church. Twelve hymns are recognized by the Benedictine editors as genuine, all of them resonant with deep, spontaneous feeling. He wrote O lux beata Trinitas (O Trinity of blessed light), Deus Creator omnium (Maker of all, the Lord), Veni, Redemptor gentium (Redeemer of the nations, come), Aeterne rerum Conditor (Creator blest, eternal King), Aurora lucis rutilat (Light's glittering morn bedecks the sky), and others.

In the fifth century, a number of poets of unquestioned ability made their appearance. Prudentius (died between 410 and 424) wrote Nox et tenebrae et nubila, Corde natus ex parentis, and the elegiac burial-song Iam moesta quiesce querela. Ennodius, Bishop of Pavia (died 521) is credited with sixteen hymns, among which are

---

381) Loehe-Hommel, *Der Psalter*, 193. 194.

Christe, lumen perpetuum (O Christ, the Eternal Light), Christe
precamur (O Christ, to Thee we pray), Christe, Salvator omnium
(O Christ, the Savior of all), and others. Caelius Sedulius (about
the middle of the 5th century) wrote the so-called Alphabet Hymn of
twenty-three stanzas, of which A solis ortus cardine (From lands
that see the sun arise) and Hostis Herodes impie (Why fear the impious Herod's might) are the best-known. At the end of the century
came Fortunatus, whose best-known hymn Vexilla Regis prodeunt
(The royal banners forward fly) is almost equaled in influence by the
Christmas hymn Agnoscat omne saeculum, the Passion hymn Pange,
lingua gloriosi, praélium certaminis, the Easter song Salve, festa dies,
the Ave, maris stella, and the Quem terra, pontus, aethera. Gregory
the Great himself closes the list of sixth century poets, nine hymns
being ascribed to him. Of these the Primo dierum omnium, Ecce
jam noctis, Lucis Creator optime, and especially the Maundy Thursday hymn Rex Christe, Factor omnium (O Christ, the heaven's
Eternal King) deserve more than passing mention.

In the Middle Ages, only a few men stand out in the earlier
period. Beda Venerabilis (died 735), whose writings are an encyclopedia of universal learning, composed the hymns Adesto, Christe,
vocibus, — Emitte, Christe, Spiritum (Send forth, O Christ, Thy
Spirit), and Hymnum canamus gloriae (Let us sing a hymn of glory).
Paul the Deacon (died 795) wrote the hymn in honor of John the
Baptist Ut queant laxis, the initial syllables of whose first stanza
were used by Guido of Arezzo in introducing solmisation:

> *Ut* queant laxis
> *Re*sonare fibris
> *Mi*ra gestorum
> *Fa*muli tuorum
> *Sa*lve polluti
> *La*bii reatum,
> *Sa*ncte Johannes!

The hymn Veni Creator Spiritus (Come, God Creator, Holy Ghost),
which was formerly ascribed to Ambrose or to Gregory, is by Duffield
referred to Rhabanus Maurus (died 856). This hymn is held in very
regard by hymnologists, some of whom give it a rank with the best
productions of Latin poetry of all times. Its stately impressiveness
and detached objectivity marks it as a product of genius.

The Choral School of St. Gall in the 9th and 10th centuries was
especially prolific in sequences or tropes, which took the place of the
long prolongation of the final syllables in the Alleluia, this being
protracted to cover the retreat of the deacon as he walked from the
Epistle-lectern and ascended the rood-loft to chant the Gospel. This
Alleluia was originally the only response between the Epistle and the

Gospel, and, since the deacon had some space to traverse, the *ia* was nearly interminable at times. Tutilo of St. Gall composed the Christmas sequence Hodie cantandus, the Omnium virtutum gemmis, and the Ascension trope Viri Galilaei. Notker Balbulus also was the author of many sequences which were widely used in the Church during the Middle Ages.[382] To Notker is commonly ascribed the hymn or sequence Media vita in morte sumus (In the midst of life we are in death), which is almost overpowering in its impressiveness. The list of the early Middle Ages is properly closed with Robert, King of France (997—1031), who composed the sequence for Pentecost Veni Sancte Spiritus (Come, Holy Spirit). Duffield names Hermannus Contractus (died 1054) as the author of both the Veni Sancte Spiritus and the Salve Regina, Mater misericordiae.

The twelfth century has several illustrious poets. To Peter Damiani is credited the hymn Ad perennis vitae fontem. He was surpassed by Bernard of Clairveaux (born 1091, died 1153), a mystic, who addressed a number of poems to the members of the suffering Savior. The most notable one is the Salve, Caput cruentatum, which proved an inspiration to Paul Gerhard. Abelard (died 1142) wrote the hymns Mittit ad virginem, Ornarunt terram germina (The earth is green with grasses), O quanta qualia sunt illa sabbata (O what shall be, O when shall be That holy Sabbath day), and others. Adam of St. Victor (died 1192) wrote Quem pastores laudavere, Salve crux, arbor (Hail, thou cross), Verbum Dei, Deo natum (He, the Word of God, the fated), and possibly about a hundred other hymns. Although his hymns are objective, they are altogether too detached, and are therefore not singable, being too abstruse. Other singers of the 12th century are Peter the Venerable and Bernard of Cluny, the latter's poem De contemptu mundi being written in leonine hexameters.

The 13th and 14th centuries brought forth some of the greatest of all Latin poets. The first of these is Thomas of Celano (died ca. 1255), who grew up under the influence of Francis of Assisi, whose biography he wrote. He composed the sequences Fregit victor virtualis and Sanctitatis nova signa, but above all the world-renowned Dies irae, Dies illa (Day of wrath, Thy fiery morning Earth consumes), which has seen so many translations and transcriptions that books have been written on the translations alone. Passages of most impressive beauty and power are the 10th and 11th stanzas: "Seeking me, Thy love outwore Thee, And the cross, my ransom, bore Thee, Let not this seem light before Thee. Righteous Judge of my condition, Grant me for my sins remission, Ere the day which ends con-

---

382) Cp. *Welche Sequenzen hat Notker verfaszt*, in *Zeitschrift fuer deutsches Altertum*, XV, 267.

trition." A still greater poet, hymn-writer, and liturgiologist was Thomas Acquinas (died 1274), who composed the Office for the Corpus Christi Festival. He wrote the beautiful sequence Lauda, Sion, Salvatorem (Sion, lift thy voice and sing), and the hymns Pange, lingua gloriosi, Corporis mysterium (Sing, O my tongue, adore and praise), Sacris solemniis juncta sunt gaudia, and Verbum supernum prodiens. To Bonaventura, his contemporary, the appealing Adeste fideles is ascribed. One more poet stands in the front rank, namely Jacoponus da Todi (died 1306), who wrote Cur mundus militat (Why should this world of ours Strive to be glorious), but especially the sequence, surcharged with the feeling of an anguished heart, Stabat mater dolorosa (At the cross, her station keeping). The list of pre-Reformation Latin poets is fitly closed with Thomas à Kempis (died 1471), who wrote Adversa mundi tolera, O qualis quantaque laetitia, and Adstant angelorum chori, and finally Francis Xavier (died 1552), who wrote the charming O Deus, ego amo Te (O Lord, I love Thee, for of old, Thy love hath reached to me). We might add the hymns of a score or more less-known writers, besides a great many anonymous compositions of unequal merit, such as Exultet coelum gaudibus, Deus-Homo Rex coelorum, Puer natus in Bethlehem, In dulci jubilo, and others.

But of all the Latin poems, five stand out from all the rest and have always affected the hearts of men with extraordinary force: the Veni Creator Spiritus is powerful, the Dies irae is grand, the Veni Sancte Spiritus is charming, the Ad perennis vitae fontem is lovely, and the Stabat mater is pathetic. It would by no means be a misfortune if hymns of this kind were known, studied, and appreciated more thoroughly in our age of jazz-band jingles.[383])

CHAPTER 4.

The Period of the Reformation.

In the Catholic Church the popular hymn or choral for the entire congregation has not been an integral part of the service since about the eighth century. The church music was entirely in the hands of the choir. No one will deny, of course, that church music made unprecedented progress in the next centuries. The Cantus firmus of the Gregorian Chant was soon supplemented with a more or less

---

383) For the last paragraphs Cp. Duffield, *The Latin Hymn-Writers and their Hymns*, Chapters III to XXVIII; Alt, *Der kirchliche Gottesdienst*, 429—438; Horn, *Outlines of Liturgies*, 81—84; Wackernagel, *Das deutsche Kirchenlied*, Book I; Chevalier, *Repertorium hymnologicum;* Daniel, *Thesaurus hymnologicus;* Marbach, *Carmina scripturarum;* Milchsack, *Hymni et Sequentiae;* Mone, *Lateinische Hymnen des Mittelalters*.

harmonious voice in accompaniment, known as discant, since it left
the path of the ancient cantus. At first there were only these two
parts, the cantus firmus accompanied by counterpoint (punctus con-
tra punctum), the former always taken from a ritual book or from a
popular tune, the latter invented, as often as occasion required, by
the singer desirous of providing change or diversion. Through the
efforts of Hucbald of Rheims (ca. 900), Reginus (920), Guido of
Arezzo, Franco of Cologne, and others, the new science was gradually
developed, harmony was introduced, the medieval school of a-capella
music took its rise. Out of the antique mnemonic system (neumae
etc.) there was developed a system of square-headed notes, with a
staff of lines and spaces. The question of long and short notes, of
beats and bars was finally decided. Musical composition began to
appear about the end of the fourteenth century in which one voice
introduced the melody or theme; another voice followed, which was
in turn pursued by a third and fourth, and sometimes by still more.
The resulting fugues (fugo) were often productions of great beauty.
Since the use of a connected text was very difficult under such circumstances, a single word, such as Amen or Hallelujah, was chosen,
and the resulting composition was called motet (from the French
mot=word). These efforts at rendering the harmony of church music
artistic reached their culmination in Palestrina (1526—1594), who
brought counterpoint into proper relation and perfection. His "Mass
of Pope Marcellus," with which he gained the favor of the church
dignitaries, is considered the most perfect product of Medieval musical art. It was followed by other works of many masters: masses,
motets, and longer hymns, in which there was often no leading part
or voice, but a series of voices running side by side or crossing each
other. Orlandus Lassus in Munich, Andrea and Giovanni Gabrielis
in Venice, Willaert, and others were among the masters of that
age, the last-named introducing antiphonal chorus singing at
St. Mark's.[384]

In the mean time, the popular church-song in the vernacular had
been gaining foothold in Germany and the adjacent countries. Since
the time of Walther von der Vogelweide, Gottfried von Strassburg,
and other minnesingers, the popular spiritual song had exerted a
great influence. Some of the earliest Leisen, as these short hymns
were called, are Also heilig ist der Tag, Christ ist erstanden, Mitten
wir im Leben sind, Nun bitten wir den Heiligen Geist, Gelobet seist
du, Jesus Christ. Some of the best Latin hymns were also translated
into the vernacular and used by the people as spiritual folk-songs.

---

384) Cp. Dickinson, *Music in the History of the Western Church,*
Chapter V.

Milchsack prints the following renderings into Middle German, as found in the collection of Flacius Illyricus: Kom du loser der heydenen (Veni Redemptor gentium), Uan des de sunne vn vp gheit (A solis ortus cardine), Uigend Herodes vngutlich, wes bistu Christo hetelich? (Hostis Herodes impie), Ik grozt dy, meres sterne (Ave maris stella), Do de konig gotliker ere (Cum rex gloriae), and Loue du schower dynen loser (Lauda, Sion, Salvatorem). Translations of Latin hymns were also published by John of Salzburg (end of 14th century), Dietrich, and others.[385] A very interesting feature of these centuries are the mixed songs, half Latin, half in the vernacular, of which a number have been preserved, the In dulci jubilo of Petrus Dresdensis (died 1440), Puer natus in Bethlehem, and Ave maris stella being the most interesting ones. These songs were in use in Germany as well as in France and elsewhere.

But all this does not change the fact that the church hymn or choral, sung by the congregation, was not included in the church services before the Reformation. There are very few service books that contain rubrics which direct the singing of even the Leisen Christ ist erstanden or Christ fuhr gen Himmel. In many places, they were permitted only at the end of the Tropes in the morning service or in the liturgical plays developed from them. The change came with Luther. "The German Reformation became great with the church hymn, and the church hymn became great with the Reformation" (Horn). The importance of Luther in this field can hardly be overestimated. He wrote his first spiritual song in 1523, after Heinrich Voes and John Esch, of Antwerp, had been martyred. Its title was "A New Song of the Two Martyrs for Christ, Burned at Brussels by the Sophists of Louvain." The end was a prophetic, triumphant outburst:

> "Summer is even at our door.
> The winter now has vanished.
> The tender flowrets spring once more,
> And He, who winter banished
> Will send a happy summer."

The same year, Luther published two hymns on two leaves in quarto size, one of which was his own: Nun freut euch, liebe Christeng'mein (Dear Christians, one and all, rejoice), and the other Es ist das Heil uns kommen her, by Speratus. This first congregational hymn of Luther was truly a "Christian hymn, setting forth the unspeakable grace of God and the true faith." In the next year appeared the small hymnal "Etlich christlich Lider, Wittenberg, 1524," containing eight hymns with the melodies, four of them by Luther: Nun freut

---

385) Alt, *Der kirchliche Gottesdienst*, 438.

euch, liebe Christeng'mein, Ach Gott vom Himmel, sieh darein, Es
spricht der Unweisen Mund wohl, and Aus tiefer Not, three by Speratus, and one by an unknown writer. In 1526 a collection of thirty-nine
hymns was published at Erfurt, and after that the number of hymns and
hymnals grew by leaps and bounds. Luther left the wonderful heritage
of thirty-seven hymns and spiritual songs. Alt divides them into five
groups. Transcriptions of Psalms are found in the following hymns:
1) Ach Gott vom Himmel, sieh darein, Ps. 12 (O God, look down
from heaven and see), 2) Es spricht der Unweisen Mund wohl, Ps. 14
(The mouth of fools doth God confess), 3) Ein feste Burg ist unser
Gott, Ps. 46 (A mighty fortress is our God), 4) Es woll uns Gott ge-
naedig sein, Ps. 67 (May God bestow on us His grace), 5) Waer Gott
nicht mit uns diese Zeit, Ps. 124 (Had God not come, may Israel
say), 6) Wohl dem, der in Gottesfurcht steht, Ps. 128 (Happy the
man that feareth God), 7) Aus tiefer Not schrei ich zu dir, Ps. 130
(Out of the depths I cry to Thee). The second group includes hymns
based upon Bible passages: 8) Jesaja dem Propheten das geschah,
Is. 6, 1—4 (These things the seer Isaiah did befall), 9) Vater unser
im Himmelreich, Matt. 6 (Our Father, Thou in heaven above),
10) Vom Himmel hoch da komm ich her, Luke 2 (From heaven above
to earth I come), 11) Mit Fried und Freud ich fahr dahin, Luke 2,
29—32 (In peace and joy I now depart), 12) Sie ist mir lieb, die
werte Magd, Rev. 12, 1—6 (Dear is to me the Holy Maid), 13) Dies
sind die heilgen zehn Gebot (That man a godly life might live),
14) Mensch, willst du leben seliglich (Wilt thou, O man, live hap-
pily). The third group comprises transcriptive translations of Latin
hymns: 15) Verleih uns Frieden gnaediglich, after Da pacem Domine,
an antiphon of the 6th or 7th century, usually ascribed to Gregory
the Great (In these our days so perilous), 16) Gelobet seist du, Jesus
Christ, after the Grates nunc omnes reddamus of Notker Balbulus
and a pre-Reformation vernacular stanza (All praise to Jesus' hallowed name), 17) Der du bist drei in Einigkeit, from the O lux, beata
Trinitas of Ambrose (Thou who art three in unity), 18) Was
fuerchtst du Feind Herodes sehr, from the Hostis Herodes impie
(Why, Herod, unrelenting foe), 19) Komm, heiliger Geist, HErre
Gott, after the antiphon Veni Sancte Spiritus, reple tuorum corda,
of which an old vernacular stanza was in existence (Come, Holy
Spirit, God and Lord), 20) Der Tag, der ist so freudenreich, after
Dies est laetitiae, ascribed to Adam of St. Victor, 21) Nun komm,
der Heiden Heiland, a free rendering of the Veni Redemptor gentium
of Ambrose (Savior of the heathen, come, 22) Wir glauben all an
einen Gott, the Nicene Creed (We all believe in one true God),
23) HErr Gott, dich loben wir, the Te Deum laudamus (Lord God,

Thy praise we sing), 24) Christum wir sollen loben schon, from the
A solis ortus cardine of Sedulius (Now praise we Christ, the Holy
One), 25) Mitten wir im Leben sind, after the sequence Media vita
in morte sumus and a medieval vernacular version, the Latin usually
credited to Notker Balbulus (Though in the midst of life we be),
26) Christ, der du bist Licht und Tag, after Christe, qui lux es et
dies, 27) Komm, Gott Schoepfer, Heiliger Geist, from Veni, Creator
Spiritus, probably by Rhabanus Maurus (Come, God Creator, Holy
Ghost). The third group includes vernacular songs recast: 28) Gott
sei gelobet und gebenedeiet (May God be praised henceforth and
blessed forever), 29) Christ lag in Todesbanden, based on the pre-
Reformation stanza and upon the sequences and antiphons Victimae
paschali and Surrexit Christus hodie (In death's strong grasp the
Savior lay), 30) Nun bitten wir den Heiligen Geist (Now do we pray
God, the Holy Ghost), 31) Gott der Vater wohn uns bei, an old
Litany of Rogation week (God the Father be our Stay). The last
group consists of hymns which were spontaneous outbursts of song:
32) Nun freut euch, liebe Christeng'mein, 33) Ein neues Lied wir
heben an, 34) Jesus Christus, unser Heiland, der den Tod ueberwand
(Jesus Christ, who came to save), 35) Vom Himmel kam der Engel
Schar (To shepherds, as they watched by night), 36) Erhalt uns,
HErr, bei deinem Wort (Lord, keep us in Thy Word and work),
37) Christ, unser HErr, zum Jordan kam (To Jordan came our Lord,
the Christ.[386])   Hymnologists seem to be agreed at present that the
hymn Der Tag der ist so freudenreich, noted above, is not by Luther.
But the hymn JEsus Christus unser Heiland, after the Jesus Christus, nostra salus of Johann Huss (Jesus Christ, our blessed Savior),
should be inserted. The St. Louis edition of Luther's works omits
also Christe, der du bist Licht und Tag, but has in addition, from
Wackernagel, Ein Lied fuer die Kinder (Nun treiben wir den Papst
heraus), Auf dem Widerwege zu singen (Der Papst und Greul ist
ausgetrieben), Wider Herzog Heinrich von Braunschweig (Ach du
arger Heinze), O du armer Judas, Eine andere Auslegung des
128. Psalms.[387])

Luther did not remain alone in this noble work. Not only in
Wittenberg, but throughout Germany and in other countries poets
began to sing of the new glory which had arisen over the Church.
The golden age in the writing of hymns had come. In the immediate
vicinity of Luther there was his friend Justus Jonas (died 1555),
who composed Wo Gott der HErr nicht bei uns haelt, wenn unsre
Feinde toben (Ps. 123), Der HErr erhoer euch in der Not (Ps. 20),

---

386) Cp. Alt, Der kirchliche Gottesdienst, 445. 446, nota.
387) l. c. 1434—1473. Cp. Saengerbote, St. Louis, 1917, Nos. 1—4.

HErr JEsu Christ, dein Erb wir sind (Ps. 79), and two additional stanzas to Luther's Erhalt uns HErr, which, however, are not very happy in their connection. Johann Agricola of Eisleben (died 1566) wrote Froehlich wollen wir Alleluja singen (Ps. 117) and Ach HErre Gott, wie haben sich wider dich so hart gesetzet (Ps. 2). Paul Eber (died 1569) struck a more popular strain in his poems HErr JEsu Christ, wahr'r Mensch und Gott, HErr Gott, dich loben alle wir, Helft mir Gott's Guete preisen, Wenn wir in hoechsten Noeten sein, and the tender In Christi Wunden schlaf ich ein. Johann Walther (died 1566), the musician, also composed spiritual songs, of which Der Braeut'gam wird bald rufen is still in use. Elisabeth Kreutziger also deserves honorable mention for her poem HErr Christ, der einig Gottes Sohn, Vaters in Ewigkeit.

When the Reformation was introduced into Prussia, in 1524, one of Luther's close friends was instrumental in furthering its cause, also by means of his poems. This was Paul Speratus (died 1554), who, in conjunction with Luther, had issued the first Lutheran hymnal. His best-known hymn is Es ist das Heil uns kommen her, a splendid presentation of the doctrine of justification. He also wrote Ich ruf zu dir, HErr JEsu Christ, ich bitt' erhoer mein, Klagen, Hilf Gott, wie ist der Menschen Not, and probably O HErre Gott, dein goettlich Wort ist lang verdunkelt blieben. His assistant in the work in Prussia was Johann Gramann or Graumann — Poliander — (died 1541), whose anthem of praise Nun lob, mein Seel, den HErren is a great favorite in the Lutheran Church to this day. Albrecht the Younger of Brandenburg-Culmbach (died 1557) wrote the appealing hymn Was mein Gott will, das g'scheh allzeit. Erasmus Alberus (died 1553) wrote in the spirit and almost with the force of Luther. His best-known hymns are Gott hat das Evangelium, Ach Gott, tu dich erbarmen, Wer Gott's Wort hat und bleibt dabei (Ps. 119), and especially the earnest and powerful Gott der Vater wohn' uns bei.

Another circle of hymnists in the period of the Reformation are those of Nuernberg, among whom Lazarus Spengler (died 1534) takes first place. He wrote Vergebens ist all Mueh' und Kost (Ps. 127), but, above all, Durch Adams Fall ist ganz verderbt, a hymn replete with the great truths of the Gospel, confessing the truth in an altogether uncompromising and unequivocal manner. Hans Sachs, the master-singer, also tuned his lyre and sang Die Wittenbergisch Nachtigall, die man jetzt hoeret ueberall. His hymns are not so well-known, although they appear in many hymnals. Among them are Warum betruebst du dich, mein Herz, O Mensch, bewein dein Suende grosz, and many songs after popular folk-songs of the day, such as

O JEsu zart, goettlicher Art, Christum vom Himmel ruf ich an, Christe, wahrer Sohn Gottes fromm, and O Gott Vater, du hast Gewalt. Sabaldus Heyd wrote O Mensch, bewein dein' Suende grosz and Wer in dem Schutz des Hoechsten ist. Johann Hesse (died 1547) is remembered on account of the tender beauty of his O Welt, ich musz dich lassen. A little later than these men, but well worthy to stand in the front rank, came Nicolaus Selnecker (died 1592). He edited "Christliche Psalmen, Lieder und Kirchengesaenge," and himself wrote some hymns which are favorites to this day, such as Lasz mich dein sein und bleiben, Ach bleib bei uns, HErr JEsu Christ, O HErre Gott, in meiner Not, and Wir danken dir, HErr JEsu Christ, dasz du gen Himmel g'fahren bist. And last, but not least, we have in this group Kaspar Bienemann (died 1591), who wrote the hymn HErr, wie du willst, so schicks mit mir, every line of which breathes childlike faith and trust.

At the same time, a number of singers arose in southern Germany, especially in Strassburg. Among these Conrad Huber (died 1577), who wrote Allein zu dir, HErr JEsu Christ and O Gott, du hoechster Gnadenhort takes a high rank. Martin Schalling (died 1608) was a pupil of Melanchthon and therefore strongly inclined toward peace at any price. But his poem Herzlich lieb hab ich dich, o HErr breathes the most devoted love for the Savior. Ludwig Oeler, who lived at about the same time, wrote the doxology Ehr sei dem Vater und dem Sohn und auch dem Heilgen Geiste.

The other parts of Germany are also represented in the list of Reformation hymnists. Nicolaus Decius (died 1541) has given us the German Gloria in excelsis, Allein Gott in der Hoeh sei Ehr, and the no less well-known German Agnus Dei O Lamm Gottes, unschuldig. loved wherever they are used. Johann Schneesing or Chiomusus (died 1567) is the composer of Allein zu dir, HErr JEsu Christ, mein Hoffnung steht auf Erden. Adam Reussner (died 1563) wrote In dich hab ich gehoffet, HErr. Bartholomaeus Ringwaldt (died 1598) had the gift of an easy, popular style in his poems, among which Es ist gewiszlich an der Zeit takes the first place. His contemporary Ludwig Helmbold (died 1598), called the "German Asaph," composed the beautiful Von Gott will ich nicht lassen. Especially well-known are the names of Johann Mathesius (died 1565) and his cantor Johann Hermann (died 1561). The former wrote Wer bei Gott Schutz und Hilfe sucht and the morning hymn Aus meines Herzens Grunde. And the latter composed hymns for all the Gospels, the book being published at Wittenberg in 1560. Some of the favorite hymns of his composing are Lobt Gott, ihr Christen allzugleich, Die helle Sonn leucht' jetzt herfuer, and Hin-unter ist der Sonnenschein. The list could easily be extended, but we must mention at least Martin Behemb (died 1622) with his hymn O JEsu Christ, meins Lebens Licht, Philip Nicolai (died 1608) with Wie schoen leucht uns der Morgenstern and Wachet auf, ruft uns die Stimme, and Valerius Herberger (died 1627), who wrote Valet will ich dir geben.

All these men were poets by the grace of God, who sang from the fulness and richness of the true understanding of God's mercies in Christ Jesus, and with such perfect objectivity that they sang the thoughts of the entire Church. For this reason their hymns, though sometimes lacking in grace and polish, have a lasting value. They are the heritage of the Church for all times.[388]

But while these men used their gifts in songs for the Church, they did not neglect the music, the choral part of the singing. Luther himself had a good knowledge of music, and he encouraged good church music in every way. He restored the Cantus firmus to its position in the choral and had the hymn sung in one voice. He by no means discarded the other voices, but used them to round out the melody in one harmonious whole. This form of composition, as used in the days of Luther, was then known as the motet, and served the highest ideals of part-choral singing. Johann Walther was Luther's right hand in preparing the music for the liturgy and in arranging the melodies for the German versions. Ludwig Senfl also deserves to be mentioned for his work along these lines.

It is usually conceded that Luther wrote the melody for Ein feste Burg himself. In general, however, he and the other hymnists of the Reformation made use of extant melodies, either by translating Latin hymns, with the original meter and inflection and retaining the melodies, or by using old church melodies from pre-Reformation times, or by composing hymns after the melodies of secular songs. Thus the ancient melody of the hymns Nun komm, der Heiden Heiland, Komm, Heiliger Geist, Komm, Gott Schoepfer, Heiliger Geist, Was fuerchtst du Feind Herodes sehr, Christum wir sollen loben schon, Verleih uns Frieden gnaediglich, were taken over by Luther, also for the hymns Nun laszt uns den Leib begraben and Christus der du bist Tag und Licht, by Michael Weisze. Gott der Vater wohn' uns bei, Nun bitten wir den Heiligen Geist, Mitten wir im Leben sind, Gott sei gelobet und gebenedeiet, have melodies of old German popular spiritual songs. Secular melodies were taken over in the case of the following hymns: Es ist das Heil uns kommen her, Christ unser HErr zum Jordan kam, Ich dank dir, lieber HErre (Entlaubt ist uns der Walde), Kommt her zu mir, spricht Gottes Sohn (Was

---

388) Alt, 446—449; *Saengerbote*, St. Louis, 1916. 1917.

woell wir aber heben an). Paraphrasing with retention of the secular melody occurred in hymns like these: O Welt, ich musz dich lassen (Innsbruck, ich musz dich lassen), Vom Himmel hoch, da komm
ich her (Aus fremden Landen komm ich her), O Christe, wo war dein
Gestalt (Rosina, wo war dein Gestalt), Wie schoen leuchtet der Morgenstern (Wie schoen leuchten die Aeugelein), Herzlich tut mir ver-
langen (Mein G'muet ist mir verwirret). The number of original
compositions, however, was by no means small. This is true not only
of Ein feste Burg, but also, according to the testimony of Walther,
of Jesaia dem Propheten and Wir glauben all an einen Gott. Nicolaus Hermann composed the melody for Lobt Gott, ihr Christen, allzugleich, Selnecker that of Wach auf, mein Herz, und singe, Philip
Nicolai that of Wachet auf, ruft uns die Stimme.[389])

Thus the Lutheran choral was introduced, and thus it spread
throughout Germany, into other countries, and beyond the sea, carrying in its wake blessings innumerable by making the people everywhere acquainted with the glories of the pure Bible doctrine which
the Lutheran Church teaches and professes.

CHAPTER 5.

Hymns Since the Reformation.

The fires of Christian poetry were by no means extinguished at
the beginning of the 17th century, nor was the ardor of the individual
poets quenched and the objectivity of the presentation lessened immediately, although the representative "We" was gradually replaced
by the more exclusive "I." "Upon the confession's song of the Reformation era followed the martyr songs of the cross and comfort." [390]) But whereas 51 writers endowed the German hymnody
from 1517—1560, an increasing host of poets more than satisfied the
needs of the Church, and some of their songs have stood the test of
time and become the precious possession of the children of the Reformation.

Johann Heermann (died 1647) stands on the boundary of the
new era. His best-known hymns are O Gott, du frommer Gott, So
wahr ich lebe, spricht der HErr, Wo soll ich fliehen hin, O Jesu
Christe, wahres Licht, and Herzliebster Jesu, was hast du verbrochen,
all of them excellent both as to form and contents. Andreas Gryphius
(died 1664) was a greater poet than Heermann, but since he did not
retain the appealing simplicity of his predecessors, his poems are not
so popular. Paul Flemming (died 1640) left as a sacred heritage the

---

389) Cp. Alt, *Der kirchliche Gottesdienst*, 518. 402—406.
390) Horn, 87.

hymn composed before his journey to Persia In allen meinen Taten. Johann Rist (died 1667) was a most prolific writer, more than 650 hymns being credited to him, some of which are veritable gems, as O Traurigkeit, o Herzeleid, Werde munter, mein Gemuete, Du Lebensfuerst, HErr JEsus Christ, and JEsu, der du meine Seele. As for Joshua Stegmann (died 1632), he composed the little hymn noted for the classical brevity of its diction, Ach, bleib mit deiner Gnade. David Denicke (died 1680) left about twenty hymns, among which Wenn ich die heiligen zehn Gebot and HErr Gott, der du erforschest mich are found in many hymnals. His friend and coeditor of the Hannoverian Hymnbook, Justus Gesenius (died 1671) composed, among other, Wenn meine Suend' mich kraenken, and the baptismal hymn Gott Vater, Sohn und Heilger Geist. To Tobias Clausnitzer (died 1684) we owe the old favorite Liebster Jesu, wir sind hier, and to Martin Rinkart the burst of triumphant praise Nun danket alle Gott. Simon Dach was an exponent of correct and easy versification, but lacked in depth. A fine burial song of his is O wie selig seid ihr doch, ihr Frommen. His friend Heinrich Alberti ranked high both as musical composer and as poet. He wrote the morning hymn Gott des Himmels und der Erden. Valentin Milo (died 1662) wrote the Lenten hymn Mit Ernst, ihr Menschenkinder.

But the culmination of 17th century church poetry was reached in Paul Gerhard (died 1676), the Asaph of the Lutheran Church. "Gerhard's songs," says Wackernagel, "mirror the transitional character of his time, when the personal feeling, the subjective expression began to be emphasized in addition to the congregation feeling, so that one must look upon him as the last and at the same time most perfect of the strict church poets who were firmly based upon the confession and creed. At the same time he opened the list of those poets, in whose songs the praise and adoration of the revealed God became secondary to the expression of the sensations which fill the soul when it considers its relation to God. He stood at the culmination of the period, and both tendencies are united in him in a most expressive fashion." He wrote about 120 hymns, many of which are regarded as classics with all reason, as the following: Ich singe dir mit Herz und Mund, O Haupt voll Blut und Wunden, Ein Laemmlein geht und traegt die Schuld, Auf, auf, mein Herz, mit Freuden, Wie soll ich dich empfangen, Nun ruhen alle Waelder, Wach auf, mein Herz, und singe, Befiehl du deine Wege. Other hymnists followed Gerhard's lead in composing songs of devotion. Louise Henriette of Brandenburg (died 1667) wrote Jesus, meine Zuversicht, Ich will von meiner Missetat, and two other hymns. Georg Neumark (died 1681) furnished both text and melody of the song of comfort

and consolation Wer nur den lieben Gott laeszt walten. In Johann
Frank (died 1677) the subjective element is expressed more strongly,
as his hymns Schmuecke dich, o liebe Seele and Jesu, meine Freude
show. Ernst Christoph Homburg (died 1681) composed 150 hymns,
of which Jesu, meines Lebens Leben and O wunderbarer Siegesheld
are the best known. His contemporary Georg Albinus (died 1679)
composed the burial song Alle Menschen muessen sterben. Johann
Scheffler or Angelus Silesius (died 1677), who became an apostate to
the Roman Catholic Church, left at least two hymns which are used
to some extent to-day, Mir nach, spricht Christus, unser Held, and
Jesu, komm doch selbst zu mir.

It was not long, however, before the rise of Pietism, followed by
Rationalism, exerted a disastrous influence also upon Lutheran
hymnody. During the 18th and 19th centuries there are only comparatively few poets whose hymns bear the stamp of classical objectivity. The hymns of Scriver (died 1693) are almost sentimentally
soft, although not without charm, as Jesu, meiner Seelen Leben.
Johann Jacob Schuetz (died 1690) sang in the heroic strain of Luther: Sei Lob und Ehr dem hoechsten Gut. Almost the same may
be said of Samuel Rodigast's (died 1708) Was Gott tut, das ist wohlgetan. Johann Daniel Herrnschmidt (died 1723) composed the stirring and appealing hymns Lobe den HErren, o meine Seele and Gott
will's machen. Christian Friedrich Richter (died 1711) composed a
total of 33 songs, of which Es glaenzet der Christen inwendiges Leben
is still in use. Then came a long line of hymnists: Johann Heinrich
Schroeder (died 1728), Eins ist not, ach HErr, dies eine; Wolfgang
Christoph Dessler (died 1722), Wie wohl ist mir, o Freund der Seelen; Ludwig Andreas Gotter (died 1735), HErr JEsu, Gnadensonne;
Bartholomaeus Crasselius (died 1724), Dir, dir, Jehovah will ich
singen and Hallelujah, Lob, Preis und Ehr; Johann Muthmann (died
1747), Zeuch uns nach dir, so laufen wir; Emilie Juliane of Schwarz-
burg-Rudolstadt (died 1706), Wer weisz, wie nahe mir mein Ende.

In the second half of the 18th century the heroic, objective strain
fell away entirely, and there are few poets which may lay claim to
recognition as church poets. Johann Ludwig Allendorf (died 1773)
wrote the song Unter Lilien jener Freuden. Leopold Lehr (died
1744) wrote Mein Heiland nimmt die Suender an. Johann Andreas
Rothe (died 1758) caught the spirit of Gerhard in his Ich habe nun
den Grund gefunden. Of the 2,000 songs credited to Zinzendorf, his
Jesu, geh voran has remained a great favorite. Erdman Neumeister
(died 1756) wrote Jesus nimmt die Suender an. To Benjamin
Schmolck (died 1737) almost 1200 hymns are ascribed, among which
Der beste Freund ist in dem Himmel is a favorite. Christian Fuerch-

tegott Gellert (died 1769) wrote a number of hymns which are the very antithesis of Lutheran force and brevity. Novalis (died 1801) is the composer of the charming Wenn ich ihn nur habe. Karl Johann Philip Spitta has many lyric gems, but none more appealing than the Es zieht ein stiller Engel.

In addition to leaving these splendid hymns and spiritual songs as a priceless heritage to the Christian Church, the poets themselves or musicians of eminent ability furnished choral tunes which, in most cases, express the very essence of the text and its sentiment, a fact which is being recognized with increasing distinctness by musicians of the first rank both in America and abroad. To sing a Lutheran hymn, which has its own tune, to the music of a modern jingle, is little short of sacrilege. It is a transgression on a par with having every long meter stanza sung to the tune of Old Hundredth. All honor to the old cantors that furnished us with such classical tunes for our congregational hymns! A few, at least, deserve honorable, if brief mention. Michael Praetorius (died 1621) wrote the melody for Ich dank dir schon. Johann Hermann Schein (died 1630) furnished the appropriate tune for Mir nach, spricht Christus. The lovely melody of Gott des Himmels und der Erden is due to Heinrich Alberti (died 1668). A musician that ranked exceptionally high as a composer of choral tunes, was Johann Crueger (died 1662), who wrote the music for HErr, ich habe miszgehandelt, Herzliebster JEsu, was hast du verbrochen, Nun danket alle Gott, O wie selig seid ihr doch, ihr Frommen, and JEsus, meine Zuversicht. Joachim Neander (died 1680) wrote the stirring tune of Lobe den HErren, den maechtigen Koenig der Ehren. Johann Schoppe, an eminent musician who invariably entered into the spirit of the hymn, wrote the appropriate tunes for O Ewigkeit, du Donnerwort, Sollt ich meinem Gott nicht singen, Werde munter, mein Gemuete, and others. Gastorius Severus in 1675 composed the consoling melody of Was Gott tut, das ist wohlgetan. Johann Rudolf Ahle (died 1673) furnished the tune for Liebster Jesu, wir sind hier, which has been a favorite since. And last, but not least, Georg Neumark (died 1681) composed the music for his hymn Wer nur den lieben Gott laeszt walten.

In later times, especially in the period of Rationalism, a tendency to substitute shallow and sentimental melodies for the old, full chorals became apparent, which has not quite died out yet. A hymnal of a Free Protestant congregation of the middle of the last century contains not only the melodies O sanctissima and Integer vitae, but also O Isis and Osiris (from the Magic Flute), Dies ist der Tag des HErrn, and Der du von dem Himmel bist.[391]

---

391) Alt, *Der kirchliche Gottesdienst*, 413.
Kretzmann, Christian Art. 22

We ought, in passing, at least take notice of Protestant religious music. The German school entered the 17th century with the choral, the motet, and various forms of organ music. Then came the influence of the great Italian masters, Palestrina, Scarlatti, and also of Orlando Lasso, which resulted in the inspiring Passions and many beautiful cantatas. The cantata was at first a musical recitation by a single person, accompanied by a few plain chords. It was not long, however, before duets, quartets, and choruses were added, introducing, in a measure at least, the dramatic element. The Passion music grew out of the recitative declamation of the Passion story during Lent and, above all, during Holy Week. The oratorio was essentially an advance upon the cantata. There is one man who, both as organ player and as composer, stands at the summit of human achievement, as Dickinson says (p. 292). This is Johann Sebastian Bach (1685—1754). He wrote every form of organ music, especially organ preludes and cantatas. His greatest glory rests upon his five Passions, of which those of St. Matthew and St. John have been preserved. One hardly knows what to admire more, the lofty and sustained grandeur or the penetrating, appealing beauty. The Passion according to St. Matthew has given to Bach his unquestioned rank. The corresponding place with reference to the oratorio is held by George Frederick Haendel (1685—1759). His Messiah overwhelmed the audience at the first rendering, and time has in no way dimmed the luster of the wonderful composition.

But while the Lutheran choral was thus being developed in Germany, and also in Norway, Sweden, and Denmark, where its spirit had been caught from the first, a style of hymn- or anthem-writing was brought out also in England, and later in America, which was preeminently subjective and often fell short of the classic ideal, but sometimes resulted in compositions of great beauty. It would manifestly be impossible to give a complete list of the English and American hymn-writers, but the following names represent the foremost hymnists. There was never such a spontaneous outburst of melody as on the Continent, but Miles Coverdale (1488—1569) and George Sandys (1577—1643) represent the religious poets in the 15th and early 16th centuries. Then came a gradual awakening with John Milton (1608—1675), Jeremy Taylor (1613—1667), John Bunyan (1628—1688), Thomas Ken (1637—1711), Nahum Tate (1652—1715), and culminating, at the end of the 17th century, in Isaac Watts (1674—1748). Then came the golden age of English hymn-writing, with Philip Doddridge (1702—1751), Charles Wesley (1708—1788), John Newton (1725—1807), E. Perronet (1721—1792), Th. Haweis (1732—1820), and John Fawcett (1717—1817). The next fifty or three-score years were hardly less prolific, with John Adams (1751—1835), Reginald Heber (1783—1826), James Edmeston (1791—1867), William Henry Havergal (1793—1870), Henry Francis Lyte (1793—1847), and William Hiley Bragge-Bathurst (1796—1877). And during the last century we have John Henry Newman (1801—1890), Horatius Bonar (1808—1880), William Mercer (1811—1873), John Mason Neale (1818—1866), Catherine Winkworth (1829—1878), Sabine Baring-Gould (1834—   ), and Miss Frances Ridley Havergal (1836—1879).

America also has a few men who are prominent in this field. During Colonial times the name of Cotton Mather (1663—1728) stood out prominently. And in the last century and a half we have William August Muhlenberg (1796—1877), George Washington Doane (1799—1859), George Duffield jr. (1818—   ), and Phoebe Carey (1824—1871).

The following list is taken from Duffield, English Hymns, and includes all the best-known hymns which are now in general use in America:

A broken heart, my God, my King (Watts);
A mighty fortress is our God (Hedge, trsl.);
Abide with me, fast falls the eventide (Lyte);
Alas! and did my Savior bleed (Watts);
All hail the power of Jesus' name (Perronet);
All my heart this night rejoices (Winkworth, trsl. from Gerhard, Froehlich soll);
Almighty God, Thy Word is cast (Cawood);
Am I a soldier of the cross (Watts);
Arise, my soul, arise (C. Wesley);
As with gladness men of old (C. W. Dix);
Before Jehovah's awful throne (Watts);
Blest be the tie that binds (Fawcett);
Chief of sinners though I be (McComb);
Christ the Lord is risen again (Winkworth, trsl. Christ ist erstanden);
Christ the Lord is risen to-day (C. Wesley);
Come, thou almighty King (C. Wesley ?);
Come, ye disconsolate (Moore);
Crown Him with many crowns (Bridges);
Day of wrath, O dreadful day (Stanley, trsl. from Latin Dies irae);
Fairest Lord Jesus, Ruler of all nature (Willis, trsl. Schoenster HErr JEsu);
From Greenland's icy mountains (Heber);
Glorious things of Thee are spoken (Newton);
Go to dark Gethsemane (Montgomery);

God moves in a mysterious way (Cowper);
Guide me, O Thou great Jehovah (W. Williams);
Hail, Thou once despised Jesus (Bakewell);
Hark! the herald angels sing (C. Wesley);
Here I can firmly rest (Winkworth, trsl. Ist Gott fuer mich, so trete);
Holy Ghost, with light divine (A. Reed);
Holy, Holy, Holy, Lord God Almighty (Heber);
How brightly shines the morning-star (Sloan, trsl. Wie schoen leuchtet);
How precious is the book divine (Fawcett);
How shall the young secure their hearts (Watts);
How sweet the name of Jesus sounds (Newton);
I am trusting Thee, Lord Jesus (Havergal);
I know that my Redeemer lives (C. Wesley);
I lay my sins on Jesus (Bonar);
In the cross of Christ I glory (Bowring);
In the hour of trial (Montgomery);
It came upon a midnight clear (Sears);
Jerusalem the golden (Neale, trsl. from Urbs Syon aurea);
Jesus, and shall it ever be (Grigg);
Jesus, I my cross have taken (Lyte);
Jesus, lover of my soul (C. Wesley);
Joy to the world, the Lord is come (Watts);
Just as I am, without one plea (C. Elliott);
Lord of mercy and of might (Heber);
My country, 'tis of thee (S. F. Smith);
My faith looks up to Thee (Palmer);
My soul, be on thy guard (Heath);
Nearer, my God, to Thee (Adams);
Now thank we all our God (Winkworth, trsl. Nun danket alle Gott);
Oh, come, all ye faithful (Oakeley, Mercer, and others, trsl. Adeste fideles);
Oh, for a faith that will not shrink (Bathurst);
O sacred head, now wounded (J. W. Alexander, trsl. O Haupt voll Blut und Wunden);
One sweetly solemn thought (Phoebe Carey);
Onward, Christian soldiers (Baring-Gould);
Open now thy gates of beauty (Winkworth, trsl. Tut mir auf die schoene Pforte);
Our country's voice is pleading (Mrs. Anderson);
Praise God, from whom all blessings flow (Ken);
Rock of Ages, cleft for me (Toplady);
Savior, breathe an evening blessing (Edmeston);

Savior, Thy dying love (Phelps);
So rest, our Rest (Massie, trsl. So ruhest du, o meine Ruh);
Stand up, stand up for Jesus (G. W. Duffield);
Sun of my soul, Thou Savior dear (Keble);
Take my life and let it be (Havergal);
The morning light is breaking (S. F. Smith);
There is a fountain filled with blood (Cowper);
Thine forever, God of love (Maude);
Thy life was given for me (Havergal);
Wake, awake, for night is flying (Winkworth, trsl. Wachet auf ruft
     uns);
While shepherds watched their flocks (Tate);
Zion, thy marvelous beauty be telling (Muhlenberg).

There are indications that the fountain of Christian poetry has not
dried up, also not in the Lutheran Church in America, and the hymns
of some poets living to-day will probably outlive the generation and
be reckoned with the heritage of the ages.

PART III.
Heortology.

CHAPTER 1.
The Festivals of the Old Testament Church.

The church-year of the Jews was not the result of slow development, but was given to them by divine commandment at the time of their becoming the people of the covenant. When the people of Israel were delivered from the bondage of Egypt, the Lord designated the spring month Abib, the month in which they left Egypt, as the first month of their year. He also gave them full and exact instructions as to the entire mode of celebration, including the choice of the sacrificial animals, the time and manner of sacrificing, and all the rites which should be observed in connection with the festivals. In the course of the forty years' sojourn in the wilderness, all the laws, regulations, and customs regarding the festivals were codified in the Pentateuch. Their briefest summary is contained in Deut. 16, 16: "Three times in a year shall all thy males appear before the Lord, thy God, in the place which He shall choose: in the Feast of Unleavened Bread, and in the Feast of Weeks, and in the Feast of Tabernacles." After the return from the exile two more festivals were added by the leaders of the Jewish Church, the Feast of Purim and the Feast of the Dedication of the Temple. In addition, there were the new moons, including the Feast of the Seventh New Moon, the Feast of Wood-Offering, and the fast-days, which were observed with punctuality and punctiliousness.

The oldest festival in the Jewish calendar is the *Passover,* with which was connected the Feast of Unleavened Bread (Ex. 12, 1—51; 13, 1—10; Lev. 23, 5—8; Num. 28, 16—25; Deut. 16, 3—8; 2 Chron. 30, 13—21; Ezek. 45, 21—24; Ezra 6, 19—22). It was instituted at the time of the exodus of Israel from Egypt. The spring month, the time of the awakening of the earth to new life, corresponding to the latter half of our March together with the beginning of April, was made the first month of the Jewish year, under the name Abib or Nisan, Ex. 13, 4. On the 14th of this month each head of a household or company, large enough to eat a lamb at one meal, was to take the animal and slaughter it. At the first celebration, the Israelites had the choice between a lamb and a kid, but in later years the rule was to take a lamb. The animal was to be a lamb of the first year, that is, one born during the preceding year. It was essential that it was without blemish, not sick, nor disfigured, nor crippled. The killing of the lamb should be done "between the evenings," Ex. 12, 6; Num. 9, 5. The Pharisees maintained that this expression designated the time before and after sunset, the Samaritans and the Karaite Jews insisted that it meant the time between sunset and darkness.[392] The use of the expression in other passages, e. g. Ex. 16, 12; 29, 39— 41; 30, 8; Num. 28, 4, show that the interpretation of the Samaritans was correct. The other custom was one which practical reasons and expediency suggested and later made imperative. Cp. the German Zwielicht, the English twilight, and especially the passage Deut. 16, 6.

At the first Passover, every house-father tended to the killing of the lamb himself. Later, when the command of God required every member of the Jewish Church to be present in Jerusalem, the rite was performed in the temple. In Egypt, the blood was used to paint the side posts and the lintel of the doors, in order that the angel of the Lord might pass by or over these houses. The lamb was then taken and roasted with fire, "his head with the legs, and the purtenance thereof," Ex. 12, 9. Nothing should remain of the roasted lamb till the next morning; any remaining parts had to be burned with fire.

In addition to the lamb, the Passover meal consisted of unleavened bread and bitter herbs. Neither leavened bread nor any form of leaven was to be seen in any quarters of the Jews during Passover and the Week of Unleavened Bread, Ex. 13, 7. The Jews use a form of unleavened bread called *Mazzoth,* in the shape of flat cakes or crackers resembling soda crackers. The bitter herbs of a green color, according to the rabbis, which were used as a condiment, were especially prescribed. Many scholars believe that the German name for Maundy Thursday, Gruendonnerstag, is derived from these green herbs.

The Passover was kept by the children of Israel in the wilderness, in the second year after they were come out of the land of Egypt, Num. 9, 1—5. Its celebration is again recorded after the conquest of Canaan, when the children of Israel were encamped in Gilgal, Josh. 5, 10. In the time of David and Solomon the keeping of this festival must have been a regular occurrence, 2 Chron. 8, 13. Later records, however, show that there were long intervals during which the people left the customs of their fathers, 2 Kings 23, 21; Ezra 6, 19; Ezek. 9, 4—6. After the restoration of the temple during the time of the Maccabees and during the Roman period the celebration again occurred with great regularity. It was then that the many ordinances of the elders were added, regulating the observance of the festival even to the minutest detail.

392) Cp. Gesenius, *sub* eber.

The great sacrifice of the Feast of Unleavened Bread, which was celebrated from the 15th to the 21st of Nisan, consisting in bringing a sheaf of the firstfruits to the Lord. It was a sheaf of barley, which was waved before the Lord, that is, it was held out between the priest and the person designated for bringing the sacrifice, and the hands were then moved back and forth, and up and down, Lev. 23, 4—14. During this whole week, special sacrifices were made to the Lord, a burnt offering: two young bullocks, one ram, and seven lambs of the first year; a meat offering: flour mingled with oil; a sin offering: one goat; all this beside the usual burnt offering, Lev. 23, 5—8; Num. 28, 16—25. The first and the seventh day of the week were set aside for convocations. It seems that every day of the week was later regarded as a Sabbath, John 20, 1, and that the entire 14th day of Nisan was included in the Days of Unleavened Bread, Matt. 26, 17; Mark 14, 12.

If any member of the Jewish Church happened to be levitically unclean at the time of the Passover, or if he was on a journey, such a person had the opportunity to celebrate a month later, on the 14th of Zif (May), being obliged, at that time, to observe all the rules and customs of the regular festival, Num. 9, 6—14. In one case, at least, it happened that the priests themselves were not sanctified and that the entire nation celebrated the Passover on the 14th day of the second month, 2 Chron. 30, 13—17.

To speak in detail of the symbolism of the Passover would lead us too far afield. For the children of Israel it was the day of emancipation or independence, it was the birthday of their nation. Almost every feature of the festival, however, served as a type of things to come under the new dispensation. The unleavened bread with its insipid and disagreeable taste symbolized to the Israelites the hardships and afflictions of Egypt, Deut. 16, 3. In the New Testament unleavened bread is a symbol of spiritual purity, just as leaven is a type of corruption and of quick results, 1 Cor. 5, 6—8; Matt. 16, 6; Luke 12, 1; Mark 8, 15; Gal. 5, 9. The fact that the bones of the paschal lamb should not be broken is interpreted by John, chap. 19, 36. And the lamb was a type of Christ, 1 Cor. 5, 7; 1 Pet. 1, 19; John 1, 29.

Fifty days after the festival of the Passover, counting seven complete Sabbaths, and taking the morrow after the seventh, Lev. 23, 15. 16, was the Day of *Pentecost* or the Feast of Weeks, Num. 28, 26; Ex. 23, 14—17; 34, 22; Lev. 23, 15—21; Deut. 16, 9—16; 2 Chron. 8, 13. It was, incidentally, the feast of the firstfruits of wheat-flour, Lev. 23, 17. 20; Ex. 23, 10; Deut. 26, 2. 10. The date of Pentecost was the 6th of Sivan (June). The people came together to celebrate before the Lord, in the early days in the place where the tabernacle stood, later in Jerusalem, all males being obliged to appear, Ex. 23, 17. Although the festival lasted only one day, it was a principal feast and was kept with great rejoicing, Deut. 16, 9—12. Special sacrifices were offered, burnt offerings: two young bullocks, one ram, seven lambs of the first year; a meat offering, of flour mingled with oil; a kid of the goats, for atonement, beside the usual burnt offerings and drink offerings. There was also a holy convocation before the Lord on the day of Pentecost, Num. 28, 26—31. The special offerings of the firstfruits consisted in two wave-loaves of fine flour, and two lambs of the first year for a sacrifice of peace offerings, Lev. 23, 15—21.

The symbolism of the Feast of Weeks has offered great difficulties to scholars, on account of the absence of definite New Testament passages in explanation of the types. We may say, however, without straining the matter of probability too strongly, that, as the fiftieth day after the first Passover brought the giving of the Law on Mount Sinai and the formal acceptance and acknowledgment of Israel as a nation, so the day of Pentecost in the New Testament witnessed the birth of the holy nation, the Christian Church. And as the Feast of Weeks served for the purpose of sacrificing the firstfruits of the year to the Lord, so the New Testament Pentecost was made memorable by the winning of the firstfruits for the Lord.[393])

The third great festival of the Jewish calendar was the *Feast of Tabernacles,* Lev. 23, 34—43; Ex. 23, 16; 34, 22; Deut. 16, 13—16; 2 Chron. 8, 13; Zech. 14, 16—21. Incidentally, it was the feast of the ingathering of oil and wine, Deut. 16, 13, just as Pentecost was the festival of the grain harvest. It was held on the 15th day of the seventh month, Tishri or Ethanim (October), and lasted seven days. The first day was a Sabbath with an holy convocation, and also the eighth day. Being the last harvest feast of thankfulness, it was the most joyous of all festive seasons in Israel. All the people erected booths made of boughs of goodly trees, branches of palm trees, and the boughs of thick trees and willows of the brook, Lev. 23, 40. The number of sacrifices offered in the course of this week was exceptionally large, to correspond with the joyful nature of the occasion. burnt offerings: thirteen young bullocks, two rams, and fourteen lambs of the first year; meat offering, flour mingled with oil; sin offering, one kid of the goats, in addition to the usual offerings. The number of bullocks was reduced by one every day until the seventh day, only seven being offered on that day. On the eighth day one bullock, one ram, and seven lambs were sacrificed, Num. 29, 12—34.

---

393) Cp. Kliefoth, *Die urspruengliche Gottesdienstordnung,* I, 155; Goodwin, *Moses et Aaron,* III, Cap. V; Baehr, *Symbolik des mosaischen Kultus,* II, 645—652; Edersheim, *The Temple,* Chapter XIII.

There are several notices of subsequent celebrations of this festival, 1 Kings 8, 2; 2 Chron. 5, 3. But the most joyous occasion which is recorded in the Old Testament in connection with the festival was at the time of Ezra and Nehemiah, when the people took olive branches, and palm branches, and branches of trees with dense foliage to make booths, and there was very great gladness, Neh. 8, 14—18.

The Feast of Tabernacles was especially rich in symbolical acts and customs, according the account of Edersheim. The ceremony of fetching and pouring out water from the pool of Siloam was one which was followed with almost breathless interest, especially since the pool at times contained "living water," from the action of a spring in the rock, from whose pool the water was siphoned over to Siloam, Is. 12, 3; John 7, 38. Another ceremony was the lighting of four golden candelabra filled with oil at the close of the first day of the feast, their combined splendor yielding a great light which shone out over Jerusalem and the surrounding country, Is. 9; Is. 60; John 8, 12; Rev. 7, 9. 10. The fact also that the festival was the feast of the ingathering at the year's end, the harvest feast of thankfulness, served as a type, Is. 25, 6—8; Rev. 21, 4.

Beside these great festivals, on which it was obligatory for all members of the Jewish Church to appear in Jerusalem, there were several minor festivals that, in some respects, possess even more interest for us than some of the others. The first of these is the *Day of Atonement,* Lev. 16, 1—34; Lev. 23, 26—32; Num. 29, 7—11. The ritual of the day was extremely complicated, and the entire responsibility rested upon one man, the high priest, who officiated alone in the bringing of the sacrifices. The festival was on the 10th of Tishri. The high priest, for this day, in the bringing of the special sacrifices wore white linen garments. He first took a bullock and killed it as a sin offering, to make an atonement for himself and for his house. He also received two goats from the people, setting one aside for a sin offering for the people and the other for a scapegoat. After killing the bullock, he took a censer full of sweet incense and filled the most holy place with its smoke. He then entered the most holy for the second time with the blood of the bullock, sprinkling it upon the mercy seat and before the mercy seat seven times. He then killed the goat of the sin offering for the people, sprinkling its blood also upon the mercy seat and before the mercy seat, thus making an atonement for the transgression of the children of Israel. He next took the remaining blood of the bullock and the goat and put it upon the horns of the altar, sprinkling it with his finger seven times. He finally took the live goat, laid upon its head, by confession, the iniquities of the children of Israel, and had him led away by the hand of a fit man into the wilderness. Thus was the Azazel, which, according to Edersheim, means "wholly put aside, wholly sent away." The high priest also had charge of the burnt offering on this day and of the fat of the sin offering, thus making full atonement for himself and for the people. On the evening of this day, the ordinary sacrifice was made.

That this festival in its chief features was altogether a type of the great sacrifice of the New Testament is evident even from Zech. 3, 3. 4; Is. 1, 18. The writer of the Epistle to the Hebrews goes into the symbolism in great detail, especially in chap. 9, 7. 11. 12. Nowhere is the fact that the Old Covenant was a shadow of things to come so apparent as in the sacrifices of the Jews, and above all in that of the Day of Atonement.

Though every new moon was a special holy day for the Jewish Church, yet that of the seventh month, the 1st of Tishri, was designated as a special festival, the *Feast of the Seventh New Moon,* or of Trumpets, or New Year's Day, since the civil year began with this day, Num. 29, 1—6; 10, 10; 28, 11—15. A holy convocation was commanded, and special offerings were made, burnt offerings: one young bullock, one ram, and seven lambs of the first year; meat offering, flour mingled with oil; sin offering, one kid of the goats, beside the regular offerings of the new moon, Num. 28, 11—15. At the morning sacrifice Ps. 81 was chanted, at the evening sacrifice Ps. 29. Trumpets and horns were blown at the temple and throughout Jerusalem all day. The symbolical meaning of this day is probably referred to Eph. 5, 14. 8.[394)

Three of the Jewish festivals at the time of Christ were of post-Mosaic origin. The first of these was the *Feast of Purim* or of Esther, Esther 3, 7; 9, 21—26. 32; 2 Macc. 15, 36; John 5, 1. It was celebrated on the 13th and 14th of Adar (March), and later extended also to the 15th, the 13th being the Feast of Esther, the 14th Purim or the Feast of Haman, and the 15th Purim proper. The festival commemorated and celebrated the delivery of the Jews from the evil designs of Haman and was therefore kept with great merriment and rejoicing. Friends sent one another presents, and expressions of good will were exchanged on all sides. The mode of celebrating is described at length in the Tract Megillah of the Talmud.

The second of the post-Mosaic festivals was the *Feast of the Dedication of the Temple* or *Chachunah,* 1 Macc. 4, 52—59. It is

---

394) Cp. Edersheim, *The Temple,* Chapter XV. For the whole section, Kliefoth, I, 143—170; Goodwin, *Moses et Aaron,* III, Cap. IV—VIII; Baehr, *Symbolik des mosaischen Kultus,* II, 613—698.

also called the Feast of Lights.[395]) It was instituted by Judas Maccabeus, 164 B. C., after the recovery of the Jewish independence. He removed the altar which had been polluted by the heathen and purified the temple. The festival was held on the 25th of Chisleu (December), and extended over eight days, with great pomp and ceremony, the Hallel being sung in the temple services each day. It also commemorated the descent of the fire from heaven upon the first altar, together with the relighting of the fire upon the purified altar. (John 10, 22.)

The last festival was the *Feast of Wood-Offering,* on the 15th of Ab (August), Neh. 10, 34; 13, 31. At this time, offerings of wood for the use of the temple were made by all the people. It is described in Tract Taan, iv, of the Talmud, and in Josephus.[396])

CHAPTER 2.

Festivals of the Early Church.

There are no festivals or holidays by divine appointment in the New Testament. The festivals of the Old Testament, including the Sabbath, were abrogated by Christ, since the mere external observance of hours and days cannot be meritorious in the sight of God, Matt. 12, 8; Luke 6, 5. And St. Paul was especially insistent upon preserving the liberty of the New Testament Church unimpaired in this respect, Col. 2, 16; Gal. 4, 10; Rom. 14, 5. He emphasized the necessity of having meetings for the preaching of the Word and for the celebration of Holy Communion, Rom. 10, 14—17; 1 Cor. 11, 20. 21, but he would have nothing of a law laid upon the necks of the disciples as a yoke to force them back into the bondage of legalistic minutiae, which neither their fathers nor they had been able to bear, Acts 15, 10.

When the Christian congregation of Jerusalem had been founded by the miracle of Pentecost, the Christians held daily assemblies in the temple and in the houses, Acts 2, 46. It was not long, however, before the first day of the week became the acknowledged day for divine worship, Acts 20, 7; 1 Cor. 16, 2; Rev. 1, 10. For the early Christians, therefore, every week brought a renewal of the memorial of Christ's suffering and death, and every Sunday reminded them of the resurrection of their Lord. Some of the earliest documents speak of the celebration of Sunday in this manner. In the Epistle to Barnabas a whole chapter is devoted to the discussion of the Sabbath,

---

395) Josephus, *Antiquities of the Jews,* XII: 7, 7.
396) *Wars of the Jews,* II: 17, 6; Edersheim, *The Temple,* Chapter XVII.

and the author closes with the words: "Wherefore we also celebrate with gladness the eighth day in which Jesus also arose from the dead, and was made manifest, and ascended into heaven." 397) The words of Ignatius, in his letter to the Magnesians, Chapter IX, are also commonly understood of the Sunday: "If then they who walked in ancient customs came to a new hope, no longer living for the Sabbath, but for the Lord's day, on which also our life sprang up through Him and His death." 398) The well-known letter of Plinius, governor of Bithynia-Pontus, also mentions a "status dies," a fixed day which it was their custom to observe regularly. That this can hardly have been any other day but Sunday, is evident from the First Apology of Justinian, Chapter 67, written only a few decades later, in which he expressly states: "And on the day called Sunday a convocation of all takes place. . . . Sunday is the day on which we all hold one common assembly, because it is the first day, on which God, having wrought a change in the darkness and matter, made the world, and Jesus Christ our Savior on the same day rose from the dead." 399) At the time of Tertullian (died 220) this day of the Christians was so strongly marked from the services of the feriae that the suspicions of some were aroused as though they were sun-worshipers (die solis laetitiam curare). Origen (died 253) devotes a large part of his 52d Homilia de tempore to the discussion of Sunday and its celebration.400) At the beginning of the fourth century, Eusebius wrote of the Dies dominica: "We celebrate every week on Sunday the mysteries of the true Lamb, by whom we have been redeemed."401) The custom of the Church was made a requirement of the state by Constantine the Great, who issued the order that the Sunday should be given over to devotional exercises.402) Since that time, the Sunday has been the day of rest and of religious exercises wherever the influence of Christianity extended.403)

The earliest festival of the Christian Church is Easter. Its celebration is also so ancient that it may well be said to extend back to the time of the apostles, although there are such as doubt that the passage 1 Cor. 5, 6—8 refers to a New Testament celebration. So far as extant documents show, there was never any question as to the celebration, but only as to the date of the celebration. The Jewish Christians celebrated the Passover on the 14th of Nisan and the Resurrection on the 16th of the month. This usually resulted in a day different from Sunday, where the Jewish calendar was not used. The Greek Christians had always celebrated the Sunday in commemo-

397) Lake, *The Apostolic Fathers*, I, 397.   398) P. 205.
399) St. Louis, Ed., 73.   400) Alt, *Der kirchliche Gottesdienst*, 24.
401) Kellner, *Heortology*, 8.   402) Alt, 25.
403) Cp. Alt, 30—32.

ration of the resurrection and therefore wanted to keep this day, even under the Julian calendar. Two customs thus soon became prevalent: the Alexandrinian Church celebrated on the Sunday after the 14th of Nisan, even if this were the 15th, the Occidental Church chose the 16th of Nisan if it was a Sunday, or, in the opposite event, the following Sunday. For a while, the discrepancy caused little comment, but when the effort to establish uniformity of practise became persistent, difficulties arose. In the year 160 A. D., Bishop Polycarp of Smyrna made a journey to Rome and attempted at that time to reach an agreement with Bishop Anicetus. He based his Quartodecimanian views upon the custom as handed down from St. John, while Anicetus stood firmly upon the tradition in Rome. In spite of the difference of opinion, however, there was no schism. The controversy became acute about ten years later, at Laodicea, and still more serious since 193 A. D., when Victor of Rome attacked the Alexandrinian practise. Synods were held in Rome, in Palestine, in Pontus, in Gaul, in Corinth, and elsewhere. Polycrates of Ephesus became just as emphatic in his denunciation of the western method as the Occidentals had been in their rejection of his. The threatened schism was averted by Irenaeus of Lyon. His suggestion that Easter should be celebrated only between March 22 and April 20 met with general approval and was resolved upon by a Synod of Caesarea in 198, but the Quartodeciminian custom persisted.

The question as to the date of Easter was finally settled by the Council of Nicea, in 325. According to the account of Epiphanius the resolution read: "The first Sunday after the full moon of spring shall be celebrated as the day of Resurrection. If the full moon be on a Sunday, the celebration of Easter shall be a week later." This was a compromise between the Oriental and Occidental views, and was adopted by all the bishops of the East and many of the West, especially of Milan, but not by the bishop of Rome. The Alexandrinian bishops were designated as the committee for fixing the exact date for every year, which was then announced in all the churches on Epiphany. The Roman bishops continued to follow their own way of computing the date of Easter. This resulted in unpleasant differences, since in 387 Easter was on March 21 according to the Roman, and on April 25 according to the Alexandrinian way of figuring. There were difficulties again, in 444 and 455, but since 532 the Eastern mode has been in force, which upholds the resolution of Nicea, according to which the earliest date of Easter is March 22, the latest April 25.[404]

---

404) Alt, *Das Kirchenjahr*, 14—18; Kliefoth, *Die urspruengliche Gottesdienstordnung*, I, 344—346; II, 95; Loehe, *Haus-, Schul- und Kirchenbuch*, II, 22—24; Horn, *Outlines of Liturgics*, 22; *Memoirs*, VII: 5.

From very early days Easter was preceded by a special period of preparation, called the Lenten season. The custom of fasting was observed very generally from an early date, but there was a great diversity as to the length of the period. Irenaeus mentions one, two, and more days. Eight days seems to have been an average period at first, but a season of forty days, after the analogy of the Lord's temptation, Matt. 4, 1—11, was soon accepted. The mode of distributing these forty days varied. In the West, the Sundays were excepted, putting Lent back; in the East only five fast days in the week were observed, thus extending the time still farther back, so that it began eight weeks before Easter. The original length of Lent in the 4th century, according to Eusebius, Cyril of Jerusalem, Ambrose, etc., having been forty days or six weeks, the extra weeks were later known as the Quadragesima and the Fast. Since the six weeks, according to the Occidental reckoning, did not include a full forty days' number of fast days, Gregory II (715—731) is said to have fixed the Wednesday now known as Ash Wednesday as the first day of Lent. The season of preparation closed with the Great or Black Week, also called the Holy Week or Week of the Passion. The first day of this week was Palm Sunday, which introduced the week of deepest sorrow and repentance in the whole year. Every day in this week has its own significance, even from olden times, for which reason even the Apostolic Constitutions made the rule that servants be free from work, in order that they might devote themselves to proper study of the passion story and to devotional exercises. It was also the rule, at least in the Orient, that the feriae of Holy Week be observed with the strictest manner of fasting. The so-called *xerophagia,* consisting of bread, salt, vegetables, and water, was the only food which was permitted.

The Thursday of Holy Week commemorated the institution of the Holy Supper. Since the Gospel of the day was John 13, 1—15, the day was also known as the Day of Foot-washing. Its present English name Maundy Thursday is derived either from the words in the Gospel: Mandatum novum do vobis, or from the custom of carrying gifts to the poor in maund(y) baskets on that day. It was the custom to have Holy Communion on the evening of this day, and the ceremony of foot-washing was found in parts of the Church from olden times. The name dies competentium is derived from the custom of having the *photizomenoi* or illuminati, the catechumens that had been prepared for Baptism, make a public confession of their faith, by saying the Creed.

Good Friday was, almost from the first, the dies crucis or dominica passionis, Parasceve, a day of deepest mourning, with a complete fast till 3 or 6 o'clock in the afternoon. The services were reduced to a simple reading of the passion story. In some churches, no form of service was prescribed, the faithful merely coming together for silent prayer. In Spain it was even custom, for a while, to close the churches entirely on this day, as a sign of deepest sorrow.

Just as the time before Easter had been a period of repentance, of fasting and prayer, so the season opening with Easter Sunday was one of great joy from the earliest times. It ended in a burst of special rejoicing, with the festival of Pentecost, fifty days after Easter. This festival may also be of very ancient date, perhaps going back to the time of the apostles, and celebrated as the birthday of the Church, though the passage 1 Cor. 16, 8 can hardly be regarded as one that refers to the Christian festival. Tertullian calls the whole time from Easter to Pentecost by the latter name, and gives to each day of the entire period the importance and dignity of a Sunday. According to Augustine, the Hallelujah was used only during this period of great joy (ut Alleluia per solos dies quinquaginta cantetur in ecclesia).

Within the fifty days of rejoicing, on the fortieth day, came the festival of the Ascension, which is mentioned by Eusebius and may have been celebrated at the end of the 3d century. Augustine gives to it equal rank with Easter and Pentecost, and Chrysostomus explains its significance at length. In the Orient, especially, the emphasis of the day was placed upon the fact that the human nature of Christ was now exalted, and therefore the work of redemption brought to its final glorious conclusion. This is also the feature which is emphasized in the Apostolic Constitutions.

In the early Church less stress was laid upon the birthday of the Lord than upon the fact that the Son of God actually became man, that His *epiphaneia* is the truth, John 1, 14; Tit. 2, 11; 3, 4; 2 Tim. 1, 10; 1 John 4, 9. Accordingly, we find a festival celebrating this fact as early as the time of Clement of Alexandria (died ca. 216). It was known as *he epiphaneia* or *ta theophania,* Festum Epiphaniae, Dies manifestationis Domini. The 6th of January was the accepted date for this festival at the end of the third century. It commemorated not only the birth of Christ, but also His baptism and, in some cases, His first miracle, thus expressing very well the general idea of the revelation and manifestation of the divinity of Christ in His humanity. The inscriptions in the catacombs show that the story of the wise men of the East and of the miracle of Cana were the chief subjects of the festival.

The celebration of Christmas as the birthday of our Lord on December 25 goes back to the middle of the fourth century. Tradition says that Pope Julius I (336—352) had the imperial archives of Rome searched for the exact date of the birth of Christ and found that this was the correct day, according to the tax lists. The careful research work of Tille [405]) and of Usener [406]) have established beyond a doubt that Pope Liberius fixed the celebration of Christmas for December 25, in 354. There is a record from the year 360, showing that it was celebrated at that time.[407]) By the year 385 it was well-known, since Jerome and others mention it. There is a Christmas sermon of Chrysostomus preserved, which he held on December 25, 386. He mentions that the East was not yet unanimous with regard to the festival, but that it was nevertheless firmly established.[408])

Just as Easter had its season of preparation, a similar period came into use for Christmas. The length of the Advent season varied according to some of the old Comites, Milan observing five Sundays, also Jerome, Rome only four. The time was regarded as tempus clausum, but not in the same degree as Lent. The custom of having four Sundays agreed with the four milleniums before the coming of Christ.

Since the beginning of the 5th century the number of festivals increased very rapidly, a fact which sheds some light upon the trend of matters in comparison with the earlier practise. Tertullian (died 220) knows only Easter and Pentecost, Origen mentions Easter, Parasceve, and Pentecost. The Law of 389 recognized also Christmas and Epiphany. By a law of Theodosius II, of 425, spectacles were forbidden on all Sundays, Christmas, Epiphany, and during the whole period from Easter to Pentecost. But in the 5th century, Perpetuus gives the list of festivals of St. Martin of Tours: Natalis Domini, Epiphania, Natalis S. Joannis (June 24), Natalis S. Petri episcopatus (Feb. 22), Pascha, Dies Ascensionis, Pentecoste, Passio S. Joannis, Natalis SS. Petri et Pauli, Natalis S. Martiani, and others. The Statutes of Sonnatius, Bishop of Rheims, 614—631, name the following festivals: Nativitas Domini, Circumcisio, Epiphania, Annunciatio Beatae Mariae, Resurrexio Domini cum die sequente, Ascensio Domini, dies Pentecostis, Nativitas beati Joannis Baptistae, Nativitas Apostolorum Petri et Pauli, Assumptio Beatae Mariae, eiusdem Nativitas, Nativitas Andreae Apostoli et omnes dies dominicales.[409]) Other lists are given in Migne.[410])

For the sake of having a summary, the following list of festivals at the beginning of the Middle Ages will serve: 1) Nativitas Domini

---

405) *Die Geschichte der deutschen Weihnacht.* 1893.

406) *Das Weihnachtsfest.* 1911.   407) Kliefoth, III, 41.

408) Cp. Horn, 22—24; Alt, *Das Kirchenjahr*, 34—43; Kliefoth, III, 41; Loehe, II, 28—40.

409) Kellner, *Heortology*, 20. 21; *Memoirs*, IV: 2.

410) *Patrologia latina*, 138, 832; 140, 640; 141, 260.

nostri Jesu Christi, 2) Epiphania, 3) Pascha, 4) Ascensio Domini, 5) Pentecostes, 6) Anniversarium Passionis, 7) Anniversarium Resurrectionis, 8) Praesentatio Jesus seu Purificationis B. M. V. (Feb. 2), 9) Dormitio seu Assumptio B. M. V. (Aug. 15), 10) S. Michaelis Archangeli (Sept. 29 or 30), 11) Omnium SS. Martyrum, 12) SS. Macchabaeorum (Aug. 1), 13) S. Joannis Baptistae (June 24), 14) S. Stephani Protomartyris (Dec. 26), 15) SS. Petri et Pauli (Orient in December, Occident June 29) — Cathedra Petri (Feb. 22), S. Andreae (Nov. 30) —, 16) SS. Jacobi Majoris et Joannis Apostoli (Dec. 27 or 28), 17) SS. Philippi et Jacobi Minoris (May 1), 18) SS. Innocentium (Dec. 28), 19) S. Sixti Papae, d. 258 (Aug. 1 or 6), 20) SS. Perpetuae et Felicitatis, d. 203 (March 7), 21) S. Flaviani seu Fabiani (May 5).[411]

The next chapter will show to what extent the introduction of festivals was carried which had begun in so gradual a manner. For during the Middle Ages the Church was secularized, and the world boldly entered in at the portals which had been erected to conquer her.

CHAPTER 3.
The Growth of the Specific Roman Catholic Church Year.

The development of the church year with the cast or specific characteristics of the Roman Catholic Church may be said to extend back to Gregory the Great (590—694). It was he who was the father of the liturgy as used in the Roman Church; it was he who developed the idea of the Mass in connection with the doctrine of purgatory, so that the final result was the abomination of the sacrifice for the living and for the dead, tam pro vivis quam pro defunctis.

The so-called great or principal festivals, Easter, Pentecost, and Christmas, were in general use throughout the Church at the beginning of the 7th century. The period of preparation for Christmas had been a Quadragesimal fast in the Gallican Church, beginning on Nov. 11. In other parts of the Church this time had also included five or six Sundays, according to Baeumer (p. 289), especially in Milan. The Roman Church ordered the fast of Advent to begin on the Sunday after St. Catherine (Nov. 25), which gave the number of days till Jan. 6 a total of forty, if one were inclined to insist upon that amount, and also wanted to include the Epiphany festival for the sake of those that held this in special reverence. The Advent season proper now includes only four Sundays and is celebrated as a time of repentance and sorrow, a fact which is symbolized by the

---

411) Baeumer, 183 ff.

wearing of violet vestments. The instrumental or orchestral accompaniment is not permitted during this season, only the voice and the organ being allowed.

The festival of Christmas was celebrated with three masses, the first one at midnight, the second at dawn, and the third at the usual time in the morning. At the festival itself and during the twelve days which followed, up to and inclusive of Epiphany (feria duodenaria, Shakespeare's Twelfth Night), white vestments were worn and used for hangings and decorations. The churches to this day are lighted up most brilliantly and some representation of the Nativity is usually found, a stable or cave with a manger which serves as the bed of the Christ-child. Joseph and Mary are in the foreground, an ox and an ass in the background. On one side are shown the shepherds with their flocks, on the other usually the wise men from the East. The Christmas cycle includes the festival of the Circumcision, on Jan. 1, which is incidentally the octave of Christmas, and is concluded with Epiphany. The latter festival has given occasion for various legendary additions to the Scriptural account, the Venerable Bede not only insisting that the Magi were kings, but also giving the names Caspar, Melchior, and Balthasar. For this reason, Epiphany was widely known as the Festival of the Three Kings. In some countries, it was called the Festival of the Star, and the custom was for the lower clergy and the choir boys to march from house to house with carols, led by a star.

The number of Sundays after Epiphany depends upon the date upon which Easter falls. If Easter is very early, there is only one Sunday after Epiphany, if it is on one of the last possible days, there are six. The color of the Epiphany period, beginning with its octave, is green. The second Sunday is commonly known as the Festival of the Name of Jesus.

The time of fasting and preparation for Easter begins with the Sunday Septuagesima, the ninth Sunday before Easter. The time from this Sunday to Ash Wednesday is known as Pre-Lent (Vorfasten), the clergy beginning their fasting on this Sunday. The days from Quinquagesima till Ash Wednesday were known as Carnival days and given over to all manner of festivities, masked processions, and theatrical exhibitions. Ash Wednesday was the signal for the beginning of the Lenten fast. The custom of placing ashes upon the foreheads of the attendents at church services, preceded by appropriate ceremonies, goes back at least to the end of the 11th century. The Sundays in Lent are known after the first words of their introitus, as Invocavit (Ps. 91, 15), Reminiscere (Ps. 25, 6), Oculi (Ps. 25, 15), Laetare (Is. 66, 1), and Judica (Ps. 43, 1). Holy Week be-

gins with Palm Sunday (dominica palmarum), on which the blessing
of the palms and the procession takes place. On this day the story
of the Passion according to St. Matthew is read. On Tuesday of
Holy Week the Passion according to St. Mark is read, on Wednesday
according to St. Luke, and on Friday according to St. John. Maundy
Thursday is a joyous festival (feria quinta in coena Domini), with
ringing of bells and Gloria in excelsis. On this day, the benediction
of oil takes place in cathedral churches, and the denuding of the altar
in all churches, also the ceremony of foot-washing where it is still
practised. On Good Friday there is a special custom of the Adoratio
crucis, followed by the Depositio crucis in a special sepulcrum. After
the Mass of the Presanctified, with elevation of the sacred host from
the place where it was deposited on the previous day, all services
cease, and the deepest quiet prevails in the church. On the Great
Sabbath, everything is quiet till Vespers, when the ceremony of the
Benediction of Fire and of Incense takes place, followed by the lighting of the Easter candle.

The celebration of Easter begins early in the morning, with the
dramatic Elevatio crucis, a joyous procession, followed by early Mass.
Still more elaborate is the great High Mass, in which the Easter
sequence Victimae paschali laudes immolent Christiani is sung with
full orchestral and organ accompaniment. The Sundays after Easter
are Quasimodogeniti or Dominica in albis (1 Pet. 2, 2), Misericordias Domini (Ps. 89, 2), Jubilate (Ps. 66, 1), Cantate (Ps. 98, 1),
Rogate (Matt. 7, 7), and Exaudi (Ps. 27, 7). The entire time is regarded as a period of great joy, symbolized also by the white color of
the vestments. The Sunday Rogate opens the Rogation Days, with
a daily procession in preparation for Ascension Day. On the latter
day, which is celebrated with three masses, the Easter candle is extinguished, as a sign that the Lord is no longer present visibly on earth.

The Festival of Pentecost is one of the festivals of the first rank
and is celebrated accordingly. A feature of the service is the beautiful sequence Veni Sancte Spiritus. The octave of Pentecost is now
celebrated as Trinity Sunday. In some places on the Continent it
was observed as special holiday since the twelfth century, but it did
not receive general recognition until 1334. A festival which is entirely characteristic of the Roman Catholic Church is the Festum
Corporis Christi. Celebrated as early as 1247, established in 1264 by
Urban IV as a general festival, ordered to be held once more in 1311,
it was introduced very generally a few years later.[412] Thomas
Acquinas wrote the office, which is a liturgical masterpiece. In
Catholic countries, the solemn procession with the host is made in

---

412) *Theol. Quart.*, 1915, Jan. and Apr.

public, but in other countries only inside the church or on the church property.

Of especial interest in the consideration of the Roman Catholic church year are the festivals of the virgin. The Festival of the Betrothal of Mary (Festum Desponsationis B. M. V. cum Josepho) is celebrated on Jan. 23. It was invented in 1546 by the Franciscans and established as a general festival by Benedict XIII in 1725, but has never received recognition as a festival of the first rank. The Festival of the Purification of Mary (Festum Purificationis B. M. V.) on Feb. 2 is considered one of the most prominent. Baronius claims an origin under Pope Gelasius (492—496), but documentary evidence shows that it was introduced by Justinian I (died 565). All the lections of the day were farced by the responsory: Lumen. The special ceremony of the day is the benediction of the candles, their distribution to the people, and the solemn procession with the lighted tapers, hence the English Candlemas, the German Lichtmesz.

Another Mary festival of the first rank is the Feast of the Annunciation (Festum Annunciationis B. M. V.) on March 25, nine months before Christmas. The Armenian Church had taken the 6th of January, that of Milan the fourth Sunday in Advent. But the fixation of the date of the nativity in the West determined also the date of the Festum Incarnationis sive Conceptionis Christi. A less important festival which follows shortly after this is the Festum VII Dolorum Mariae, on the Friday before Palm Sunday. It seems to have been celebrated in some places as early as the 14th century, becoming general in the 15th century (about 1423). The seven dolors of Mary are 1) The circumcision of Christ, 2) The flight into Egypt, 3) Losing the child Jesus in the temple, 4) The bearing of the cross, 5) The crucifixion, 6) The taking down from the cross, 7) The burial.

The Festival of the Visitation (Festum Visitationis B. M. V.) on July 2 was originally a Franciscan celebration, since 1263. In 1389 Pope Urban VI established it for the entire Church. To encourage the celebration, the pope granted a hundred days' indulgence to every one attending the early service of the day. Upon this followed the smaller Festival of Mary from Mount Carmel (Festum Mariae de Monte Carmelo) on July 16. It is the special festival of the Carmelites, who claim to have received a scapular by the hands of the virgin herself, in the year 1251.

A festival which was celebrated with extraordinary pomp and show almost from its establishment, is the Festival of the Assumption (Festum Dormitionis, Assumptionis, Depositionis, Pausationis Mariae) on Aug. 15. It is based entirely upon apocryphal material, and its earliest traces go back to the time of Epiphanius (died 403). The festival is first mentioned in the middle of the seventh century, and the event is merely spoken of as dormitio or pausatio. But at the Council of Aix-la-Chapelle (818) the Assumptio S. Mariae is given as a festival, and after the time of Peter Damiani (died 1072) it has been generally accepted as the truth, though the assumption has not yet been declared a dogma by the pope. A festival of equal importance is that of the Nativity of Mary (Festum Nativitatis B. M. V.) on Sept. 8. In the Greek Church, the day has been observed since the middle of the seventh century. In the West it was celebrated quite generally in the tenth century. Since the Council of Lyon (1245) and Gregory XI (1271—1276) it is one of the chief festivals of the Roman Church. On the next day, Sept. 9, the celebration of the Festival of the Name of Mary (Festum Nominis B. M. V.) is ordered. It is a minor day, celebrated since 1513 in Spain and made a general festival by Innocent XI in 1683.

The Festival of the Joys of Mary (Festum Septem Gaudiorum Mariae) is on Sept. 24. It was established by Pope Benedict XIII in 1727, receiving further sanction by his successor in 1745. The joys of Mary which are commemorated on this day are 1) The annunciation, 2) The visitation, 3) The birth without labor pains, 4) The adoration of the wise men, 5) The resurrection, 6) The sending of the Holy Spirit, 7) The crowning of Mary by the Father and the Son. A special festival of Mary is also the Festival of the Rosary (Festum Rosarii B. M. V.) on Oct. 1, with Oct. 3 or the first Sunday in October as alternates. It was a Dominican festival for a long time, but received the approval of Gregory XIII in 1573. It was extended over the whole Church by Clement XI in 1716. Its object is to make propaganda for the telling of the rosary in honor of the virgin Mary.

The Festival of the Presentation of Mary (Festum Praesentationis B. M. V.) on Nov. 21 was celebrated in the Orient since the eighth century. In 1372 Philip of Maizieres brought the office of the day to Pope Gregory XI, who approved its celebration. Sixtus V (1585) established it as a general festival. The date is not exactly eighty days after that of the nativity, but has probably been set purposely.

Of equal importance is the Festival of the Immaculate Conception (Festum Immaculatae Conceptionis) on Dec. 8. In the 11th century, Anselm of Canterbury (died 1109) was strongly interested in both the doctrine and the festival. In spite of opposition, the celebration gained a foothold, being upheld especially by the Franciscans. In 1854 Pope Pius IX made the doctrine a dogma of the Church, thus establishing also the festival beyond contradiction.

Of the small festivals of Mary which have never gained more than local importance, the Festum Mariae ad Nives (Aug. 5), the Festum Translationis Almae Domus Lauretanae B. M. V. (Dec. 10), and the Festum Patrocinii B. M. V. (third Sunday in November) may be mentioned.[413]

A feature of the Catholic calendar are also the many saints' and martyrs' days which have generally been accepted. The following may be mentioned as the more important ones: the Festival of Peter and Paul (Natales Apostolorum Petri et Pauli) on June 29 and 30; All Saints (Festum Omnium Sanctorum) on Nov. 1; the Festival of the Chair of Peter (Festum Cathedrae Petri) on Jan. 18; the Festival of the Chains of Peter (Festum Catenarum Petri) on August 1; the Festival of the Conversion of St. Paul (Festum Conversionis Pauli) on Jan. 25; St. James the Elder, on July 25; St. John the Evangelist, on Dec. 27 and May 6; St. Andrew, on Nov. 30; St. Bartholomew, on Aug. 24; St. Thomas, on Dec. 21; St. Matthew, on Sept. 21; St. Philip, on May 1; St. James the Younger, on May 1; SS. Simon and Judas, on Oct. 28; St. Matthias, on Feb. 24; Divisio SS. Apostolorum, on July 19; St. Mark, on April 25; St. Luke, on Oct. 18; Barnabas, on June 11; Timotheus, on Jan. 24; St. John the Baptist (Festum Decollationis) on August 29; St. Stephen, on Dec. 26; Festum Innocentium, on Dec. 28; Mary Magdalene, on July 22. In addition to these more important festivals, there are so many days in commemoration of bishops and teachers of the Church, of martyrs, confessors, and saints, of the cross of Christ and other relics that the number of days in the calendar for one year is not sufficient for them all, and in many instances two or more festivals are celebrated on the same day.[414] Fortunately, not all these festivals are celebrated in all the dioceses, only a relatively small number being prescribed for all the churches. Urban VII, in the constitution Universa per orbem, Sept. 24, 1642, fixed the following holidays: 1) Feasts of our Lord — Christmas, Easter, and Pentecost, with the two following days, New Year, Epiphany, Ascension, Trinity, Corpus Christi, Invention of the Cross; 2) Feasts of our Lady — Candlemas, Annunciation, Assumption, Nativity; 3) Saints' Days — St. Michael, May 8; Nativity of St. John the Baptist, SS. Peter and Paul; St. Andrew, St. James, St. John, St. Thomas, SS. Philip and James, St. Bartholomew, St. Matthew, SS. Simon and Jude, St. Matthias, St. Lawrence, St. Silvester, St. Joseph, St. Anne, All Saints', and the patron saint of the country; lesser saints' days were omitted. Later regulations reduced the saints' days to minor festivals.[415]

---

413) Cp. *Lehre und Wehre*, 1912, Dec.; Kliefoth, III, 173—176; Alt, *Das Kirchenjahr*, 60—76.   414) Alt, 76—106; 300—430.
415) Kellner, *Heortology*, Part I; Alt, 432.

The present chapter would hardly be complete without a reference to the liturgical customs which were in use in many dioceses during the Middle Ages and have, in part, been retained to this day. Luther's criticism of the Rorate masses during Advent as giving occasion for grave transgressions of the sixth commandment seems to have had good foundation.[416] During the time of Advent certain parts of the liturgy were developed into the Ten Virgin Plays. From a lesson of the third Sunday in Advent, which was also used in the Vigils of Christmas, and in which Isaiah, Jeremiah, Daniel, David, Moses, Habakkuk, Simeon, Zacharias, Elizabeth, John the Baptist, Vergil, Nebuchadnezzar, and the Sibyl were introduced with their prophecies, the Prophet Play was developed.

At Christmas, the tropes Quem vidistis, pastores, dicite and Quem quaeritis in praesepe, together with other sections of the services offered the outline for Plays of the Nativity. On Dec. 28, the Festival of the Innocents, the lower clergy, the choir boys, and the school children were permitted to elect a boy bishop, who then was led through the streets to the church, where he celebrated Mass. The liturgy of this day in a few cases also offered the tags for a Rachel Play, which was later combined with the Magi Play.

The Feast of Fools, celebrated by the subdeacons on Jan. 1, was unsavory from the first and rapidly degenerated into a burlesque of the Mass which was altogether blasphemous, especially where the recitation of the "ox and ass" prose was introduced. The Play of the Three Kings was developed from the liturgy of Epiphany, and offered a welcome chance for the display of pomp. As the Play of the Star it was retained in many places on the Continent for centuries. Much more reprehensible was the Feast of the Ass on the octave of Epiphany. It was not only that an ass bearing a virgin was led into the church, but also that blasphemous hymns and sequences were permitted for the enjoyment of the people, a fact which caused the sober and serious citizens to condemn such practises without reserve.

The Great Sabbath having been regarded as the day of commemoration of Christ's descent into hell since early times, its last service gave occasion for a Descent Play, with a procession resembling that of Palm Sunday and the Tollite portas dialog from Psalm 24 at the door. This play later became the prolog to the more elaborate Resurrection Play, which was developed from the Quem quaeritis trope of Easter day, together with other parts of the liturgy.

The afternoon service of Ascension Day was used for a dramatic representation of the scene spoken of in the Gospels, a carved picture of Christ being elevated into the loft above the triumphal arch. This

---

416) 22, 508; 21a, 1439; Daniel, Codex liturgicus, II, 22.

ceremony was followed by that of the casting out of Satan from heaven, also that of the bread from heaven and the water of life. The sending of the Holy Spirit on Pentecost Day was symbolized by the liberating of a dove, or by throwing down burning tinder or flower petals from above.

As noted above, many of these customs developed into such serious abuses and blasphemies that serious-minded people, both from among the clergy and the laity, protested earnestly, and several councils felt constrained to pass resolutions suppressing them. Fortunately, the Reformation acted as a leaven also in the Roman Church, and the blasphemous practises have, for the most part, been discontinued. But in remote parts, the last remnants of liturgical plays and usages are still to be found, and many forms of superstition that may be traced back to ceremonies of festival days, are still to be found.[417)

CHAPTER 4.

The Church Year of the Orient.

The long struggle for supremacy between Rome and Constantinople was reflected also in the divergent development of the church calendar. The chief festivals, indeed, are celebrated in both the Orient and the Occident, but the cultus in either case found a different expression, and the trend of the East was much stronger toward symbolism than that of the West. The love of the Oriental for gorgeous display manifested itself also in the arrangement of the services throughout the year. And just as every Sunday served for the full dramatic representation of the entire order of salvation, beginning with the creation of the world and closing with the coming of Christ to judgment, so the festival services were made an occasion to symbolize the special act of God which was commemorated on each day.

The Greek Orthodox Church takes the leading part in this respect. The more the preaching of the Word fell into disuse, the more the dramatic content of the liturgy was emphasized. The church year is commonly represented as beginning with Easter, which is celebrated with extraordinary displays of joy and splendor. As the midnight bell heralds the new day, a remarkable change takes place in the churches and in the congregations assembled in them. The church is still filled with the darkness of sorrow and mourning, but when the procession of triumph, headed by the priests, has returned from its walk around the church, the interior blazes forth with a great

---

417) Cp. *The Liturgical Element in the Earliest Forms of the Medieval Drama*, Minneapolis. 1916; *Lehre und Wehre*, 1917, Nov. ff.

multitude of lights. The Easter greeting is spoken by the bishop, and the doors of the altar screen are opened, revealing the high altar and all the furnishings of the apse, which are otherwise hidden from the eyes of the multitude. For the entire week the doors remain open, symbolizing the rending of the temple vail at Jerusalem. The procession continues inside the church, and the choirs burst out in anthems of joyful devotion. A feature of the celebration is the ring-ing of the church bells and the presenting of eggs as symbols of the resurrection. The celebration of Easter extends over three days as festival days of the first rank, but the entire octave is given over to special services of praise and thanksgiving.

The octave of Easter is known as Thomas Sunday, having lost the old distinction of names which referred to confirmation, the first communion, and the white baptismal dresses. Reference, however, is still made to the fact that the day was formerly celebrated as the Sunday of the Apostles, the lesson being Matt. 28, 16—20 and Acts 5, 12—20. The following week is known as that of the Ointment-bearers, since the Matin lessons tell the story of the three Maries at the sepulcher. The third Sunday after Easter is known as the Sun-day of the Paralytic, after the Gospel of the Matins, Luke 24, 1—9. The Gospel of the chief service, John 5, 1—15, also commemorates the healing of a sick man. The fourth Sunday after Easter is called the Sunday of the Samaritan Woman, after the Gospel of the day, John 4, 5—42. The fifth Sunday after Easter is the Sunday of the Blind, after the Gospel of the day, John 9, 1—38.

The celebration of the Paschal season proper closes with the thirty-ninth day after Easter *(apodidotai to Pascha)*. The fortieth day after Easter, as in the Western Church, is celebrated as Ascen-sion Day. On this day it is customary to hold a solemn procession, which in Jerusalem has the Mount of Olives for its endpoint and in other places is usually undertaken to the nearest hill or mount. The Sunday after this festival is the Sunday of the Holy Fathers, in com-memoration of all the fathers of the seven Ecumenical Councils. The Saturday of this week is the Oriental All Souls' Day, with processions to the cemeteries.

The festival of Pentecost is not signalized by the same display of pomp and splendor as Easter, but it is also a festival of the first rank, with a full three days' celebration. The Sunday of All Saints' as the octave of Pentecost in a way closes the celebration of the Holy Ghost's outpouring, but its principal significance is its being set aside to commemorate all saints and martyrs, and to serve as an introduc-tion to the season without great festivals. The total number of Sun-days in this long period till the beginning of Lent is thirty-five. The

one extraordinary festival in this entire season is the Christmas festival, which includes the three days beginning with Dec. 25. Instead
of the account of St. Luke (chap. 2), that of St. Matthew describing
the coming of the wise men from the East is used. On January 1
occurs the Festival of the Circumcision, and on January 6 that of
Epiphany, or Theophany. On the latter day, which commemorates
the baptism of Jesus, a solemn procession is formed and made to the
nearest river, where, after the proper benediction, the baptism in
Jordan is celebrated.

The three Sundays immediately preceding Lent again have special names, the first of them being known as the Sunday of the
Pharisee and the Publican, after the Gospel lesson Luke 18, 1—14,
the second as the Sunday of the Prodigal Son, the Gospel being
Luke 15, 11—32, and the third as the Sunday of Christ's Final Advent, with the Gospel lesson Matt. 25, 31—46. The week of this
Sunday is the Carnival Week of the Greek Church, and the use of
milk, butter, cheese, and eggs is permitted, while during the fast of
Lent only cheese is permitted. The first Sunday in Lent is, on this
account, known as the Sunday of Cheese. The second Sunday in
Lent is called the Sunday of Orthodoxy, with reference to the confession of Nathanael in the Gospel, John 1, 43—51. On this day there
occurs the solemn procession with all the saints' statues and icons,
after which the great anathema is pronounced upon all heretics which
were excommunicated by the seven Ecumenical Councils. The third
Sunday in Lent is distinguished only by the first readings of the
Gospel according to St. Mark. The seventh and last Sunday in Lent
is Palm Sunday, on which the procession of palms is held. Every
day in Holy Week is set apart for chief services. On Thursday, the
institution of the Lord's Supper is celebrated, also the ceremony of
the washing of feet, but principally the benediction of the Holy
Chrism which has been prepared on the first days of the week. The
celebration of Good Friday is distinguished by special anthems, but
especially by the reading of twelve Gospel lessons concerning the
Passion, taken from the four Gospels, after the form of a harmony.
On Good Friday as well as on the Great Sabbath everything in and
about the church is expressive of deep repentance and mourning, until once more the midnight bell ushers in the glad day of Easter.[418]

This complete calendar, as here briefly sketched, was the result
of a gradual development for centuries, some festivals having meanwhile gained in prominence and others lost. Under the latter Byzantine Empire, the festivals, according to Kellner, were the following:
Christmas, Epiphany, Hypapante (Presentation), Easter, Pentecost,

— Orthodox Sunday (1st Sunday in Lent), Palm Sunday, Holy Saturday, Easter Octave, New Year's Day, Sept. 1; — St. Basil, Jan. 1; St. George, April 23; Constantine, May 21; Nativity of John the Baptist, June 24; Feast of the Apostles, June 30; Transfiguration, Aug. 8; Assumption of Mary, Aug. 15; Beheading of John the Baptist, Aug. 29; Nativity of our Lady, Sept. 8; Invention of the Cross, Sept. 14; Chrysostom, Nov. 13; Presentation of our Lady in the Temple, Nov. 21, and others.[419])

Neale divides the festivals of the Greek calendar according to their importance: A. *Great Festivals* — 1) Easter; 2) Christmas Day, Epiphany, Purification, Annunciation, Palm Sunday, Ascension, Pentecost, Transfiguration, Repose of the Mother of God, Nativity of the Mother of God, Exaltation of the Holy Cross, Presentation of the Mother of God; 3) Adodecata: Circumcision, Nativity of John the Baptist, SS. Peter and Paul, Decollation of John the Baptist. B. *Festivals of the Second Class* — 1) With additional canon at Lauds in honor of the Mother of God: SS. Basil, Gregory, and Chrysostom, Jan. 30; St. George, April 23; St. John the Divine, May 6; St. John Chrysostom, Nov. 13; St. Sabbas, Dec. 5; St. Nicolas of Myra, Dec. 6; 2) Middle Festivals of the second class: days of apostles, certain great doctors or wonder-workers, etc.; 3) Little festivals: a) those that have the great doxology, b) those that have not.[420])

The Armenian church year, as might be expected, shows some similarity to that of the Orthodox Greek Church, but its whole structure points to a greater age and a more conservative stand. It is not only more primitive, but it is unusually well-balanced and harmonious, even the later festivals having been added in a way which causes them to appear as parts of a consistent whole. The calendar of the Armenians is divided into sections in accordance with the great festivals: 1) from Easter to Pentecost, 2) from Pentecost to the Festival of the Transfiguration, 3) from Transfiguration to the Assumption of Mary, 4) from Assumption of Mary to Elevation of the Cross, 5) from Elevation of the Cross to the Pentecostal season preceding Epiphany, 6) the season of fasting before Epiphany, 7) from Epiphany to Lent, 8) Lent to the Great Sabbath. A feature of the spring season are the processions for the benediction of the fields, which take place on the seven Sundays after Easter, on Ascension Day, and on the Saturday before Pentecost, as well as on Pentecost itself. There are also other processions, as on Easter and Pentecost for the benediction of the graves, on Transfiguration to the nearest mountain or hill instead of Tabor, on Assumption of Mary both in the morning

---

419) *Heortology*, 28.   420) *Essays on Liturgiology*, IV.

and in the afternoon, the latter for the benediction of the fields. A number of festivals are either peculiar to the Armenians or have assumed special characteristics. Among these are the following: Commemoration of the prophet Jeremiah, on the Saturday after Pentecost, Gregorius Illuminator on the following Saturday, Festival of the Relics of Gregorius Illuminator two weeks later, Festival of the Two Hundred Fathers of the Council of Ephesus, Festival of the Three Hundred and Eighteen Fathers of the Council of Nicea, Festival of the Seventy Disciples of Christ, and others. The Sundays in Lent have the same names as those in the Roman Catholic calendar.[421])

The Nestorians have their church year divided into six sections: I. The twelve weeks from New Year till Christmas (four weeks of Moses, four weeks of dedication — from the tabernacle of Moses to the temple of Serubbabel —, four weeks of annunciation); II. From the Nativity of Christ to Epiphany, with a period of fasting of twenty-five days; III. From Epiphany to Lent (nine weeks devoted to the ministry of Christ); IV. The period of fasting before Easter (ending with Holy Week and the Great Sabbath); V. From Easter to Pentecost (during which Friday after Easter the "Friday of Confessors"); VI. From Pentecost to the Festival of the Cross (including six Sundays devoted to the commemoration of the apostles, and the last three to a preparation for the Elevation of the Cross). The Festival of Transfiguration is an important festival in the Nestorian calendar.[422])

The Coptic and Abyssinian church year has not been changed much since the tenth century. In the 8th century, the following festivals were observed: Annunciation (March 25); Olivarum sive festum palmarum; Pascha; Festum ascensionis; Pentecoste; Nativitas Domini; Immersio i. e. baptismus Domini (Epiphany); — lesser festivals: Circumcisio Domini; Candlemas; Maundy Thursday; Holy Saturday; Low Sunday; Festum transfigurationis (Aug. 6); Festum crucis (Sept. 14). Of these festivals, that of Epiphany is the most characteristic, being celebrated in a strictly Monophysitic manner.[423])

---

421) Alt, 225—280.　　　422) Alt, 286—290.
423) Kellner, *Heortology*, Part I; Alt, 291—296.

CHAPTER 5.

The Reformed Church Year.

There are several factors which separate the calendar of the Reformed churches from that of the Catholic Church on the one hand and the Lutheran Church on the other. One of these is the legalistic imprint which characterizes the Protestant churches that had their origin in Switzerland and in England and Scotland, although the Reformed Church of Germany is not far behind in this respect. The other factor is this that, with the exception of the Anglican (and the Protestant Episcopal Church) all Protestant denominations of this class have abrogated the old church year, either entirely or in its chief parts.

The legalistic phase of the question is especially strongly marked with reference to the discussion of Sunday or Sabbath. The idea that the Old Testament Sabbath is continued in the New Testament Sunday is very strongly developed among many of these denominations. The Presbyterians, the Congregationalists, the Baptists, the Free-Will Baptists, the Mennonites, the Methodists, the Evangelical Adventists, and others claim full validity for the ceremonial law, so far as the keeping of a certain day in the week is concerned.[424] In England a law given in 1562 prohibited all marketing, buying, and selling on the Lord's Day, all labor being forbidden that was usually performed on the week days. The Puritans became the strongest advocates of the movement to enforce the provisions of the Old Testament Sabbath, both in England, so far as their influence extended, and later in America. The duties of piety and religion, both publicly and privately, were enjoined. No tradesman, artificer, workman, laborer, shoe-maker, butcher, baker was allowed to ply his trade. The ban was placed even upon the showing forth and exposing to sale of wares, merchandise, fruit, herbs, etc. The purpose of all these measures was to "keep the divine institution from being polluted." In Scotland the Sabbath laws were insisted upon and enforced with appropriate punishments to such an extent that the Sunday was given over entirely and alone to the hearing and reading of the Bible, all other activities being omitted absolutely. In the Puritan days of New England the same state of affairs obtained. In the early days, the colonies were practically church states, and the ceremonial law of Moses was observed as strictly as the civil law, in fact the latter were based upon the former. And to this day, this conception of Sunday, as found in the ancient Blue Laws, crops up in the legislation of many states, cities, and towns, not on the basis of a natural law

---

424) Guenther, *Symbolik*, 289—291.

which demands a day of rest, but on the basis of the Old Testament commandment.

The Reformed church which adhered most closely to the ancient church calendar was the Anglican Church. As the founders of this church were conservative in the selection of their liturgy, so they were also conservative in the retention of established festivals. In 1559, the Anglican Church celebrated the following festivals: Circumcision, Epiphany, Conversion of St. Paul, Purification of the Blessed Virgin Mary, St. Matthias, Annunciation, St. Mark, Philip and James, John Baptist, Peter, James, Bartholomew, Matthew, Michael, Luke, Simon and Jude, All Saints', St. Andrew, St. Thomas, Christmas, St. Stephen, John the Evangelist, Innocents, Mary Magdalen (1549), Clement (1552), Barnabas (1549, 1559), George, Lawrence, Lammas (1552 and 1559). Easter was celebrated as a matter of course.[425] The influence of the Puritans and of the Presbyterians in the 16th and 17th century was not without its effect upon the Anglican calendar, but the result has been chiefly salutary, by weeding out many festival days whose celebration savored strongly of Romanism. The church year of the Church of England, as recognized also in the Scotch, Irish, and American branches, has the following order: 1) Advent, with four Sundays and the days of the apostles, Andrew, on Nov. 30, Thomas, on Dec. 21; 2) The Christmas season, with Christmas, St. Stephen, St. John the Evangelist, Innocents, Sunday after Christmas, and the Circumcision; 3) The Epiphany season with its six possible Sundays, and Conversion of St. Paul on Jan. 25, Purification on Feb. 2, St. Matthias on Feb. 24; 4) The season of preparation and Lent, with Septuagesima, Sexagesima, Quinquagesima, and the five Sundays in Lent; 5) Palm Sunday and the Holy Week, during which Monday, Tuesday, Wednesday, and Thursday before Easter, Good Friday, and Easter Even are commemorated; 6) Easter Day and Easter Monday and Tuesday, also Annunciation on March 25, and St. Mark on April 25; 7) The five Sundays after Easter, Ascension, Whit-Sunday with its Monday and Tuesday, Trinity, with special days at some time during that season: SS. Philip and James on May 1, St. Barnabas on June 11; 8) The twenty-five Sundays after Trinity. The following festivals are included in this period: St. John Baptist on June 24, St. Peter on June 29, St. James on July 25, St. Bartholomew on Aug. 24, St. Matthew on Sept. 21; St. Michael and All Angels on Sept. 29, St. Luke on Oct. 18, SS. Simon and Jude on Oct. 28, All Saints' on Nov. 1.[426]

So far as the other Reformed denominations are concerned, a

---

425) Blunt, *Annotated Book of Common Prayer*, Part I.
426) Alt, *Das Kirchenjahr*, 459.

distinction must be made between those that were influenced from Zurich and Basle and those that were influenced from Geneva. Zwingli placed the chief emphasis upon the celebration of Sunday, a feature which has not been abandoned since. He was not in favor of many other holidays, retaining only the Nativity of Christ, Easter, Ascension, and Pentecost. The Church Order of Ulm was even more radical, designating Sunday as the only day to be celebrated and merely permitting a commemoration of the Lord, the apostles, and the martyrs, on the days formerly devoted to their celebration. The Hessian Church Order of 1526 is almost as exclusive, allowing only Sunday for celebration in the proper sense of the word, but designating Christmas, Circumcision, Epiphany, Presentation of Christ, Annunciation, Good Friday, Easter Day, Ascension, Whitsunday, Visitation of Mary as commemorative days. Of apostles and martyrs, only John the Baptist and St. Stephen are mentioned. By 1566 it seemed to become evident that such an extreme and radical position was not to be recommended, for the same Church Order names the following festivals: Christmas with the second day, Circumcision, Epiphany, Purification, Annunciation, Easter with the second day, Ascension, Pentecost with the second day, John the Baptist, and Visitation. On the days of the apostles, Mary Magdalen, Michael, Conversion of St. Paul, Maundy Thursday, Good Friday, and on the third festival day of the great Christ feasts, there should be early morning service only. But the monthly day of prayer and penitence was very strongly recommended.

In Switzerland and Germany the final result of agitation from various sides has yielded the following: 1) Christmas Eve and Christmas, two days, 2) New Year's Eve and New Year, 3) Palm Sunday, Great Thursday, and Good Friday, 4) Easter, two days, 5) Ascension, 6) Pentecost, two days, 7) Trinity. The division of the church year into periods, such as Advent, Epiphany season, Lenten season, Easter season, Pentecost season, is observed at least in the prayers recommended for the several Sundays.

The denominations which were influenced by Calvin were even more radical in rejecting the festivals which were traditional in the Church. Calvin acknowledged only the Sunday as a holiday, to be kept with extraordinary solemnity. He also had daily service with preaching in the large churches, and the same on Monday, Wednesday, and Friday, or at least on Wednesday in the smaller churches. These views became authoritative in the French Reformed Church, as well as for the Puritans and Presbyterians of England and Scotland, and later, of America. They also influenced the Baptists, the Methodists, the Congregationalists, the Campbellites, and the many Protestant denominations that have sprung up in the last few centuries. With all of them, the Sunday is the one recognized holiday which is held with all solemnity. In some of these churches, a monthly or yearly watch-night is held and the midweek prayer meeting is, with many, an established institution. There are also regular missionary meetings, and the Methodists celebrate the first Sunday in every new year for the Renewal of Covenant.

But the influence of environment cannot be denied, and the instinctive liking for festival celebrations cannot be entirely suppressed. Accordingly, both Christmas and Easter are celebrated in most of the Reformed denominations of this country. Lent is also being regarded more and more as a season of preparation, the practise of noon-day services by no means being restricted to the Lutherans. Holy Week is solemnized by special services and by references to the events between Palm Sunday and Easter. And this practise is to be commended most heartily, being far preferable to the habit of dedicating the several Sundays, not only to all manner of causes, but also to all manner of fads. Rally Day and Mothers' Day were well enough, but to go to the extreme which has been reached in some quarters at the present time and make the church platform a forum for the rehashing of the previous week's editorials and the discussion of every question under the sun but that of the redemption through Christ augurs ill for the Church of the future. A more stable church calendar may do much to stem the tide which threatens to carry all before it.

CHAPTER 6.

The Lutheran Church Year.

When Luther undertook the great work of liberating the Church from errors of doctrine and life, he was actuated only by true zeal for the honor of Christ. He was never unmindful of the history of the Church nor of the obligations which historical associations laid upon the Christians of this latter day. And for that reason he did not become guilty of iconoclasm, also with reference to the church year and its festivals. The ancient festivals in honor of Christ and the Triune God he retained as a matter of course. And as for the other festivals, he was careful to keep all such as had any value for the devotion and edification of the Christian congregation, while he carefully expunged all parts or references which savored of Romish idolatry. In his "Order of Divine Services in the Congregation" of 1523 he writes: "All festivals of saints ought to be omitted, or, if there were a good Christian legend, be introduced on the Sunday [nearest] after the Gospel as an example. But the festival Purification and Annunciation of Mary I should retain; Assumption of Mary into Heaven, commonly called Ascension of Mary by the people, and Nativity of Mary one must keep for a while, although the liturgy is not pure. The Festival of John Baptist is also pure. Of the legends of the apostles none is pure but that of St. Paul, therefore they may be used on the Sundays, or, if desired, be celebrated separately." [427]) He makes a similar distinction in the Formula Missae of 1523: "But we of Wittenberg intend to celebrate only on the Sundays and on the festivals of our Lord Jesus Christ, for we believe that the festivals of the saints should all be discontinued, or if there be anything worthy of speaking in them, it may be included on the Sundays in the sermon. The festivals of Purification and Annunciation we consider Christ festivals, just as we do Epiphany and Circumcision. Instead of the festivals of St. Stephen and St. John the Evangelist it pleases us to make use of the office of Christmas. The festivals of the Holy Cross should be condemned. Others may follow their own conscience or the weakness of other people, as each one's spirit will suggest and counsel." [428]) In the same strain Luther writes three years later, in his "German Mass and Order of Services" of 1526: "But with the festivals, as Christmas, Easter, Pentecost, Michaelis, Purification, and the others, we must continue as heretofore, Latin, until there are enough German hymns for them. . . . Lent, Palm Sunday, and Holy Week we retain; not as though we compel any one to fast, but that the reading of the passion story and the Gospels, which were fixed for this time, be retained. . . Holy Week shall be like other weeks, only that the passion story be preached an hour every day through the week, or as many days as it pleases, and he who wishes may receive the Sacrament. For everything should be done for the sake of the Word and the Sacrament in the service." [429])

Luther discusses the question also in other passages of his writings. In his Sermon on the Second Article he mentions Christmas, Holy Week, Easter, Ascension, and Pentecost.[430]) In another case, he speaks of the keeping of Vigils.[431]) In his Exposition of the Epistle to the Galatians, 4, 10, he refers to Wednesday and Friday as days of commemoration, and to Easter, Pentecost, and the days of the martyrs. But the passage which is of the greatest interest in this connection is that of the Instruction of the Visitors to the Pastors in the Electorate of Saxony, of 1528, since so many of the German Church Orders were based upon these instructions. The passage reads: "Therefore the festivals, as Sundays and others, as is the custom of each pastor, should be observed. For the people must have some cer-

---

427) 10, 225, No. 15.   428) 10, 2238, § 11; Daniel, II, 83.
429) 10, 257, §§ 50. 51.   430) 10, 1107.   431) 3, 1208.

tain times that they may come together to hear God's Word. The
pastors also should not become guilty of altercation, in case one cele-
brates a holyday and the other does not, ... nevertheless they shall
not abrogate all holydays. It would be well if they all, with one
accord, would celebrate the Sundays, Annunciation, Purification,
Visitation of the Pure Virgin Mary, St. John the Baptist, Michaelis,
the festivals of the apostles, that of Mary Magdalene; unless those
festivals have already been discontinued and could not well be reintroduced. But above all, Christmas, Circumcision, Epiphany, Easter, Ascension, Pentecost shall be held, but with the omission of un-
Christian legends or hymns, since these festivals are thus ordered.
For it is impossible to teach all parts of the Gospel at once, for which
reason the doctrine has been divided into the church year. . . . In the
week before Easter the usual celebration shall be observed that the
passion story may be preached, and it is not necessary that this old
custom and order be changed." [432])

Luther himself followed the principles here enunciated by him,
as we see from his postils and other writings. Of the season of Advent and its ceremonies he judged that "they were instituted and
ordered in the very best manner and in good Christian intention, to
thank God for the fact that His dear Son became man." Christmas
he called "the beautiful, pleasant festival of the holy birth of our
Lord Jesus Christ." Of the two festivals immediately after Christmas he at first spoke harshly: "The preacher should discontinue the
stories of St. Stephen and St. John as not pertaining to this festival
[Christmas], and preach only of the birth of the Savior"; but later
he himself preached a sermon on the martyrdom of St. Stephen and
called the narrative "a very fine history." New Year's Day he wanted
to have observed only as the Festival of the Circumcision, and said
of it: "The Festival of the Circumcision is a very comforting festival." On the Festival of Epiphany Luther would have preferred
the commemoration of the baptism of Christ: "This festival should
really have its principal name from the baptism of Christ and this
preaching of the holy baptism especially be done on it." It was not
altogether clear to him which feature should be emphasized more
strongly. "On this festival there is much to preach, namely the history of the wise men, also of the baptism of Christ, also of the first
miracle which Jesus performed at Cana of Galilee." Later the pericopes were so arranged as to give due attention to each of these
stories. Of Palm Sunday Luther writes: "The Palm Sunday should
be observed with the procession and the liturgy as of old, but the
benediction of the palms should be omitted." For Maundy Thursday

432) 10, 1663. 1664.

and Good Friday we have sermons by Luther, as also for the "solemn, joyous Easter festival." Of Rogation Week he writes: "They who first instituted it may have meant well, but is has turned out poorly." For this reason he opposed its celebration. For Ascension Day Luther has a sermon in one of his postils, and in regard to Pentecost he declares: "On this holy and joyous festival of Pentecost we commemorate and thank our dear God for the great, endless blessing which He has done on earth in this that He has revealed to us poor men down from heaven His dear holy Word." On Trinity Sunday he preached: "The present festival is instituted for this reason, that we learn as much as possible from the Word of God, what God is in Himself."

In regard to the minor festivals we also have remarks of Luther. His opinion of the Corpus Christi Festival is especially unfavorable: "Therefore I have never been more opposed to any festival than to this one, because the pope used Scriptures wrongly for it. . . . On no other day is God and His Christ blasphemed more gravely than on this day, and especially with the procession, which should be abrogated above all things." Of the Dedication Festivals or Kirmessen, as they were then in use, Luther says: "The Kirchweihen should be altogether discontinued, since they are nothing but regular taverns, markets, and gambling dens, for the furthering of God's dishonor and the damnation of souls." The Feast of the Annunciation he wanted to have regarded as a festival of the Savior, "which should by preference be called the Festival of the Conception or Incarnation of Christ." He says of it: "This festival is observed on account of the article in the Creed, when we say: I believe in Jesus Christ. . . . born of the virgin Mary." In the same way, Luther regarded the Festival of Purification as a feast of the Lord: "We observe this day as a festival of our Lord Jesus Christ, who revealed Himself on this day, when He was carried into the temple at Jerusalem and there presented to the Lord." The Roman leaven in the Festival of the Visitation Luther excluded, asserting that the conception of Christ, the Son of God, and the Magnificat are proper subjects for consideration on this day. The Festival of the Assumption was ruled out summarily, having basis neither in Scriptures nor in reasonable probability. He says of it: "The Festival of the Assumption of Mary is thoroughly papistical, that is, full of idolatry, and instituted without Scriptural grounds." The Festival of John the Baptist Luther retained. Michaelis was also regarded very highly by him, and he called it "the festival of all holy and chaste angels." It was a matter of course with him to remove all superstition. For the feasts of saints and martyrs Luther showed little interest. He says of the festivals All Saints' and All Souls': "I wish that these two festivals would be abrogated in all countries, on account of the abuse which takes place on them." In regard to the legend of St. Barbara Luther uses very emphatic language: "The legend of St. Barbara we will omit . . . it is all a mass of lies." [433])

Luther himself has sermons, in his postils, not only for the great festivals, Christmas, Epiphany, Easter, Ascension, Pentecost, but also for the following minor festivals, many of which he preferred to have discontinued, using, incidentally, Scripture passages for the basis of his discourse instead of legendary material: St. Andrew, St. Barbara, St. Nicholas, Conception of Mary, St. Thomas, St. Stephen, St. John the Evangelist, Circumcision, Conversion of St. Paul, Purification or Presentation of Christ, St. Matthias, Annunciation, SS. Philip and James, Invention of the Cross, Corpus Christi, John the Baptist, SS. Peter and Paul, Visitation of Mary, St. Margaret, Mary Magdalene, St. James the Elder, Feast of St. Anne, St. Lawrence, Assumption of Mary, St. Bartholomew, Decollation of John Baptist, Birth of Mary, St. Matthew, Michaelis, SS. Simon and Jude, All Saints', St. Martin, St. Catharine, and others.[434]) Whenever Luther held a sermon on a festival day whose abrogation he favored, he gave his reasons for rejecting the legend and used the pericope of the Gospel lesson prescribed for that day as his text.

Thus Luther worked in a fine, conservative, tactful way in eradicating the evils which had crept into the Church with the multiplicity of the festivals. And the sound principles which he thus advocated were accepted by the Lutheran Church and incorporated in its confessions. "It pleases us well that universal ceremonies be kept for the sake of uniformity and good order, as we also in our churches observe the Mass, the celebration of Sunday, and the other great festivals." [435]) "The most ancient institutions of the Church, as the three great festivals, etc., the celebration of Sunday, which were invented for the sake of good order, uniformity, and peace, etc., we observe gladly." [436]) Thus the Lutheran Church "tried the traditional church year by the canon of Holy Scripture, rejected all the pseudo-festivals, declared against any mere outward fasts, and disburdened herself of the great mass of saints' days. Thus only the great festivals, with those days of Mary which are founded on Scripture, remained; and of the memorial days, the day of John the Baptist and the apostles' days without the legends, the days of SS. Stephen and Lawrence as commemorative of the martyrs of the Church, and the day of the archangel Michael as a representative of the triumphant

433) Cp. Daniel, *Codex liturgicus*, II, 15—65; Luther, 12 and 13.
434) 11, 1908—2414.
435) Apologia Conf. Art. de Ecclesia. Mueller, 159, §§ 33. 34.
436) Apologia. Art. de Traditionibus Humanis. Mueller, 212, § 38.

THE LUTHERAN CHURCH YEAR.

Church. . . . Some Kirchenordnungen retain also the day of Mary Magdalen. . . . Reformation Day was added very early." [437])

This calendar, as thus outlined, is used in the Lutheran Church to the present day, with local variations, in a true evangelical spirit. Loehe names the following festivals and holydays: A. *Movable Festivals.* Septuagesima, Sexagesima, Quinquagesima or Esto Mihi, Ash Wednesday, Invocavit, Reminiscere, Oculi, Laetare, Judica, Palmarum, Dies Viridium or Maundy Thursday, Dies Parasceves or Good Friday, Easter, Quasimodogeniti, Misericordias Domini, Jubilate, Cantate, Rogate, Ascension, Exaudi, Pentecost or Whitsunday, Trinity; B. *Fixed Festivals.* Circumcision, Jan. 1; Epiphany, Jan. 6; Conversion of St. Paul, Jan. 25; Purification, Feb. 2; St. Matthias, Feb. 24; Annunciation, March 25; SS. Philip and James, May 1; Birth of John the Baptist, June 24; SS. Peter and Paul, June 29; Visitation of Mary, July 2; Mary Magdalene, July 22; St. James the Elder, July 25; St. Lawrence, Aug. 10; St. Bartholomew, Aug. 24; St. Matthew, Sept. 21; Michaelis, Sept. 29; SS. Simon and Jude, Oct. 28; All Saints', Nov. 1; St. Andrew, Nov. 30; St. Thomas, Dec. 21; Christmas, Dec. 25; St. Stephen, Dec. 26; St. John the Evangelist, Dec. 27; Innocents' Day, Dec. 28.[438])

In the American Lutheran Church, all the chief festivals are observed very generally, and the second festival day is still recognized. Many of the minor festivals, however, are referred to in the second service of the nearest Sunday. An effort is being made in some quarters to observe the festivals in a proper manner and, if possible, on the proper day, and this effort deserves the earnest support of all those that recognize the beauty of the Lutheran calendar and the possibility of true edification which a proper observance of the festivals offers. The chances are that a tactful and proper reference to the beauties of many festivals will stimulate interest and counteract the danger of monotony. The older service books of the Lutheran synods in America, the Book of Worship of the General Synod, the Kirchenbuch of the Council, the Agenda of the Missouri Synod, as well as the new Liturgy and Agenda of the last-named body and the Common Service Book of the Lutheran Church make proper provision for the celebration of all the fixed and movable, and of all the chief and minor festivals. If the observance of these festivals is untainted by high-churchism and they are always conducted in a strictly evangelical spirit, it will surely redound to the glory of God and the Church.

---

437) Horn, *Outlines of Liturgies,* 28.
438) *Agende,* 1—4; *Haus-, Schul- und Kirchenbuch,* II, 111—113; Kliefoth, *Die urspruengliche Gottesdienstordnung,* IV, 310—369; Alt, *Das Kirchenjahr,* 466—544; Richards-Painter, *Christian Worship,* Chapter VIII; Fuerbringer, *Leitfaden,* 6. 7.

PART IV.
The Liturgical Content of the Lutheran Services.

CHAPTER 1.
The Morning Service or the Communion.

The division of the chief service of the Lutheran Church, formerly called the Mass, and now known as the Morning Service or the Communion, into two groups of acts, the sacramental and the sacrificial, is commonly accepted by liturgiologists. The definitions of Melanchthon in the Apology of the Augsburg Confession are short and to the point: "Sacramentum is a ceremony or external sign or act, by which God gives that which the divine promise, attached to the ceremony, offers . . . Sacrificium is a ceremony or act that we offer to God, by which we honor Him." [439]) The sacramental group, then, includes the forms and acts by and through which God deals with His people: the message of the atonement in the Gospel and the fruit of Christ's redemption in the Sacraments are actually given to the believer. The means of grace provide, appropriate, and seal unto us our salvation. Thus the sacramental idea of communicating grace has the precedence in Christian worship. But upon it are based the acts of the sacrificial group, the fruit of the lips and the fruits of Christian activity in actual participation in the service, Acts 2, 42. In practically all denominations outside of the Lutheran Church, there is more or less confusion as to the dividing line between the two groups. Since the time of Tertullian, with his "sacrificium offerri," the idea that the congregation, through its priests, offers up a sacrifice in the Eucharist, gained ground, and that is the conception which underlies the sacrifice of the Mass to the present day. In the Reformed churches, on the other hand, the conception of the Eucharist as of a mere memorial supper is commonly held. Their purpose is merely to commemorate the Lord's death, to remember His vicarious sacrifice by a commemorative feast. The Lutheran Church holds the golden means, giving to the means of grace their full sacramental value, but giving proper opportunity to the people also to partake in the worship, in the sacrificial group of the service acts, in the prayers, hymns, and confessions. It has been stated that it would be preferable to avoid these terms by saying that the objective element of worship is found in the Word and the Sacraments, and the subjective

---

439) Mueller, 251, §§ 6. 8.

element in prayers and singing,[440]) but the terms sacramental and sacrificial are in such general use and can be explained so easily that there is no valid reason for discontinuing them.

In general, the chief service of the Lutheran Church may be divided into two large groups: I. *The Word Group or Homiletical Part:* a) Introit, Kyrie, Gloria; b) Salutation, Collect, Epistle, Gospel; c) Creed, Sermon, Hymn; II. *The Eucharist or Sacramental Part:* a) Salutation, Preface, Sanctus, Exhortation; b) Lord's Prayer, Consecration, Distribution; c) Postcommunion.[441]) Dr. Jacobs makes the following division: I. *Preparatory Service,* a) Confession, b) Declaration of Grace. — *The Service Proper, Part I: The Word.* Div. I: a) Introit, b) Kyrie, c) Gloria in excelsis; Div. II: a) Salutation, b) Collect, c) Epistle, d) Hallelujah, e) Gospel, f) Glory be to Thee, O Lord; Div. III: a) Nicene Creed, b) Sermon, c) Offertory, d) General Prayer. *Part II: The Communion.* Div. I, Introduction: a) Salutation, b) Preface with Sursum, Gratias, Dignum, c) Sanctus with Hosanna, d) Exhortation; Div. II, Consecration: a) Lord's Prayer, b) Words of Institution, c) Pax; Div. III, Distribution: a) Agnus Dei, b) Distribution Proper; Div. IV, Postcommunion: a) Nunc dimittis, b) Versicle, c) Collect, d) Benedicamus and Benediction.[442]) The "Sketch of the Lutheran Liturgy" given in *An Explanation of the Common Service,* p. 68, differs only in minor points from this presentation, being in such detail as to satisfy all ordinary requirements.

After an opening hymn, usually a hymn of invocation to the Holy Ghost, by whom only we can render true worship to God through Christ, 1 Cor. 12, 3; Eph. 2, 18, the service is opened with an Invocation to the Triune God, Matt. 28, 19; 18, 20; Ex. 3, 5; Eccl. 5, 1, which is responded to with a hearty Amen by the congregation, expressing the firm conviction that Christ will fulfil His promise. John 14, 23. Immediately there follows the Preparation. This part is based upon the Preparatio in missam or the Confiteor, as it was used in the Middle Ages. At that time the congregation was not included in this section of the liturgy, the Confiteor being nothing but a liturgical dialog between the officiating priest and his assistants. The meaning of the preparation was that the priest was being prepared for his sacerdotal functions; in confession and prayer he doffed his usual clothing, and in donning his priestly vestments he became worthy of offering sacrifice for the sins of the living and of the dead. In this sense the Confiteor was absolutely to be condemned, for which

---

440) Richards-Painter, *Christian Worship,* Chapter I.
441) Richards-Painter, Chapter X.
442) *Lutheran Movement in England,* Chapter XXIV.

reason Luther as well as most of the early Church Orders omitted it. After various experiments of the liturgiologists of the 16th century, the consensus favored a general confession with absolution at the very opening of the services, the confession of the present order being taken from Mecklenburg, 1552. In this sense it is a splendid preparation for the drawing near which the Christian does in public worship.

This drawing near with a true heart is done in accordance with the Exhortation, Heb. 10, 22. The heart and mind should be properly prepared to confess, conscious of man's depravity and many failings, Ps. 32, 5; 1 John 1, 8. 9. The first step in confessing is made in the Versicle, taken from Ps. 124, 8. God's mercy is invoked and His willingness to forgive is stated. Then comes the Confession proper, with its open statement and acknowledgment of both inherited and actual sin, followed by the Prayer for Grace, in which the congregation joins the pastor, asking for pardon and also for the fruits of this remission, as shown in growth in spiritual knowledge and sanctification. The climax of the preparatory service is reached in the Declaration of Grace, held in a jubilant tone and declaring to each believer full pardon and remission, and the promise of God for increase in saving knowledge and in sanctifying power, John 3, 16; 1, 12; Mark 16, 16.

The first part or general division of the service proper is the Office of the Word, which is composed of three parts, the Psalmody, the reading and preaching of the Word, and the Offerings. The character of the day and the nature of the spiritual food it offers is indicated by the Introit. This is a remnant of the primitive psalmody which was probably taken over into the early Church from the services of the synagog. Its name was probably derived from the fact that it was chanted or sung by the choir at the great entrance of the officiating priests with his assistants. The Psalm was sung antiphonally between the clergy officiating at the altar and the choir. Luther favored the return to the entire introductory Psalm (quamquam psalmos mallemus). In his order of 1526 he advocates the singing of an anthem or a German Psalm and gives as an example a setting of Psalm 34.[443] At the present time the Introit consists of an Antiphon, which is a Scripture passage expressing briefly the leading thought or theme of the day, and the verse or verses from the Introit Psalm, in harmony with the thought of the day. In order to distinguish this psalmody from that of the Jewish Church, the Introit is followed by the Gloria Patri or small doxology to the Holy Trinity. If the fundamental thought of the day shall be emphasized very strongly, the Antiphon and the Introitus may be repeated after the

---

443) 10, 235.

Gloria Patri, a feature which is especially effective on great festival days. The importance of the complete Introit for the full liturgy can hardly be overestimated, as is shown by the fact that many Sundays bear the names of the first word of the Latin Introit, e. g. Estomihi, Invocavit, Reminiscere, Jubilate, etc. This importance may be brought out still more strongly by having the Introit sung or chanted by a good choir, for which Lochner pleads. It enhances the impressiveness of the worship in a most remarkable way if this is done, and most city churches will find in their midst a sufficient number of trained voices that could do this very effectively. The Gloria Patri at the close will rise like a jubilant sacrifice of the lips to the throne of God, Rom. 16, 27; Eph. 3, 21; Phil. 4, 20; Rev. 1, 6.

With the Kyrie a new thought is introduced into the service. It is based upon Scriptures, Ps. 51, 1; 123, 3; Matt. 9, 27; 15, 22; 20, 30; Mark 10, 47; Luke 18, 35—43, and it is found in some of the earliest liturgies, as in that of St. James, St. Mark, and others. It is a plea for the removal of misery and suffering, a "confession of wretchedness to be borne as a consequence of sins now forgiven" (Jacobs). "The congregation, realizing its infirmity from indwelling sin, calls upon God for that grace which has been announced and offered in the Introit" (An Explanation of the Common Service). At the same time, it finds its one solace in the Lord of Mercy, who out of love of fallen mankind was made incarnate by the Holy Ghost and born of the virgin Mary at Bethlehem, and whose birth was hailed and acclaimed with the victorious shouting of the multitude of the heavenly host.

This sequence of thought is brought out in a very striking manner by the Gloria in excelsis, Luke 2, 14, which now follows. The introduction of this hymnus angelicus into the order of service is ascribed to Bishop Telesphorus of Rome, about 126 A. D. Athanasius states that the hymn, with its stately extension Ainoumen se, Laudamus Te, was sung by the virgins as a morning hymn, and it is found complete in the Apostolic Constitutions.[444]) Of the first part of the hymn Luther says truly: "It did not grow, nor was it made on earth; it came down from heaven," but the last part, regardless of the author of the addition, is such a sublime doxology, such a rich outburst of praise and thanksgiving in honor of the Father in the glory of the creation and reconciliation, in adoration of the Son as the Redeemer, and in magnification of the Triune God in the fulness of His majesty, that the entire hymn represents practically a unit of surpassing power and loveliness. The versification of this hymn by Decius, "All glory be to God on high," and that of Luther, "All praise and glory be to

---

444) Book VII, § 47.

God," may be substituted on smaller festivals and in week-day services, but the intonation by the pastor should never be omitted.

The first part of the service, the psalmody, with petition, prayer, and praise, now having been concluded, the second part of the service, the Application of the Word, begins. According to ancient usage, the new liturgical division is introduced with the Salutation, Judg. 6, 12, Ruth 2, 4, and the Response of the congregation, 2 Tim. 4, 22. It is an exchange of greetings found in the early Greek liturgies. Pastor and congregation extend to each other the wish and prayer for the presence of the Lord to fill their hearts, minds, and spirits with true devotion for prayer and praise, for hearing the Word and receiving the Sacrament. On great festivals or upon other extraordinary occasions, the Salutation may be followed by a special Versicle, emphasizing the theme of the day. Hereupon follows the Collect, or several Collects on great feast days. The collects, as Neale points out,[445] are liturgical prayers; they must therefore be short, embrace but one main petition, consist of but one sentence, ask through the merits of the Lord, and end with praise to the blessed Trinity. The construction of the collect should be the following, according to the same authority: 1) Invocation, 2) Antecedent reason for petition, 3) Petition itself, 4) Benefit we hope to obtain, 5) Conclusion. The collects in the ancient Roman Sacramentaries, especially those of Gregory, are models in this respect. The collects which were produced under the influence of Pietism are usually the very opposite, full of bombastic phrases and platitudes. Much has been written in regard to the meaning of the collect. "It collects and concentrates the thought of Gospel and Epistle";[446] "collected by authority of Scriptures and used for reading in churches";[447] "prayers in which the wants and perils or wishes and desires of the whole people or Church are together presented to God."[448] The last explanation is that which is also quoted in the original Latin by Kliefoth[449] and is probably the best definition. The Collect represents the prayers of the people collected in a short form; it shows concentration of mind and singleness of purpose; it is brief and concise in form and Scriptural in content, pleading God's promises; it is congregational in use and application, voicing the needs of God's kingdom among men.[450] The congregation signifies its assent by an emphatic Amen.

Immediately after the Collect comes the reading of the Epistle. This has been the custom in the Church since the earliest times, Col. 4, 16. Justin and Tertullian bring evidence for the further de-

---

445) *Essays on Liturgiology*, II.
446) *Explanation of the Common Service.*   447) *Memoirs*, VI: 3.
448) Horn, *Outlines of Liturgics*, 73.
449) V, 28.   450) *Memoirs*, V: 5.

velopment of the system of readings. And the Apostolic Constitutions [451]) and the early liturgies show that readings from the Law and from the Prophets were in use beside the Pauline Epistles and the Gospels. Later, the lessons from the Old Testament were transferred to the minor services, especially to Vespers, the reading of the Psalms was fixed for the canonical hours, and the disadvantages of the lectio continua were removed by a system of pericopes whose father was Jerome. The Lutheran Church has retained the Epistle pericopes according to the ancient system. With all its faults, which Luther freely points out, the advantages are so great for both pastor and people that the practise should not be discontinued. At the same time, the new pericopes which have been selected both abroad and here (Eisenach, Synodical Conference, etc.) may well be chosen in alternate years. The chanting of the lessons is no longer in general use and it is doubtful whether it would be wise to reintroduce it, in spite of the earnest efforts of Lochner and other liturgiologists. While it may readily be granted that a dramatic recital of the lessons is not the proper thing for the church services, it must also be conceded, on the other hand, that the chanting of a long passage requires much ability and more practise, and even then tends to be monotonous. The lessons are a form of proclaiming the Word and should be treated accordingly.

At the end of the Epistle, the congregation answers with a joyful Hallelujah, praising the Lord for the unspeakable gift contained in His Word. It is at this point in the services that the graduals, sequences, proses, tracts, hymns or tropes were inserted, which were discussed in a previous chapter. If a congregation have a good choir, proper sequences may be sung after the Hallelujah. So far as other choir music is concerned, its most fitting position is here, but it must be in harmony with the thought of the day. "Special music at any other place in the service should be discontinued." [452])

The reading of the Gospel has always received special liturgical consideration in the service. The announcement of the reading is hailed with the sentence "Glory be to Thee, O Lord," and the "Praise be to Thee, O Christ" at the close signifies the grateful acceptance of the Word by the congregation. The congregation has seen, with the eyes of faith, the Word of God Incarnate, and its sentence of glory rises up to the throne of grace. It seems almost self-evident that the liturgist will turn to the congregation during the reading of the lessons. And since the fact that the congregation should be able to hear the Word is essential, it would seem advisable for all congregations to have a lectern on the side of the chancel opposite the pulpit, in

---

451) II, §§ 39. 57.   452) *Explanation of the Common Service*, 35.

order that the pastor may be nearer to the congregation at this important point in the liturgy.

After the Gospel comes the Creed, the proper Creed for the chief service being the Nicene Creed. Its use in the service may be traced back to 488 or even 476 A. D., when Peter the Fuller, Patriarch of Antioch, introduced it. The custom entered Europe by way of Spain, in 589 A. D. It was used in Rome under Benedict VIII in 1014. Luther retained its use for the chief service and transcribed it into verse-form for the German order. The Apostolic Creed is the Creed of Baptism, but may be used in minor services. It is especially effective if the pastor intones the Credo and the entire congregation sings or chants the Creed as its confession, based upon the reading of the Gospel which has gone before, and voicing the fundamental rule or confession of faith before all men.

After the Creed, a hymn which should be chosen with reference to the thought of the day, prepares for the Sermon. Its position at the climax of the homiletical part needs no apology or defense in the Lutheran Church. The principle of Luther that it is better neither to sing nor to pray nor to come together if the Word is not preached, is subscribed to without question to this day, wherever the spirit of Luther is still to be found. When we come to that point that special music is emphasized and the subject of the sermon is inserted into the so-called program (?) with an apology, to which is added the promise that it will be only a short talk of no more than 10—15 minutes, we shall cease to have a mission as a church. The Sermon closes with the Votum, Phil. 4, 7.

With the Sermon, the homiletical part of the service has reached its climax. But the third section of this group is also of no little importance, since it brings the sacrificial element of the congregation's attitude toward the Word, in the question of the proper application of the principles of sanctification. In the Offertory, Ps. 51, 17—19. 10—12, the assembled congregation confesses its grateful and humble acceptance of the Word which has just been proclaimed, all the faithful offering themselves, their substance, and the sacrifices of prayer, praise, and thanksgiving to the Lord. The Word has been appropriated by them and has become effective in them. It is hardly necessary to affirm that the Lutheran Offertory has absolutely nothing in common with the oblation of the Mass which is practised by the Roman Church at this point. Even the Offering of Gifts, which in most churches takes place during the Offertory or during a Voluntary or Hymn immediately following it, has nothing in common with any oblation in the Romish sense. It is merely a free-will offering for the Church, its missions, and all other enterprises.

The General Prayer of the Common Service is a splendid example of concise and still complete statement of petition. It is taken from the Strassburg Order of 1598, and in its chief parts has been traced back to 1553. It is a model prayer according to the apostolic injunction that supplications, prayers, intercessions, and giving of thanks be made for all men, 1 Tim. 2, 1. 2.. The General Prayer is very properly concluded with the Lord's Prayer, as containing the petitions for all spiritual and temporal wants, for all time. A hymn of praise and adoration is next sung by the congregation, thus ending the Office of the Word. If there is no communion, the Doxology and the Benediction are used, and the congregation leaves the house of worship after silent prayer.

As a rule, however, the Holy Supper should be celebrated in the chief service. As an introduction to this solemn service, a hymn is sung which expresses the earnest expectation and devotion of the believers with reference to the Eucharist. During the singing of this hymn, the pastor comes to the altar and arranges the sacred vessels with their contents in their proper place, the ciborium and the paten with the proper number of wafers on the left side, and the flagons and the chalice with the wine on the right hand side. At the close of the hymn, the first part of the service of the Holy Communion is begun, the Preface. The Salutation and Response are sung to indicate the opening of a new part of the service. The Prefatory Sentences, Sursum, and Gratias are held in an elevated tone, in conformity with the solemnity of the occasion. And then comes the impressive, beautiful Preface proper. The simple Preface was in use in the Liturgy of St. James and may have a still greater antiquity. In the fourth century, Prefaces were composed for all the festivals and their seasons, which are now called Proper Prefaces. They are Eucharistic Prayers of thanksgiving of singular beauty, seeming to gain, with every new sentence, in joyful cadence until each one reaches its culmination in the burst of triumphant melody on the part of the congregation, the Hymnus seraphicus or Sanctus, Is. 6, 3; Ps. 118, 26. Its first part is heaven's hymn of praise, its second is earth's hymn of praise, and both together form such an exalted strain of glorification and thanksgiving that the soul is transported to taste some of the joy of the great Beyond. The second part of the hymn, usually called the Benedictus, resolves the whole Sanctus into a hymn of praise to Christ as God, John 12, 41. The Exhortation, after Luther and Volprecht of Nuernberg, 1525, makes a break in the liturgical service and may fitly be omitted, especially as there should always be a preparatory service for those that wish to partake of Holy Communion.

The second part of the Communion service proper is the Administration, which is opened with the chanting of the Lord's Prayer. Of this prayer Cyprian properly said: "What prayer can be more spiritual than that which was given us by Christ, by whom also the Holy Spirit was sent? What petition more true before the Father than that which came from the lips of His Son, who is the Truth?" It should be noted, however, that it is not a prayer of consecration at this point, on the order of the Invocation or Epiklesis of the Eastern Church. But since the praying of the Lord's Prayer was always considered a peculiar privilege of believers, who alone can pray it in spirit and in truth, it was considered especially fitting before the meal which is a confession and declaration of union and communion between believers. By reciting it, they become conscious of their adoption and feel that they may come to the Lord as fellow-members of the same body.

Immediately after the Lord's Prayer follow the Words of Institution, taken verbally from the Gospels, without transcriptions and additions. These words teach the sacramental use, the sacramental presence, the sacramental benefit, and the sacramental institution. Since they are the words of administration, they are also very properly the words of consecration. It is by means of these words, taken from Scriptures themselves, that the bread and the wine on the altar are set apart for sacred use and the eating and drinking is distinguished from ordinary use, becoming a Sacrament. It is necessary, therefore, that the liturgist speak or chant the words with a loud and distinct voice, to distinguish the pure Sacrament from the abomination of the Mass, where the Secreta as well as the Words of Institution are murmured and in places whispered. The celebration in the Lutheran Church is that of the congregation, and the pastor is merely acting in their stead, as the steward over God's mysteries. At the close of the consecration, the pastor turns to the congregation and chants the Pax, Luke 24, 30; John 20, 19—21; Rom. 16, 16; 1 Pet. 5, 14. It is the greeting of the risen Lord to the believers who are about to partake of His holy body and blood.

As the pastor turns back to the altar, the congregation chants the Agnus Dei, John 1, 29, during which the communicants begin to come forward. The Lamb of God who, by His vicarious sacrifice, gained a complete redemption for us, is implored to grant His mercy and His peace to those that are now partakers of His heavenly meal. The Agnus Dei is an ancient morning hymn, which has been in use in the Church since early times and inserted into the communion service by Sergius I (687—700). The distribution is made with the words: Take and eat, this is the body of Christ, given for thee; Take and drink, this is the blood of the New Testament, shed for thy sins. On account of Reformed errors, the word "true" was inserted before "body" and "blood" by liturgiologists at the end of the 16th century.

It serves as an emphatic assertion, especially in places and circumstances where such a confession is necessary to prevent the intrusion of false ideas.

The third part of the Communion service, the Postcommunion, is ushered in with the exalted strains of the Nunc dimittis, Luke 2, 29—32. The believer, having received the fulness of God's grace and mercy, having partaken of the body and blood of his Savior, and having thus seen the salvation of the Lord, feels that he may now depart in peace. The Nunc dimittis is fitly closed with the Gloria Patri, the doxology being due to the Triune God for the manifestations of mercy, glory, and power. The Thanksgiving Collect, preceded by the Thanksgiving Versicle, as found in Psalms 105, 106, 107, 118, 136 is then chanted. It expresses the heartfelt gratitude of the believer for the benefits he has received and asks for the further manifestation of sanctifying grace.

The service closes with the Benedicamus, the Salutation and Response, and the Versicle of Benediction, Ps. 41, 13; 72, 18. 19; 89, 52; 106, 48; 150, 6. It is a joyful heart's cry: Bless the Lord, O my soul, and forget not all His benefits. The congregation is dismissed with the Aaronic Blessing, Num. 6, 24—26. This is not a mere pious wish, but the actual imparting of the blessing of the Triune God to the believers, who may now go down into their houses justified, rejoicing in the goodness of the Lord. This is emphasized by the final Amen of the congregation.[453])

CHAPTER 2.

The Minor Services: Vespers, Matins, and Confession.

The canonical hours were observed by the Church at a very early date, those in the Orient being the following: *Mesonyktion* or Nocturnum, at midnight; Matina (Matutinum and Laudes), at 3 A. M.; Prime, at 6 A. M.; Terce, combined with the Typikon, at 9 A. M.; Sext, at 12 noon; Nones, at 3 P. M.; Vespers (combined with Vigils before fasts), at 6 P. M.; Completorium, at 9 P. M. The number eight in this connection was based upon Neh. 9, 3. The Western Church having at all times had a predilection for the mystical number seven, preferred to have only seven canonical hours, the Noctur-

---

453) For the entire discussion, cp. *Memoirs*, I: 3; V, 6; *An Explanation of the Common Service*, 19—68; Lochner, *Der Hauptgottesdienst*, 80—277; Kliefoth, *Die urspruengliche Gottesdienstordnung*, V, 1—135; Schuette, *Before the Altar*, 48—77; Fuerbringer, *Leitfaden, Liturgik*, 11—25; Horn, *Outlines of Liturgies*, 32—90; Alt, *Der kirchliche Gottesdienst*, 483—512; *Public Worship in the Lutheran Church*, by A. G., in *Theol. Quart.*, I, 37 ff.

num being combined wither with the Completorium or with Matins and Lauds. The Breviary contains the prayers and Psalms for these services, whether they be held as Officia publica, in monasteries and cathedral churches, or as Officia privata, which all members of the clergy, being canonici and therefore under the canon, are obliged to keep.

The nature of the services and the circumstances of every-day life soon made it necessary to reduce the number of services for the general public during the week to two hours of devotion, Matins and Vespers. On Sundays, Vigils, Matins, and Prime together became Early Mass, Terce and Sext were combined for the chief service, and Nones and Vespers were united for the afternoon service. The people then had sufficient opportunity to attend services, and all occasion for offense was removed. This state of affairs continued till the 16th century.

The Lutheran reformers, with Luther as their leader, many of whom had been inmates of monasteries, retained the service of the canonical hours, especially Matins and Vespers. The service now known as Matins or Morning Prayer is a combination of Matins, Lauds, and Prime, that which is called Vespers or Evensong is a union of Vespers and Compline. For both of these services Luther and his coworkers, as well as the liturgiologists till the end of the century, retained the four major parts: Hymnody, Psalmody, Lessons, Prayers, as well as the so-called minor parts: at Matins the Invitatory with the Venite, and at Matins and Vespers both the Versicles, Antiphons, and Responsories. The ancient order of Matins had been: Pater Noster, Ave Maria, Credo, Invitatory, Venite exultemus, Hymn, Nocturn (of twelve Psalms, recited two and two together, under one antiphon), — in double festivals the antiphons are doubled —, Farced Lections (insertion of Kyrie eleison, Tropes), Nocturns end with Verse and Response, Lord's Prayer, Absolutions, Benedictions. The Lections or Homilies were taken from the Church fathers for use in the Nocturns. The Te Deum, which really indicated the close of Matins, was followed immediately by Lauds, which contained the following parts: Psalm 93 and 100, 63 and 67 under one Gloria, Benedicite, a short Chapter, Hymn, Versicle and Response, Benedictus, Collect for the Day. At Vespers, the order was much the same: Pater Noster, four or five Psalms, each under its own Antiphon, short Chapter, Hymn, Verse and Response, Magnificat with its proper Antiphon and Collect. In Advent and Lent, the closed seasons, the Preces and Psalm 51 were used after the Magnificat.[454] Luther retained all that was not in itself wrong, but

454) Neale, *Essays on Liturgiology*, I.

shortened both services so as to have three lessons in each, with the proper Responsories, the Old Testament lessons being commended for use in the morning and the New Testament lessons in the evening.[455]

In proposing the retention of these additional or supplementary (not subsidiary) services, Luther acted with his customary conservatism, carefulness, and tact. He says, in his Formulae Missae of 1523: "On work-days, I see nothing that might not be suffered, but that the Masses be abrogated. For the Matins of three lessons and the horae canonicae, Vespers and Compline de tempore, excepting on the great festivals, are nothing but words of Holy Scriptures, and it is a good thing, yea, necessary that the boys become used to reading and hearing the Psalms, and whatever other lessons are read from Scriptures. But if something new should be introduced here, the long chanting might be changed according to the discretion of the pastor, in this way that three Psalms be sung at Matins and three at Vespers, with one or two Responses. . . For this reason lessons must be prescribed to be read daily: one early from the New or Old Testament, the other in the afternoon, whether it be from the Old or New Testament, with a short explanation of that lesson in a known language." [456] And in the Deutsche Mess of 1526 he writes: "Early at five or six at Matins a few Psalms are sung. Then the Epistle of the day is preached, chiefly for the sake of the servants, that they also be supplied and hear the Word of God, in case they could not be present in other services. Then an Antiphon and the Te Deum laudamus or Benedictus antiphonally with the Lord's Prayer, Collect, and Benedicamus Domino. . . . In the afternoon, at Vespers, before the Magnificat, the Old Testament is preached in due order." [457] He then explains his plan in detail, especially as to the necessity of instruction in the Catechism and in the Word of God by systematic reading and exposition.[458] Thus Luther, and his coworkers with him, emphasized the element of instruction from the Word of God as the most essential part in the services.

In recent years, the American Lutheran Church has paid more attention to the additional services. And the result is highly satisfactory, both from an aesthetic and artistic and from a devotional point of view. In city churches, where the majority of the people live near the house of worship, the introduction of such services should redound to great benefit. In schools, colleges, and seminaries it is a matter of feasibility and expediency at the same time. The fact that the principal Psalms and the chief parts of Scriptures that may be read in public are thus taken through in the course of a year, makes

---

455) Horn, 136.   456) 10, 2253. 2254.
457) 10, 233.   458) 10, 234, §§ 22—25.

the introduction of the ancient services highly desirable. And the chances are that a closer acquaintance with the beautiful contents of the services will awaken and maintain both interest in them and love for them.

The service of Matins opens with the Versicles Domine labia (O Lord, open Thou my lips), Ps. 51, 15, and the Deus in adjutorium (Make haste, O God, to deliver me) Ps. 70, 1. Both the praising of the Lord for the gifts of the day and the supplicating for their gracious vouchsafing are expressed in these opening sentences. And the Gloria Patri addresses the prayer to the Triune God, whose praise is expressed in the Hallelujah, and faith in whose willingness to help is confessed in the Amen.

Immediately after the opening the Invitatory, Ps. 95, 6, is chanted, with the Venite, Ps. 95, 1—7, added. This Psalm is always used at Matins with the Invitatory, having been in use in that capacity since ancient times. Even if other Psalms (1—109) are chanted in order in the course of about a month, this Psalm always forms a part of the worship. It was introduced for the use of Matins by Pope Damasus (died 384).

After a Hymn, which should express the central thought of the season or the day, has been sung, the Psalms are read or chanted, those from 1 to 109, as noted above, being used in Matin services. Each Psalm has an Antiphon preceding and following it as an Invitatory, which should also conform to the character of the season. The Gloria Patri is sung after every Psalm. After the Psalms come the Lessons which are chosen so that every part of Scripture suitable for public reading is used in the course of the year. The lectio continua will follow a Comes which will embrace every book of the Bible. After each Lesson the Response "But Thou, O Lord, have mercy," is sung or said.

After this follows either a Hymn or the Responsory, the latter serving to connect the Lessons with the church year. It is in the form of a farced verse with a short Gloria Patri. The Responsory is in use since ancient times, since it is mentioned by Gregory of Tours (died 595) and Isidore of Seville (died 636).

The Sermon, which comes next, was introduced according to the maxim of Luther in regard to the necessity of the instruction in the Word of God. After the Sermon, which will be in the nature of a homiletic discussion or brief exposition, comes the Canticle Te Deum laudamus, whose authorship was formerly ascribed to St. Ambrose. Instead of this canticle the Benedictus may be sung, with which is usually connected an Antiphon. Under circumstances, the Athanasian Creed, often called the Hymn of St. Athanasius concerning the Holy Trinity, or the Psalm Quicunque vult, may be substituted.

The Prayers are next in order, consisting of the Kyrie, a cry over the misery and distress of fallen mankind, but also of faith in the merciful help of the Lord, the Lord's Prayer, and the Collects. So far as the latter are concerned, either the Collect for the Day or that for Grace may be used. To give proper variety to the services, the Suffrages or the Litany, of which Luther thought so highly, may be inserted here. The service closes, like the chief service, with the Benedicamus, followed by the Benediction of St. Paul, 2 Cor. 13, 14.

The services at Vespers have the same general order as Matins, the main difference being that the Hymnody precedes the Prayers. In the evening the faithful Christian first of all seeks for forgiveness, the assurance of God's mecry after the work of the day, and then praises Him for all His goodness and commends his soul to the Lord for safe keeping during the night. There is no Invitatory nor Invitatory Psalm. The Canticles of Vespers are the Magnificat, Luke 1, 46—55, and the Nunc dimittis, Luke 2, 29—32, both of which have been in use in the Church since the early centuries, the latter being mentioned in the Apostolic Constitutions. The Collect at the end of Vespers is the beautiful Collect for Peace, preceded by the Versicle "The Lord will give strength unto His people." The peace of God, which passeth all understanding, is the last thought of the Christian, wherewith he commends his soul into the hands of his heavenly Father for the night.[459]

A service which is characteristic of the Lutheran Church is the service of Confession, held either on Saturday evening (Beicht-Vesper) or on Sunday morning just before services, preparatory to the communion service. So long as private confession was still practised, for 250 to 300 years, the need of a special congregational service was not so great. But since the period of liturgical deterioration, this old beneficial custom has fallen into disuse, and it seems impossible to arouse the necessary interest in America for its reintroduction. In a measure, at least, we have a substitute for the ancient custom in the present usage of personal announcements for Holy Communion. The service itself is very simple in character. After a hymn of confession and repentance, a Versicle or appropriate Prayer is read by the pastor, followed by a short address to the communicants. The General Confession is then spoken and the Absolution pronounced, the service closing with a Hymn expressing the faith of the congregation in the certainty of the absolution and the mercy of the Lord.[460]

---

459) Cp. *Explanation of the Common Service*, 71—91; Horn, *Outlines of Liturgics*, 133—139; Kliefoth, *Die urspruengliche Gottesdienstordnung*, V, 164—199; *Memoirs*, II: 5.

460) Cp. Kliefoth, *Liturgische Abhandlungen*, II: Beichte und Absolution; *Memoirs*, VI: 5.

CHAPTER 3.

Liturgical Forms for Occasional Sacred Acts.

The Lutheran Church is justly proud of the beauty of its occasional acts, not only of the forms which are the heritage of the ages, having merely been cleansed of the various false and dangerous additions and excrescences which had accumulated under the influence of false doctrines, but also of those which have been composed or compiled by well-trained Lutheran liturgiologists in the past 400 years. The influence of these sanely conservative and eminently chaste forms has extended even beyond the denominational boundaries, being freely acknowledged by critics that may be considered exceptionally competent in this field.

The most ancient form for occasional acts in the Christian Church is that for Baptism. Of the manner of application in apostolic times, and of the ceremonies accompanying the act of baptizing, we know nothing beyond the simple account of Scriptures. The rite of Baptism was performed with water in the name of the Father, and of the Son, and of the Holy Ghost, Matt. 28, 19; Acts 2, 41. At the time of the Didache the form of Baptism was still very simple, for the regulation reads: "Concerning Baptism, baptize thus: Having first rehearsed all these things, 'baptize in the name of the Father, and of the Son, and of the Holy Spirit,' in running water; but if thou hast no running water, baptize in other water, and if thou canst not in cold, then in warm. But if thou hast neither, pour water three times on the head 'in the name of the Father, Son, and Spirit'." [461] This passage is interesting, not only on account of its great antiquity, but also on account of the fact that is presents one of the oldest proofs for a mode of Baptism by other methods than immersion. Justin Martyr's account also describes a very simple rite: "Then [after proper instruction] they are brought by us to a place where there is water, and are regenerated in the same manner as we also were regenerated. For in the name of God the Father and Lord of the universe, and of our Lord Jesus Christ, and of the Holy Ghost, they then receive Baptism with water." [462] In the Apostolic Constitutions the formula is much longer. It embraces the following parts: Renunciation, Creed, Anointing, Benediction of Water, Act of Baptism, Imposition of Hands, Lord's Prayer, Prayer of Thanksgiving. According to Tertullian,[463] the ceremonies of Baptism included: Invocation of the Holy Ghost and Benediction of the Water, Renunciation, Immersion (threefold), Creed, Anointing, Imposition of Hands.

---

461) Lake, *The Apostolic Fathers*, 319. 320; Cabrol, *Monumenta*, 52.
462) *First Apology*, Chapter XLI. 463) *De corona*, III.

In the early centuries, the ceremony of Baptism was performed principally for adults and the forms and descriptions which are extant from the early days have the baptismus adultorum in mind. It was only gradually that the baptismus clinicorum paved the way for a general baptismus parvulorum. This does not by any means imply that paedobaptism was unknown, just as the fact' that immersion was generally practised does not exclude and invalidate the administration of the Sacrament by a different mode. Paedobaptism was in use before the middle of the 3d century, as the testimony of Irenaeus, Origen, Fideus, and others shows,[464) and was practised within the congregations. But the Baptism which is most commonly mentioned and described is the Baptism of adult proselytes. Their Baptism was not a matter of a short ceremony, but included a number of steps, commonly under three heads: *christianous poiein, katechoumenous poiein, exorkizein,* extending over a certain length of time. During this season of preparation, the candidates were obliged to submit to various scrutinia, among which may be mentioned the impositio manuum, the oratio super electos, the gustus salis, the exorcismus, the Ephphatah ceremony, the abrenuntiatio, and finally the symbolum or confession of the Creed. The Baptism itself included: 1) Benedictio fontis, 2) Consecratio fontis, 3) Signum crucis, 4) Demissio cerei in aquam, 5) Infusio de chrismate, 6) Symbolum, 7) Immersio, 8) Signatur in cerebro de chrismate, 9) Datio Spiritus septiformis, 10) Signatio in fronte.[465) It was not long before the ceremonies of the catechumenate were combined with those of Baptism, the usages Christianum facere, catechumenum facere, and exorcizare taking place at the door or in the atrium, and the ceremonies of sabbatorum die mane with abrenuntiatio and symbolum, as well as Baptism proper, inside the church.

The ritual of Baptism remained practically unchanged throughout the Middle Ages. According to the Agenda Moguntinensis of 1513, the following parts belonged to the Ordo ad baptizandum pueros: I. Introduction, ad januas ecclesiae: Inquiry after name, Small Exorcism, Sign of Cross and Prayer, Gustus salis and Pax with Prayer, Great Exorcism, the Lessons, Pater Noster with Ave Maria and Apostolic Creed, Ephphata ceremony, Entrance into church; II. Rite of Baptism: Abrenuntiatio, Credo, Anointing (in pectore, inter scapulas in modum crucis), Admonition to sponsors, Baptism (with child's head pointing to east, north, and south respectively at the three infusions), Prayer of Thanksgiving, Clothing in Chrisom or White Robe.[466) A similar order of baptismal ceremonies is given by Hoef-

---

464) Gibbons, *The Faith of Our Fathers,* 308. 309.
465) Hoefling, *Das Sakrament der Taufe,* I, 450.
466) Daniel, *Codex liturgicus,* I, 183—188.

ling.[467]) Other ceremonies that were found in some ordines were the Kiss of Brotherhood or Peace, Placing of a Lighted Taper into the Hand of the Child, and others. The ceremonies of the two exorcisms, the gustus salis, and the infusio de chrismate, were those whose significance was emphasized very strongly. In fact, as Gwynne says (Chapter XXVIII), these ceremonies became so elaborate as to obscure Baptism itself.

In spite of this fact, however, Luther retained the ceremonies in his first compilation of the Order of Baptism, for they were not essentially wrong or damnable. Luther's first attempt at a German order is his "Taufbuechlein verdeutscht" of 1523. It was in substance nothing but a translation of the liturgy of Baptism as then in use at Wittenberg. It contains the Small Exorcism, Signum crucis with Prayers, Gustus salis with "flood" Prayer, Large Exorcism with Prayer and Pax, Lesson Mark 10, Lord's Prayer, Ephphata Ceremony, Ingression; Abrenuntiatio, Credo, Act of Baptism, Anointing (cross on head), Clothing with Chrisom, Placing of Lighted Taper in Hand.[468]) After Luther had issued a second short order or outline of liturgy for Baptism, in which he omitted some of the ceremonies upon which the Papists had placed so much stress,[469]) he came out in 1526 with an order which discarded all the usages that were in any way connected with superstition. But he retained the division into two parts. His order included: Small Exorcism, Sign of Cross with Prayer for Mercy and "flood" Prayer, Large Exorcism, Lesson from Mark, Lord's Prayer, Ingression to baptismal font; Renunciation and Creed, Act of Baptism, Putting on Chrisom, and Final Prayer.[470])

Most of the Lutheran Church Orders adopted the form of 1526. The Saxon of 1539 inserted the Admonition to the Sponsors at the beginning of the second part,[471]) that of Cologne of 1543 placed the Admonition to Parents and Sponsors at the beginning of the entire ceremony, concluding this on the second day. Many forms soon omitted the exsufflation, the signation, and the exorcism. They all agree, however, in retaining the division into two parts, and the most prominent Church Orders have the admonition to the sponsors at the end, since it is not an integral part of the ceremony. The questions are usually addressed to the child, the sponsors being expressly asked to answer in the name of the infant. The tendency in our days is toward abbreviation of the liturgy, but it is to be hoped that the

---

467) *Das Sakrament der Taufe,* II.
468) 10, 2136—2143; Sehling, *Die evangelischen Kirchenordnungen des 16. Jahrhunderts,* I, 19. 20.
469) 10, 2134—2137.   470) 10, 2144—2147.
471) Sehling, I, 266. 267; Daniel, II, 208—214.

prayers and the lesson will be retained, as well as the introduction, not only because they are hallowed by centuries of sacred associations, but also because they represent the most perfect efforts of our Church's best liturgiologists.[472]

Closely connected, liturgically speaking, with the Sacrament of Baptism is the rite of Confirmation. In the early Church, Confirmation was the concluding ceremony of the rites connected with Baptism, being, in effect, the acknowledgment of the catechumens that had been baptized during the baptismal seasons (especially Easter and Pentecost), as full members of the congregation, and entitled to receive Holy Communion. The rite of anointing and the imposition of hands which signified this public admission into congregation membership later developed into an independent ceremony which could be performed by the bishop only. The rite of Confirmation, according to the Pontificale Romanum, includes the following parts: Spiritus S. superveniat. . . ., Adjutorium nostrum . . . ., Oremus: Sempiterne Omnipotens . . . ., Signo te signo crucis et confirmo te chrismate salutis . . . ., (in maxilla caedit) Pax tecum . . ., Confirmo hoc Deus . . ., Ostende nobis Domine . . . ., Oremus . . . ., Benedicat vos . . . . The secondary liturgical customs are: Clothing in white garments, girdling with zona, crowning with corona or cappa, giving of burning candle, lotio pedum, giving of milk and honey, osculum pacis.[473] Confirmation was formally declared to be a sacrament at Lyons in 1274 and at Florence in 1439. Pope Eugene IV (1431—47) confirmed the entire rite in his bull "Exultate."

To Luther, Confirmation was at first an abomination, because it had been declared a sacrament. His opposition to it, which he voiced in his book "Of the Babylonian Captivity," [474] permitting it to be called no more than a "sacramental ceremony," and expressed also in a letter to Nicolaus Hausmann, dated March 14, 1524,[475] influenced his coworkers, and is found in the Lutheran confessions.[476] For these reasons, Luther did not compile a form for Confirmation, and most of the early Church Orders omit the rite entirely. At the Ratisbon Colloquium, Melanchthon, Bucer, and Pistorius proposed the rite as a good observance. In the General Articles for Electoral Saxony only the thorough indoctrination of the children is urged be-

---

472) Cp. Hoefling, *Das Sakrament der Taufe;* Schuette, *Before the Altar,* 31—37; Jacobs, *The Lutheran Movement in England,* Chapter XXI; Loehe, *Haus-, Schul- und Kirchenbuch,* II, 250; *Memoirs,* III: 11.

473) Hoefling, I; Daniel, *Codex liturgicus,* I, 200—208.

474) 19, 90. 91.   475) 21a, 600.

476) Apologia. Art. de Numero et Usu Sacramentorum, § 6; Articuli Smalc. Tract. de Potestate et Primatu Papae, § 73. Mueller, 203. 342.

fore admitting them to the Eucharist. The Strassburg Order of 1534 has similar directions, that of Cassel of 1539 has an Order for Confirmation or Imposition of Hands. The Wittenberg Reformation of 1545 advocated an evangelical use of the ceremony. Chemnitz devoted an entire Locus to Confirmation, mentioning the following parts: 1) Indoctrination; 2) Admonition, renunciation, and confession of faith; 3) By catechumen: personal profession of doctrine of faith; 4) Thorough examination; 5) Admonition that this implies dissent from all false teaching; 6) Exhortation to persevere; 7) Public prayer. The Lutheran Church has adhered to these principles, dividing the act of Confirmation into three parts: 1) Examination; 2) Profession and vow; 3) Prayer with imposition of hands.[477]

Without in any way considering the fact that the Roman Church introduced a number of false doctrines regarding Holy Matrimony, the rite itself, as in use at the beginning of the 16th century, was in need of revision, in order to remove various false sentences and wrong questions. The formula for the solemnization of holy marriage at that time had two parts, the rite of giving in marriage taking place at the door or in the vestibule, and the Mass with sacrifice for the bridal couple in the church. The Ordo ad matrimonium sollenniter celebrandum of 1587 has the following parts: 1) Ad fores ecclesiae: Questions in regard to obstacles (forbidding the bans), the act of marriage with ring ceremony and prayer; 2) In ecclesia: Mass with prayers over the wedded, benediction.[478] This is the form which had been in use for centuries and, in its essential parts, is in use to-day.

In his "Traubuechlein fuer die einfaeltigen Pfarrherren" of 1534 Luther retained the division of the formula into two parts. After the proclamation the act of giving in marriage was performed "before the church," with the ring ceremony. In the church, "before the altar," the Scripture lessons with regard to holy matrimony were read, and the service closed with benediction and prayer.[479] This order for the solemnization of holy matrimony was generally accepted or regarded as fundamental. Some of the Church Orders, indeed, made the bipartite division of the form more prominent by having the two parts take place on separate days. But the text and the order of the several parts of the formula remained, even after the external division was no longer observed and the entire ceremony took place before the altar. The joining in matrimony came first, then the reading of the lessons, and finally the benediction. Thus the orders of Calenberg of

---

477) Cp. Hoefling, I and II; Jacobs, Chapter XXII; *Memoirs*, III: 2; Schuette, 38—40; Loehe, II, 259; Kliefoth, *Liturgische Abhandlungen*, III; *Lehre und Wehre*, 1905, Feb. Mrz; *Hom. Mag.*, 1910, II ff.

478) Daniel, *Codex liturgicus*, II, 262—265.

479) 10, 723—725; Sehling, I, 23. 24.

1569, of Electoral Saxony of 1580,[480]) of Osnabrueck of 1588, and others. The idea was that the Word concerning the institution of holy matrimony should follow the act of joining in marriage in a confirmatory capacity, and the other lessons should precede the benediction as fundamental for the proper understanding of the obligations of marriage.[481]) But since it cannot be denied that there is an element of abruptness about the rite in this form, aside from the fact that natural sequence of thought would seem to demand that the Scriptural doctrine be stated first, as an introduction to the ceremony, other Church Orders preferred to place the lessons first, then the giving in marriage, then the benediction. This sequence seemed more logical to the Order of Brandenburg of 1540, of Lueneburg of 1598 and 1643, of Pommerania of 1568, and of Wuerttemberg. In America, the form of questions to the copulands as given by Luther is generally employed, though the form of the Book of Common Prayer, in an abbreviated wording, is also in use.[482])

So far as Ordination is concerned, Luther could not and would not sanction the form which was in use for the consecration of priests and all other members of the clergy, since it implied the assenting to various false and blasphemous doctrines. He gave the reasons for his position in his book "Of the Babylonian Captivity." [483]) In the Smalcald Articles he also states the truth on the basis of Scriptures and on historical grounds.[484]) For this reason, the form of Ordination which Luther adopted and which was used so extensively in Wittenberg, had nothing in common with the Roman ordo for the consecration of a priest. Luther's form is given as follows: Hymn Veni Creator Spiritus; Collect; the Lessons of Ordination: Acts 13, 3; 20, 29; 1 Tim. 3, 1 ff.; Titus 1, 6; Questions addressed to the ordinand; Admonition and Lord's Prayer; Prayer and Benediction; Hymn Nun bitten wir den Heilgen Geist.[485]) The essential features of this form have been included in most Lutheran formulas, the only difference being that the questions to the ordinand are longer and enumerate more of the pastor's duties. In many formulas an admonition addressed to the congregation is included, since an ordination or installation offers the best opportunity for broaching this subject and dealing with it more extensively than is done upon other occasions.[486])

---

480) Sehling, I, 366. 367.
481) Kliefoth, *Liturgische Abhandlungen*, I, 95.
482) Cp. Kliefoth, *Liturgische Abhandlungen*, I; Loehe, II, 86. 272; Schuette, 65—71; Jacobs, Chapter XXII.
483) 19, 109. 344.　　　　484) Mueller, 342.
485) 22, 647; *Agenda of Wittenberg of 1565;* Daniel, II, 517—522; Kliefoth, *Liturgische Abhandlungen*, I, 462. 463.
486) Cp. Schuette, 40. 41; Loehe, II, 292; Kliefoth, I; Sehling, I, 26.

There are numerous other liturgical acts for which forms have been compiled, such as the Visitation of the Sick, the Burial of the Dead, the Dedication of Churches, Schools, Organs, Bells, Altars and other Church Furniture, Cemeteries, Anniversaries of Marriage, Installation of Church Officers, and many others, for which the various Church Books and Agenda give appropriate and simple forms. The principle which governs every form of dedication is this that the use of Scripture consecrates and hallows all acts of this kind, and that every form of superstition and false doctrine must be kept away from things which are intended for the use of worship in the churches. The words of the apostle: "Let all things be done unto edifying. . . Let all things be done decently and in order," 1 Cor. 14, 26. 40; "It is sanctified by the Word of God and prayer," 1 Tim. 4, 5, must govern all these acts, so that their proper execution may redound to the glory of God and the edification of the Church.

CHAPTER 4.

The Symbolism of the Lutheran Cultus.

Divine worship in the Christian Church is not an *adiaphoron*. The Lord expressly commands that His Word be heard, John 8, 47. He has only severe censure for those who forsake the Christian assemblies, Heb. 10, 25. He expressly enjoins public prayer, 1 Tim. 2, 1. 2. 8. He graciously promises His divine presence at such assemblies, Matt. 18, 20. He records with approval the public services of the early Christians, Acts 2, 42—47.

But though He has prescribed the *general* content of public worship, though He is present in the sacramental acts of divine service, declaring and appropriating to the believers the means of grace, and though He graciously receives the sacrificial acts of the assembled congregation, in confession and prayer and offerings, He has not commanded a definite form or order of divine service. It is a matter of Christian liberty whether a congregation wishes one or many prayers, one or several hymns, one or two sermons or homilies, whether the chief assembly be held in the morning or in the evening, whether the service be held on Sunday or on a ferial day.

To argue from these facts, however, that it is a matter of complete indifference as to how the form of Christian worship is constituted would be bringing liberty dangerously near to license. The Lord says: "Let all things be done decently and in order," 1 Cor. 14, 40; and again: "Let all things be done unto edifying," v. 26. It cannot really be a matter of indifference to a Christian congregation

when the order of service used in her midst shows so much similarity
to a heterodox order as to confuse visitors. One may hardly argue
that such *adiaphora* do not matter one way or the other, when it has
happened that a weak brother has been offended. And a Lutheran
congregation cannot justly divorce herself, not only not from the doctrinal, but also not from the historical side of its Church. It is a
matter of expediency, as well as of charity and edification, that every
Lutheran pastor and every Lutheran congregation have outward significant symbols of the inner union, of the one mind and the one spirit.

In addition to these facts, there is the further consideration that
the outward acts of the Church, commonly known by the appellation
"the liturgy," have a very definite significance, which, in many cases,
renders the acts of public service true acts of confession of faith.
And the symbolism of many of the Lutheran sacred acts, if correctly
performed, is such that the beauty of these treasures of our Church
may be brought to the joyful attention of our congregations.

This is true especially of the morning worship in the Lutheran
Church, commonly known as The Service or The Communion. For
this is not, as some people have supposed, a haphazard combination
or a fortuitous conglomeration of heterogeneous material, but an artistic unit with definite and logical parts, a "spirituo-psychological,
well-ordered, and articulated whole," as Lochner says.[487] The order
of service is a beautiful work of art, presenting a gradual climax of
such wonderful dignity and impressiveness that the mere presence in
such a service should result in the edification of the faithful.

The service opens most appropriately with the Confession of sins.
There is no better explanation of this preparatory step than that
given by Augustine *In enarratione ad Psalm. CXIX,* when he writes:
"Intrate in portas eius in confessione. In portis initium est; a confessione incipite. Unde in alio psalmo dicitur: Incipite Domino in
confessione. Et quia? Quum iam intraverimus non confitebimur?
Semper confitere; semper habes quod confitearis." [488] Having made
his confession and having been given the first assurance of the forgiveness of God, the believer enters into the Lord's presence.

He is now greeted by, and, in most cases, takes part in, the Introit of the day. It makes him acquainted with the special character
and idea of the day, and he answers with the *Gloria Patri,* the confession of the coeternal Godhead of our Lord and the Holy Ghost with
the Father.

Standing now within the portals of the temple, the congregation
lifts up its voice in the *Kyrie.* This has been explained as follows:

---

487) *Der Hauptgottesdienst,* 41.
488) Daniel, *Codex liturgicus,* I, 23.

"The congregation, realizing its infirmity from indwelling sin, calls upon God for that grace which has been announced and offered in the Introit." [489] Since, however, such a confession at this point would interrupt the sequence of thought in the service, it is preferable to say with Horn [490] that "the *Kyrie* is not specifically a confession of sin, but a cry of need," and with Lochner [491], that the *Kyrie* is the common, humble confession of the entire misery and woe of the human race, on account of which God's only-begotten Son became man. For this wonderful deed Christ and the entire Godhead is then greeted and proclaimed in the *Gloria in excelsis,* the angels' hymn of glory, sung for the first time at Bethlehem and in use in the Church since the time of Hilarius Pictaviensis.

The words of humble entreaty and petition having now been spoken, and the sinner having been greeted with the assurance that his sins are fully and completely forgiven in and through Christ, to whom he has given joyful homage and adoration, he now joins with the entire congregation in the Collect. It will be well to quote Calvoer here, who writes of this prayer: "Praemittere solet sacerdos collectis: Oremus! Excitatur hoc ipso fidelis populus ad comprecandum devote, neque hoc solum, sed ut populus quoque sciat, quae sint sua et quae sint sacerdotis solius partes, ut quando simul orare, quando vero sacerdotis functionibus in sacro silentio attendere debeat. Legit enim minister ecclesiae, concionatur, consecrat eucharistiam, distribuit eam accedente verbo ad elementum, dimittit ecclesiam cum benedictione, in quibus coetus collectus non tam se habet active quam passive, non simul haec talia cum ministro peragens, sed recipiens haec sacra potius ab eodem, ipsa sacerdotalia mera relinquens. At in collectis, quum sint totius collectae aut coetus preces, jungit suam operam populus; quae cum omnia rite ac ordine peraguntur, acclamat sacerdos populo: Oremus!" [492] It is therefore entirely correct for an old Agenda to explain: "Collecta dicitur oratio, in qua sacerdos totius populi vel ecclesiae necessitates et pericula, seu vota et desideria, quasi collecta, Deo repraesentat; unde dicit: Oremus, quasi adstantes invitet ad hanc orationem adjunctis votis animisque faciendam." The Collect also serves to concentrate the thought of the Epistle and Gospel.

For now the Lord comes to the congregation in His Word. In the Epistle, which contains primarily doctrine and admonition, His apostles address the faithful, and in the Gospel the great signs and miracles of our Lord are proclaimed, or He speaks to us in His own

---

489) *Explanation of the Common Service,* 27. 28.
490) *Liturgics,* 61.   491) *L. c.,* 111.
492) In Kliefoth, *Die urspruengliche Gottesdienstordnung,* V, 29.

words. Very properly, therefore, the congregation stands before Him in meek and humble devotion, responding to the Epistle with the Hallelujah or a hymn embodying the great Gospel-news of the day, and to the Gospel with the recital of the Creed in chorus.

Having thus publicly stated their acceptance of the truth of God's Word, the faithful are prepared for the next great part of the service, the Sermon, with its application of the doctrines contained in the lessons *de tempore* to their hearts and minds. It is the first part of the great climax of the service, the recital of the wonderful deeds of God for the salvation of fallen mankind or the earnest admonition of the faithful to lead lives commensurate with the exalted state of the elect of Christ. The congregation answers with the Offertory or Offering, accepting the doctrines that have been proclaimed, and vowing faithfulness to the Lord with all their heart and soul.

It is a mistake to assume, with Kliefoth, that The Service is properly divided into the sacramental act of the Word and that of the Communion. The old Lutheran liturgists very properly called the whole service The Communion, and though the celebration of the Lord's Supper is, in a way, the culmination of the service, since only the actual adult members of the church are permitted to partake of the heavenly meal, yet the means of grace are on the same level. The Eucharist is the second part of the great climax. The audible Word is supplemented by the visible Word. The faithful having received the assurance of the grace of God in the sermon, they now become partakers of that meal in which assurance is made doubly sure, being supplemented by the body and blood of the Savior, sacramentally received.

This miracle requires adequate preparation, and so, after the conclusion of the Church Prayer, which is made from the altar as the place of prayer, the faithful lift up their hearts in a prayer of thanksgiving, the Eucharistic Prayer, for God's unspeakable mercies. The prayer is followed by one of the most impressive hymns of praise, the Holy, Holy, Holy. The Consecration having been introduced with the Lord's Prayer and consummated with the Words of the Institution, the administration of the Holy Supper takes place, while the congregation devoutly sings the Agnus Dei.

And now the believer, having received the final assurance of pardon, joins with the congregation in the joyful hymn of Simeon: "Lord, now lettest Thou Thy servant depart in peace." He prays with a thankful heart for strength to live as it becometh a disciple of Christ, and, having received the blessing of the Lord, goes back to his home rejoicing in the fruits of his salvation.

Just as the Service, however, is thus a beautiful and harmonious unit, with a symbolism whose full significance is unknown to, or not appreciated by, the majority of the church-goers, because they have never been made acquainted with it, so also other acts of worship performed in the church have a meaning, which should be brought out by the ministrant. Properly interpreted and correctly understood, they become a source of pleasure to the congregation present, instead of wearying by the monotony of frequent repetition.

When Luther wrote his "Taufbuechlein verdeutscht," in the year 1523, he very properly retained the form in general use in the church, since the ceremonies prescribed in the various agendas were not in themselves wrong. The outward ceremonies, including the exorcism, the administration of salt, the Ephphatha-ceremony, and others, have since been omitted, but the text has been retained almost in its entirety. Thus also the symbolism of the form may well be preserved. Since ancient times the ceremony of baptism was divided into two parts. The renunciation and the profession of faith took place in the vestibule, "ad januas ecclesiae." Most of the English parish churches had north and south porches, which were used for this part of the ceremony. When the words had been spoken, "The Lord preserve thy going out and thy coming in from this time forth and even forevermore," the celebrant, preceding the sponsors with the child, came into the church, where the rite of baptism was administered at the font, which stood near the entrance.

We still have the division of the act of baptism into two parts, and might well indicate the symbolism of the rite. The pastor may meet the sponsors with the child at the foot of the chancel-steps, where the first part of the sacred act takes place. When the blessing of entrance has been spoken, the pastor should lead the sponsors with the child to the font, where the Sacrament is administered. Thus the symbolism is preserved. The child, having been born under the curse of inherited sin, and therefore subject to eternal death and damnation, is brought to the place where the mercy of God is dispensed in the means of grace. It is welcomed at the entrance of the chancel, and then taken into the place where the Lord of mercy gives the blessings of the Gospel through baptism, thus signifying its admission into the communion of the congregation.

The form of the marriage ceremony is similarly indicative of the doctrinal position of the Lutheran Church. According to Luther's "Traubuechlein fuer die einfaeltigen Pfarrherren" of 1534, the marriage ceremony was divided into two parts. The rite proper, the giving into wedlock, took place in the vestibule, "vor der Kirchen." Then the procession moved to the altar, where the reading of the lessons and the benediction were rendered. The symbolism of this original form, if applied to-day, is immediately apparent. Marriage is a thing of this world and is primarily under the jurisdiction of the State, "ein weltlich, irdisch Ding," as Luther so often points out. This fact is brought out by the rubric, according to which the rite of joining in wedlock was performed in the vestibule, in the porch, or before the doors. The solemnization and blessing of the marriage is, however, a matter of the church, and therefore takes place at the altar.

There is another circumstance to which attention should be called. According to the understanding of Scriptures, a valid betrothal is tantamount to a marriage *in foro ecclesiae*. It is far better, therefore, and liturgically the one correct thing, to have the bride and groom come to the altar together, to emphasize this fact. The form according to which the groom awaits the bride-to-be at the altar cannot be defended in a Lutheran church.

The original symbolism of the sacred act may also be retained, even in our days. If there be an address by the pastor, he should meet the young people at the lowest step of the chancel and perform the joining in wedlock there. After that he should proceed to the altar, read the lessons, and pronounce the blessing over the bride and groom at the step of the altar. In case there be no address, the lessons ought to precede the act of marriage, which takes place at the entrance to the sanctuary, while the benediction is pronounced in the chancel, at the step of the altar.

If space permitted, much might be said in regard to other occasional acts according to the beautiful forms of the Lutheran Church. Many a church dedication is spoiled by the fact that the symbolism of the rite was not brought out or that Roman superstitions were unwittingly introduced. It may also be well to consider whether, perhaps, it would not be better to have the ordination take place, whenever this is possible, in the midst of the congregation or mission field which the ordinand is to serve, to emphasize the fact that the call makes the pastor and avoid the suspicion as though we held the doctrine of the character indelibilis.[493]

---

493) Cp. Kliefoth, *Liturgische Abhandlungen*, I; *Die urspruengliche Gottesdienstordnung*, V, 25. 26. 42. 50; *Synodalbericht*, Nebr., 1898. 1903; Lochner, *Der Hauptgottesdienst;* Loehe, *Agende*, Vorwort.

CHAPTER 5.

Liturgical Decorum of the Pastor.

The questions which we broach in this chapter are not a matter of indifference to the conscientious, faithful pastor. Decorum is a thing which few of us, if any, can afford to disregard. There are not many of us that do not know of instances where the mannerisms of a certain minister impaired the entire performance of his work before the congregation. It may be permissible for a genius to have his own fads and fancies, and people will bear with oddities for the sake of the general excellence of his ministry, but we are by no means all geniuses, and therefore our actions must largely be governed by a decent respect for the opinions of mankind.

The fact that a pastor is obliged to perform the work of a liturgist presupposes that he be familiar with liturgical dress for himself and his church. As soon as pastors and organists will go to the delightful trouble of informing themselves as to liturgical tradition and interpretation, and will be willing to impart this information to the congregation, an impetus will be given to Lutheran liturgical consciousness whose importance will be most far-reaching. It is not only that the colored vestments and the various linen coverings are very beautiful and most conducive to a visual, vivid portrayal of the church year in its large divisions, but there is also another good feature. A uniformity of liturgical custom in our churches, also in this respect, would beautify the services, satisfy the inherent ritualistic tendencies of the people, and incidentally do a great deal toward creating a consciousness of unity. While it remeains unalterably true that it is the substance upon which all depends, it is no less true that the beauty of the dress in which the substance is offered has a good deal to do with the appeal to the intellect and to the hearts of men.

The liturgical crimes that are perpetrated in the name of sacred art are entirely inexcusable. Every pastor should be acquainted with the purpose of each sacred vessel, including the burse and the palla, and he should be just as familiar with the proper vestments for altar, pulpit, and lectern. The indiscriminate draperies found in many churches, in all kinds of nondescript or unliturgical colors reflect sadly upon the knowledge of ecclesiastical art in our Church. The proper seasonal colors are green, violet, red, white, and black, and any first-class dry-goods store in a large city will be able to procure a good silk damask in the proper shades. The pastor should furnish a calendar for the proper change of vestments for the use either of the janitor or the Altar Guild. In some churches even the fact that the white linen cloth over the mensa should be in use at all seasons of the year seems to be unknown. And the Eucharistic cloths are either conspicuous by their absence or otherwise torn, mutilated, or — what is worse — dirty. There is no excuse for this. Some one in the congregation, preferably an Altar Guild should have charge of this, under the supervision of the pastor, in order that the proper cloths are in proper condition. Trifles make perfection, said Michaelangelo, but perfection is no trifle.

The pastor's own dress for officiating in church is also not a matter of indifference. The heterogeneous array of pulpit gowns that might be assembled from a number of Lutheran churches in a district would serve as a fine object lesson. So far as materials are concerned, it is true, of course, that there may be a difference. The finest silk warp henrietta and nun's veiling is priced so high that a poor pastor cannot afford it, and silk, which is also not cheap, is correct only for doctors' gowns. But even if a pastor can afford only serge, he can insist upon having his gown made after an approved pattern. The Intercollegiate Bureau and Registry of Academic Costume will cheerfully answer any questions with regard to the proper gown, either for pulpit use or for the holder of any academic degree. Then there are the bands, the remnant of the ancient peritrachelium, indicating that the wearer is an ordained pastor and may administer the Sacraments. Their use should not be discontinued, but it would certainly be best to have a uniform style. They may be made of the finest linen, six (or eight) inches long, and two inches wide, and may be hem-stitched and ornamented with a small cross. All other embroidery is out of place in the bands.

The pastor should be very careful about having his vestments on properly and buttoned or hooked correctly, also the bands clean and adjusted so that they are in the center. Any slouchiness in dress or appearance will draw the attention of the audience to the person of the liturgist, and this should be avoided by all means, since the liturgist should efface himself when officiating at the altar.

It seems almost superfluous to mention that the pastor must be thoroughly familiar with the liturgy, not only for the usual Sundays, but also for extraordinary occasions. Any hesitation or stumbling will mar the easy flow of the service and call attention to the unpreparedness of the liturgist. Only when a perfect liturgy is perfectly used is the result truly edifying. A knowledge, not only of the right forms, but, at least to some extent, of the history of liturgics, is therefore essential for proper liturgical deportment. The preparation of the liturgist will consist also in this that he understands the rubrics, for liturgical accuracy demands a perfect and consistent following of the rubrics. Only if the liturgy in all its parts is perfectly understood and thus used, will it prove uplifting also for the pastor. Above all, the liturgist must be prepared in advance in order that he may not change, at his own discretion, the prescribed form. Liturgical prayers should not be extemporaneous, and an attempt to compose prayers before the congregation will usually be a shame and an impertinence. The chaste and Scriptural forms of our collects and church prayers, hallowed with the worship of ages, should be retained by all means. The same is true of other liturgical forms. The ancient responsories and formularies, especially the Apostolic Benediction, should not be mutilated by additions or transcriptions. The garbled use of Scriptural formulas, Dr. Krauss rightly says,[494]) is exasperating.

The preparation of a liturgist for a service includes something more. He is to officate in the chancel, and therefore should see that everything is in place and in order before services begin. It happened in a communion service recently that the chalice had been forgotten in preparing the altar, and the officiating pastor was obliged to use a glass goblet in distributing the wine. Therefore the pastor will see that everything needed during worship is in place. He will usually order the wafers and the wine himself, to be sure that the right quantity and quality are there. When the number of communicants is exceptionally large and the number of flagons is insufficient to hold all the wine, he will provide other silver vessels, in order to avoid the use of bottles on the altar. The aesthetic sense of more than one communicant has been jarred by seeing the pastor pour the communion wine from bottles during services — with a gargling noise. It is also a matter of wisdom, even if sanitary reasons do not compel it, to have special cloths for both paten and chalice. With all due care, the hands of the administrant will sometimes touch the lips of communicants, and it is best to remove even a trace of moisture on the fingers. And so far as the distribution of wine is concerned, where it has not been found necessary to introduce the individual cup (which should be resorted to only in extremities), it is best to keep a number of small squares of antiseptic gauze on hand, in order that the cup may be wiped out along the rim after three or four communicants have received the wine. It is self-evident, also, that the administrant will slowly turn the chalice while distributing the wine.

Other matters that require the attention of the liturgist before the service are the marking of the lessons and placing the Bible on the lectern, in order that no time be consumed in paging over the sacred Book, the putting of all papers used during the service within easy reach, and otherwise getting the chancel in order. All service books shall be accessible at all times and in the place where the pastor

---

494) *Memoirs*, V: 2.

happens to be officiating. No hesitation, no disagreeable pauses should mar the easy flow of worship.

A word is also necessary with regard to personal habits before the altar. "Do not make your toilet in public. Attend to your ears, nose, eyes, teeth, in the privacy of your own room. Scratch your head with your comb or fingers all you please, — but never do so in public. Use your sacristy for these things, but not your pulpit. . . . You should never need, or use, artificial perfumes. Particularly in the sick-room or in the public service your breath should not smell of tobacco or liquor." [495])

When the service opens, it is best for the pastor, especially if the duties connected with public worship tend to make him nervous, to become so completely absorbed, with his whole personality, in the business at hand, that he loses all self-consciousness and becomes entirely the "minister of the Lord." When approaching the altar, do not swagger leisurely as in a sense of officiousness on the one hand, or, on the other, do not hastily strut about as if in a nervous excitability. Since you are here handling divine things, let yourself be as inconspicuous and your actions as unnoticeable as possible. . . Avoid any action that may interfere with the devotional spirit of the congregation assembled. Proper decorum before the altar is, I believe, possible only if at all times and everywhere the minister exercises watchful discipline over himself, and when, in the act of ministering divine things, he concentrates his mind, not on himself and his audience, but on his work, the business before him.[496])

In a Lutheran church, the symbolism is better preserved if the pastor does not occupy a chair in the chancel. He has his place before the altar, at the lectern, at the font, on the pulpit, only when the part of the service requires his presence there, when he is actually employed in the administration of the means of grace. During the singing of hymns, the liturgist has no more right in the sanctuary than any other member of the congregation. He may either withdraw to the sacristy, or sit with the congregation, or have sedilia placed at the entrance to the chancel.

The movements of the liturgist, his coming and going, must be as inconspicuous as possible, without, however, letting him appear, at any time, quam deus ex machina. A vicious fault is that indulged in by some pastors when they leisurely look over the congregation during any part of the liturgy. Such a survey makes even friends of the pastor squirm, mentally and physically.

In the liturgical reading, there should be no injection of the dramatic element, but it should be done intelligibly, with proper in-

---

495) *Theol. Quart.*, XXI, 226.   496) *L. c.*, 226.

flection and emphasis, not with exasperating monotony or in the tone of one racing against time. During the lessons and liturgical prayers, the liturgist should not look up from the page. In the sacrificial part of the service, there should be no sanctimonious turning up of the eyes to the ceiling. A matter which cannot be emphasized too often is this that the pastor should face the people in all sacramental functions, and the altar in all sacrificial parts. The call: Let us pray, will of course be addressed to the congregation, but the collect following is prayed in the name of the congregation, with the assembly. When the introit is a prayer, it is read facing the altar, when it is a call of rejoicing or an admonition, it is addressed to the people. The sacred vessels should always be covered before the pastor leaves the altar at the close of the service. Decency and order is required at all times. A word of warning regarding announcements must also be sounded. They should be as brief as possible and contain only the actual church announcements. Everything else belongs on the Bulletin Board or in the Parish Paper. Above all, the pastor's tendency toward facetiousness must not be indulged in making announcements.

In addition to these rather aphoristic remarks, one might bring many with reference to the general decorum of the pastor upon all occasions. For he should exert the same care in the occasional acts that he uses in the chief service. And while he will not personally perform acts not consistent with the dignity of his office in the presence of the congregation, he will quietly and inconspicuously insist upon their being done. In short, the pastor, also as liturgist, will endeavor to show himself a good steward of the manifold mercies of God.[497]

CHAPTER 6.

Organ Music in Church Services.

The Protestant churches of America have, either by agreement or consent, given to the organ a very prominent place in the services. Whereas the Puritans consistently opposed the use of musical instruments in church worship, many of the present Reformed bodies have brought the organ forward into such prominence, both architecturally and liturgically, that a discussion of the place of the organ in the Lutheran service would seem by no means superfluous, especially since an increasing number of Lutheran congregations are taking up the idea, not only of giving to the organ a very conspicuous position

497) Cp. *Memoirs*, V: 2, 7, 8; *Theol. Quart.*, XXI (1917), 218—230; Muehe, *Die pastorale Wuerde im Kirchendienste;* Lochner, 142. 264. 265.

in the church-building, but also of yielding or assigning to it the most prominent part of the service.

The broaching of this matter may seem to some a needless emphasizing of trifles. It may be conceded, of course, that the matter of organ music of every kind is an *adiaphoron*. There is no commandment of God which gives to the organ either a primary or a secondary position, or makes music either essential or subsidiary for divine worship. And yet, it is not a matter of indifference. In many Reformed churches, organ music is placed on a par with the means of grace, and more. In many service "programs" the organ music and the names of the sólo singers are displayed in prominent type, while the subject of the sermon, if one be held at all, is announced with a most apologetic air, accompanied, in many cases, with the express assurance that the sermon will not occupy more than ten or, at most, fifteen minutes. It means, in effect, that the audience should not let the few words of the pastor or speaker interfere with its enjoyment of the musical numbers on the "program." There may be no harm intended if such "special music programs" be announced for a Lutheran church in place of the regular service with preaching, but there certainly is danger of harm. A Lutheran congregation will strive to bring out its doctrinal position also in its *cultus,* and will avoid everything that may be misconstrued as though the Lutherans had abated one whit from their position toward the means of grace. The Word and the Sacraments must always occupy the most prominent place before the congregation, and everything that will detract the attention of the audience from these most important parts of the service must be avoided with the greatest care.

In order, however, that this principle may be upheld in the Lutheran Church, it is necessary that the organist (and the music committee) be acquainted with the liturgical history of the Christian Church, especially since the sixteenth century. It may not be necessary to take a full and thorough course in liturgics, though such a course would by no means seem superfluous, but it would certainly be advisable to take up the history of church music from the beginning, with special reference to the liturgy. And the organist should understand that the liturgy represents not merely a form of worship, but is a confession of faith. There is such a thing as catering to the spirit of the times, and, incidentally, losing some of the greatest treasures of the Lutheran Church.

So far as the history of church music in the narrower sense since the Reformation is concerned, the early Church Orders restricted its use, and apparently with the best of reasons. To the liturgists of the sixteenth and seventeenth centuries it was an evidence of the decay of the choral that an organ was absolutely required in services. "To say the truth," says the learned, but eccentric Flacius, "the strange, manifold squeaking (*Quinkelierung*) of the organ does not fit so well into the church as some people seem to think." Instead of finding rules for the introduction of organs, as we should perhaps expect, we find a number of directions which not only correct abuses of the organ as a factor in the liturgical service, but actually restrict its use. According to some Church Orders, the organ was not to be used on Good Friday, or from the second Sunday in Advent till Christmas and from Laetare till Easter. The Pomeranian Agenda also included Rogation Week, with the exception of Ascension Day. It was also not customary for the organ to accompany all the hymns or the entire hymns. In many instances the organ merely intoned the melody and the congregation sang the hymns alone. This was true especially with regard to the German Creed. In addition to these restrictions, the attempts at artistic playing were frowned upon. All efforts which savored of concert playing were not looked upon with favor. Motets or other strange pieces in the service proper were not permitted, the organ being strictly in the service of the congregation and its singing. The organist might give evidence of his art in the postlude. Emphasis was placed especially on one point, namely, that the preludes, interludes, and postludes, also other voluntaries, should not encroach upon the time reserved for prayers and the sermon. Above all, secular music was strictly taboo, secular songs and fantasies, as well as popular melodies being under the ban.[498])

These orders were given with good liturgical understanding, not in Puritanical opposition to music as such. One principle must be maintained in the Lutheran Church, namely, that the organ should not occupy an independent position in worship. Its subsidiary character must be expressed at all times. It should serve the congregation above all in the singing of the hymns. The organist will therefore prepare himself very carefully for each service. His music must be selected with the purpose of bringing out the lesson or the character of the day. This will be apparent even in the prelude or voluntary before the beginning of worship. The hymns must be studied both as to text and music to emphasize the spirit in them. All the shadings of joy up to the veriest exultation, all the blendings of sorrow, longing, repentance, and whatever other disposition is brought out in the text, must be correctly interpreted in the music. The preludes for the several chorals especially must agree with the character of the respective hymns. Interludes should not be longer than to afford a

---

498) Cp. Kliefoth, *Die urspruengliche Gottesdienstordnung,* IV, 280. 281.

breathing-space for the congregation. Above all, extemporaneous playing and improvising is inexcusable at the organ during regular church-services. An artist of the first rank may attempt it at a church concert, but for any one else to test the patience of the congregation in such a manner is little short of an insult. The sacredness of public worship and the exclusive emphasis which we must place upon the means of grace forbid such performances. In many hymns, interludes may be omitted entirely, a long pause being sufficient to indicate the close of a stanza. The organist should avoid chopping two stanzas which form one sentence, or a closely knit paragraph, apart. This is evidence of great thoughtlessness on his part, and seriously interferes with the devotion of the audience.[499])

A Lutheran organist will remember, above all, that the classical choral melodies of the sixteenth and seventeenth centuries should always occupy first place in his *repertoire*. He will do well, therefore, to discuss the selection of the melodies with the pastor. To replace the glorious tunes of the "golden age" in Lutheran church music with some of the shallow, sentimental melodies of modern Gospel-hymns or operas, is little short of sacrilege. The grand old melodies of that age were written for the hymns, or the hymns were written for the melodies, and to divorce them means a lowering of devotional propriety. Only by a consistent combination of forces can the organist serve the edification of the congregation.[500]) The words of Kliefoth may well be mentioned here: "The organ deserves special attention in its relation to the singing of church-hymns and the liturgy. That idea, indeed, as though the organ enabled the congregation to learn to sing or sing better, must be dropped. . . . To educate the congregation in the ability to sing the organ is neither needed nor is it adapted for that purpose; but it is good and appropriate for accompanying good church-singing, which is learned by singing and in no other way. And since the organ occupies this accompanying position only, it must be retained in this position. In the service of the congregation only such music has the right of existence as is in the service of the Word. The organ dare not play an independent *role* without such singing. Long preludes, postludes, and interludes must be discontinued, but, above all, the insertion of self-composed fugues and other devices, by which the congregation assembled for services is changed into a concert audience. When the service is over, the organist may exhibit his art and play a fugue or other composition." [501])

---

499) Fuerbringer, *Leitfaden, Liturgik,* 26.
500) Cp. "Lutheran Tunes for Lutheran Congregational Singing," in *Lutheran Witness*, XXXVII, 118.
501) *Die urspruengliche Gottesdienstordnung*, V, 356. 357.

Lochner, in the discussion of this question, calls attention to several points: First, that a long prelude between the reading of the Gospel and the singing of the Creed is out of order, as well as interludes during the Creed; and secondly, that the interludes between the stanzas of the Communion hymn should not be too long. This is more tiresome for the congregation than the singing of several hymns.[502])

A question which is broached by Kliefoth, as well as by Lochner, is that of having the organ be silent during the liturgical singing, especially during the chanting of the pastor. The argument which has usually been advanced, that the organ was to *assist* the liturgist, is one which will not hold good, for the liturgist is supposed to know the music of the litrugy thoroughly before attempting to sing it before the altar. The other reason advanced, that the solemnity of the service be enhanced and the devotion be stimulated, has more to sustain it. The proper playing of the melody not only serves the purpose of impressiveness, but also has a quieting effect upon the mind. Without encouraging mere sentimental rhapsody, it assists in devotional edification. Local circumstances must therefore decide the question as to the accompaniment of chanting by the organ. If the liturgist has a good voice for singing, the organist will do well to accompany the chanting with soft chords. If the pastor's voice is not reliable, he should chant either without accompaniment or, better still, read the passages. The rules given by Kraussold are: "1) The organist should use soft stops only. 2) The recitative chant of the pastor should be norm for the length of the chords. 3) The chanting should never be accompanied *in continuo,* the organ being silent where there is no change in harmony. 4) The pedal must not be used during the recitative chanting of the pastor." [503])

As far as music of the choir is concerned, it must always be in accordance with the purpose of the day. Its proper place is after the Epistle-lesson, instead of the Hallelujah otherwise chanted by the congregation. But choir-singing may also be used during the distribution of Holy Communion. And it must never be forgotten that the choir should be active as choir only, solo singing, unless it be as a movement of a larger composition, being out of place in a Lutheran service, just as much as any other individual and independent activity outside of the means of grace. Everything that reminds of the concert hall must be avoided in a Lutheran service. This includes the placing of the choir in the altar space or on any prominent elevation before the congregation. It is quite proper, however, to place the choir on the balcony of the transept. It must never be forgotten that

---

502) *Der Hauptgottesdienst,* 171. 266.
503) Lochner, *Der Hauptgottesdienst,* 75. 79.

the Lutheran church choir is a part of the congregation, and represents the congregation in the singing of any hymns of praise. To give to the choir the position of the lower clergy savors of a polity which is not in harmony with Lutheran democracy.

A word may finally be said in regard to selections from operas which are rendered in many churches, the "Bridal March" from *Lohengrin,* the "Intermezzo" from *Cavalleria Rusticana,* and several other melodies being the chief martyrs in this respect. A Lutheran liturgist and a Lutheran organist with tact will immediately feel the impropriety of such music upon the occasion of a church-service. Operatic music for the operatic stage, but church-music for the church! The distinction between religious concert-music and church-music must be upheld most rigidly if we wish to preserve the glorious heritage of the Church, the matchless choral and the wonderful achievements of Bach and other masters.[504]

---

504) Cp. Lochner, 34—38. 84. 85; Dickinson, *Music in the History of the Western Church,* Chap. VI.

INDEX AND GLOSSARY.

Egyptian style, Sag Harbor, L. I. 95